Strategic Management

A focus on creating and sustaining a flow of profitable transactions, in other words, the creation of sustainable competitive advantage, is the seemingly simple, yet complex goal of strategic leaders and managers. Allen C. Amason and Andrew Ward approach the topic of strategic management with this focus in mind. Rather than simply teaching theory and research, Amason and Ward seek to convey the fundamental keys to how strategy works.

This book is designed to help students think critically and understand fully how to strategically manage their future firms. In so doing, it will enable them to adapt and learn, even as their circumstances change, and to apply sound logic and reasoning, even in new and unfamiliar settings. By conveying enduring and fundamental principles of economic and human behavior rather than simply reporting on the latest innovations, this book succeeds in preparing students to excel in the business environment over time, regardless of how it evolves.

Allen C. Amason is Professor of Management and Dean of the Parker College of Business at Georgia Southern University.

Andrew Ward is the Charlot and Dennis E. Singleton '66 Endowed Chair of Corporate Governance and Professor of Management at Lehigh University College of Business.

"This may be the best strategic management textbook that I have seen in recent years. Amason and Ward cover the standard topics that need to be addressed—and do so in a clear, straightforward manner. Then, in a conclusions section at the end of each chapter, offer insightful commentary on the chapter topic. Students should find this book interesting, useful, and perceptive."

Gary Castrogiovanni, *Florida Atlantic University*

"Allen C. Amason and Andrew Ward have written a fabulously readable and totally up-to-date book. It draws from classic, time-tested concepts but in a way that is completely contemporary and fresh. I especially admire the in-depth discussion of analytic frameworks along with more behavioral and social aspects of executive leadership. The book will serve both students and instructors of strategic management exceedingly well."

Donald C. Hambrick, *The Pennsylvania State University*

"Amason and Ward's *Strategic Management (second edition)* is a wonderful book, current, thoughtful, innovative, and comprehensive. Its focus on leadership and its role in value creation is especially noteworthy. Well written and easy to follow, the book does a masterful job in capturing current thinking while being accessible. Cases and vivid examples make the book fun to read and easy to apply. I strongly recommend it."

Shaker A. Zahra, *University of Minnesota*

"Amason and Ward's book provides a solid presentation of tools and insights necessary for a fine strategy text. It also nicely balances analytics of strategy and the management of strategy."

Philip Bromiley, *University of California, Irvine*

"Allen C. Amason and Andrew Ward have taken the associated theory and research relating to strategic management and presented it in a straightforward and understandable manner that challenges each reader, regardless of career level, to question his or her past strategy decisions and methods of determining those decisions."

Craig Loyal Sarna, *Account Executive, GE Capital Solutions*

"Thinking and acting strategically are key to any successful manager or business. This book bridges the gap between just learning about strategic management and applying strategic thinking and models to everyday business challenges and situations. This practical text provides an experienced voice to the research, adding a needed and integral set of skills to any manager's repertoire."

Julie Staggs, *Senior Client Consultant, Stamats, Inc.*

"Amason and Ward do an exceptional job of shining a spotlight on the subtle difference between a text 'on' strategic management and a book 'about' strategic management. Students using their text will have the confidence and desire to take responsibility for value creation, rather than simply understand it."

Jim Martin, *Regional Director, Senior Vice President, Eagle Asset Management*

Strategic Management

From Theory to Practice

SECOND EDITION

Allen C. Amason and Andrew Ward

Routledge
Taylor & Francis Group

NEW YORK AND LONDON

Second edition published 2021
by Routledge
52 Vanderbilt Avenue, New York, NY 10017

and by Routledge
2 Park Square, Milton Park, Abingdon, Oxon, OX14 4RN

Routledge is an imprint of the Taylor & Francis Group, an informa business

© 2021 Taylor & Francis

First edition published by Routledge 2011

British Library Cataloguing-in-Publication Data
A catalogue record for this book is available from the British Library

Library of Congress Cataloging-in-Publication Data
Names: Amason, Allen C, author. | Ward, Andrew (Andrew John) author.
Title: Strategic management : from theory to practice / Allen C Amason,
    Andrew Ward.
Description: Second Edition. | New York : Routledge, 2020. | Revised edition of
    Strategic management, 2011. | Includes bibliographical references and index.
Identifiers: LCCN 2020012829 (print) | LCCN 2020012830 (ebook) |
    ISBN 9780367430054 (hardback) | ISBN 9780367430061 (paperback) |
    ISBN 9781003000594 (ebook)
Subjects: LCSH: Strategic planning. | Management.
Classification: LCC HD30.28 .A425 2020 (print) | LCC HD30.28 (ebook) |
    DDC 658.4/012—dc23
LC record available at https://lccn.loc.gov/2020012829
LC ebook record available at https://lccn.loc.gov/2020012830

ISBN: 978-0-367-43005-4 (hbk)
ISBN: 978-0-367-43006-1 (pbk)
ISBN: 978-1-003-00059-4 (ebk)

Typeset in Berling and Futura
by Apex CoVantage, LLC

Accompanying website: www.strategicmanagement.business

Dedication

Allen C. Amason's Dedication: Writing a book takes a significant investment of time, effort, and energy. Focusing all of those things on any single project like this ultimately means focusing less on others. And so, I dedicate this book to those who have loved and supported me most throughout the process of writing this book and building my career as a scholar, teacher, and manager: my late wife, Cricket; our children, Chase, Shana, Jaclyn, Alex, Christopher, Yanna, and Hunter; and our grandchildren, Ronan, George, and Rhett. I love you all.

Andrew Ward's Dedication: Writing a book that attempts to summarize a whole field is daunting, and I know that there will be some areas that we haven't done sufficient justice to. However, to reach the point of being able to even attempt this task has taken a great deal of mentorship throughout the years, as well as many years' experience of teaching the subject. Accordingly, I would like to dedicate this book to the teachers, practitioners, and scholars who have mentored me during the course of my career; the many students who I have had the pleasure of teaching, guiding, and mentoring; and my family, who have supported me in this chosen profession.

Brief Table of Contents

Accompanying website: www.strategicmanagement.business

Detailed Table of Contents

Accompanying website: www.strategicmanagement.business

About the Authors

Allen C. Amason, Ph.D. is Dean of the Parker College of Business at Georgia Southern University. He earned his Ph.D. in Strategic Management and International Business from the Moore School of Business at the University of South Carolina and served on the faculties of Mississippi State and the University of Georgia, where he was Chair of the Terry College Department of Management.

Dr. Amason's research focuses on strategic decision making and the role of top management in the strategy process. He has published more than 40 articles, books, and chapters in various scholarly outlets, served on the editorial boards of several top journals, and was Associate Editor for the *Journal of Management Studies* and the *Journal of Management*. He is past-President of the Southern Management Association. Professor Amason's teaching and consulting focuses on strategic management and decision making. He has served on the boards of various organizations and done C-level consulting on issues related to strategy and strategic decision making with a variety of widely recognized and leading firms in the U.S. and around the world.

He holds a bachelor's degree in finance, from Georgia Southern, and, prior to her passing in 2019, was married for 36 years to his high school sweetheart and Georgia Southern alumna, Cricket Amason. They have 4 children, the youngest of whom is the subject of his book *Expensive Yanna: An Adoption Story*.

Andrew Ward, Ph.D. is the Charlot and Dennis E. Singleton '66 Endowed Chair in Corporate Governance and Professor of Management. From 2010 to 2018 he also served as the Associate Dean for the College of Business at Lehigh University with responsibility for all graduate programs (Ph.D., Master's, and MBA) for the college. Prior to joining Lehigh University, he was a member of the management faculty at the Terry College of Business at the University of Georgia and previously at the Goizueta Business School of Emory University.

Dr. Ward conducts research on issues related to corporate governance including CEO successions, CEO compensation, the roles and concerns of the chief executive officer, CEO/board relations, reputation, and leadership and has published articles in several leading academic journals, including *Academy of Management Journal, Administrative Science Quarterly*, and *Organization Science*. Dr. Ward's work has been featured in numerous publications including *Harvard Business Review, Business Week, The Washington Post, The Financial Times, Directorship, Directors and Boards, Investor's Business Daily*, and *Leaders Magazine*. His first book, *The Leadership Lifecycle: Matching Leaders to Evolving Organizations* (Palgrave, 2003) examines how leadership needs change over the course of an organization's life. His book *Firing Back: How Great Leaders Rebound After Career Disasters* is co-authored with Dr. Jeffrey Sonnenfeld of Yale University and was published by Harvard Business School Press in 2007. *Firing Back* has received national and international media attention with reviews in *The New York Times, The Washington Post, The Los Angeles Times, The Financial Times, Forbes, Business Week*, and *The Economist* among other publications.

A native of England, Ward received his undergraduate degree from the University of Surrey, his MBA from the Goizueta Business School of Emory University, and his Ph.D. from The Wharton School of the University of Pennsylvania.

Acknowledgements

We are extremely grateful to Munzer Abu-ghosh for his extensive research assistance.

Preface

Welcome to the Second Edition of *Strategic Management: From Theory to Practice*. As a potential reader or adopter of this text, you may ask: Why another book on this subject? Certainly, there is no shortage of alternatives, all authored by good scholars who are also knowledgeable in their field and passionate about their work. The answer is that this book is fundamentally different from those others. Moreover, the things that make this book different will also make it an especially valuable tool for teaching, for learning, and for the practice of good strategic management. Indeed, students and instructors alike are likely to find this approach novel, accessible, and most of all valuable, as they grapple with the complexities of the business world.

What makes it so different? Stated plainly, it is a book ***on*** strategic management rather than a book ***about*** strategic management. The difference is subtle but important and reflects a basic question that every teacher of this material should ask, specifically, why do students take this course and what must they take away from it in order to have a successful experience? It is my belief that students expect to leave this course as better strategic thinkers and managers. They want to be able to do the things, to make the decisions, and to deliver the results that will enable their success. In essence, they come to this course wanting to become successful or to become more successful. So, this text is organized and oriented in such a way as to help.

Rather than try to convey all that theory has to say on a subject, the book seeks to translate what theory has to say into principles and practices that students need to know in order to accomplish what that they want to accomplish. As mentioned, it is a subtle difference but it is an important one. It reflects an approach that is grounded firmly in theory and research but that is ever so practical in application. It reflects roughly 50 years of combined experience on the part of the authors, teaching strategic management to executives and executive MBAs, as well as to traditional MBA, Ph.D., and undergraduate students. And it reflects a desire to communicate, in a straightforward and plain-spoken way, a model that has too often seemed overly esoteric and academic to students and executives alike. In essence, the approach is to render strategic management practical by making it accessible and to leverage its utility by leveraging its generalizability. Everything in the book, then, from its coverage to its organization, reflects this philosophy.

Chapter 1 is an introduction built on a simple foundation—namely, that it is all about performance. There is a song by Sean "Diddy" Combs entitled "It's All About the Benjamins." Few books or articles capture the practical essence of our discipline as well as this simple phrase. In business we keep score by measuring performance, and performance is a function of strategy. Of course, strategy and strategic management can mean different things to different people, and the study and practice of strategy can involve all manner of complexity and nuance. But tying it all together is the focus and the impact on performance.

Chapter 2 then addresses the question unanswered in Chapter 1: What is performance? While seemingly simple, the issue of performance has been elaborated and complicated by the myriad different measures that are employed to capture it and by the context in which it is evaluated. Thus, great attention is paid to the technical challenges and trade-offs in performance measurement. Here too, though, the point is to simplify and make accessible and to show performance from a variety of perspectives. Moreover, the discussion is connected to strategic management to illustrate the responsibility and challenge of the role.

Chapter 3 begins the process of meeting that challenge, and strategic management is presented as a set of "tools" that can help. Covered in this chapter are the principal components of the model. However, the point is not to be comprehensive or exhaustive. Indeed, we intentionally gloss over some fine-grained distinctions and lump together some things that others would prefer to keep separate. We do this because the purpose is to simplify and make practical, to focus on questions of "why" rather than questions of "what," and to provide an overarching framework for the practice of strategy.

Chapter 4 covers the first step in that application analysis of the environment. While similar in many ways to other texts, this analysis is different in some fundamental ways as well. The first is the way the environment is defined. With a goal of practical accessibility, we define competition as those who interfere with the relationship a firm has to its customers. We define the competitive environment as the sum of those first-order connections that affect the relationship of a firm to its customers. Finally, we cast environmental analysis as the input to the rest of the strategic process. Through the analysis of past, present, and future, environmental analysis must produce the insights that will motivate every step thereafter.

Chapter 5 takes that input and answers the question: Now what? How does a strategist take the output from the environmental analysis and convert it into strategy? The chapter focuses on some common tools for this, such as SWOT, the value chain, and VRIN (value, rarity, inimitability, and non-substitutability) analyses. These tools along with examples of how they are best applied are meant to provide a mechanism for answering the "What now?" question that often arises in the real practice of strategic management.

Chapter 6 focuses directly on competitive advantage and flows naturally from the issues in Chapters 4 and 5. However, rather than discuss competitive advantage as an organizational-level construct, we discuss it as it exists at the transaction level. The point is to facilitate better connection between the "why" and the "how" of strategy. How does the practice of strategy with all of its various models and tools actually connect to performance? The answer is by enabling more and more profitable transactions. This approach also provides a practical measure of competitive advantage that is both tangible and immediate and that links directly to financial performance.

Chapter 7 introduces the concept of multi-business strategy. Viewing competitive advantage at the transaction level focuses attention on environmental conditions and organizational attributes. Those conditions and attributes are specific to individual business units. But what does strategy have to say about diversified firms with multiple business units? Answering that question requires a discussion of synergy and of the "better-off" principle. In essence, a diversified firm should be more valuable than the sum of its individual business units or its corporate strategy will have been unsuccessful. How a firm gains and manages that synergy so as to be better off is the subject of this chapter.

Chapter 8 deals with implementation and marks the final step in the framework. A good comprehension of implementation requires understanding two distinct topics: fit and change. It also requires understanding that the relationship between these things is paradoxical. Designing a firm so that it is tightly fit to the current strategy and the demands of the current environment can facilitate performance in the short term. However, it also limits flexibility and adaptability in the long term. Yet performing well over time requires that attention be paid to both. This chapter, then, is meant to explain both topics in a practical and accessible way, while also introducing the subsequent dilemma and offering insights on how to manage it.

Chapter 9 is part addendum, part insightful application. It discusses the impact of megatrends that have helped to shape the world's economy and the various business models, operating norms, and strategic paradigms that characterize the business world today. As we discuss, the challenge with these megatrends is that, while they are extraordinarily powerful forces, they are difficult to identify and understand in advance. Thus, we spend time looking forward and thinking about the megatrends that, while only emerging today, may well shape the business world tomorrow.

Chapter 10, the final chapter, is offered both as a summary of the book and as a point of connection between the practice of strategy and leadership. Chapter 10 does not flow directly from the previous chapters but rather derives from the sum of them, by showing the generalizable nature of strategic management. It does this by comparing similarities in the strategic management framework to issues in entrepreneurship and international business. It also connects some of the basic dynamics and functions of leadership and governance to the larger strategic management framework. Some will surely object to presenting these topics and disciplines so briefly and as subsets of strategic management. But the treatment is intentional and meant to illustrate that, by truly understanding the framework and principles of strategy, anyone can move and work efficiently across a range of contexts and settings.

The sum total of the book, then, is a straightforward walk through the principles and practices of strategic management. Like other books, this one draws from theory and research as it explains the tools, models, and logic of the discipline. However, the language, perspective, and approach are subtly and yet fundamentally different. The result is a text that should be interesting, accessible, and useful to students at every level—undergraduate, MBA, and executive. Moreover, it is an approach that should be refreshingly different and yet still very comfortable for researchers, teachers, and students alike. Additional supplemental material to accompany this book is available at www.strategicmanagement.business

Chapter 1

An Introduction to Strategic Management

GOOGLE: A STORY OF GREAT SUCCESS

September 4th of 2018 marked 20 years since the incorporation of Google. Founded in 1996 by Larry Page and Sergey Brin, two graduate students at Stanford University, Google is one of the world's most valuable companies and most iconic brands. Its first and still best-known product is its search engine. Page and Brin designed their new and better search engine around a superior system for analyzing the relationships among websites. The result was a program that enabled searches that were more efficient and more relevant than previously available. Hence, Google was created; the domain name was registered in September of 1997, and the company was incorporated in 1998. It went public through an IPO in 2004 and it was cemented into the English vernacular in June of 2006, when the company name itself, "Google," was recognized as a transitive verb by the *Oxford English Dictionary*.

The story of Google's founding and growth is fascinating for any number of reasons. The name was derived from the number googol, which is 1 followed by 100 zeros. This name was picked to signify the massive amount of information the service was designed to organize. The founders met in 1995, when one (Brin), a second-year graduate student at Stanford, was assigned to host the other (Page), a prospective graduate student, during a visit to the Stanford campus. The chemistry was apparent almost immediately, as the two talked, argued and debated throughout their first meeting. The pair ran their newly created search engine out of their dorm rooms initially and, by 1998, their program was handling over 10,000 search requests per day. Since then, the growth of the company has been nothing short of phenomenal. The initial public offering or IPO in 2004 generated approximately $1.9 billion. Twenty years later, Google's market value was nearly $700 billion. Even famed investor Warren Buffet has stated that he made a mistake by not seeing the value and investing in Google early on. Indeed, an investor who purchased just a dozen shares of Google stock (worth about $1,000) at the time of the IPO, would have seen that investment grow to approximately $25,000 today.

But the lessons of Google's success are really less about these fascinating historical details than they are about a consistent strategy for the company and the market and the relentless pursuit of opportunities to execute, learn, and adapt. At its essence, the strategy for Google has been, and continues to be, making the internet increasingly accessible to everyone. In so doing, it has been able to drive revenues and profits, by driving visitors to websites and platforms on which it sells ads. And Google has driven a lot of revenue. In 2004, Google's revenues were $3.2 billion; by 2017 that number had grown to $110 billion. Of course, in 2017, Google was merely one subsidiary of a recently created parent company named Alphabet. But the majority of Alphabet's revenues and earnings continued to come from Google and from the basic strategy of organizing and providing access to information, so as to drive traffic, clicks, and advertising.

The challenging part is that few customers know, or care, which search engine they use, how any particular search engine works, or even how their use of search is monetized into revenue by the provider. Customers just want information, whether that information is an answer to a specific question, a response to a curiosity, or simply something to entertain an open or restless mind. People want information and Google's success depends upon those people using Google's platforms to find it. So, the people at Google work every day to improve the efficiency and breadth of their search engine. As a practical matter, that means continuously tweaking, expanding, and refining their algorithms, so that every query returns the very answer the customer wants, even when that customer isn't sure what he or she is expecting. Google also works to make sure that, whenever or wherever customer needs arise, there is a Google platform available and accessible to facilitate the search. So, in addition to its core search engine, Google has developed a range of related products, things like YouTube, Gmail, Chrome, Maps, Translate, Android, Docs, Calendar, Photos, Files, and Scholar. Google has even invested in hardware, in the form of the Pixel phone, Pixelbook computer, and Google wireless wi-fi routers. What ties these products together is that they all provide accessibility to people who need information. By connecting these different products and platforms to Google's constantly adapting and evolving search algorithms, Google provides users with usable information quickly and efficiently. What Google intends with all this, and what has indeed happened, is that millions and millions of users around the world have simply found Google to be the best, or at least the most convenient and accessible, alternative when seeking information. Hence, Google achieves billions and billions of user interactions each day. And each user interaction is an opportunity to generate revenue.

But what does it mean to say that users have found Google to be the best alternative? Well, that really depends upon the customer. Because every customer is different, each will naturally want, value, and seek different things. Some will choose based on the speed of the response, the variety of the responses, or perhaps the relevance in relations to their queries. To others though, the best may mean merely the simplest and the most accessible. So, when using a Google device, they might simply accept the default browser, Google Chrome, as the best. They might find Google Maps the easiest to use and so simply choose to use it, even if they are using an Apple device. Having created a Google account, to store files or photos, they might also choose to have a Gmail account, for reasons of convenience. What it means to be the best will vary from person to person and from user to user. So, Google must invest heavily not only in the underlying technological infrastructure to manage and deliver information but also in the broad array of platforms necessary to satisfy customers of all types, regardless of the information they are searching for and the way they connect in trying to reach it. What is more, Google must do all of this in the face of competitors who are constantly introducing new products and services designed to lure away its customers. It must do what it does in the face of changing customer tastes and preferences; in just a few short years, customers have shifted from stationary computers to mobile devices. The next shift could radically alter the way users search for information. So, Google has to be relentless in finding ways to remain the best, across every meaningful dimension, lest it lose users and so lose its revenue stream.

But Google's sights are set on more than merely today's customers and today's revenue streams. What happens to Google's revenues when advertisers are no longer willing to pay for visits and clicks? Could such a thing ever happen? Well, ask someone in the encyclopedia business about how their business changed with the proliferation of web-based search. Alternatively, ask someone involved in the manufacture, sale, and use of LORAN (long range navigation) equipment how their business was impacted by the evolution of satellite-based GPS (global position system) technology or how the demand for cathode ray tubes changed with the introduction of flat panel displays. Every product gives way, ultimately, to time and to changes in technologies and tastes. Just as what was popular yesterday is often no longer popular today, likewise will today's leading products and services one day be displaced by different, and better, alternatives. Google understands this and so actively invests the profits from its current businesses in longer-term innovations that will, one day, provide the profits for the future.

Many of these innovations are housed and nurtured in Alphabet's Other Bets division. In 2016, Alphabet made $4.4 billion (or 7% of total operating costs) worth of other bets. What sorts of bets is Alphabet making and what sorts of subsidiary companies are included under this new holding company? One example would be Google Fiber, which provides super high-speed internet connectivity in about 20 different cities around the U.S. Another example would be Google Ventures, which makes early-stage investments in start-up companies across a range of industries, including agriculture, robotics, and life sciences. There is Capital G, which is also an investment company. But whereas Google Ventures invests in early-stage firms, Capital G invests in more established but still young technology firms, with significant growth potential. Capital G has made some impressive investments and its portfolio includes firms like Lyft, Airbnb, credit karma, and glassdoor. There is Nest Labs, the maker of home automation equipment, most notably the Nest programmable thermostat and smoke alarm. Calico Labs is a biotech research and development company focused on aging and age-related diseases, and Verily Life Sciences is a research firm focused on data science and healthcare, with the goal of organizing the world's health data so as to enable healthier lives. All of these "other bets" grew out of, and were funded by the original Google, and together, they produced more than $800 million in revenue in 2016.

But the value of these investments lies far beyond their immediate revenues. Indeed, many will likely never prove profitable or sustainable in the long term. Nevertheless, they have value in the here and now by creating options for the future. With each of these innovative new initiatives, Google is learning about the future, learning about emerging, new technologies, and learning about the evolving nature of the competitive environment. As society evolves, as customer behavior changes, as technologies, habits, fads, and fashions rise and fall, Google will be positioned to adapt and respond because of its presence across these many other bets. Stated differently, by investing in this wide range of nascent businesses and industries, Google is purchasing options in the future. Some of those options may expire, unused. But others may provide a valuable claim on exciting and profitable new opportunities.

So, the real story of Google's impressive and ongoing success is partly about its founders, its origins, its name, and its growth, but it is mostly about an innovative strategy built on two fundamental truths. The first is that customers seek superior value and Google has created an extraordinary array of coordinated products and technologies designed to deliver value, through billions of transactions, so as to generate billions in revenues and profits. The second truth is that nothing lasts forever, not even a superior search engine supported by a brand hegemony as strong as Google's. Google understands this and so purposefully reinvests a portion of its cash flow into things that will help it to learn, to adapt, and to one day create another great success story.

A QUEST FOR PERFORMANCE

Reflect for a moment on this story and consider some questions. How is it that some firms perform so well, while others struggle and fail? What is it about a firm that allows it to thrive, despite ongoing challenges from its competitors and ever-increasing demands from its customers? While the story of Google's founding and growth is a stirring example of a company that has had great success and that is building for the future, what can be said of so many other companies that also had their moment upon the stage but then failed to sustain that momentum and ultimately disappeared? What separates a company like Google from so many others like Compaq, AoL, Gateway, Blackberry, Sun Microsystems (Facebook is now headquartered in the complex that formerly housed Sun), or NEXT, the company founded and run by Steve Jobs, prior to his return to Apple? What is it that enables the successful firms to perform well, to outpace their rivals and to continue to provide good value and good returns to their customers and stakeholders?

To use an old expression, performance really is the bottom line. Performance is the crux of business and of business education. While different people will adopt different definitions of performance and while some dimensions of performance will matter more to some than to others, performance itself is still the standard by which businesses are judged. Thus, the ability to understand, predict, and ultimately direct a firm's performance is the goal of every business student, every manager, and every investor. Why do investors devote so much effort to the research and study of specific firms and industries? The answer is that they want to distinguish the exceptional opportunities from the marginal ones and the marginal ones from the ones that offer little potential. Moreover, they want to do this all before these differences become common knowledge in the marketplace.

Why do students study the principles of economics, marketing, management, and finance? Why do managers invest in continuing education and why do they commit resources to the research and analysis of their markets and competitors? The answer in each case is that they want to build firms that perform well and that, like Google, are considered outstanding among their peers.

STRATEGIC MANAGEMENT

This book is about that quest for performance. More specifically, this book is about how the principles and practices of strategic management can be used to enable better performance. Understood most simply, strategic management is a discipline, like marketing or accounting, within the larger academic field of business education. Over the years, strategic management has been defined in a number of different ways (see Box 1.1). While these definitions reflect the different perspectives and approaches common during the period in which they were written, they all describe a basic and fundamental phenomenon, the quest for superior performance.

Box 1.1
Some Prominent Definitions of Strategic Management

- *The definition of the long-run goals and objectives of an enterprise, and the adoption of course of action and the allocation of resources necessary for carrying out these goals.*

  Alfred Chandler (1962)

- *Strategy is the pattern of objectives, purposes, or goals and the major policies and plans for achieving these goals, stated in such a way as to define what business the company is in or is to be in and the kind of company it is or is to be.*

  Kenneth Andrews (1987)

- *The fundamental pattern of present and planned resource deployments and environmental interactions that indicate how the organization will achieve its objectives.*

  Charles Hofer and Dan Schendel (1978)

- *What business strategy is all about is, in a word, competitive advantage . . . the sole purpose of strategic planning is to enable a company to gain, as efficiently as possible, a sustainable edge over its competitors.*

  Kenichi Ohmae (1982)

- *Strategy is a set of important decisions derived from a systematic decision making process, conducted at the highest levels of the organization.*

  Daniel Gilbert et al. (1988)

- *An integrated and coordinated set of commitments and actions designed to exploit core competencies and gain competitive advantage.*

  Hoskisson et al. (2008)

The common thread running through these definitions is the creation of superior value. Successful firms create superior value for their customers and are rewarded by those customers with profitable sales. As illustrated in the story of Google, profitable and valuable firms thrive by creating superior value for customers. Those customers in return provide the firm with a stream of revenues and profits. Profits, of course, mean jobs for managers and employees and returns for owners and investors. Good managers then understand that value creation is the key to performance, and so they formulate and implement strategies designed to create value and to capture the resulting profits. These managers understand one of the most fundamental realities in business: real value creation does not happen by accident; rather it is the result of a purposeful and deliberate process.

Strategic management is that process by which managers integrate the firm's functions into streams and patterns of action designed to fit the constraints and demands of the market. To the extent that it is done well, the process is beneficial to the customers, owners, and stakeholders of the firm. Moreover, to the extent that it drives the process of change and adaptation, it enables the firm to stay ahead of the competition and continue to receive those benefits in the future.

BASIC DEFINITIONS

While Box 1.1 provides some prominent historical definitions, strategic management is essentially a framework for analyzing the environment, for integrating the firm's activities, for learning and adapting to change, and for creating value in both the present and into the future. As discussed later in the book, it is a framework that can be used in every type of organization, large or small, new or old, domestic or international, even for-profit and not-for-profit. It is a framework that can be understood and applied systemically, with discrete components, logical steps, and some simple but powerful models and tools. Beyond all of that though, it is a framework that, when applied, becomes the process by which managers integrate the firm's functions into streams and patterns of action designed to identify and fit the contours of a competitive and evolving environment. Finally, and to the extent it is done well, strategic management is a process that creates value for customers, for owners, and for all the stakeholders of a firm.

While the number of various and different definitions of strategy has been a source of confusion to some, strategic management is, in its essence, a company's manifest plan of action for the ongoing creation and appropriation of value. Strategic management is at once a short-term and a long-term process that involves both plans and actions. It must reflect the immediate realities of the business environment, yet it must also provide impetus for future direction and for innovation, adaptation, and change. It is most often the province of top management, yet it is also relevant and important to every employee, and everything an organization does that affects its performance in the present or future is ultimately strategic. Strategic management is, at once, a framework to guide thinking and a process to guide action. Owing then to its complex and multifaceted nature, Henry Mintzberg (1987) once described strategic management as being part plan, part ploy, part pattern, part position, and part perspective.

Plan, Ploy, Pattern, Position, and Perspective

Strategic management is certainly part planning. For many years, virtually every strategic management text made the point that the word strategy derives from a Greek military term *"strategia"* and actually means a plan of action. Strategic management is a high-level cognitive activity, a forward-looking and visionary process that incorporates understanding about the environment, the firm, and the ongoing developments and changes in each. It is the process by which threats and opportunities are identified, analyzed, and accommodated. It is willful and intentional, analytical and creative. Indeed, planning is fundamental to strategic management.

Of course, plans are not always all that they appear to be. They are sometimes more significant for their symbolic value than for their practical value. They are sometimes designed to signal capabilities rather than intentions. They are sometimes intended to lure a competitor into a poor decision or to create an illusion of strength to mask some vulnerability. In this sense, strategies are as much ploys as they are plans. A ploy is simply an article of deception, used to gain an advantage over a competitor, but it can be a powerful and substantial component of a firm's strategy.

Strategic management can also be understood as a pattern. Some strategies are best understood in terms of the interaction of the firm with its environment. These interactions follow a template or pattern that becomes the manifest strategy. That pattern is instilled throughout the company and promoted in the marketplace as the key to its value proposition. The term **business model** has grown popular in recent years and refers to the pattern of connections among a firm, its customers, its suppliers, and its partners (Amit & Zott, 2001). A business model then is the pattern of action that defines a firm's strategy. Think about a company like Google and contrast it against other successful companies like SAP, Oracle, and Cisco. All are considered technology companies. Yet, each has a different business model. Each offers different products and goes to market in different ways. As such, each follows a particular pattern in how they do business. It is this pattern that is seen by the marketplace and experienced by customers and employees, and it is this pattern that is understood to be the firm's realized strategy.

But strategic management is also about positioning the firm within an attractive and manageable environment. Granted, such positioning may result from an intentional plan or emerge from a natural pattern. Still, such positions often become the focus and substance of the firm's strategy. Many firms seek positions that allow them to avoid competition. Regulated monopolies, for instance, are protected from competition. While they are constrained by their environments, their strategy is also a function of their protected position. Even in competitive environments, a large portion of a firm's strategy is dictated by the realities of its surroundings. Thus, positioning is also a key component of strategic management.

Finally, strategic management is largely a matter of perspective. In other words, firms differ in how they view the world and their place within it. Much as individuals have distinct personalities and characters, so too do firms have distinct perspectives that govern what they do and how they believe they should do it. Some firms are aggressive, while others are much less so. Some seek a leadership position in their industries while others are content to merely make a good margin, away from the spotlight. Some firms have a reputation for engineering excellence, while others are known for their marketing prowess. This collective view of the firm itself, of the environment, and of how the firm should operate within that environment is a large part of strategy.

These five faces of strategy are at once all important and accurate. At the same time, each is alone inadequate and incomplete. At any single moment in time, strategic management may involve them all. Strategy can be a unifying theme that gives coherence and meaning. But coherence and meaning are worth little if they fail to fit the changing realities of the marketplace. Strategy certainly involves the setting of goals and objectives. But goals and objectives are worth little without the skills and resources needed to accomplish them. Strategy is a systematic process for guiding decisions and actions. But a systematic process that cannot adapt and change will inevitably fail. Thus, good strategic management must incorporate all five of these facets. Strategy is, at once, part plan, part ploy, part pattern, part position, and part perspective.

Just as importantly, while strategy is all of these things, we should never forget that the end result of strategy is action. Eloquent statements of intention and well-conceived plans are certainly helpful, but day after day it is the action that gives a strategy its life. Look at the mission statements of several high-performing and low-performing firms. What you will find is a remarkable similarity across the two groups, the differences in performance notwithstanding. Yet, look at the types of actions these firms take and you will begin to see some significant differences. So, at the end of the day, strategy is all about action; strategy is all about what the firm really does to produce superior performance. And it is on that ability to produce superior performance that the success of a strategy is ultimately judged.

COMPETITIVE ADVANTAGE

For all of their complexity and in all their various manifestations, all strategies seek the same fundamental thing, *competitive advantage*. What is competitive advantage? It is frequently defined as the ability of one firm to perform better than its rivals. According to this definition, firms that perform above the average for their industry have a competitive advantage. Although simple and popularly appealing, this definition is not especially useful to a manager in practice. For instance, who are the rivals against which a firm should be compared? Do they seek to accomplish the same things and do they measure their performance in the same way, such that a fair comparison is possible? What happens if a firm is publicly owned while its rivals are privately owned; how do we compare their performance then? What is the appropriate time period over which to measure and compare this performance? Do we measure performance annually, quarterly, or in some other, more immediate fashion? Does the fact that one firm had greater profit than another in the previous year say anything about its competitive advantage in the here and now and into the future? While the ability of one firm to perform better than its rivals is certainly a reflection of competitive advantage, it is not a definition of competitive advantage with much practical value. Indeed, in the case of some firms, thinking of competitive advantage in this way has proven to be detrimental. Consider the stalwart IBM; for many years IBM was a model of success, easily dominating all of the competitors in its immediate industry. The problem was that the industry itself was changing and the firms leading that change were little or nothing like IBM. Thus, the competition that overtook IBM came from firms and technologies that did not appear to be rivals, at least not at the time.

Competitive advantage also is frequently described in metaphorical terms, as a sporting contest, for example. Defined in this way, competitive advantage is the key asset or ability that allows one team to best another. While similarly popular and appealing, this metaphor can also be misleading because it fails to capture two important characteristics of business competition. The first is that the pursuit of competitive advantage never ends. Consider history and you will find few, if any, examples of perpetual success. Even the strongest firms, with the most dominant positions, like Sears once had in retailing and consumer products, like General Motors once had in automobiles, or like Research in Motion (Blackberry) once had in cellular phones, all eventually faltered with the emergence of new technologies and markets.

As history illustrates, unlike a sporting event, the competition in business is ongoing and because the game never ends, there is never a final winner. Wal-Mart, for instance, is still on top of the discount retailing business at present. However, history teaches that sustaining this success, in the face of evolving technologies, demanding customers, and emerging new competitors will be a daunting task. Today Amazon and Dollar General both pose significant threats to Wal-Mart's dominance, even though neither operates in a way that is exactly like that of Wal-Mart. Consider also the case of Netflix. Netflix itself was an industry disruptor, destroying the dominant video-rental company Blockbuster, whose competitive advantage was based on real estate and having a Blockbuster video rental store within a few minutes' drive of the majority of the U.S. population. Netflix undermined this competitive advantage by mailing DVDs directly to customers' homes, leading to a rapidly growing customer base, strong revenue trends, and good profits and leading to the destruction of Blockbuster which couldn't adapt itself to this new business model.

However, it quickly became apparent that Netflix's own business model was in danger of becoming obsolete with evolving technologies, such as online streaming, and the proliferation of alternative services for movie distribution threatened to undermine its competitive advantage and its potential for growth. Netflix, however, was able to see this next evolution and let go of its original business model to successfully adapt to this new method of distributing movies and furthermore lead the shift in the focus of competition in the industry to the focus on original content, creating demand not just for its ability to deliver entertainment content produced by other firms but to produce compelling content of its own attracting and tying consumers to its service over the alternative distribution offered by other companies. Thus, every firm faces an ongoing stream of new threats and demands that must be satisfied over and over again if they hope to establish and continue a legacy of success.

The second area where the sporting contest metaphor falls short is that in a sporting contest, the competitors are known. In business, however, new competitors arise constantly and often in ways and areas that are unexpected. A competitive advantage and the profits associated with it may actually attract new competitors. Vanquish one and two more may arise to take its place. Schneider National is the nation's largest carrier of freight in the truckload, long-haul segment of the trucking business. Yet, some of its most intense competition comes not from other large, well-known carriers but from the hundreds of small, relatively unknown, independent operators, who enter and exit different markets quickly. The same is true in the music business, where a few large and well-known record labels like Polygram, Universal, and EMI once dominated the industry. The real threat for each of these firms though was not the challenge posed by other similar firms but the emergence of new and independent labels, along with technologies that enabled artists to produce, record, and distribute their own music directly. The challenge then is to sustain competitive advantage in the face of the competition that is known today and the competition that will become known tomorrow.

This discussion is meant to illustrate that while the term competitive advantage is often used, it is rarely understood in its fullness. And that is a problem; if strategic management is to be understood as the pursuit of competitive advantage, then we must have a good sense of what competitive advantage really is. All strategic management, throughout an organization, should point to competitive advantage because competitive advantage is the key to performance. Every goal and objective, every intention and action, every plan, ploy, and perspective should ultimately point toward competitive advantage, its development, maintenance, and expansion. But what is competitive advantage? How can we define it so that it is practically meaningful to all involved in a firm's strategic management?

FOCUSING ON TRANSACTIONS

In his 1985 book entitled *Competitive Advantage*, Michael Porter defined this key construct as growing "out of the value a firm is able to create for its buyers that exceeds the firm's cost of creating it." While this definition says little about beating competitors or winning games, it nevertheless captures the essence of competitive advantage in a way that is especially insightful and practical. Defined in this way, competitive advantage is achieved in some small measure every time a firm sells a product or delivers a service at a profitable price.

Of course, a lot of firms sell a lot of products and deliver a lot of services at profitable prices. How, then, can such a simple and common action be a measure of competitive advantage? To understand, consider all that is implied by this simple definition. If a customer is to buy a product or service, at a profitable price, it is because she perceives some value in it, over and above its cost. For example, when Coca-Cola sells a drink, the customer receives value in excess of the price that she pays. That excess is what economists call **consumer surplus**. If the price she pays is also more than Coca-Cola's total cost in the product, then the company has earned a surplus, called a profit. The transaction then yields value to both parties.

However, this profitable transaction did not occur in a vacuum. Rather, it occurred in an open and competitive environment, where this customer had any number of other options for her money. She could have chosen to buy a Pepsi or she could have chosen to buy nothing at all, preferring to save her money. By choosing a Coke, she also chose, simultaneously, not to buy from a competitor, at least not in this particular instance. Thus, for the sake of this one purchase, Coca-Cola held an advantage over the competition. This advantage is even more significant when you consider that buyers have scarce resources. Even if our imaginary customer was quite wealthy, her resources are still finite. Thus, she can never again spend the same money that she just spent on that drink from Coca-Cola. She may make other purchases, with other money, at some other points in the future. But for the sake of this one transaction, the competition ended when she made her purchase, and the advantage in that competition went to Coca-Cola.

Why should a text in strategic management begin with such a basic and granular lesson in the economics of a single transaction? Because students, managers, and professors alike are prone to neglect these basics in favor of other, more grandiose issues. IPOs, globalization, emerging technologies, cost of capital, visionary leadership, and intellectual property—these are the sorts of things that attract headlines and attention. However, while these sorts of issues are certainly important, we should never lose sight of the fact that strategic management is really about competitive advantage and competitive advantage emerges when a firm is able to create value for customers over and above its costs. What that really means is that strategic management must begin with the customer and it is in the eye of the customer that competitive advantage must be understood. After all, if customers do not buy a firm's products or services at prices that exceed the costs, then nothing else really matters.

Moreover, it is through real and specific actions that firms actually create products and services that customers want and are willing to buy. Thus, competitive advantage emerges and is sustained when a firm's actions create products and services that customers value over and above the available alternatives and over and above the firm's costs. This practical reality often gets lost amidst discussions of esoteric terminology and advanced analytical procedures. So, it is important to remember that the ultimate arbiter of strategic success is the customer. All else aside, if customers do not buy the product or service in sufficient volume and at a sufficient price, then the firm will not succeed. This is the very issue being discussed and debated around the future of Tesla. Yes, the company has created some of the "coolest" cars on the road, utilizing state-of-the-art battery and motor technologies. Tesla cars are extraordinarily efficient, exquisitely designed, loaded with features, and just plain fun to drive. But none of that will matter if Tesla cannot find a way to sell a sufficient number of cars at sufficiently high prices to make and sustain a profit, without the benefit of subsidies. Can Tesla turn cutting-edge engineering and cool design into a revenue stream that is consistently greater than its costs? Every successful strategy must begin with the intent of creating value through individual and specific transactions with individual and specific customers.

The relationships depicted in Figure 1.1 form the basis of competitive advantage and so lie at the very heart of strategic success. For instance, while Harley-Davidson makes and sells motorcycles and motorcycle-related products, the strategy of

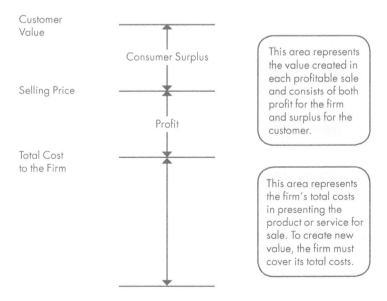

FIGURE 1.1 Competitive Advantage as Value to the Customer

Harley-Davidson is to create value for its consumers by defining an image and a lifestyle of a Harley owner, which differentiates Harley from any other competitive product. While BMW, Honda, and many others make motorcycles of similar, and perhaps in some dimensions even better, qualities and capabilities, Harley owners for the most part don't consider these other brands when making their purchase as they are buying into the lifestyle and persona of Harley-Davidson as much as they are buying a motorcycle. This Harley-Davidson lifestyle creates a large consumer surplus for the consumer, enabling Harley-Davidson to charge premium prices for their motorcycles and motorcycle-related products, which in turn creates profit for the company. Putting this in the context of Figure 1.1, this means that Harley-Davidson is providing products and services that customers value over and above the available alternatives and over and above Harley-Davidson's costs; implied in this are two fundamental requirements. First, Harley-Davidson must understand the competitive environment in which its products and services will be seen and evaluated. Second, Harley-Davidson must understand its own capabilities for supplying what customers will want.

Understanding the competitive environment involves asking questions like, who are the target customers and what is likely to motivate their purchases? What alternatives exist to buying from Harley-Davidson and what do those alternatives offer? What events or trends in the marketplace or in society might affect the willingness of those customers to buy a Harley in the future? These questions are essential to understanding how customers will perceive the product in the context of the competitive landscape and lead Harley-Davidson to realize that they are "more than just a motorcycle" to their customers, such that their Harley-Davidson often becomes a central part of the identity of their customers who align themselves with the brand. As such, Harley-Davidson's managers spend their time not just on everything that goes into manufacturing motorcycles but also on nurturing the lifestyle aspect of Harley ownership, through things such cultivating the Harley Owners Group, or H.O.G., and organizing events where H.O.G.s can gather and share experiences on and about their Harley-Davidson. Indeed, so focused is Harley-Davidson on their customers rather than on simply the manufacture of the bikes themselves that the first key objective in their strategic plan for 2027 is to "Build 2 Million New Riders." Not motorcycles, but riders. As they state in this objective, "It's building new riders that will keep us cruising for another century and beyond, and our efforts are squarely on inspiring new riders who will one day carry the torch for our sport and our brand."[1]

But the managers at Harley must also know something about their own firm. They must know how to produce products that the customers want. They must understand the available technologies and the conditions of the labor market and they must be able to make informed choices about how best to operate. They must understand the relative costs associated with different levels and means of production and they must plan for the evolution and adaptation of their own processes that will necessarily have to occur as the market changes. Finally, they must bring all of this information together in such a way that it yields action and so leads individual customers, acting of their own volition and in their own best interests, to pay a price greater than Harley-Davidson's total costs. When that happens, Harley-Davidson will have competitive advantage. The challenge then is simply to do it all over, again and again and again, day after day and year after year.

Competitive advantage then is best defined as the reason a customer pays a particular firm a profitable price for its products or services. Thought about differently, competitive advantage answers the question, what makes a firm's product or service advantageous relative to the other options? Going forward then, competitive advantage is what will make a firm's service or product advantageous relative to the options that will emerge in the future. By focusing on competitive advantage, at this level, strategic management concerns itself with the customer and the competitive environment within which he or she makes decisions. Alternative suppliers, relative prices, new technologies, reputations for quality and service, these are all parts of the competitive landscape. As such, they are all parts of strategy. But, by focusing on competitive advantage at this level, strategic management also concerns itself with the firm, its capabilities, and its resources. Technologies, inventory, engineering and marketing talent, these are all areas in which a firm may exploit a capability to gain advantage. As such, they too are all a part of strategy.

Competitive advantage then is about creating value in specific transactions, for specific customers, in a specific competitive context. Understood in this sense, competitive advantage is not simply a state of being. Rather, it is a distinction that has to be earned over and over again, with each transaction. It is defined less by a firm's relationship with its competitors than by a firm's relationship with its customers. It is the source of a firm's success and the target of a firm's competitors. As such, it must be constantly developed, nurtured, and grown, because when left alone it will naturally erode and decline.

STRENGTHS, WEAKNESSES, OPPORTUNITIES, AND THREATS

One of the most commonly recognized terms in strategic management is SWOT. The SWOT framework derives its name from two basic issues that every strategy must address. As explained earlier, competitive advantage occurs when customers view a product or service as being sufficiently valuable that they actually pay a profitable price for it. To understand this transaction, we must understand the competitive environment in which it takes place. We must also understand the capabilities and resources required to produce the product or service. These facets of the transaction, the external and the internal, are represented by the letters of SWOT. The S and W represent the internal analysis of the firm, its various Strengths and

Weaknesses; the O and T represent the external analysis of the environment, its various Opportunities and its Threats.

There will be much more to say about each of these later. For now, it is sufficient to know two things. First, a SWOT analysis is merely a tool for identifying some key issues. Simple lists of strengths and weaknesses, opportunities and threats, will provide few insights from which to build meaningful strategy. Yet, such lists are an important part of understanding the conditions of the environment and the capabilities of the firm. Second, neither the environmental nor the organizational side of the analysis alone can tell the whole story of strategic success. Great products and services do not exist in a vacuum. They are attractive only in a particular context, in relation to specific customers and specific alternatives. Good strategy involves analysis and understanding of both the firm's capabilities and resources and its competitive environment.

It is important to understand this from the outset as two major branches of strategic management theory have evolved to address these two different phenomena. **Industrial organization economics** addresses the environment and the competitive landscape of the firm. The **resource-based view** addresses the firm, its capabilities, and its resources. Both are necessary, but alone neither is sufficient to fully explain competitive advantage. As such, neither is, alone, sufficient to guide strategy. Rather, good strategic management must be informed by and incorporate both.

When done well, then, strategic management is a framework for managing the interaction of the firm, with all of its weaknesses and strengths, with its environment, with all of its threats and opportunities. Competitive advantage emerges at this intersection of the two. As Hofer and Schendel (1978) define it (see Box 1.1), strategic management is about the interaction of the firm with its environment, with the intent of creating an ongoing stream of products and services that customers will value and purchase at prices in excess of the firm's costs.

COMPETITIVE ADVANTAGE AND FIRM PERFORMANCE

In the strictest sense, management's ultimate responsibility is to enhance the value of the firm. But what does it really mean to enhance the value of the firm? To understand this concept, it is important to understand that the value of the firm, at any moment in time, is a reflection of expected earnings. Coca-Cola is a valuable company because the strength of its brand, the size of its market, and the record of its performance lead people to believe that the likelihood of future earnings is great. Because owning a portion of this company means owning a claim on a portion of those earnings, increases in expected earnings translate into increases in the value of the firm itself. The same is true of decreases in expected earnings. When the market expects that a firm's earnings will decline, the value of that firm declines as well. When Twitter announced a drop of 1 million users in the summer of 2018, its stock price plunged by more than 20%. That translates into $5 billion in market capitalization that was lost because of the drop in expected revenues. While investors might not have understood the intricacies of all Twitter's efforts to eliminate fake or offensive accounts or to provide greater user security, they did understand that a significant reduction in users was likely to translate into lost revenue and increased losses that would diminish the value of the company. And so they sold their stock, hoping to cash out before that value declined.

Even for new firms, which have not yet had any earnings, the same basic logic applies. Back in 2012, the highly anticipated initial public offering of Facebook valued the firm at about $104 billion. It was one of the largest IPOs ever, and the valuation reflected the expectation of future earnings at that point in time. Given Facebook's enormous user base, strong brand name, and nimble technology, investors believed future earnings would be sufficient to justify the enormous market capitalization. In essence, these investors were betting that Facebook's resources, talent, brand strength, and effort would lead to competitive advantage and that competitive advantage would lead to profits sufficient to provide a good return on the capital invested. Now viewed through the lens of retrospect, those assessments appear to have been correct and Facebook has proven capable of driving strong revenues and profits through its site and business model. Indeed, an investment of $1,000 (about 26 shares at the IPO price of $38) would have been worth over $5,000 in the summer of 2019.

Competitive advantage relates directly to firm value because it relates directly to earnings. Firms with a strong competitive advantage are in a position to earn more than their competitors and, as a consequence, to be more valuable. Of course, earnings can be affected by any number of different things. A new competitor may arise, imitating a firm's product and thereby reducing its share of the market. A new technology may emerge that makes your service less attractive, thereby making it more difficult to sell. Customer tastes may change, leaving a firm with a product that was once highly sought after but that now is all but forgotten. Demographic patterns may shift, changing the size and nature of the target market. An employee could act negligently, causing harm to others and exposing a firm to litigation and penalties. Someone could manipulate the numbers to make the firm appear more profitable, only to be found out and to undermine the trust of investors, increasing the firm's cost of capital. In each example, these various occurrences would reduce the expectation of future earnings and so reduce the value of the firm.

Similar scenarios could be imagined where changes within the firm or the environment would enhance the expectation of future earnings and so enhance the value of the firm. A firm could create a new process, allowing it to make a product more inexpensive and so sell it more profitably. A firm could reorganize its board to alleviate concerns that future earnings could be threatened by litigation or poor oversight. A firm could expand into a new market, increasing its revenues and economies of scale. Shifts in demographic patterns or customer tastes could make a firm's products or services much more popular and attractive than they had been heretofore. These sorts of changes would all increase the expectation of future earnings, thereby increasing the value of the firm.

By focusing on competitive advantage, strategic management is concerned with all of these potentialities and then some. As explained earlier, strategic management is concerned with the environment and how changes within it could create opportunities or threats. Strategic management is concerned with the firm itself and with the various strengths and weaknesses of its products, processes, people, and technology. Finally, strategic management is concerned with the firm's position within society and how the firm itself is viewed and evaluated by customers, investors, regulators, and employees, to name just a few of the stakeholders in the firm. Because the ultimate responsibility of management is to enhance the value of the firm, strategic management lies at the heart of managerial responsibility. The value of the firm is a reflection of current and expected earnings, and both of these are a reflection of competitive advantage. Focusing on value creation and on competitive advantage then provides a sort of strategic **balanced scorecard** for gauging performance in the day to day. Deliver these two things, and all the other measures of performance that are so frequently tracked and reported will take care of themselves. Thus, the development, maintenance, and ongoing cultivation of competitive advantage is the ultimate responsibility of strategic management and the underlying key to firm performance.

THE END OF THE BEGINNING

As you go through this book, you will encounter a number of different topics, frameworks, models, and examples. However, it is important to remember that all of these will point in some way towards competitive advantage. It is also important to remember that competitive advantage results from action. Each framework, each model, each analytical tool should have some implication for action. As you read, stop frequently and ask yourself, how can this impact action? What will actually change, within the firm or between the firm and its customers, as a result of this concept, analytical tool, or way of thinking? How will approaching things in a particular fashion create new value or help the firm to sustain the value it is currently creating? These are the sorts of questions that demand answers. Too often strategic management is presented in an abstract fashion, as a science or a field of study, interesting in its own right but far removed from the practical details of managerial life. That is unfortunate because strategic management is the most practical of disciplines. It is the framework through which all of the functions of an organization are integrated; it is the underlying theory of how a firm will pursue superior performance. In that sense, strategic management is the key to firm success and the capstone of business education.

The chapters that follow will present strategic management in a systematic fashion, starting with Chapter 2, which will look in detail at organizational performance and the various definitional and measurement problems associated with it. Performance is certainly the crux of business. Yet, performance itself is a messy concept, difficult to measure and paradoxical in nature. Chapter 3 will examine the use and utility of different components of the strategic process, like the mission, vision, and the processes of formulation and implementation. These so-called "tools of the trade" are common parts of the business lexicon, yet their purpose is often misunderstood and their importance often unrealized. Ultimately, their value is linked inextricably to competitive advantage and to the firm's ability to employ its resources in a way that delivers value to the customer.

The next section, focused on an in-depth examination of the main tools of strategic analysis, begins with Chapter 4, which introduces environmental analysis as a key step in the strategic process. Environmental analysis has both static and dynamic elements and involves research into the contours of the marketplace. Environmental analysis should yield insights into the opportunities and threats in the near and the more distant future. To capitalize on those insights, firms must understand their own strengths and weaknesses, and the analysis of the firm is the subject of Chapter 5, which introduces the resource-based view and develops a framework for analysis of the organization. The strategies that emerge from environmental and organizational analyses are the subject of Chapter 6. These business-level strategies are designed to produce competitive advantage, which is itself manifested in transactions that lead to profitability.

Following the discussion of business-level strategy, Chapter 7 introduces the concept of corporate-level strategy. Many firms pursue multiple business strategies through multiple strategic business units. Corporate strategy is the process by which all of those strategies are linked and organized in support of the firm as a whole. All strategy though comes to life through the process of implementation, which is the subject of Chapter 8. Implementation has two main implications: its immediate effects on performance and its longer-term effects on the options available for the future. Both are critical to long-term success and so are discussed in detail.

The final section examines some special topics for strategic managers. As firms are faced with dynamic environments and the pace of change continues to accelerate, managers need to not only focus on the immediate day-to-day actions that generate competitive advantage but also be thinking about those factors that will shape their environment in the future, potentially endangering the sustainability of generating that competitive advantage. Chapter 9 looks specifically at major disruptive megatrends that have shaped and that will continue to shape the contours of the business world and society at large. Considering these megatrends, and how they will affect a firm's environment, helps managers prepare the firm to adjust and pivot its strategy to take advantage of the opportunities provided by the disruptive effects of these trends and sustain competitive advantage over the long term.

Finally, our concluding Chapter 10 looks briefly at a range of topics such as entrepreneurship, internationalization, leadership, and corporate governance. It also recognizes that, ultimately, strategic management is a human process, subject to the same limitations and biases of ordinary human behavior. Good strategic management acknowledges this and takes it into account in the design of organizational structures and systems and the ongoing management of strategic processes. In this context, leadership, governance, and ethics are not tangential topics but rather essential elements to strategic management.

As noted, this is more than just one more book *about* strategic management; this is a book *on* strategic management. All of the topics you encounter in it, from those introduced in this first chapter to those covered in the final chapter, are meaningful because of their implications for value creation and firm performance. Ultimately, managers are charged with protecting, building, and leveraging the worth of their organizations. And strategic management, despite all of its popularity and academic rigor, is merely a tool for meeting that challenge. Learn it and learn to use effectively and you will be a better and more valuable manager.

KEY TERMS

Balanced scorecard is the name given to a performance measurement framework developed by Robert Kaplan and David Norton. The framework employs a variety of different strategic and non-financial performance metrics, in combination with traditional financial measures, to produce a single "balanced" measure of performance and condition.

Business model is a term used to describe the template or pattern of how a firm interacts with its customers, suppliers, and partners.

Competitive advantage is the reason a customer chooses to transact with one firm over another. Understood in this way, competitive advantage is episodic and best understood through the eyes of the customer.

Consumer surplus is the gap between the value a customer places on a good or service and the price that he or she pays. In essence, it is the difference between the actual price and the price a customer would have been willing to pay.

Industrial organization (IO) economics is an area, within the larger field of economics, concerned with the competitive forces that affect firm behavior and performance. Established by the work of Chamberlin, Bain, and Mason, IO economics proposes that firm performance is a function of strategic conduct, which is a function of industry structure.

Resource-based view (RBV) holds that competitive advantage, and the economic rents or profits associated with it, is a function of each firm's unique and valuable bundle of resources. Such advantages can persist as long as these resource bundles are not effectively imitated or substituted.

QUESTIONS FOR REVIEW

1. Why study strategic management?
2. What the common theme that runs through the most respected definitions of strategic management?
3. How can strategy be at once part plan, ploy, pattern, position, and perspective?
4. What is the connection between value creation and competitive advantage?
5. What does it mean to say that competitive advantage must be understood through the "eye of the customer"?
6. What is the connection among strategic management, competitive advantage, and overall firm performance?

NOTE

1   www.harley-davidson.com/us/en/about-us/company.html

Chapter 2

Understanding Organizational Performance

VALUING FACEBOOK

As mentioned in Chapter 1, Facebook's initial public offering (IPO) in February of 2012 was one of the most anticipated ever announced. Facebook would become a publicly traded firm, and observers expected the IPO value to be one of the highest ever. Facebook's rise, from its founding in 2004, to more than a billion users and an IPO in 2012, to a market capitalization that topped $600 billion in 2018 is another astonishing business success story. Nevertheless, at the time it went public, the real question facing the markets and investors was, what was Facebook actually worth? What would be the actual price, and the underlying valuation, for the new stock and what sort of growth in revenues and earnings would be needed to support that stock price and valuation?

Facebook's regulatory filings at the time showed that it produced $3.7 billion in revenue with a $1 billion profit in 2011. Revenue growth had been 88% over the previous year, which indicated that it was still a fast-growing enterprise. While some analysts were pleased with Facebook's position, others expressed disappointment with what appeared to be slowing revenue growth. If revenue growth were to continue to lose speed, the company would be unlikely to produce profits sufficient to support a record valuation and the stock could be worth significantly less. The predictions varied widely, with most analysts placing the overall value of Facebook within a range from $75 billion to over $100 billion.

Within days of the announcement, financial analysts and investment firms began releasing competing assessments with various different projections and valuations. Instead of the valuations becoming more similar, they grew further apart. Some experts valued Facebook as low as $50 billion, while others valued it as high as $125 billion. Facebook itself valued its employee shares at a price which translated to a value of $74 billion. All of these various differences reflected differing perceptions about future user levels, future ad revenue growth, and future sources of additional revenues. Moreover, many of these various and differing projections reflected the different valuation methods used by the different experts.

Ultimately, Facebook went public at a price of $38, which yielded approximately $16 billion in new cash to the company and translated to an overall valuation of $104 billion, making it the largest IPO in history. However, in the weeks and months that followed, Facebook's stock dropped, reaching a low of just over $18 per share by late August 2012. At that price, Facebook's overall valuation was about $41 billion, less than half of its value on the day of the IPO. Yet, the company was substantively no different in August than it had been in February. The business model, user base, and brand were still virtually the same. The strategy, which was to build users and connections and then to leverage those users and connections to target refined market development and advertising efforts was largely unchanged. The management team that built the company was still intact and still engaged in the day-to-day management of the company. On top of all this, the financial strength of the company was perhaps even greater in August than it had been in February, because of the new cash generated through the IPO. And yet, somehow the company was worth less than half in August than it had been in February of the same year.

How do we explain this? Was Facebook overvalued initially or was it undervalued later? Or, is it possible that the true value of the company was somewhere in between? Was the company performing better in February than it was in August, or did the range of valuations merely reflect estimates of future performance that failed to occur? The drop in Facebook's value following its IPO, along with all of the fluctuations and discrepancies in the pre-IPO estimates of its price, point to the difficulties in predicting, valuing, and quantifying organizational performance. As noted previously, strategic management really is all about the quest for performance, which means that performance is the crux of strategic management thinking, focus, and effort. But performance itself is inherently problematic. First of all, the term itself can mean different things to different people and in different contexts. Second, performance is difficult to assess in isolation. Without a reference point to use in comparison, what does it even mean to say that a firm has performed well? Finally, the definition and measure of performance is fixed to a particular point in time.

In the case of Facebook, the valuations during the IPO were based upon estimates of the future and of future performance. As the timeframe changed, so too did those estimates. As a result, the value of the company was reduced significantly. With even more time having passed though, and now viewed through the lens of history, it seems that the subsequent discounting was in error. Indeed, by February 2015, Facebook's stock was trading at nearly $75 per share, and by July of 2018 the price was over $200 per share, giving Facebook an overall market valuation of more than $600 billion. Of course, issues related to concerns with user security, fake news, and government regulation would lead to steep declines in the stock price and market value in the fall of 2018. Nevertheless, the initial offering price of $38 per share appears now to have been a very good investment, and assessments of Facebook's revenue and profit-generating potential, which led to that initial decline in its market value, appear now to have been incorrect. Learning to apply strategic management then means learning to deal with the complexities surrounding the definition, understanding, and measurement of organizational performance.

UNDERSTANDING ORGANIZATIONAL PERFORMANCE

Thinking about organizational performance is at once simple and complex. While most will readily claim to know what performance is, they will also likely have difficulty defining it precisely. Thus, as we begin this chapter, it is important to acknowledge three things. First, performance is a multi-dimensional construct, with a variety of different and sometimes conflicting facets. There are many different ways that performance can be defined and measured, and each of those definitions and measures can produce different indications of how a firm is actually doing. Second, performance can be paradoxical. The pursuit of good performance along any one dimension might well lead to diminishing returns on others. Some have argued, for instance, that good performance in the present can actually produce mindsets and behaviors that hinder good performance in the future. Finally, despite all of these complexities, performance is still the key to business success and the standard against which management is evaluated. As such, it pays for managers and students alike to understand what various different measures of performance mean and what implication each has for strategy and the pursuit of competitive advantage.

VALUE AS A MEASURE OF PERFORMANCE

As mentioned in the previous chapter, the ultimate responsibility of management is to enhance the value of the firm. So, would that mean that the most valuable firm is also the one that is performing the best? Unfortunately, it is not that simple. Simply look at the case of Facebook. How could market value fluctuate so dramatically, while everyday strategy and execution continued largely unchanged? While market value is an **unbiased estimate** of the value of a **publicly held firm**, it is still just an estimate and so is subject to measurement error. But even if we could measure market value perfectly, how would we compare the value of a publicly held firm to the value of a **privately held firm**? For a publicly held firm, market value is most simply understood as the market value of each share of stock times the number of shares outstanding. The problem is that the shares of a privately held firm have no established market price. How do we estimate the value of such a firm? And, if we cannot easily estimate the value of all firms, how can value be a practical measure of performance?

Estimating value presents other problems as well. What, for instance, does value represent? Fundamentally, value is supposed to reflect the present value of all future earnings. Take, for example, a small restaurant. Its various holdings of equipment, inventory, and other assets may amount to $300,000. This value reflects the costs of the equipment, assets, and inventory, less the accumulated depreciation resulting from age and use. The business itself, however, is more than the sum of these tangible assets. Suppose that this restaurant also has a great reputation for tasty food, good prices, and fast, friendly service. Suppose that it is situated in a great location, with lots of visibility and traffic. In that case, the earning potential of those assets may be substantial. Indeed, suppose that this small restaurant generates profits of $100,000 per year. By discounting those profits to their present day value, at a risk-adjusted opportunity cost of capital of 17.5%, we get a value of $566,091, a substantial increase over the $300,000 figure obtained from the book value of the tangible assets.

This simple example illustrates several important points about the determination of value. First, valuation is based principally on future events. A buyer of this restaurant would certainly want to know the history of the business and to know how well it has performed. However, he would not be buying that history. Rather, what he would be buying is ownership of the profits to come in the future. Anything that affects that future would affect the value of his investment. A demographic shift that produced a change in the traffic patterns around the restaurant might decrease the value of the business. The addition of new menu items that produced new sales but that did not require new equipment might increase the value of the business. However, in both cases, these events would occur in the future.

This was a part of the problem with estimating the value of Facebook. Much of the difficulty resulted from assumptions about the growth of future revenues and earnings. The future is uncertain, and it is especially uncertain in the case of new businesses and new business models. Thus, different assumptions about Facebook's growth and profitability led to different valuations, and different valuations led to different expectations of the stock's price. Value then is really a forward-looking measure. And, as a forward-looking measure, estimates of value are subject to insufficient information, human bias, and outright error.

Notice too that several of the key variables used in the determination of this restaurant's value are subjectively derived. As just discussed, because the value is based on estimates of future profits, there will be some subjective assumptions in those estimates. How much will the business grow? What sorts of events might occur that will increase or decrease demand and costs? How will the competitive landscape change and what sorts of actions might the owners take to enhance or diminish their competitive advantage? These sorts of issues and the impact they will have on profitability must be evaluated, estimated, and quantified before they can be used to estimate value. At the same time, the discount rate (of 17.5% in the earlier example) is a key to calculating the present value of the profits. In this case, a change in the discount rate of 2.5%, above or below the estimate of 17.5%, would result in a change of $158,704 in value, with a 20% discount rate yielding a value of $497,894 and a 15% discount rate yielding a value of $656,598.

The discount rate is meant to reflect the risk of the investment and the opportunity cost of the capital needed to buy and own the business. While there are a number of very good models to aid in the calculation of this discount rate, the actual rate itself is specific to each individual or firm. In this instance, the original owner, with all of his knowledge and experience, would see relatively little risk in the business. As such, he would employ a relatively low discount rate, which would result in a higher value. A buyer, though, would see the business as being much less secure and certain. Thus, he might use a higher discount rate, which would result in a lower value. Each individual, then, might look at the same business and at the very same stream of profits and value them differently. As noted from the Facebook case, different experts produced substantially different valuations, largely because they used different sets of assumptions and discount rates. Value, then, while extremely important in assessing a business, is far from a perfect, practical measure of performance.

PROFITABILITY AS A MEASURE OF PERFORMANCE

Because value reflects profits, many use profitability as the ultimate measure of performance. Indeed, in classical economic theory managers are to maximize profits and to take whatever actions they can, within the bounds of the law and accepted practice, to increase earnings. Unfortunately, though, profitability is as problematic as value, although for different reasons. As such, profitability too fails to measure performance perfectly and fully.

The problems with profitability are threefold. First, profit can be measured both in absolute and in relative terms. Second, while profitability occurs on a continuous basis, it is calculated and reported in discrete increments. Finally, unlike value, profitability is a backward-looking measure; it merely reports that which has already occurred but gives little insight into what is occurring now or what might occur into the future. Each of these problems are discussed later. However, it is important to remember that discussing problems in the measurement of profitability should not be seen as a criticism of profit itself. Firms must create profits; their very survival depends upon it. However, in understanding performance, it is important to recognize the strengths and weaknesses of the myriad different ways in which performance can be measured and reported.

Profit is important because it is the excess of revenues over costs. As depicted in the last chapter, in Figure 1.1, firms profit as they create products that customers value and buy at a price over and above the firm's costs. Firms that are creating profits have some measure of competitive advantage in their markets. Customers are choosing, of their own volition, to buy from the firm and to buy at a price that provides the firm a profit. But as we expand our view to include many transactions, between many firms and many customers, the picture becomes more complex. Consider two firms, one of which sells $10,000,000 in product and profits $350,000 from those sales and the other of which sells $2,000,000 in product and profits $100,000 from those sales. Which of these two firms is more profitable and which is performing better? It is really difficult to say. The first, while creating more profit in an absolute sense, performed less well in a relative sense. The first firm earned only 3.5% on each dollar of sales; the second firm earned 5% on each dollar of sales. Similar comparisons could be made by comparing profits as a proportion of assets or profits as a proportion of equity.

For example, suppose the first firm is in a knowledge-intensive industry, where labor costs are high but fixed asset costs are low. Suppose as well that this firm had booked assets of $3,000,000. That would yield a profit of 11.7% on each dollar of asset. Now suppose that the second firm was a retail establishment with a $1,000,000 investment in a stand-alone store and specialized equipment. This firm would have profited only 10% on each dollar of asset. Depending upon how the assets in these two examples are financed, with different levels of equity or debt, we could similarly imagine different levels of return for each dollar of equity. None of these ratios is inherently better or more insightful than the others. However, they all reflect profit as a percentage of a baseline, whether that baseline is sales, assets, or equity. As such, they will all provide somewhat different information and a somewhat different picture than merely reporting profit in absolute dollars.

Another problem with profit arises from the fact that profits are earned continuously; with each sale and with each expense, profit changes, even if only slightly. Yet, when we report profit on a periodic basis, we essentially stop the continuous, day-to-day activity and report a single number at a particular moment in time. This difference in the nature of how profit is earned and how it is reported can lead to both confusion and occasionally misrepresentation. For example, confusion can arise over the impact of extraordinary, one-time events (see Box 2.1: Earnings Take a Hit). One-time charges or an extraordinary loss like those associated with the insurance payments that follow large-scale, natural disasters can wipe out the earnings from otherwise stable operations. Such events can also increase earnings too, as when a firm sells off a location or wins a judgment against a competitor for copyright infringement. In both cases, the revenues realized might be significant, yet non-recurring. As such, they can affect the profits in one period, but not in others. As a result, they can create the impression that is inconsistent with the ongoing reality of the firm.

Such events are actually quite common and can usually be accommodated through adjustments in the financial reports and notes explaining the impact on expenses and profits. Sometimes, though, these sorts of one-time events can be so exceptional that they defy a simple explanation. For example, after the collapse of the mortgage market in late 2007–2008, and the subsequent fall in asset values, many firms had to write down or write off the value of some assets. These one-time charges affected earnings in the period in which the write-offs were taken, even though they reflected activities that accumulated much earlier. These sorts of events can change dramatically the profits a firm reports without changing any of the fundamental characteristics of the firm's competitive advantage.

Reporting profit on a periodic basis can also provide opportunities for misrepresentation. Why would managers intentionally misrepresent their firm's profit?

Box 2.1
Earnings Take a Hit

In early January 2018, JPMorgan Chase, one of the largest banks in the country, reported that fourth-quarter earnings would be down from the previous year. The culprit in this earnings decline was a one-time charge of $2.4 billion, related to the 2017 tax law. Jamie Dimon, CEO of JPMorgan Chase, is on record saying that the overall effect of the new tax law would be "a big significant positive and much of it will fall to our bottom line in 2018 and beyond." However, in the immediate term, the effect of such a large, one-time expense was to reduce earnings by nearly 40% when compared to the year before.

Emily Glazer, Wall Street Journal 1/12/2018

Because doing so may work to their benefit in the eyes of investors, regulators, or parties with whom they are bargaining. For years, Major League Baseball has suffered from a highly acrimonious relationship between the owners and the players' association. Part of the acrimony is attributable to the claim by the owners that the franchises themselves are barely profitable. The players' association challenges that such claims are merely ploys, on the part of management, to reduce the players' salaries. The owners charge that the players are simply greedy and fail to comprehend the complexity of measuring profit and loss in a major league franchise (see Box 2.2: The Profitability of Major League Baseball). Public utilities have similarly

---

Box 2.2
The Profitability of Major League Baseball

For years, Major League Baseball (MLB) has been marked by the contentious relationship between its players and its franchise owners. While the players and the owners should share a common interest in maintaining a healthy and profitable league, the two groups have frequently disagreed over the basic issues of profitability among the teams and the league. Consider that MLB generated over $10 billion in revenues in 2017, more than in any previous year. Nevertheless, the league claimed its teams lost a total of $93 million.

While some teams are clearly more profitable than others, accounting for the actual profitability of a baseball franchise is a murky process. Some teams are based in large markets and have the ability to generate enormous revenues, but these teams may also have exceptionally high player salaries and other costs. Meanwhile, there is the competitive balance tax, sometimes referred to as the "luxury tax" which charges teams a percentage of every salary dollar above the league cap. There is the effect of revenue sharing, whereby every team pays a percentage of its revenues into a common pool. That pool is then shared evenly across the league. Of course, one of the largest sources of revenue for MLB is the money generated from ticket sales, merchandise, and concessions. But attendance was down in 2017, below 70 million total for the first time since 2002, even as television revenues are up.

This complexity has impacted the relationship between the owners and players by making it difficult to tell whether teams are in fact profitable. The owners, along with the league itself, often claim the teams are under financial stress. And, as a result, they will argue that they cannot afford to pay more to the players. Indeed, prior to spring training in 2018, there was talk of another strike as players claimed collusion among the owners to suppress free agency and salaries overall. In support of their claims, the players pointed to record revenues of the league, the enormous TV contracts, new stadiums and related real estate developments, and the skyrocketing prices that have been paid for MLB franchises, as evidence that they are being shortchanged.

Over the years, the players and the owners have made their cases and drawn their respective lines in the sand. At the root of the matter, though, is a fundamental disagreement over the profitability of the franchises themselves.

sought to understate their profits in the hopes of getting favorable rate decisions from their governing public service regulators. Such firms will argue that, without rate increases, they will have to operate at a loss. The regulators will often respond by saying that the firms are doing a poor job of managing their costs and could be profitable if they would simply do a better job of reducing their expenses. The United States Postal Service is a classic example of this.

Finally, managers will sometimes seek to misrepresent their profitability to analysts and investors. Christopher Milliken, the CEO at OfficeMax, was forced to resign in 2005, along with 6 other executives who also either resigned or were fired. The company had intentionally misrepresented payments to and rebates from some vendors, the effect of which was to overstate income by $5 to $10 million. The board of directors ousted CEO Martin Grass in 2003 for similar irregularities at the drug store chain Rite Aid. Ultimately, the Securities and Exchange Commission filed suit against Grass and 2 other top executives, charging that they had intentionally misrepresented earnings by a total of $1.6 billion, over a period of several years, leading up to Grass' dismissal. Recent research shows that severe restatements of earnings are highly correlated with CEO turnover, suggesting that the restatements are often the result of managerial misrepresentation (Land, 2010).

Among the tricks that managers have used to misrepresent earnings is "booking" revenue in a current period that rightly belonged in some future period. This can be done in a number of ways; a firm may ship orders early, overloading their customers with inventory but allowing the firm to show the sale and the revenue earlier. They might also sell a multi-period contract but recognize all of the expected revenue from that contract at the time of the sale. Both practices are unethical and potentially illegal because they have the effect of overstating the firm's profits in the current period. Higher profits, or the perception of higher profits, may make the firm appear more valuable and so make management appear to be doing a better job. This seems to have been the underlying motivation at Rite Aid, which is why the SEC filed suit. Indeed, many of the now infamous ethical scandals in the 1990s, and then again in the 2000s, involved similar schemes to overstate earnings for the sake inflating firm value.

Finally, even when profit is reported accurately and interpreted correctly, it remains a historical measure, reflecting past activity. As such, it is of dubious value for judging performance in the present or going forward. Profit is certainly an indicator of competitive advantage, good management, and good fit with the environment. However, competitive advantage is based on a number of different things. Changes in customer tastes or in the competitive landscape could render a firm that was profitable in the previous year unprofitable in the current one. Profit is certainly associated with good management, but it would be a mistake to think the two correspond directly. Some industries are simply less attractive than others. The grocery and related products business, for example, is very competitive, with little overall growth and persistently strong cost pressures. As such, it is a business where some very good managers compete over some very small margins. The medical diagnostic and testing business, on the other hand, has seen tremendous growth over the past two decades. With dramatic increases in the amounts spent on medical care, and the ever growing complexity of diagnostic procedures, this business has seen strong growth and rising profits. In comparing these two industries, it is important to understand the structural differences that underlie the differences in profitability.

The point of looking at these two common performance measures is not to criticize them outright. Quite the contrary, both are essential components of overall performance. Rather, the point is to illustrate the broad and multifaceted nature of performance itself. To be understood properly, performance must be considered over time, from a variety of perspectives, and in its proper context.

PERFORMANCE OVER TIME

One of the most challenging issues in understanding performance is the need to consider it over time. Think of all the firms that were once dominant players in their respective markets, profitable firms with strong reputations and highly sought after products and services that slipped from their positions of leadership. Arthur Andersen, Kmart, RCA, Sears, Xerox, Kodak, and PanAm could all be examples of firms that once had every advantage but, for some reason, slipped back into the pack or stumbled and fell altogether. How could a firm with all the advantages of Kmart be overtaken by a small chain from an unfamiliar town in northwestern Arkansas? How, with all of the market power and money associated with its position in the photography and film business, could Kodak fail to seize control of the digital photography business when it emerged? How could Arthur Andersen, one of the most respected names in the business of accounting and auditing, stumble to the point of exiting an industry that was virtually synonymous with its name? The explanations will be discussed in detail in Chapter 9. For now, though, these examples should serve as a lesson that, in the business world, the competition never ends. As explained in Chapter 1, the metaphor of a game, with winners and losers, breaks down when applied to business because in business, the game never ends.

Danny Miller (1990) has written insightfully on this phenomenon whereby successful firms fall prey to their own complacency, inertia, limited vision, and defensiveness, relating it to the mythical story of Icarus. Icarus was the son of Daedalus, a gifted architect and builder, who was exiled on the island of Crete. To escape the exile, Daedalus fashioned wings, made of wax and feathers, for himself and his son Icarus. Icarus, upon learning to use his wings, flew so high that the heat from the sun melted the wax of his wings. As a result, Icarus fell into the Aegean Sea and died. This mythical story depicts a paradox. Icarus' greatest asset was also his ultimate undoing. The power of his wings allowed him to soar to heights otherwise impossible. Yet, in soaring to these heights, Icarus died.

Miller applies this fabled lesson to successful companies and argues that the same pattern applies. Successful firms, insulated by the resources accumulated from their past success, can grow complacent and cease to exercise the vigilance and drive that made them successful in the first place. They may become so enamored of their own products and services that they fail to continue learning and innovating. They may become so conceited amidst the shower of praise from professors, consultants, customers and writers in the popular press that they fail to consider new and unfamiliar competitors. Finally, they may become so invested in and defensive of the status quo that, in trying to protect their current advantage, they fail to invest in the sorts of learning and adaptive behaviors necessary to ensure competitive advantage in the future.

By understanding competitive advantage as the continuous pursuit of value creation and appropriation, we can begin to see that performance is ongoing. Competitive advantage does bring profitability, but competitive advantage is a distinction that must be earned one customer at a time, over and over again. Naturally, firms must perform in the present, but not at the expense of the future. At the same time, firms that cannot perform in the present do not last to see the future. This tension between the short and the long term is subtle and paradoxical. Persisting too long in one strategy, even as successful as that strategy may be, can provide an opportunity for new competitors. Good performance is certainly desirable and will often bring with it substantial rewards. Those rewards, however, can dull the hunger, the creativity, and the innovativeness needed to ensure performance in the future. Moreover, that performance and the rewards associated with it can attract competition and provide a target on which new competitors can focus. As will be discussed in greater detail later, to perform well over time, firms must learn to be their own toughest competitors, constantly challenging convention, constantly seeking dissenting points of view, and constantly reminding themselves that the contest never ends.

For now, it is enough to remember that virtually all measures of performance are momentary snapshots of an ongoing phenomenon. See Table 2.1, which lists the 10 U.S.-based firms with the largest asset base, the highest total revenues, and the greatest overall profits for the years 1980, 1996, and 2017. While there is some stability, there is also substantial turnover on each of these lists. What is so impressive about this turnover is that it occurred despite the fact that these are some of the most well-endowed firms in the world. These firms on the list in 1980 enjoyed all the advantages of incumbency. They had great name recognition; they enjoyed great bargaining power with their customers and suppliers; they could afford the best minds, the best research, the best locations, and the best advertising. Yet, somehow, they were overtaken by firms with far fewer advantages. What are we to make of this, and what is the lesson for strategic managers? It is simply this: although we

Table 2.1
A Changing of the Guard

The 10 Firms With the Highest Profits in:

	1980	1996	2017
1.	Exxon	General Motors	Apple
2.	IBM	General Electric	Berkshire Hathaway
3.	General Motors	Exxon-Mobil	Verizon
4.	Mobil	Altria Group	AT&T
5.	Chevron	IBM	JPMorgan Chase
6.	Texaco	Ford	Comcast
7.	Amoco	Intel	Wells Fargo
8.	General Electric	Citicorp	Pfizer
9.	Gulf Oil	Merck	Microsoft
10.	BP America	DuPont	Exxon Mobil

The 10 Firms With the Highest Revenues in:

	1980	1996	2017
1.	Exxon	General Motors	Wal-Mart
2.	General Motors	Ford	Apple
3.	Mobil	Exxon	Berkshire Hathaway
4.	Ford	Wal-Mart	Exxon Mobil
5.	Texaco	AT&T	United Health Group
6.	Chevron	IBM	McKesson
7.	Gulf Oil	General Electric	Amazon.com
8.	IBM	Mobil	CVS Health
9.	General Electric	Chrysler	AT&T
10.	Amoco	Altria Group	General Motors

The 10 Firms With the Most Assets in:

	1980	1996	2017
1.	Exxon	Fannie Mae	Fannie Mae
2.	General Motors	Citicorp	JPMorgan Chase
3.	Mobil	Ford	Bank of America
4.	IBM	Bank of America	Freddie Mac
5.	Ford	General Electric	Citigroup
6.	Chevron	Prudential Insurance	Wells Fargo
7.	Texaco	General Motors	Goldman Sachs
8.	Gulf Oil	Salomon Brothers	Morgan Stanley
9.	Amoco	JP Morgan	Prudential Financial
10.	General Electric	Chase Manhattan	Berkshire Hathaway

measure it in discrete increments and at particular moments, success is ongoing. A firm cannot simply perform once and then rest in that success. In time, competitors will adapt and overcome; customers will grow restless and demand better services, lower prices, or both; and markets will adjust their aspirations, taking for granted in the future that which was seen as extraordinary in the past. Understanding performance means understanding this temporal dimension; it means understanding that performance occurs over time.

PERFORMANCE FROM A VARIETY OF PERSPECTIVES

In addition to thinking about performance over time, it is also important to think about it from a variety of perspectives. As illustrated earlier, no single measure tells the whole story. Rather, a number of different measures must be considered, simultaneously. Table 2.2 provides a list of and descriptions for a number for various ratios used to measure performance (see Table 2.2: A Sampling of Ratios Used to Measure Performance). For any single firm, these different measures will provide different information. A firm that is highly leveraged with debt, for instance, may have a high return on equity but a much lower return on assets. A firm with growing sales and substantial profitability may still be performing poorly in terms of cash flow as it fails to collect the money for its sales. Earnings per share is a function both of the earnings and the number of shares outstanding. Moreover, earnings per share is of little value in the consideration of private firms or firms that are not actively traded. Because no single measure tells the whole story, it is important to use multiple measures and to think carefully about what each measure actually reveals.

In addition to the measures in Table 2.2 and the two described at the beginning of the chapter, there are a number of others that are commonly used to assess performance. Two of these, Tobin's q and economic value added (EVA), are discussed here.

Tobin's q

Tobin's q is formed by dividing a firm's market value by the replacement cost of its assets (Lindenburg & Ross, 1981). Tobin's q is somewhat unique, conceptually, in that it gets at the value of a firm's intangible assets based upon their earning capacity in the future. Consider, for instance, the example given earlier of a restaurant with assets valued at $300,000. Recall that this hypothetical firm had a market value estimated at between $500,000 and $600,000, nearly twice the book value of the assets. What accounts for the difference, and from where does this value come? As explained, the book value of the assets, in this case $300,000,

Table 2.2
A Sampling of Ratios Used to Measure Performance

Measure	Description	Interpretation
Return on Sales (ROS)	$\dfrac{\text{After-tax Profit}}{\text{Total Sales}}$	Return on total sales; percentage per dollar of sales
Return on Assets (ROA)	$\dfrac{\text{After-tax Profit}}{\text{Total Assets}}$	Return on total investment; percentage per dollar of assets
Return on Equity (ROE)	$\dfrac{\text{After-tax Profit}}{\text{Total Firm Equity}}$	Return on total equity; percentage per dollar of owner's equity
Gross Profit Margin	$\dfrac{\text{Total Sales} - \text{Cost of Goods}}{\text{Total Sales}}$	Proportion of each dollar of sales retained as operating profit
Net Profit Margin	$\dfrac{\text{Total Sales} - \text{Total Expenses}}{\text{Total Sales}}$	Proportion of each dollar of sales retained as profit
Earning per Share (EPS)	$\dfrac{\text{Net Profit} - \text{PS Dividends}}{\text{Common Shares Outstanding}}$	Profit available for distribution to the shareholders
Price/Earnings Ratio (P/E)	$\dfrac{\text{Stock Price per Share}}{\text{After-Tax Earnings per Share}}$	Stock price as a multiple of earnings; indicates anticipated earnings
Cash Flow per Share	$\dfrac{\text{After-Tax Profit} + \text{Depreciation}}{\text{Common Shares Outstanding}}$	Liquidity to fund operations over and above current costs
Current Ratio	$\dfrac{\text{Current Assets}}{\text{Current Liabilities}}$	Liquidity over and above current liabilities
Debt to Total Assets	$\dfrac{\text{Total Debt}}{\text{Total Assets}}$	The proportion of the firm's assets financed by debt
Debt to Total Equity	$\dfrac{\text{Total Debt}}{\text{Total Equity}}$	The amount of financing in debt as a proportion of total equity

reflects the costs of the assets to the firm, less any accumulated depreciation. However, those costs are poor indicators of the actual earning value of the assets. Earning value is difficult to assess directly because it is context-specific; in other words, it varies from firm to firm and from situation to situation. The restaurant in the example is valuable because of its reputation, its location, and the quality of its product. Change the location or change the way the business is managed and you change the earning value of the assets. Consider the case of a single asset, a Gibson Les Paul Standard guitar. This guitar may have a book value of about

$2,000. However, in the hands of a famous and talented musician, like Joe Walsh, the asset would take on much greater value. In the same fashion, a formula for the production of a sweet, dark-colored, carbonated soft drink might have modest value. However, in concert with the legal copyright to the name Coca-Cola and the marketing and distribution presence to promote and deliver that soft drink around the world, the formula becomes much more valuable. This increase in value, over and above the book value, is intangible and specific to the individual application and firm. At any moment in time then, a firm's value is a combination of (1) the actual book value of its assets and (2) the intangible value added to those assets by the managers, people, brand recognition, and strategies of the firm. Intangible value then can be a powerful measure of organizational success and performance.

Calculating Tobin's q requires estimating two values: the market value of the firm and the replacement costs of the firm's tangible assets. Unfortunately, neither value is especially easy to measure with precision. Market value, for example, can be established with the following formula:

Firm market value = Market value of common shares
+ Market value of preferred shares
+ Book value of total debt (short and long term)

Common shares are easily valued if they are regularly traded. The average number of shares outstanding, over a given period of time, times the average price per share over the same period of time provides a good measure of the value of the common shares. Valuing other types of shares, such as preferred shares, presents a somewhat larger challenge. When they are actively traded, preferred shares can be valued in the same way as the common shares. Preferred shares are not, however, always traded actively. In that event, it is often necessary to consult some other sources of information, such as the Standard & Poor's preferred stock yield index. This index value, in conjunction with the preferred dividend paid on the stock, can be used to establish a value for the preferred shares. More simply, preexisting databases like COMPUSTAT will often report a preferred stock value for the firms in its database. The final component of market value is the cost of the firm's debt, including both short-term and long-term obligations. These values are available directly or can be extracted from a firm's balance sheet. The sum of these values provides a good estimate of the market value of the firm.

The denominator in the calculation of Tobin's q is the replacement costs of the firm's assets. Of course, the calculation of this number is highly problematic, as it involves estimating the cost of all the firm's assets in current terms. While a number of procedures have been proposed for estimating these replacement costs, they are all rather cumbersome. Fortunately, research has shown that the book value of total assets is a relatively unbiased estimate of replacement costs

(Perfect & Wiles, 1994). The book value of total assets is readily available from a firm's balance sheet. Using the book value of total assets as an estimate of total asset replacement costs, the calculation of Tobin's q becomes, simply, market value divided by book value. This ratio represents the intangible value added to the firm's assets by its people, its strategy, its unique organizational configuration, and its managerial skill.

As important and powerful as this measure may be, it is important to recognize that it too has limitations. The calculation of market value, for instance, is easy enough in the case of large, publicly traded firms. It is much more difficult and much less certain for firms that are not actively traded. Moreover, even among actively traded firms, the determination of market value is subject to daily variation, as the price of the stock rises and falls. Such variation in the share price translates directly to variation in the value of Tobin's q. Additionally, it is also important to remember that the book value of a firm's assets reflects the accumulated depreciation of those assets. Firms with older assets will naturally have a smaller denominator and, consequently, a higher q. Still, taking into account the strengths and weaknesses of the numbers from which it is derived, Tobin's q is a valuable indicator of firm performance.

Economic Value Added

The other measure of performance mentioned is *economic value added* or EVA. The measurement of EVA reflects the desire to capture what economists call rents or *economic profit*. Economic profit reflects returns over and above those expected based upon the value of the assets and capital employed. Essentially, economic profit differs from accounting profit in that it takes into account the cost of the firm's capital. EVA is calculated as net operating profit after taxes (NOPAT) less the firm's weighted average cost of capital (WACC). The importance of including the cost of capital into the calculation of profit is that it raises the bar for what constitutes good performance. Without including the cost of capital in the assessment, a manager might invest in marginal projects that produce a return in excess of their direct costs yet ultimately still lose money. Because the costs of capital are real, management should invest only in projects that produce a positive return over and above those costs.

Unfortunately, calculating EVA is complicated. The first value, NOPAT, is a function of earnings before interest and taxes (EBIT) and the taxes on those earnings. EBIT is equal to revenues minus cost of goods sold, selling, general and administrative expenses, and depreciation. Taxes on EBIT are reported in the company's financial statements. However, when a direct examination of those statements is impossible or when future taxes are being considered, it is necessary to estimate. Estimating the taxes on EBIT is difficult to do with precision as they involve a number of variables including interest expense, interest income, and non-operating income. However, a good estimate can be obtained by multiplying EBIT by the statutory marginal tax rate. While this simple approach will not account for deferred taxes or changes in deferred taxes, it will provide a close estimate that can be easily derived. NOPAT is then equal to EBIT less the taxes on EBIT.

The second component of EVA is the weighted average cost of capital. The precise calculation of the WACC is also complicated and so is frequently simplified in practice. Calculating WACC involves calculating the cost of the firm's debt as well as the cost of its equity and then weighting each based upon the proportion of capital in the form of either debt or equity.

Estimating the cost of debt is complicated by a number of factors. Specifically, firms may have debt from a number of different sources. A bank loan at an interest rate of 6% is easy to value. However, if a firm also has issued bonds, then the cost of that debt will vary with the quality of the bonds' rating. A rating of A+ might translate to an interest rate of 5.5%, while a rating of B– might translate to an interest rate of 10%. There is also the issue of tax deductibility. If the interest expense is deductible from income, then it reduces the tax burden on the firm, effectively reducing the cost of the debt. Taking these into account, it is necessary to multiply the after-tax cost of the debt by the proportion of debt in that particular form. For example, consider a firm with $1 million in high-quality bonds, on which it is paying 7%; a secured bank loan of $500,000, on which it is paying 7.5%; and lease arrangements on assets totaling $800,000, on which it is paying 8.5%. For the sake of simplicity, assume that all of the interest expense is fully tax-deductible. The total amount of debt carried would be $2.3 million and the weighted average cost of this debt would be 7.6%. Recall, however, that this interest expense is tax-deductible, meaning that, for a tax rate of 30%, every $100 in interest results in a tax saving of $30. Thus, we adjust the cost of the debt by the inverse of the tax rate (1 – tax rate), or in this case, 1.0 – .3 for 70%, which is then multiplied by the WACD of 7.6%, for a true WACD of 5.3%.

Calculating the cost of equity is similarly complicated and involves the capital asset pricing model (CAPM). The CAPM is simply:

Cost of equity = RFR + FR (E (MRR) – RFR)
Where: RFR is the risk-free rate of return
       FR is firm specific variability or risk
       E(MRR) is the market rate of return.

While appearing complex, this formula can be practically useful. For example, the risk-free rate of return is generally estimated as the interest rate on guaranteed government securities. A good estimate of the market rate of return is the actual rate of return for various stock market indices, like the Standard & Poor's composite index.

The calculation of the firm-specific risk, referred to as β or beta, requires regression analysis. The regression formula for beta is:

$R_{i,t} = a + b_i R_{m,t} + e$
Where: $R_{i,t}$ is the actual return on the firm's stock over a set period of time
a is a constant, equal to $(1 - b)$
b_i is the estimated value of beta
$R_{m,t}$ is the market return
e is the error, associated with estimating $R_{i,t}$

Fortunately, beta is provided for most publicly traded companies through various research services. So it can be known without actually doing the analysis described earlier. Still, knowing beta is essential to knowing the value of a firm's equity because beta represents the variance in a firm's stock price as a proportion of the variance of the total market. So, knowing beta allows us to know that a 10% change in the overall value of the stock market will produce a change of beta * 10% in the value of the firm's stock. Stocks with a high beta are risky, and that risk translates into higher equity expenses. Calculating the cost of equity simply involves plugging in the appropriate values. If the risk-free rate of return is 4%, if beta is 1.5, and if the market rate of return is 8%, then the cost of equity is equal to:

.04 + 1.5 (.08 − .04) or .10

Conceptually, that means that an equity investor would require a 10% return as compensation for the risk of investing in this firm rather than in the risk-free instrument.

With the cost of equity and the cost of debt computed, the WACC is computed simply by adding the percentage of total capital in the form of debt, weighted by its cost, to the percentage of total capital in the form of equity, weighted by its cost. Suppose that our hypothetical firm had a total capitalization of $5,000,000, with 46% of its capital in the form of debt and 54% in the form of equity. The weighted average cost of capital would then be:

46 (5,000,000*.053) + .54 (5,000,000*.1),
A WACC of $391,900

EVA then is simply the NOPAT less the WACC. If this firm had net operating profits of $1,150,000 and a tax rate of 30%, then calculation of EVA would be:

Operating profit	$1,150,000
Taxes	−$345,000
Cost of capital	−$391,900
EVA	$413,100

Focusing on EVA has some advantages in that it corrects for the biases inherent in the consideration of profit and profit rate. Remember that those firms with the highest profit may not be those with the highest profit rate. As a firm attempts to maximize profits, it may invest in projects that produce revenues in excess of direct cost but that fail to cover fully the cost of capital. As a firm attempts to maximize profit rate, it may under-invest and pass up what could be profitable projects. Focusing on EVA allows a firm to overcome these problems and align the dual desires of maximizing profit and maximizing shareholder value.

Both of these measures, along with many others that are used to measure performance, have various advantages and disadvantages. EVA is a very powerful tool for evaluating performance but requires considerable time and sophistication to calculate. Tobin's q is a simple and powerful indicator of success but cannot be applied easily to private firms. Market value and accounting profit are also both valuable but limited by the range of issues discussed earlier. All of these measures, along with the ratios in Table 2.2, can give us a sense of how a firm is doing, but none of them alone is sufficient to tell the whole story.

Unfortunately, many students, professors, managers, and analysts alike become enamored of single performance measures to the detriment of a better overall understanding. In an insightful and interesting article, Collingwood (2001) documents how firms often alter their strategies, sometimes in ways that actually compromise overall value, just to make certain that their quarterly earnings reports correspond to projections and match expectations. As Collingwood explains, given how closely many stockholders and analysts follow the projections and the performance that follows them, executives have begun to manage the process by managing both the projections that make it into the marketplace and the rate at which earnings or losses are reported. By meeting or just slightly beating the expectations of the market, a firm can ensure itself of a stable or growing market for its stock. Unforeseen variation, whether over or under expectations, can signal unforeseen problems or raise expectations unrealistically. Thus, companies devote considerable time and energy to the careful development of projections and the management of their activities so as to meet the subsequent expectations. Not only is this effort a drain on organizational resources but it also focuses attention, disproportionately, on short-term results, which may or may not be important to the overall financial health of the firm or the strength of its competitive advantage.

Indeed, in an effort to stem the momentum of this fascination with the setting and meeting of periodic projections, some leading companies, like Coca-Cola, AT&T, McDonalds, and Gillette, have ceased providing the earnings guidance information that becomes the basis for analysts' quarterly earnings forecasts. Coke made the decision to opt out of this process in 2003. The chairman and CEO at the time, Douglas Daft, explained the move saying:

> "We are quite comfortable measuring our progress as we achieve it, instead of focusing on the establishment and attainment of public forecasts,"

Mr. Daft said. "Our share owners are best served by this because we should not run our business based on short-term 'expectations.' We are managing this business for the long-term."

Miller (1990)

Interestingly, the immediate effect of this decision for Coke, and for other firms that made similar decisions, was a small reduction in share price. However, the absence of quarterly earnings guidance has not affected stock volatility overall (Chen et al., 2011). Indeed, in August 2018, President Trump suggested scrapping quarterly earnings reports altogether, in favor of a biannual reporting cycle. The argument is that less frequent reporting would reduce costs and provide more latitude for long-term thinking.

So, performance is an ongoing and long-term phenomenon. Yet, the success of any effort to manage for the long term is difficult to measure. So there is the dilemma. It is difficult to measure and value that which has not yet occurred. Yet, it is equally difficult to make long-term judgments about performance, based only on what has happened in the most recent past. Thus, as has been explained throughout this chapter, performance must be understood and measured from a variety of different perspectives.

PERFORMANCE IN CONTEXT

The final comment about performance and its assessment relates to the relative nature of success itself. What does it really mean to say that a firm is successful and performing well? Consider the following example: assume that one firm shows a profit of 10% on its sales, while the second firm, with comparable revenues, shows a profit of only 5%. Which of these firms performed best? Well, that depends upon a number of things. For example, consider the differences among the software, airline, and restaurant industries. Adobe Systems, Intuit, and Microsoft reported profit margins of 28.6%, 19.9%, and 16.4%, respectively, in 2017, while the industry as a whole reported a return on sales of 10.43%. During the same period, Delta, American, and United reported net profit margins of 7.9%, 3.1%, and 5.6%, respectively, while the industry as a whole reported an average return on sales of 6.7%. Finally, in the restaurant industry, Bloomin' Brands, Buffalo Wild Wings, and Chipotle Grill reported profit margins of 2.7%, 3.2%, and 3.9%, while their industry reported an average return of 8.1%. While the differences in these profit numbers are significant, much of that difference can be attributed to the specific competitive conditions in the industries. As a consequence, it is difficult to compare the firms without contextualizing the data. While Chipotle provided a lower return than 5 of the 6 firms in the software and airline industries, it was still the best of those in the restaurant industry. And while Microsoft earned a better return than any of the firms in the restaurant or airline industries, its return was lower than both Adobe and Intuit. Thus, in assessing the performance of any particular firm, it is important that appropriate industry benchmarks be chosen against which to assess any gain or loss.

Determining appropriate industry benchmarks is easier said than done, however. Consider the airline companies mentioned earlier: are they representative of the industry as a whole? Southwest Airlines, for instance, reported a profit margin of 17.2% for the same time period, while Jet Blue reported a profit margin of 6.7%. Of course, Delta, American, and United are much larger than either Jet Blue or Southwest. So, are the two groups comparable? In considering the airline industry, should we lump together Southwest, Alaska Air Group, Spirit Airlines, and JetBlue, together with Delta, American, and United? That question will be answered in greater detail in the next chapter. Asking it now though raises an important issue. What is the appropriate industry benchmark for assessing the performance of a firm? For the moment, it is enough to remember that the most meaningful insights can be drawn from comparisons to similar firms. So, when assessing the performance of a firm like Delta, it is important to look at Delta's performance in relation to other similar firms; the more similar, the more meaningful the comparison.

But industry variation is just one of the several contingencies that should be considered in assessing a firm's performance. An equally important consideration is the historical context of the firm. For example, Hilton Worldwide Holdings reported a net profit margin in 2017 of 13.77%. While that is an outstanding number, it is well above the average of the previous 5 years, which was 6.5%. Perhaps the 2017 profit was attributable to something unique to that year and outside the company's normal activities. Suppose Hilton's 2018 profit margin is 8%, should that return be viewed as an improvement on the historical average or as a decline from 2017? Just as it is hard to judge a firm's performance in the absence of industry benchmarks, so too it is difficult to judge performance without the context of historical precedent.

As these examples demonstrate, contextual considerations are key in the assessment of performance. The same amount of profit or the same rate of return can appear completely different when judged in relation to historical trends. A firm with consistently rising earnings might see a period where earnings remain relatively flat as a disappointment. On the other hand, a firm with consistently declining earnings might see a period where that decline levels off as a success. Empirical research has shown the importance of past performance to the mental state of the firm's managers and other stakeholders (Amason & Mooney, 2008; Audia et al., 2000).

After a sustained period of growth and profitability, managers and stockholders may feel entitled to the continuation of such growth. As a result, they may become careless in the assessment of future initiatives and overextend their own expertise and ability. Miller (1990) describes this pattern as the "builder" becoming the "imperialist." Pushed by the expectations of continued growth in revenues and profits, managers will often overreach and make poor investments. Alternatively, success can promote a sense of hubris and detachment among the firm's top management, allowing the firm to drift along with its own momentum but failing to learn and adapt with the environment. What this research suggests is that current performance is, in some ways, a reflection of the past. Evaluating performance in the present, then, requires understanding the historical context from which that performance emerged.

Purpose, Values, and Mission

Of course, no consideration of context would be complete without a consideration of the firm's purposes and intentions. Consider, for example, Porsche. Porsche is an automobile maker, just like Ford. However, Porsche's 2017 revenues of €21.68 billion are a small fraction of Ford's 2017 revenues of $156.78 billion. Does that mean that Porsche is less successful? Quite the contrary, Porsche's size is a reflection of its basic intent, to be an extraordinary maker of high-end sports cars. Porsche's own statement of philosophy says:

> Our vehicles should always be something special. We also expect extraordinary results when it comes to the profitability of the company. To achieve this, today and in the future, we rely on employees and managers who think just like Ferry Porsche did and who are always willing to go that extra mile.

Ford, on the other hand, has a different purpose. Ford talks about being an efficient, global company, with practices that will supply consumers, and satisfy constituents all over the world.

> Ford's vision is people working together as a lean, global enterprise for automotive leadership. Where leadership is measured by the satisfaction of our customers, employees, investors, dealers, suppliers, and communities.

These two companies define themselves very differently. As a result, what is important to one may not be important to the other, and what is considered success for one may not be considered a success for the other. Perhaps the most basic, yet important, contingency to the consideration of organizational performance is the basic purpose of the firm. Viewed in this light, assessing performance means asking the question, is the firm accomplishing its own purposes? Is it doing well that which it set out to do? Understanding a firm's purposes requires understanding something about its *values* and *mission*.

Corporate values and missions, which will be discussed in detail in the next chapter, lie at the very root of the strategic process. While basic economic theory suggests that firms should maximize profits and so shareholder wealth, the reality is that firms are driven by a number of varied motivations. At some point, all firms must earn a profit, if they are to survive. But, as the example of Porsche and Ford illustrates, there are many paths to profitability and many different ways of operating that a company may choose to follow. These basic choices are a reflection of the company's values. Chick-fil-A, for instance, states clearly that:

> We exist to glorify God by being a faithful steward of all that is entrusted to us and to have a positive influence on all who come in contact with Chick-fil-A.

This purpose, which reflects the Christian values of the restaurant chain's founder, Truett Cathy, supersedes the profit motivation in a number of tangible ways. For example, all Chick-fil-A stores are closed on Sunday. In real terms then, Chick-fil-A is sacrificing 14%, or 1/7th, of its potential revenues and profits for the sake of its corporate values. These values are fundamental to Chick-fil-A's purpose and so are an integral part of how the company defines and measures its own performance.

Starbucks provides another example of values impacting strategy and potentially changing the way performance should be defined and measured. Starbucks states plainly that social responsibility and community involvement are fundamental to its purpose. Specifically:

> We have always believed Starbucks can—and should—have a positive impact on the communities we serve. One person, one cup, and one neighborhood at a time.

The Starbucks Foundation offers millions of dollars in grants to help low-income and at-risk youth. Starbucks offers "fair trade" and "farm direct" coffees, which are more costly but which provide a greater return to the farmers and so a greater degree of stability to the economies in which the coffees are grown. Starbucks invests in a variety of different community programs designed to promote volunteerism and economic development of underdeveloped neighborhoods. Of course, all of this activity costs real money and so demonstrates the commitment of the company to a value system that supersedes the profit motivation alone. Naturally, without profit, none of these good works would be possible. Still, the way Starbucks goes about making its profit and the types of activities in which it engages reflect more than just the desire to maximize profit. Rather, these things all reflect a desire to earn profit in a particular way and for a particular purpose. Like Porsche, Chick-fil-A, and Starbucks, all companies have an underlying value system that drives their decision making and affects how they define success and good performance.

In assessing the performance of those companies, it is important that we keep those values in mind.

Value systems, like those just described, give rise to the company's mission. These statements of fundamental purpose are also known as credos, principles, or purpose or vision statements. Regardless of the name, the mission is the underlying reason that the firm exists; it makes clear the goals and aspirations of the business itself. It articulates the principles upon which the firm's culture rests. It stands as a guiding light amidst the turmoil of everyday activity. In his book on corporate mission statements, Jeffrey Abrahams (1999) explains that a mission statement is:

> an enduring statement of purpose for an organization that identifies the scope of its operations in product and market terms and reflects its values and priorities. A mission statement will help a company to make consistent decisions, to motivate, to build an organizational unity to integrate short-term objectives with longer-term goals and to enhance communication.

Mission statements will often make explicit the priorities of the firm. The desires to enhance stockholder value, employee development, community involvement, or customer satisfaction are common to most, if not all, firms. However, not all firms prioritize those various goals in the same way. Ben & Jerry's Homemade Inc., the Vermont ice cream maker that is now a division of Unilever, Inc., was famous for its commitment to social causes and to its employees. The Ben & Jerry's mission articulated three basic priorities, a product mission, a social mission, and an economic mission. Specifically, Ben & Jerry's mission stated:

> Ben & Jerry's is founded on & dedicated to a sustainable corporate concept of linked prosperity. Our mission consists of 3 interrelated parts:
>
> **Product Mission:** To make, distribute, and sell the finest quality, ice cream, with a continued commitment to incorporating wholesome, natural ingredients and promoting business practices that respect the earth and the environment.
>
> **Economic Mission:** To operate the company on a sustainable financial basis of profitable growth, increasing value for our shareholders and expanding opportunities for development and career growth for our employees.
>
> **Social Mission:** To operate the company in a way that actively recognizes the central role that business plays in society by initiating innovative ways to improve the quality of life, locally, nationally, and internationally.

> Central to the mission of Ben & Jerry's is the belief that all 3 parts must thrive equally in a manner that commands deep respect for individuals in and outside the Company, and supports the communities of which they are a part.

Ben and Jerry's desire was to run their business in such a way that these missions were linked and sustainable. The satisfaction of the social mission depended upon the satisfaction of the economic mission. The satisfaction of the economic mission depended upon the satisfaction of the product mission. Yet, the product mission linked back to the social mission, as it was the unique culture of the company and quality of the ice cream that made the product so attractive and so profitable. The satisfaction of this 3-pronged mission, then, had demonstrable effects on the way that Ben & Jerry's operated. Ben & Jerry's often paid above-market prices to their suppliers, reasoning that in so doing they were both contributing to their communities and ensuring a sustainable supply of raw materials. Ben & Jerry's refused to use milk from dairies that used artificial growth hormone, as part of their commitment to the quality of the product. They also capped the salaries of the highest-paid employees at no more than 7 times that of the lowest-paid employees. All of these decisions were reflections of the company's purpose, as articulated in its mission.

The problem at Ben & Jerry's was that not everyone shared this vision of linked priorities. As the firm grew, so did the need for outside investment. Like many entrepreneurs, Ben & Jerry sought that investment through an offering of stock to the public. Unfortunately for the company, many of these new investors were attracted by the prospect of above-average returns. As such, these investors favored satisfaction of the economic mission over the others. Thus, as Ben & Jerry's grew and as the competition in its industry intensified, the company began to get away from its own basic values. Amidst the malaise that followed, Ben & Jerry's was taken over by a large diversified conglomerate, Unilever.

The story of Ben & Jerry's can serve as a powerful reminder that not all missions are fully compatible and that different **stakeholders** will define performance in different ways. All firms must make a profit and produce a return over and above their costs if they want to survive. However, many firms like Ben & Jerry's, Porsche, and Chick-fil-A intentionally chose not to maximize volume, profit, or shareholder value. Instead, they chose to try and make money by operating in a way that is consistent with other principles. As a consequence, what these firms view as good performance may be somewhat different than what others view as good performance. Provided that there is agreement among the various constituents of the firm, that choice is perfectly all right. For our purposes and for the purposes of this text, then, it is enough to remember that performance must be considered in context. All firms do not seek to do the same things, nor do they seek to do those things in the same way. Thus, an essential dimension of performance measurement and assessment is the degree to which the performance definition fits the purposes of the firm.

Before leaving the subject, it is important to make one final comment about missions and mission statements. As discussed in Chapter 1, mission statements are often written for public consumption, designed to sound good and to make the company look good but to have little tangible meaning and to provide little in the way of specific operational direction. If this is so, why should missions come up here, amidst this discussion of real performance? To understand, it is important to acknowledge that there is often a disconnect between what firms say and what firms do. In their book on corporate mission statements, Jones and Kahaner (1995) comment on the fact many firms have at times said one thing, only to later do another. Not all firms invest equal time in thinking through their mission and writing it out for others to see. Even among those firms that do write well-crafted statements of purpose, not all invest equal effort in assessing those missions carefully. In light of this, it is important to remember that, even when there is no formal articulation of a mission and no explicit statement of purpose or direction, there remains some underlying logic, some unspoken principle that drives the company's strategy and gives coherence to the decisions and actions of its people. It is that basic set of values that must be taken into account when assessing the firm's performance.

TAKING STOCK OF PERFORMANCE

Chapter 1 made clear that performance is the crux of business and of business education. Strategic management then is a tool, a systematic framework of cause and effect relationships and associations that, when understood well, can facilitate that quest for performance. Before we can begin to understand the principles and applications of strategic management, however, we first need to understand performance itself. On the one hand, performance is a simple idea. Buy low and sell high; maximize revenues and profits and, in so doing, maximize shareholder value. These pithy statements have a clear intuitive appeal. As has been discussed throughout Chapter 2, however, the reality is that it is never quite that easy. Performance means different things to different people. Performance can be measured in a variety of different ways. Performance can change with time. All of these realities must be internalized and integrated into our understanding if we are to make good use of all that strategic management has to offer.

Good strategists understand all of this and so consider multiple measures of performance, depending upon the situation and their goals. Some focus on growth; others focus on profitability. Still others focus on stock price or on intermediate measures, like market share, productivity, or asset usage. All of these various measures provide good information that can be useful in the proper context. Some devise composite measures in an effort to distill different types of information into a single measure. Recall that the balanced scorecard was mentioned in Chapter 1. A balanced scorecard takes into account a host of different and different types of measures in an effort to capture in a single indicator, the true and overall performance of the firm, relative to all of its various stakeholders and interests. While the thought of a single measure of performance that transcends context and setting is appealing, it may not always be practical or even possible. What is possible, though, is a better understanding of firm performance. Good strategists understand the strengths and weaknesses of different performance measures. Good strategists fully comprehend the implications of setting and the impact of goals. Good strategists focus on performance, but they do so while understanding the importance of viewing performance from multiple perspectives, over time, and in the proper context.

KEY TERMS

Economic value added is a measure of financial performance incorporating both accounting measures of profitability and the firm's overall cost of capital. The result is a measure that reflects economic profit or the return over the minimum required by investors.

GAAP or "generally accepted accounting principles" refers to the set of rules and guidelines that govern how accountants should record and report financial information. The GAAP framework is established and maintained by FASAB or the Federal Accounting Standards Advisory Board.

Privately held firms are those whose ownership stock is not traded publicly or listed or traded on any public exchange.

Publicly held firms are those whose ownership stock is available to the public and is listed and traded on a public exchange.

Stakeholder refers to an individual or firm holding a stake in an organization's future and performance. The term usually implies a set of interests beyond purely economic interests, as would be characteristic of absentee stockholders.

Tobin's q is a measure of financial performance and is the ratio of the market value of a firm, divided by the replacement cost of its booked assets. To the extent that the ratio is greater than 1, it suggests that management and strategy are adding value to the firm's assets.

QUESTIONS FOR REVIEW

1. Why is the value of a firm problematic as a measure of performance? Why would the best performing firm not also be the most valuable?
2. How could a potential buyer and owner of a business look at the same resources, the same market, and the same financial history and yet still draw different conclusions about the actual value of a business?
3. Why must strategic managers be so familiar with the specifics of performance and performance measurement? Should technical issues like this best be left to financial specialists?
4. Describe some of the potential problems associated with an over-reliance on various performance measures like profitability, stock price, or market share.
5. Are some performance measures more easily manipulated than others? Why would anyone care to manipulate measures of firm performance?
6. What is the advantage of utilizing more complex measures like Tobin's q or EVA rather than simpler, more accessible measures?
7. Why is it so important to consider industry factors and company history in assessing performance?
8. What is a balanced scorecard? Could different companies include different measures in their own balanced scorecard of performance?

Chapter 3

Tools of the Trade

THE TOOLS OF THE TRADE

Chapter 1 introduced strategic management as the framework of thoughts and actions by which firms pursue superior performance. While accurate and reflecting the complex and multifaceted nature of strategy, definitions like this are not especially helpful to those who would ask, so how does one actually do strategic management? Indeed, students and executives alike are often left bewildered and unsure by the somewhat esoteric nature of strategy. They understand the terminology and grasp the concepts, but they are frequently unable to translate the framework from the conceptual to the practical. As a consequence, strategy remains for many little more than an academic undertaking, a thought-provoking exercise that has little direct connection to the reality of day-to-day action.

Although common, views like this are unfortunate. Strategy is actually all about action. Strategy points towards and culminates in genuine commitments and behaviors that create value for the customer and competitive advantage for the firm. Strategy is a theory of sorts; it is a systematic and organized body of assumptions, principles, and relationships that can help to explain events and predict outcomes. As Lewin noted, "nothing is quite so practical as a good theory" (Hunt, 1987), and strategic management is a good theory because it relates so well to practice. In other words, strategy is valuable because it is practical. Understanding strategy can provide insights into why things happen as they do, and those insights can facilitate the prediction of cause and effect.

For example, how likely is it that a potential competitor will encroach on your firm's business? To answer the question, it is necessary to consider the issues in light of some known principles and relationships. Suppose this competitor had recently expanded its operation and so had excess capacity. Suppose too that this competitor was getting pressure from its customers, who were quite large and so had substantial bargaining power because of their purchasing volume. In this instance, you could predict with some certainty that this potential new competitor would need to increase volume so as to better amortize the costs of the newly expanded facility over a larger number of units. Moreover, in reducing the cost per unit, this competitor could more effectively respond to pressure from its own customers.

Understanding this framework of interactions, the sequence of cause and effect relationships explained by the theory, would allow you to understand and predict the motivations and actions of your competitor and to take substantive, concrete actions to prepare for the actions that he might take. Understanding the environment, the competitors and customers within it, and your firm in relation to these parties can allow you to devise a strategy to increase the strength of your competitive advantage and, along with it, your firm's performance. Because strategic management is all about performance, it must also be especially practical. Indeed, to truly be effective, every strategy should be understood at the level at which it becomes actionable. In other words, grand ideas and broad statements about intentions, directions, and strategies are worth little until some action is taken on their behalf.

As the internet was quickly becoming a major platform for commerce, business, and leisure, there was a need for an effective and easy way for people to find their desired information quickly, easily, and with little hassle. Both Yahoo and Google were developing technologies to advance the effectiveness and performance of internet search engines. At the turn of the millennium, both Google and Yahoo were competing vigorously to dominate the rapidly growing territory known as the World Wide Web. At that time, both companies seemed evenly matched in this battle to become the dominant way people navigated the web. Although both companies had the same ultimate objective, through its more effective execution of using its proprietary algorithms and simple user interface to produce the results that best match the user's search, Google came to dominate to the point where "google" has become a common verb and Yahoo failed to gain the traction needed to remain competitive. At the outset, both companies were capable, had the financial wherewithal, had the technical competence, and had the will, but only Google became the "go-to" search engine and dominated the increasingly lucrative search engine market. Therefore, it was Google's superior execution of their strategy, rather than the strategy alone, that ultimately mattered. Even the best strategy and all the good intention in the world will not produce the desired results if it is not coupled with **the ability to execute**. Google's success and Yahoo's failure speak directly to one of the most important elements of success, planning execution with strategy. So, the recipe for a successful strategy must include carefully crafted execution and implementation plans. Google completely and clearly understood the problem, developed both their strategy and their implementation plan, then executed and realized the potential of their strategy. That is why Google successfully came to dominate search and Yahoo with all of its technical resources, brand recognition, and market reach failed to do so.

Execution is simply the aggregation of the implementation of numerous tactics and actions, and these tactics and actions are driven by strategy. Good strategic managers understand that strategy and action are inextricably linked. Thinking about strategy requires understanding the link to action, as well as the reciprocal link from action back to strategy.

This chapter then focuses on the nuts and bolts of strategy, the so-called tools of the trade. The word tools, here, is appropriate for a couple of reasons. First, the topics covered in this chapter are not strategy themselves but are the means through which strategy is devised, formulated, tested, implemented and ultimately made real. Strategic management is an ongoing process, but that ongoing process involves the use of some essential tools. Second, the term tools is appropriate because, like real tools, these things are applicable across a range of settings. Every firm is unique. Yet, there are similarities that allow for the application of common tools. Goals and objectives, for instance, are tools of the trade. Every firm has goals and objectives, whether explicitly stated or not. Thus, goals and objectives can be a level starting point for comparing one firm to another. This point was made in the previous chapter in discussing performance. Absent some understanding of a firm's goals, it is hard to evaluate its performance. Yet, because every firm has some goals and objectives, we can compare different firms on their ability to meet their own goals. Every firm exists within an environment. Thus, environmental analysis is a good place to start in the assessment of firm strategy. That assessment is accomplished through the use of some common tools.

The various component parts of the strategic management process then are really just a means to an end. The end, of course, is competitive advantage and the superior performance that accompanies it. But achieving the end requires diligent attention to the use of each component part, each tool of the trade. This chapter then will review briefly some of the basic elements of the strategic management process and discuss how each relates to the practical management of the firm and to competitive advantage.

Figure 3.1 provides a general overview of the strategic management process. While all of the components are important and necessary, none of them alone is sufficient for understanding the whole. For example, strategic management does begin with the mission or statement of the firm's purpose. However, such mission and purpose statements are not complete strategies. Indeed, even a good mission statement, if it is unconnected to the other components of the process, will have little or no effect on the performance of the whole. Similarly, analysis and understanding of the environment is essential to success. However, strategic management is more than just environmental analysis. Implementation and processes of learning and adaptation are often cited as the keys to strategic success. Yet, implementation does not exist in a vacuum. Thus, every one of these components is dependent upon

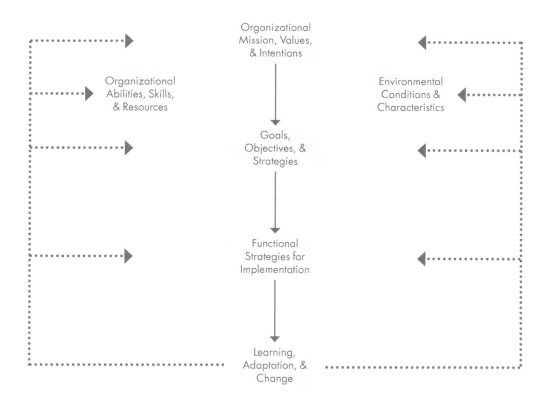

FIGURE 3.1 The Tools of the Trade

and related to the others. The key to both understanding and using the strategic management process is the ability to understand each of these components individually as well as collectively.

ORGANIZATIONAL MISSION, VALUES, AND INTENTIONS

At the top of the model is the *mission* of the organization. In the previous chapters, the mission was introduced and linked to the organization's purpose. While there are a number of different names by which this particular tool is known, including mission, vision, statement of purpose, and value statement, the idea is more or less the same. That idea is that, beyond the obvious need to produce a positive return on investment, the organization's mission is the reason the firm exists, the foundational statement of principle by which the firm is guided. For Porsche, it is to be a small, craft-oriented maker of superbly engineered automobiles. For Chick-fil-A, it is to be a family-friendly and Christian-oriented provider of chicken-based fast food. Every firm has a mission of sorts, whether it realizes it or not. Some managers are diligent to think through the implications of their mission; others are not. However, every firm is guided by some principle, and that principle is conveyed throughout the firm in subtle ways. Thus, it is important to think carefully and deliberately about the mission and the message that it sends. Consider again, for instance, a portion of Porsche's statement of purpose:

> Money alone cannot produce inventiveness. It is far more the pressure of having to prove oneself against the competition again and again. Porsche relishes its role as David amongst the Goliaths in this world.

One clear implication of this statement is that Porsche has no intention of being among the world's largest automobile makers. As a consequence, there are segments of the automobile business in which Porsche simply does not care to compete. In making inexpensive and highly standardized cars, for instance, Porsche would be at a persistent disadvantage to its larger and more automated competitors. Thus, one implication of this mission is the orientation towards unique, high-quality, and customer-focused products. Those products are designed to compete, not on their price, but on the basis of their engineering, styling, and attentiveness to idiosyncratic detail. This is what Porsche believes it can do well; this is what Porsche, its managers, and its owners choose to do, and this is what makes Porsche unique and attractive and what enables it to charge substantially more per unit than many of its competitors.

This fundamental mission also serves as a guidepost to Porsche employees and other stakeholders. Whether making decisions about new products or markets, new technologies or manufacturing methods, or a new inventory and financing system, all operational decisions are tested against this philosophy. Where an action is inconsistent with the mission, it is rejected. Similarly, investors understand that Porsche will never have the lowest labor costs, the quickest development cycle, or the fastest assembly line. Those sorts of characteristics, while desirable for many companies, are inconsistent with Porsche's basic philosophy.

Another example would be the Minnesota Mining and Manufacturing Company, better known as 3M. By the end of 2017, 3M operated in over 70 countries and had 91,000 employees and total worldwide sales in excess of $32 billion. Yet, as large and successful as it has become, 3M still takes care to remain faithful to a set of principles developed in 1948. In that year, William L. McKnight, president and soon to be chairman of the board, laid out a set of principles that remain the foundation for the company's operations:

> As our business grows, it becomes increasingly necessary to delegate responsibility and to encourage men and women to exercise their initiative. This requires considerable tolerance. Those men and women to whom we delegate authority and responsibility, if they are good people, are going to want to do their jobs in their own way.

> Mistakes will be made. But if a person is essentially right, the mistakes he or she makes are not as serious in the long run as the mistakes management will make if it undertakes to tell those in authority exactly how they must do their jobs.

> Management that is destructively critical when mistakes are made kills initiative. And it's essential that we have many people with initiative if we are going to continue to grow.

These principles have been elaborated into a detailed set of value statements, conduct guidelines, and operational and performance metrics, all of which are designed to promote sustainable economic growth and community involvement that transcends the technological, demographic, and cultural changes that are bound to occur over time and over the range of many different markets. 3M is dedicated to innovation. That dedication reflects the belief that customers, markets, technologies, and economies are in a state of constant change. The only way to remain fit to these changing conditions is to change as well. The problem is knowing how and when to change. To better understand that, 3M makes use of its 91,000 employees. Each employee brings to the table his or her own unique interests, experiences, skills, and understandings. As such, collectively this group of people represents tremendous potential for experimentation, learning, and development. Thus, 3M seeks to engage their efforts with selection, socialization, compensation, and promotion systems designed to encourage creativity, innovation, and new product development. 3M employees are encouraged to spend paid time creating, and they are rewarded when their creations succeed as new products. But just as importantly, they are not punished for their failures. Consistent with its basic principles, 3M appreciates that finding those few truly successful innovations means enduring any number of failures. Thus, it commits to the process of innovation by cultivating a culture where creativity and invention can thrive.

What really makes these principles effective tools, however, is not just the quality of the values they depict but also the closeness with which they are linked to real and practical actions. In the Porsche case, the value of being a small, quality-oriented firm translates directly into specific operational tactics, focused marketing practices, and real performance measurement implications. The consistency between the values and the practices reinforces for Porsche's employees, managers, owners, and other stakeholders the type of firm that Porsche intends to be and the types of strategies that it intends to pursue. Similarly, Google's original mission statement, to *"organize the world's information and make it universally accessible and useful"* is simple, yet implies the basic philosophy of ongoing innovation and creativity at the heart of the corporate culture that has real and practical implications for how the company operates across all disciplines and from strategy to execution (see Box 3.1: Innovation at Google). Again, for this corporate philosophy to be meaningful, it must show up and have a real effect on action. To the extent that it does, it is a meaningful part of the strategic process. From the very start, as explained in Sergey Brin and Larry Page's original founders' letter to shareholders upon going public, Google was always going to make "smaller bets in areas that might seem very speculative or even strange when compared to our current businesses." As these smaller bets became bigger, and more indirectly connected to the core business, Google formed a parent company, Alphabet, to be a holding company not only for Google but for these other wide-ranging bets in areas ranging from glucose-sensing contact lenses to driverless cars. At the core of its competitive advantage is the relentless commitment to innovation, R&D, and creativity. As Larry Page explained in his letter explaining the formation of Alphabet,

> We did a lot of things that seemed crazy at the time. Many of those crazy things now have over a billion users, like Google Maps, YouTube, Chrome, and Android. And we haven't stopped there. We are still trying to do things other people think are crazy but we are super excited about. We've long believed that over time companies tend to get comfortable doing the same thing, just making incremental changes. But in the technology industry, where revolutionary ideas drive the next big growth areas, you need to be a bit uncomfortable to stay relevant.

Box 3.1
Innovation at Google

Google and its parent company, Alphabet, are developing new technologies and creating new products and services. Innovation, creativity, and imagination are not only encouraged but are ingrained into the culture. Google's headquarters in Mountain View, California, is designed to be a hub of innovation, expression, and team creation. True to its mission, their culture of innovation resonates in the 3,200-hectare corporate campus. If you are lucky enough to visit their offices, you will find that it somehow feels like a children's playground. The objective behind these aesthetically pleasing office designs and open spaces is for the very purpose of creativity and imagination. The culture is supported by the actual layout and design of the campus to wake up the child within and recapture the ability to dream, imagine, create, and invent. It sounds simple, but encouraging employees to dream and creating the environment for them to achieve is at the heart of Google's competitiveness and its ability to innovate and continue to develop new products and services to stay ahead of its competition. So, in a sense, innovation is Google's core competency. But establishing creativity and innovation as a core competency requires aligning all the company's activities, culture, beliefs, actions, and employees' hearts and minds with the company's direction. Moreover, the company's vision and mission also support innovation as a core competency and competitive advantage. Google's mission is simple yet profoundly effective and powerful "*organize the world's information and make it universally accessible and useful.*" A simple statement that puts no bounds and no limit to realizing the company's mission. Another key element to Google's culture of innovation is the ability for any employee to access and share information freely, which builds trust and commitment to the mission. Feedback and sharing points of view on ideas, projects, and product development is encouraged and provides seeds for future ideas, advancements, and breakthroughs. These key elements are simple to understand yet challenging to align across the entire organization. Together, they enable Google to remain at the cusp of innovation and to develop the next generation of innovative products and services. For example, Google is pioneering drone technology—a small versatile aircraft that has the ability to fly and maintain its position in air (hover) and thus access areas that are not easy for a vehicle to access. Google is also working on advancing driverless cars, or what are called autonomous vehicles, which will also challenge the concept of transportation as we know it today. In 2015, Alphabet Inc, Google's parent company, was established by then Google CEO Larry Page as a creativity and idea "incubator" to allow the company to focus on innovations away from its core business. Alphabet also has a corporate venture capital arm, Google Ventures, which invests in "up and coming" technologies in fields such as life sciences, healthcare, artificial intelligence, robotics, transportation, cyber security, home automation, and agriculture.

As noted in Chapter 1, some of the "crazy ideas" that Alphabet is focusing on include autonomous (driverless) vehicles, artificial intelligence and machine learning, drone technology, and smart-home technologies. In 2016, Alphabet tested its first drone delivery at Virginia Tech University, where the drones delivered burritos into an open designated area for students to pick up. Alphabet continues to advance its drone technology and capabilities to reach practical and commercial use. The applications are endless, starting with food, grocery, and package delivery. Alphabet's innovations in the drone and driverless vehicle technologies are likely to have a significant impact on the future of transportation and parcel deliveries and the future strategic direction of Alphabet itself.

ORGANIZATIONAL ABILITIES, SKILLS, AND RESOURCES

Most business students and practitioners have heard of the SWOT framework and analysis. The acronym is formed from the first letters of the words Strengths, Weaknesses, Opportunities, and Threats. The logic of the analysis is simple yet deceptively powerful. Competitive advantage emerges when a customer sees value in a product or service and so pays the firm, providing it a profitable price. As explained in Chapter 1, that value that the customer sees is a reflection of two things. First are the options available within the environment; the customer can buy the product from your firm, buy a substitute product from a competing firm, or buy nothing at all. The attractiveness of the product, the attractiveness of the substitutes, and the attractiveness of doing nothing or doing something entirely different is a reflection of the environment. There is also then the issue of how the firm and its products are received. Given the other alternatives, what is it about your firm that makes it attractive? Is it truly a better product or is it merely a less expensive one? This determination reflects the unique qualities of your firm, as they affect this particular purchase. The SWOT framework captures both of these components. The strengths and the weaknesses deal with the qualities, skills, abilities, and resources of the firm. The opportunities and threats deal with the characteristics of the environment and the nature of environmental change.

To really understand the strengths and weaknesses side of the SWOT analysis, it is important to understand why strengths and weaknesses are important. To help with this, it is important to return to the definition of competitive advantage supplied in Chapter 1. Recall that competitive advantage is the value a firm is able to create for customers over and above the costs of creating it. Defined this way, competitive advantage is achieved momentarily every time a firm sells a product or delivers a service for a profitable price. The competitive advantage is then the reason that the customer saw this particular firm's product or service as being advantageous or desirable over and above all of the other available options, including doing nothing. For example, when a customer chooses one hotel over another, he or she does so for a reason. That reason is at least a part of the hotel's competitive advantage. When an airline chooses a vendor for its in-flight food and drink service, it does so for a reason. That reason is at least a part of the vendor's competitive advantage. To understand competitive advantage, we must understand what advantage customers see in particular firms. The attributes and abilities that lead to those advantages are the strengths of the SWOT analysis. Alternatively, the absence of the sorts of attributes and abilities that lead to perceptions of advantage are weaknesses.

Unfortunately, students, managers, and academics alike conduct SWOT analyses and yet fail to fully apply these criteria. As a consequence, they end up with little more than unorganized lists of characteristics that firms may use to describe themselves but that have little or no connection to real competitive advantage.

Some examples here would probably be useful. Consider Wal-Mart, one of the largest and most profitable companies in the world and a leader in the business of discount retailing. What are Wal-Mart's strengths and weaknesses? To answer the question, we need a sense of Wal-Mart's competitive advantage. To get that sense, we have to ask ourselves, what is the value that Wal-Mart creates? For most of us, the answer to that question is the ready availability of a wide variety of staple goods at the lowest possible, or nearly the lowest possible, price. We go to Wal-Mart because we expect that it will have the goods that we want and have them for as low a price as anyone else. As such, Wal-Mart creates value by providing us with products quickly, reliably, and inexpensively, thereby saving us time and money. But what strengths allow this? Well, to do what Wal-Mart does, a firm would have to be large, so as to buy in bulk, at discount prices, and to be able to carry a wide array of items. It would have to be able to move those items around efficiently, so as not to add costs unnecessarily. It would need a substantial infrastructure in procurement, inventory, and logistics as well as a host of good locations to make the purchase of these products convenient. All of these attributes, size, inventory, and logistical infrastructure, as well as the number and location of the stores would be strengths of Wal-Mart, strengths that lead to competitive advantage. But more importantly, these strengths would be just as essential to any firm seeking competitive advantage in this market. Moreover, the absence of these strengths would represent weaknesses.

However, consider the approach taken by Amazon, which has evolved into a serious threat and fierce competitor for Wal-Mart. Rather than focus on store locations, Amazon, like Netflix before it in its own competition with Blockbuster, focused instead on the internet as the point of convenience for the customer. However, like Wal-Mart, one of Amazon's primary sources of competitive advantage lies in logistics. Despite having been founded in 1994 as an online bookstore, Amazon has grown to be able to compete with Wal-Mart because it has established a core competency in logistics and web merchandizing that allows it to compete on price, variety, and delivery across seemingly every conceivable type of consumer merchandise.

As a result, in 2015, Amazon surpassed Wal-Mart as the most valuable retailer in the United States and in 2018 became the second company in history (the first being Apple) to surpass the $1 trillion mark in market capitalization. Only recently has Amazon expanded into the "brick and mortar" store segment with its acquisition of Whole Foods Market for $13.4 billion in 2017, which is expected further escalate the competition between Wal-Mart and Amazon.

The point of this is that strengths and weaknesses cannot be judged in a vacuum. Rather, certain attributes and capabilities are strengths because they lead to competitive advantage in specific markets. At the same time, the absence of certain attributes or capabilities in specific markets are weaknesses when they inhibit the attainment of competitive advantage. Actually doing a SWOT analysis then requires understanding the value of specific attributes and capabilities in their proper context. It is not enough to simply list various characteristics on which firms may differ or various capabilities that a firm may or may not have. Rather, the "analysis" part of the SWOT analysis requires discerning the *key success factors* of a particular market and then assessing the firm's position relative to those factors. Where firms have much of what is needed, they are in a position of strength; where they have little or none of what is needed, they are in a position of weakness.

ENVIRONMENTAL CONDITIONS AND CHARACTERISTICS

To judge the strength or weakness of various organizational attributes in their proper context requires understanding something about that context. Thus, the other half of a SWOT analysis, the analysis of the environmental opportunities and threats, is just as important as the analysis of the firm's strengths and weaknesses. Indeed, so important is the subject that all of Chapter 4 is dedicated to the analysis of the environment. For now, however, a brief overview would be helpful.

Effectively analyzing opportunities and threats is a two-step process. In the first step, the environment must be clearly identified. The reason for defining the environment is to narrow the focus of the analysis. Not all aspects of the environment are equally important to all businesses. For instance, fluctuations in international currency markets are more relevant and important to firms that do business in multiple countries. The price of labor is more important to those firms that employ large numbers of people. Changes in population patterns may be more important to those who sell retail than to those who sell wholesale. The environment must be defined clearly and carefully or the environmental analysis will quickly become unwieldy and virtually meaningless.

To facilitate the process of careful and clear definition, it is important to view the environment as a series of concentric circles (see Figure 3.2). At the center of the circles is the firm itself. As will be discussed later, a firm is like an organism; it is an

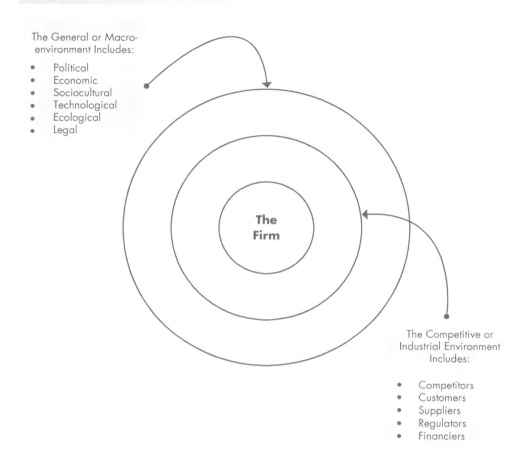

The General or Macro-
environment Includes:

- Political
- Economic
- Sociocultural
- Technological
- Ecological
- Legal

**The
Firm**

The Competitive or
Industrial Environment
Includes:

- Competitors
- Customers
- Suppliers
- Regulators
- Financiers

FIGURE 3.2 The Organizational Environment

open system that must exchange resources with its environment if it is to survive and grow. Thus, the next ring, just beyond the boundary of the firm, includes that set of actors with whom the firm interacts most regularly. This part of the environment has been referred to as the competitive environment or the industrial environment. Included in this group are those firms that supply products that customers see as substitutable. This group includes the customers who buy or who might buy the products or services supplied by the various competing firms. This group would also include the primary suppliers to a firm's industry. Thus, Microsoft and Intel would both be a part of Dell's competitive environment because both supply basic components that Dell needs in its pursuit of competitive advantage. Beyond the industrial environment is a circle representing what is called the general environment or the macro-environment. Included in this circle are all manner of potentially important forces, the effects of which may be broadly felt but are difficult to influence. For example, the general state of the economy is a macro-environmental force that can impact firm performance. Yet, the state of the economy is difficult to affect. Changes in technology or in demographic patterns, and other megatrends that we will examine in Chapter 9, are also macro-environmental forces. These sorts of forces or conditions collectively make up the general environment in which firms must operate and with which firms must contend (Castrogiovanni, 1992). The analysis of these general forces can be facilitated by the acronym PESTEL. The PESTEL framework, which we will cover in more detail in Chapter 4, divides the general environment into Political, Economic, Sociocultural, Technological, Ecological, and Legal forces that shape the firm's overall environment.

Finally, it is important to remember that every firm has a slightly different environment. Even for two firms as similar and as commonly thought of as Coca-Cola and PepsiCo, the environments are slightly different. Why? Well, because Coca-Cola is a part of PepsiCo's environment but is not a part of its own. Likewise, PepsiCo is a part of Coca-Cola's environment, yet it is not a part of its own. So it is important that the environment be defined carefully and on a firm-by-firm basis.

With the environment defined, the SWOT analysis turns to the identification of opportunities and threats. Here again, though, care must be taken or the analysis will become little more than a list of observations, unrelated to any particular business or environment and irrelevant to the formulation of strategy. As with the assessment of strengths and weaknesses, analysis of the environment should relate directly to competitive advantage. As competitive advantage is the reason a customer chooses one particular product or service, environmental analysis needs to focus on the context in which that customer's choice is made. Opportunities are instances for firms to gain new competitive advantage, either by attracting new customers or by getting additional business from existing customers. Threats are hazards to competitive advantage, forces that might interfere with the existing relationship between the firm and its customers or between the firm and customers it would like to pursue.

Again, an example would be helpful. Delta Airlines, based in Atlanta, is one of the so-called major U.S. air carriers. Over the years, Delta has been profitable and unprofitable, as the state of its environment has changed. How might we assess the environment of Delta? Well, we would begin with a definition of the first concentric circle, the industrial or competitive environment. Delta's industrial environment includes its customers and potential customers; it includes the other major U.S. carriers like American and United, as well as international carriers such as British Airways, Emirates, and Korean Air as well as a host of other regional carriers like AirTran and JetBlue which fly overlapping routes. Delta's industrial environment includes its principal suppliers like Boeing, Airbus, the airline pilots' union, and the suppliers of jet fuel. With this portion of the environment delineated clearly, the analysis then turns to the relative ***bargaining power*** of these various groups. What options, other than buying from Delta, are available to customers? How much control does Delta have over its supplies and suppliers? How loyal are customers to a given carrier and what costs are associated with switching from one carrier to another? What is the position of the competition and what resources do they have for competing with Delta? It is through the systematic assessment of these issues that the most immediate opportunities for, and threats to, Delta's competitive advantage are assessed.

With the industrial environment assessed, attention then turns to the second concentric circle, the macro-environment. For Delta, the macro-environment includes such forces as the general economy, the various demographic trends that relate to dispersion of the population and of business. The macro-environment would include the governmental entities that regulate the airline industry (the FAA), the security of airports and the screening of passengers (the TSA), and the various local governments that own and operate the major airports that Delta serves. All of these entities or forces have the potential to impact Delta greatly. For example, jet fuel is a big portion of Delta's operating expense. It is also one that can range widely over relatively short timeframes given the volatility of the underlying oil price, for instance, between 40% of Delta's operating expenses in 2014 and 16% in 2017. As mentioned, jet fuel is tied to worldwide oil prices, which are also subject to geopolitical considerations that Delta has no control over. Yet, they have a profound impact on Delta's bottom line.

Other examples could also be given for how changing actors, forces, and events could affect the nature of the relationship between Delta and its customers. For example, the entry to the Atlanta hub market of discount carrier AirTran, during the mid 1990s, substantially limited the price customers were willing to pay on routes served by both carriers. Similarly, dramatic increases in fuel costs have forced Delta to raise ticket prices. This affects the nature of Delta's competitive advantage by affecting the attractiveness of flying in general versus alternatives consumers might have such as driving or not traveling at all. All of these examples illustrate the importance of the environment to competitive advantage. Thus, all of these various forces, events, and actors should be carefully identified and their potential effects carefully considered as part of any SWOT analysis.

More will be said about the assessment both of strengths and weaknesses and of opportunities and threats in subsequent chapters. This was merely an overview. However, the key point should not be missed; a real analysis of SWOT goes far beyond the simple listing of various characteristics. Indeed, few of the tools of strategic management have the potential to be so powerful and yet are so often underused as the SWOT analysis. When done well, SWOT can provide the key to understanding strategy. As such, it is worth the time to do it well.

GOALS, OBJECTIVES, AND STRATEGIES

From this point forward, the strategic process becomes increasingly deductive. In other words, while the consideration of the mission and purpose, the development of competencies and resources, and the definition of the environment are all largely *voluntaristic*, or the result of self determination and free choice, the act of actually forming strategies from these other parts of the process is more *deterministic*, or the result of structured analysis. To illustrate what this means, let us return briefly to the example of Delta Airlines. Delta's vision statement reads:

> We are dedicated to being the best airline in the eyes of our customers. We will provide value and distinctive products to our customers, a superior return for investors and challenging and rewarding work for Delta people in an environment that respects and values their contributions.

With one of the most far-reaching route structures, Delta has committed itself to the execution of this vision on a worldwide scale. However, commitments such as this are discretionary. In other words, Delta's management chose, at some point, to be a high-value carrier, providing a full range of services across a worldwide route structure in an effort to be distinctive and desired in the eyes of its customers. But those choices were discretionary; they were made voluntarily. Thus, they are referred to as voluntaristic decisions. Similarly voluntary was the development of Delta's various strengths and weaknesses. Delta chose to headquarter in Atlanta. It chose to develop an inventory of over 600 aircraft and over a dozen different aircraft models. It chose to grow through acquisition, having acquired Northwest Airlines in 2009, another major worldwide carrier. It also chose how to advertise and market itself and what sort of reputation to try and create in the minds of its customers.

With these various strengths and weaknesses in place and with the environment and its various opportunities and threats identified, the process of actually forming strategies and setting goals becomes less discretionary. The decision to compete worldwide, through a vast "hub and spoke" route system, placed Delta in direct competition with a number of other large carriers. The presence of that competition and the similarity of the products and services offered by Delta and its competitors provide customers with a number of alternatives from which they can choose. What that means for Delta is that they must respond either with lower prices for comparable service or with new and improved services at comparable prices, if they hope to maintain competitive advantage. For example, Delta is free to try new initiatives such as better seating, better in-flight entertainment, different pilot training programs, or different vendors for fuel and supplies. However, the success of those initiatives is a function of how they are actually received by the environment. Customers may or may not be willing to pay more for the extra services. New training programs or vendors may or may not have the desired impact on costs or on reliability. Competitors may or may not imitate Delta's changes. The success of any company action is determined at least partly by the conditions of the environment. Delta may choose to set its own goals for market penetration or earnings, for instance, but its success in reaching those goals will be determined by both its own actions as well as the reactions of the marketplace. Success then is a function of how specific strategies and actions *fit* within the environment.

What should emerge from the SWOT analysis is a set of reasonable objectives, along with the necessary plans for reaching those objectives. For example, based upon its own SWOT analysis, Delta may choose to pursue more intermediate-distance routes. These routes may reflect an opportunity in that they are currently underserved by other carriers. Moreover, Delta, with its fleet of diverse aircraft, its extensive reservation infrastructure, and its large staff of flight and ground crews, is highly capable of expanding into new areas of service. Delta then may set as a goal the establishment of some number of new routes or the generation of some amount of revenue from these new routes over the next several years. Delta might also undertake a strategy of aggressive pricing on these new routes, so as to dissuade other competitors from entering the market. Delta might invest in new aircraft, designed expressly for intermediate distance flights, to further its ability to defend the new market from competition. These goals, objectives, and strategic actions would all reflect the analysis of the SWOT and the desire for Delta to mold its offerings to fit the opportunities in the marketplace.

But are there specific ways in which goals should be stated? Should managers worry about confusing goals and objectives with strategies? Are there specific periods of time over which goals or objectives should be set? The answer to these questions is no, not really. Over the years, many teachers of strategy have sought to make all sorts of fine-grained distinctions between goals and objectives, to set specific time limits on the horizon over which plans should be made, and to distinguish goals from strategies. While some of these distinctions may reflect important principles, others serve little purpose. Indeed, after more than 40 years of this effort, the result has been a myriad of confusing terms, definitions, categories, and rules that hinder real understanding. Thus, for the purpose of this text, goals, and objectives are synonymous and any strategy for achieving goals and objectives can be either good or bad, under given circumstances. There are no specific periods of time over which plans must be made, and the strategic process includes both the setting of goals and taking of actions necessary for accomplishing them.

There are, however, general principles that govern the establishment of goals and objectives as well as the formulation of plans and strategies. The first of these, as mentioned already, is that goals and strategies should flow from the conclusions of the SWOT analysis. To be effective, strategies must fit the environment for which they were fashioned. In other words, strategies should be developed around specific opportunities, to accommodate specific threats, and be built upon specific organizational resources. While general notions about being the first or being the best are fine, they are not likely to lead to real competitive advantage because they lack specificity. A good way to test for specificity in the setting of objectives and the formulation of strategies is to ask the question, what will change as a result of them? Specifically ask, who will do what differently? Then, ask the question, how will these new actions create value for customers? Well-designed objectives and well-formulated strategies will lead to actions that create value for customers. In the earlier example, Delta will begin flying new routes; it will reposition some people or perhaps hire some new ones. It will shift some assets or again buy some new ones. All of this activity will have the effect of providing a new travel option to customers who lack that option currently.

The second general principle is that goals, objectives, and strategies should be specific in the short term but general in the long term. At the heart of this principle is an idea called *logical incrementalism* (Quinn, 1980), which reflects the reality that over the course of time, conditions in the environment, as well as within the organization itself, may change. Thus, in setting goals and in articulating strategies, managers should be specific in the near term, where those specifics can be supported with good data and analysis. Yet, in the long term, where data are uncertain and analysis is based largely on conjecture, goal setting and strategy making should be more general. The question will be asked, of course, what is the long term? The answer depends upon the business and the business environment. Some firms exist in relatively stable environments and can foresee several years clearly. Others are in highly uncertain environments, where it is hard to see much of the future at all. Just how long the long term really is will vary from firm to firm and from setting to setting. However, the principle remains the same; as firms can more clearly see and anticipate future events, they should be similarly more specific about their goals, objectives, and strategies. As they are less able to clearly see and anticipate future events, they should be more general as to their goals, objectives, and strategies.

Failing to follow this principle can lead to two problems. First, if goals, plans, and strategies are too imprecise in the short term, then they will have little or no effect on company actions and performance. As discussed earlier, strategy is important because it is so practical. Strategies then matter and have their desired effects only to the extent that they change the way things get done. Towards this end, strategies that are to produce effects in the short term must be articulated clearly and directly, and they should be oriented around clear and direct short-term objectives. If, on the other hand, goals, plans, and strategies are too specific in the long term, they may cause the firm to commit to courses of action that might well become burdensome or seem, at some point, out of date. Even more problematic, committing too much too early might lead a firm to make poor decisions because of the lack of information. Thus, it is important that firms not commit too much too soon but, instead, reserve the option to change for as long as that option exists.

The last general principle to keep in mind is that all of the parts of the process—the environment, the organization, the goals, objectives, and the strategies—are tractable. All are subject to change over time. Environments change, some more quickly than others, but all do change. To stay fit to them, firms must adapt and change as well. New resources must be acquired and new skills learned; new capabilities must be developed and outdated capabilities shed. The organization itself must be viewed as a means to an end, not an end unto itself. Visions and missions, strengths and weaknesses, strategies and goals all can and must change with time if the firm is to survive amidst a changing environment. IBM has learned this lesson twice, as twice it has had to completely remake itself, adapting to an all new environment, developing different competencies, and acquiring new skills. As it made these changes, it developed new goals, objectives, and strategies for how best to take advantage of its new strengths and weaknesses and its new opportunities and threats. IBM was once a dominant force in the mainframe computer business. Changes in the environment led to a shift away from mainframe computing to personal computing. To fit itself to this new environment, IBM had to restructure and retool. It had to acquire the new strengths needed to create value in this new environment. With a new and different set of strengths and weaknesses, opportunities and threats, IBM had to develop new strategies and set new goals and objectives. Even having made these changes, IBM could not rest. Just around the corner was another set of dramatic changes. As the personal computer industry grew, so did the intensity of the competition. Indeed, so intense was the competition that IBM chose to shift its focus again, this time away from hardware manufacturing altogether. Instead, IBM focused on software and consultation services, and with this shift came another new environment and with that environment the need for different competencies and skills. IBM has repositioned itself and developed its core competency in key growth areas such as artificial intelligence (AI), cyber security, cloud computing, blockchain, quantum chips, and the Internet of Things. It is currently one of the main companies working on commercializing AI. IBM developed the "Watson Supercomputer," named after IBM's founder Thomas J. Watson, a high-level natural language "questions and answer" system that combines AI and sophisticated analytical algorithms. While Watson became famous for playing *Jeopardy!* and beating two of the most successful *Jeopardy!* champions, Ken Jennings and Brad Rutter, its capabilities are being used in many areas from medical diagnosis to customer service applications.

Remember then, goals, objectives, and strategies are simply the solution to the set of variables presented in the SWOT analysis. They are the answer to the question, "what now?" which should be asked once the environment and the firm's resources are well understood. Thus, they should relate back to the firm, its resources, and the context of its environment. In addition, they should be articulated directly, where they are needed to guide immediate action, and generally, where they are meant merely to set general direction. Finally, they should be revisited and reassessed regularly and revised whenever necessary, so as to keep the firm well fit to its ever-changing environment and to keep the firm focused on what really matters, which is the creation of value for the customer.

FUNCTIONAL STRATEGIES AND IMPLEMENTATION

More than any other tool, functional strategies and implementation relate directly to customer value. Yet, for all of its importance, this tool is often over-looked or treated cursorily by strategy texts. Part of the problem is terminology. Just what is implementation? Is it really strategy or is it simply the process through which strategy takes life? Are functional strategies synonymous with implementation, or is one the plan while the other is the execution? As before, debates over these sorts of issues create more confusion than understanding. So, for the purposes of this text, implementation is a fully participating part of strategy. Moreover, implementation of strategy takes place through a series of interrelated functional strategies, which detail how the specific work of the organization will be done.

Perhaps the easiest way to think about implementation is to think of it as that part of a strategy that customers really see. It is the physical manifestation of the strategy and the end result of the analytical process. In many ways then implementation is the strategy as it emerges in the real world.

Best Buy, an electronics retailer with an annual sales of $39.4 billion in 2017, has seen its sales decline more than 12% since 2013. It is facing stiff competition from a number of discount retailers such as Costco, Sam's Club, BJ's, and traditional "low-price" retailers such as Wal-Mart. In addition, almost everyone having access to the internet, with its ability to let customers easily shop around and find the lowest prices for any particular product, has placed further pressure on lower-price brick-and-mortar retailers such as Best Buy. One key for Best Buy strategically is avoiding becoming merely a "showroom" for Amazon and other online retailers that do not have the overhead costs of the brick-and-mortar store and that focus only on selling products at the lowest price. Best Buy combats this threat through implementing policies such as a price match guarantee, matching the price of any key online and local competitor, as well as having its own website which offers free shipping, 1-hour store pick up, and even same-day delivery. Further, it adds value to the customer through services such as its Geek Squad, which offers installation and set-up as well as support and repair services that online retailers would find difficult, if not impossible, to match.

On the face of it, this sounds pretty straightforward. In reality, however, it is actually quite complicated. First of all, there is more to implementation than just the things that customers see. For example, Wal-Mart's competitive advantage lies in its ability to offer a tremendous range of products conveniently and at costs as low or lower than its competitors. Customers know that many of the things they need can be found, found easily, and found inexpensively at Wal-Mart. That is what customers care about, and that is what they see. And so Wal-Mart gains a place in the consumer's mind when they are seeking low prices on a wide range of goods, including electronics sold by Best Buy. Yet, what enables Wal-Mart to offer this availability and the low prices is an advanced logistical and inventory management system that ensures rapid turnover, minimizes carrying costs, and provides for near-immediate replenishment of the store shelves. These systems are largely invisible to customers. Yet, it is through the working of these systems that Wal-Mart's competitive advantage is realized. Implementation then includes all of those things that are unseen but that must happen to produce that which the customer sees. Of course, herein is another of the vexing problems for strategic management. One of the reasons that implementation is so complicated is that just about everything affects just about everything else. Staying with the example of Wal-Mart, consider the inventory and logistical system that supports Wal-Mart's competitive advantage. Could Wal-Mart's competitive advantage be imitated through the replication of this system? Many have tried, but few have been successful. The problem lies in the fact that the implementation is more than just the computer hardware and software, more than just the warehouses and trucks. It is also the human component and the know-how of making it all work. It includes the right people, motivated by the right compensation system, supported by the right training, and communicating in the right timeframe. It takes the right equipment and the financial wherewithal to get that equipment into the proper alignment. It includes the critical mass of throughput necessary to provide economies of scale and a network of suppliers conditioned to work with Wal-Mart's systems. Like putting together a puzzle, implementation requires more than just the right pieces, it requires putting those pieces together correctly. Any breakdown along the chain, any missed pieces in the linkage between the concept and the customer, and the implementation will fail and the competitive advantage will suffer. So while Best Buy may develop its own similar capabilities, it has built-in cost disadvantages from a smaller scale even if it can imitate other aspects of Wal-Mart's capabilities. However, even a company like Wal-Mart that has a very strong competency in logistics and benefits greatly from economies of scale with its suppliers also has to continue to strengthen its core competencies and find new and innovative ways to keep its competitive advantage. For example, as we mentioned earlier, Amazon has become Wal-Mart's main competitor in the retail sector. Amazon has developed a core competency in logistics and internet/software capability and has transformed from an online bookstore relying on UPS for deliveries to a world-class logistics company itself. Developing this core competency allows Amazon to compete head-to-head with Wal-Mart on price, convenience, and variety. Wal-Mart is strengthening its online presence and internet capability, whereas Amazon has entered into the physical storefront space as well with the acquisition of Whole Foods Market. So what about Best Buy? How does Best Buy survive amidst this ferocity of competition from Amazon, Wal-Mart, and other low-price retailers? By specializing and differentiating. For many customers in this category, price is not the only consideration, particularly when the customer is less tech-savvy and wants support and advice as well as low prices.

Best Buy, through focusing on consumer electronics and supporting customers through in-store staff to guide customer choices and their Geek Squad service to help customers install and effectively use the latest technology, as well as its price match guarantee, carves out a niche in the minds of many consumers for being a better option within its category. As this juxtaposition among Best Buy, Wal-Mart, and Amazon shows, there is no such thing as a "good" or "successful" company in absolute terms. World-class companies are always finding new ways to capitalize on their core competencies and to develop new ones to maintain their competitive position.

To borrow a phrase from Thomas Edison, then, functional strategies and implementation are more perspiration than inspiration. Whereas the analysis of the environment, the crafting of missions, and the formulation of strategies is a creative and cerebral endeavor, implementation is about really doing the work that brings the strategy to life, as it was intended. It is tedious and detailed work, work that often happens behind the scenes and with little fanfare. Yet, in every instance, the real success of strategy hinges on the implementation. For Wal-Mart, the key to success is the ability to continue supplying a vast array of goods inexpensively. For Delta, the key to success is the ability to continue flying passengers reliably and less expensively than its competitors. For Porsche, the key to success is the ability to produce cars that are seen as well engineered, well built, and able to perform better than others. For every company, the key to success is the ability to actually do those things that produce value for the customers.

Doing that requires managing all of the specific functional details in such a way that they "fit" together with one another as well as with the strategy. Recall that fit was discussed earlier in the context of strategy and the environment. The same sort of meaning applies here. Whereas there are many different environmental conditions and many different types of strategies, some strategies work better in some environments than others. The linkages among the environment, strategy, and different sorts of competitive advantage will be discussed in detail in Chapters 4 and 5. For now, though, it is enough to remember that to be successful, every strategy must fit the contours of its particular environment. The same is true of implementation. While there are many different types of strategies and many different organizational functions, some sets of functions will work better in combination with some strategies than with others. Thus, the details of the implementation must fit the particular strategy.

In Chapter 8, we will discuss the linkages between specific functions and specific types of strategies. For now, however, it is sufficient to remember that implementation requires real action and the expenditure of real resources. To be successful, those actions and expenditures must be consistent with the nature and intent of the strategy. From the customer's point of view, then, implementation is the strategy. And, so, fit between implementation and strategy is the key to strategic success and to competitive advantage.

LEARNING, ADAPTATION, AND CHANGE

As mentioned in Chapter 1, business is ongoing. It is less like a single game than it is like an entire season. But even calling it a season fails to capture fully the fact that in business, the contest never really ends. The Roman Empire was perhaps the greatest political and military power the world has ever known. With an empire that spanned the known world and stood for centuries, Rome was and remains in a class by itself. Yet, for all this power, the empire that was Rome eventually fell. There are many examples of companies that were once in dominant positions, but were not able to adapt or in some circumstances even acknowledge the changing wants and needs of their customers or the rise of newer more nimble technologies that ended up disrupting the industry structure and creating a new way of doing business. A lot of these companies that were once household names ended up withering away, going bankrupt, or getting bought and "gutted out" to transform the business model.

Blockbuster was the premier company for video rentals. When DVDs came out and replaced VHS tapes as the dominant distribution media for movies, it was not hard for Blockbuster to evolve and adapt, because it was a change that fit with their current business model of having movies on shelves in a store that people came to and rented for a day or two. It was not a structural change in the distribution model or customer behavior that was out of line with their business model or strategy. However, the switch from VHS tapes to the more durable DVDs did allow the advent of Netflix, which used the U.S. mail service to deliver DVDs to customers to rent via a subscription model, and led rise to new competition. But, failing to see the evolution of both the technology for watching movies and the resultant change of customer behavior, Blockbuster failed to adapt to this new environment. In 2000, Netflix, beginning to gain traction as a young business, approached Blockbuster with the opportunity for Blockbuster to buy them out. Blockbuster, stuck in its established mode of video rental distribution through its retail stores, did not see the implications of this evolution in distribution and changing customer demands and turned down the chance to purchase Netflix for $50 million, stating that it will never work. Their position was that "no one wants to pay for a subscription for DVDs to be delivered to their home." When the next evolution in movie-delivery technology occurred later in the decade with the switch from physical DVDs to streaming content over the internet, Netflix was able to evolve, but Blockbuster, with its main competitive resource being physical stores, was trapped by what was formerly its primary source of advantage turning into a liability and soon went out of business. Netflix was able to foresee where the business was going and aligned their core competency development with the technological advances in personal computing and internet usage. Netflix was ready and had developed its strategy, core competencies, and business model to adapt to the new revolution in the entertainment industry. The end result is that Netflix, previously offered to Blockbuster for $50 million, is now worth over $150 billion, while Blockbuster, at the time worth many times the value of Netflix, is now gone.

However, triumphing over Blockbuster is not the end of the game for Netflix. As mentioned earlier, business is constantly evolving, and it is a never-ending competition to secure and maintain competitive advantage. The nature of media content is evolving once again, and Netflix is among the group of companies, including Amazon, that are disrupting movie and TV production and distribution away from the traditional studios, such that Netflix, Amazon, and others are moving beyond distribution and into content production, leading consumers to "cut the cord" from the traditional cable and media companies as consumers switch away from traditional television to watch more content through streaming on any one of a number of devices rather than being tied to a television. This latest disruptive change in how programs are created, watched, and broadcasted and the way value is created for the customer in this space is truly disrupting long-established players in the industry.

In 2018, The Walt Disney Co. finalized a $71.3 billion deal to buy the entertainment operations of Rupert Murdoch's 21st Century Fox Entertainment and news empire. Disney would take over 20th Century Fox movie and television studio, Fox's 22 regional sports channels, cable entertainment brands FX and National Geographic, and Fox's portfolio of international operations. Fox will keep its news networks such as Fox News. The Murdoch family recognized that with the pace of change and technology innovations in the entertainment industry, Fox's movie and cable TV operations will face an increasingly uncertain future, and Disney, with its prowess in content, is looking to both further strengthen this capability and combine it with different means of distribution. How the competition in this industry will play out will be an interesting strategic game as the players both compete against and cooperate with each other in content and distribution.

The final element of our model then is a "tool" or series of tools designed to enable ongoing learning and adaptation. At this point, some might ask, is learning, adapting, and changing really a strategy, or is it quite the opposite? After all, having a strategy suggests purposeful intent, a plan for how to get from point A to point B. How then can we reconcile the mandate to learn, adapt, and change with the whole process of planning? The answers to these questions are complicated and will take some time to answer. Thus, Chapters 8 and 9 of this text will be devoted to them more completely. For now, though, it is important to understand that learning and adaptation are as fundamental to the strategy process as any other element, as important as a mission statement and as practical as implementation. Thus, it is very important that managers attend to these tools as regularly and as genuinely as they would any other.

The way they do that is by never being satisfied and never getting complacent. Danny Miller compares managerial behavior in successful firms to the paradox of the mythical figure Icarus. Managers, prideful of their own success, complacent and buffered from the shocks and jolts of a competitive world, unwilling to risk their positions of leadership for all but the most promising of undertakings, lose touch with their customers and their markets. As such, they fail to see the signs of impending change. They fail to listen when customers say that they want something different. They fail to understand how competitors can deliver better products at lower prices. They fail to grasp the promise of new technologies or to understand why strategies that worked before are no longer working. As they grow successful, these managers lose the motivation, the will, or the time to learn and to take risks, often with catastrophic results. The key to avoiding this paradox is, obviously, keeping the drive, maintaining the hunger, and avoiding the trappings of success that lead to complacency and risk aversion. Of course, maintaining that hunger is easier said than done. Indeed, in some ways, it is contrary to basic human nature.

Thus, mechanisms that can help must be institutionalized and integrated throughout the structure, culture, and decision-making practices of the firm. Six specific mechanisms will be discussed briefly here and in greater detail later. These are (1) minimal consensus, (2) minimal contentment, (3), minimal affluence, (4) minimal faith, (5) minimal consistency, and (6) minimal rationality (Hedberg et al., 1976). Minimizing anything is another of those concepts that has grown increasingly unpopular in the nomenclature of the day. In this instance, however, doing only that which is necessary, committing only that which is required, could be the key to sustaining competitive advantage.

The first of these principles, minimal consensus, focuses on the propensity to emphasize agreement above all else. Dissent can be healthy as it forces consideration of assumptions and the examination of points of view long held. To sustain competitive advantage, a firm must remain vigilant and sensitive to divergent points of view and alternative sources of information. Thus, the premature or overzealous pursuit of consensus can be detrimental in the long term, while seeming beneficial in the short term. The ability to tolerate, and even encourage, open dissent without losing control and falling into acrimony is a key to avoiding the trap of complacency and the paradox of success.

Minimal contentment focuses on that tendency to allow things to go on as they always have. The greater the contentment of the firm's people, the stronger the contrary force must be to effect some change. Thus, in a firm of talented people, backed up by substantial resources, minor signals that something is changing can be overlooked or misinterpreted.

Minimal affluence is an especially difficult concept because all organizations seek to earn as much as possible. Indeed, strategic management is about the pursuit and increase of competitive advantage and competitive advantage relates directly to earnings. However, earning money and holding onto money are not one in the same. Indeed, in addition to maximizing their earnings, firms may also seek to maximize their inventory of earnings, in essence, their affluence. The problem is that such stocks of **_slack resources_**, as they are called, can buffer the organization from the very sorts of feedback it needs to promote adaptation and change. A modest decline in sales might be met with muted concern by a firm with a deep well of resources. For a firm that is on the brink of profitability, however, a decline in sales would set off urgent alarms. The point is to maintain a sense of imperative sufficient to encourage vigilance and the prospecting for new opportunities.

Minimal faith relates to the confidence that firms have in their own plans. Planning is a necessary reality for any organization. However, planners can some-times forget that some things are truly unpredictable; some things simply cannot be anticipated and, so, all plans must be subject to change as events warrant. On June 23rd, 2016, in a vote that took all the pollsters by surprise, the British people voted to leave the European Union (E.U.) in a move known as Brexit. With no country ever leaving the E.U. before, this created massive uncertainty for everyone, from E.U. citizens who had settled in the U.K. and U.K. citizens who had moved to Europe, to politicians, to businesses. The complexity of unwinding all the laws, regulations, and institutions that tied the U.K. to the E.U. was something that few politicians or business people, let alone voters, had considered. With a tight 2-year timeframe from when the British government triggered the exit with a letter to the E.U. on March 29th, 2017, to a stated formal leaving of the E.U. on March 29th, 2019, the realization of the near impossibility of a smooth exit threw businesses of all kinds into massive uncertainty and turmoil. Businesses could not be sure of their plans, and even the creation of multiple contingency plans for different eventuali-ties of how trade would operate between the U.K. and other countries both inside and outside the E.U. after Brexit did not provide any certainty. Furthermore, the continued failure of the U.K. government to negotiate an exit treaty with the E.U. exacerbated this uncertainty when the March 29th, 2019, date came and went and the parties agreed to extend the deadline for Brexit to occur.

Minimal consistency, in a strange sort of way, is really about minimizing the costs of inconsistency. Because a firm must stay fit to its environment and because that environment will inevitably change, change on the part of the organization is inevitable as well. However, change costs money and can be a source of substantial discomfort. As such, change is often avoided, put off, and delayed until the need becomes so great that a revolution takes place. Revolutions can be costly to under-take and difficult to control. Yet, paradoxically, the only way that they can be truly avoided is by undertaking numerous and regular evolutionary changes over time. By enabling such small, evolutionary changes, a firm can prevent the revolution-ary changes that it so wants to avoid. But embracing evolutionary change requires foregoing a measure of consistency.

Minimum rationality is the final principle, and it too often seems contrary to traditional wisdom and thought. Indeed, the pursuit of rationality appeals to our desire for certainty and control. It can lead us to over-objectify subjective phenom-enon, to value known commodities too highly, and to discount risky ventures too sharply. Unchecked, rationality can become a straightjacket, limiting the range of organizational motion and the scope of a firm's vision. It can lead to a focus on processes and procedures, on measures and methods, to the detriment of other more important issues. Peter Drucker addressed the pathological pursuit of rationality in his famous distinction between "doing things right" and "doing the right things." Managers must take care to remember that long-term success comes more from doing the right things than it does from doing things right. Thus, managers must take care to not over-emphasize rationality and not to cut off creativity by insisting that things be done by the book.

The key to avoiding the paradox of success and to sustaining competitive advantage is the institutionalization of principles like this. Each should be instilled at every stage of the strategy process and promoted throughout the organization so as to prevent calcification around any particular mindset and to encourage ongoing adaptation, learning, and change.

ADDITIONAL THOUGHTS AND CAVEATS

One of the biggest stumbling blocks to understanding in the study, teaching, and application of strategy is the tendency to allow these tools of the trade to become more important than the actual trade itself. Many students, teachers, and managers alike become so fixed on the form of the process, so absorbed in the details of the analysis, that they lose sight of competitive advantage, of the customer, and of the reality strategy is meant to create. Peter Drucker has said that the real purpose of a business is to create and keep customers. Regardless of how a firm measures its performance, a growing stream of satisfied customers will always translate into good returns. Thus, these tools, and the whole process of strategy, are valuable only insofar as they facilitate the creation of satisfied customers, what we are calling competitive advantage. Towards that end then, it is important to close this chapter with some additional thoughts and caveats.

Starting From Scratch Is the Exception

It is rare indeed that this process starts *tabula rasa*, with a blank slate. Almost always, there are processes, investments, and people already in place. In these instances, creating new strategy means initiating and managing change. While change is problematic in its own right, the issue here is broader than the need to deal with change. Winston Churchill once said, "we shape our buildings, thereafter they shape us." The "building" that is the organization is both an instrument of, and a constraint on, strategy. Firms must work with what they have; they must make use of their own resource base, broad or narrow as it may be. Whatever the future holds for Delta, in the near term it will remain in the airline business because it has so much invested in an asset base that ties it to that industry. While divestment of those assets is possible, it is surely not easy, nor could it likely be accomplished quickly and without substantial loss. Thus, any strategy that Delta formulates must take into account its substantial assets in place.

But assets need not be tangible to constrain the strategic process. Firms invest great effort selecting, hiring, and training their people to fit a particular strategy. While this can aid implementation, it can also serve to constrain the ability of the firm to adapt and change. The shift from a mainframe-based to a personal computer–based company, and then to an AI (software) and services-focused company, for instance, involved a considerable and concerted effort by IBM to develop new human resources and to divest some old ones. While IBM's people were very good, the things at which they were good were not the things needed for the new strategy. Thus, the formulation and implementation of the new strategy hinged on the ability of the firm to shift away from some resources and into others.

Even in those rare instances where strategy making can be initiated from scratch, in the establishment of a new firm, for instance, there remain constraints. The skills, talents, and biases of an entrepreneur, for instance, constrain and govern the strategy. The strategies of new firms are especially susceptible to pressures wrought by the availability of resources. Whereas a new firm might desire to grow through the traditional means of raising financing and then using that financing to fund its investment, the realities of the marketplace and the limits on the capital the firm can raise may necessitate a different strategy, like franchising. Moreover, whatever these initial trade-offs and decisions, they set precedent and become the constraints on the strategy process in the future. This is a phenomenon known as ***imprinting***. Founders imprint upon their organizations a particular strategic image, and that image continues to characterize and constrain the firm well into the future.

Thus, at any point in time, not only must the strategic manager contend with the firm, its intents, its strengths, and its weaknesses, not just with the various opportunities and threats in the environment, but they must do so while working with the resources at hand. To borrow an old phrase, they must play the cards as they have been dealt. Over time, resources can change; old assets can be sold and new assets acquired. However, all of that takes time. Thus, the strategy process almost never begins from scratch.

Whose Job Is Strategic Management?

The second caveat relates to involvement. Just whose job is strategic management, really? On one hand are those who would say that strategy is the province of top management. The CEO and the top management team are the ones best positioned to think strategically, to see the big picture, and to prescribe direction. As evidenced by the number of studies on CEOs and top management teams, this view seems to dominate the scholarly literature on strategy. While partially correct, this view overlooks the fact that the CEO and the other top managers are often isolated by the organizations and bureaucracies that surround them, cut off from direct customer feedback, from regular interaction with the environment, and from day-to-day knowledge of the firm's operations. As such, they are often unaware of many things very near the heart of their own competitive advantage.

On the other hand are those who argue for an egalitarian process. Viewed from this perspective, strategy making involves a leader who is primarily a facilitator, with broad and inclusive sharing of ideas and with consensus on and commitment to the outcomes being as important as the outcomes themselves. The object of this approach is both to engage the diverse and specialized expertise of people throughout the organization as well as to create a sense of buy-in to the final strategy. The problem with this approach is in the execution. Such broad and inclusive processes are slow and cumbersome. Moreover, without some means to resolve conflicts, such processes can produce acrimony and resentment, which can hinder implementation later on.

The best answer to the question of involvement then lies somewhere in between these two extremes. Strategic management does involve seeing the big picture and thinking ahead. It does involve looking beyond the current state of affairs and past the provincial lines of specific units or departments. It also requires, on occasion, leading people in directions that they might not have otherwise chosen. For all these reasons, the responsibility for strategic management falls disproportionately and unavoidably on top management. Yet, top management is rarely able to know everything that must be known, to foresee everything that must be foreseen, and to decide everything that must be decided on its own. There are simply too many variables and too much complexity for the process to rest in the hands of just a few.

As a result, there must be participation throughout the organization. For example, as discussed earlier, implementation is the process through which the intentions of strategy become real. Those involved with implementation then are often invaluable sources of information about what really works and what does not. Competitive advantage is really about creating value for customers. Thus, those involved directly with customers are often invaluable sources of information about technological and demographic trends, as well about competitor actions and customer preferences. Engineers, designers, and logisticians all can be tremendous sources of information about the possibilities and constraints of a new strategy. Indeed, strategy is made better when the process includes information from all of these various specialties and functions. The challenge for top management is to create a process that seeks and gets all of this diverse input but that does so without stifling the real work that all of these various people are charged to do.

Herein then lies what Hamlet would call "the rub" of participation. The issue of involvement is fundamental to the process because changing who participates will very much change the nature of the strategy. Yet, involvement is often decided in an ad hoc fashion and based upon dubious criteria. Those who are most important to the process may sometimes be those with the least amount of time to spare. Broad and diverse participation is important, but not everyone needs to participate on every decision. It is very likely that the best practices and minds will be distributed throughout the organization. However, a relative few of those minds will be tasked with thinking about the organization as a whole. Thus, the issue of involvement represents a challenge of balancing many important but competing criteria. A streamlined and quick process has advantages, but it may sacrifice comprehensiveness and depth. A centralized and focused process may offer advantages, but it might neglect some possibilities and alienate those charged with implementation. These trade-offs are inevitable, just as the responsibility for resolving them falls inevitably on top management. Still, in deciding who participates, whether that decision is made implicitly or explicitly, management shapes the nature of the strategy and so affects the nature of the competitive advantage.

Intended Versus Realized Outcomes

Strategy does not always emerge as expected. Events intervene, conditions change, people adapt, learn, and grow, and all of this variation affects the way strategy works. A closer look at Amazon's history and evolution shows various twists and turns that clearly illustrate this concept. Amazon was established in July 1994 by Jeff Bezos as an online bookstore that relied completely on UPS and the United States Postal Service for deliveries. But in a mere 20 years, the simple company that started out with humble beginnings quickly and efficiently evolved into one of the most innovative, impactful, and highly valued companies in the world. The evolution of Amazon from an online bookstore into the massively diversified business it is today did not come all at once and was a process of reacting to opportunities, market conditions, and competitor moves. Another key factor for its growth and evolution was the advancement in technology. Amazon harnessed these developments and strategically focused on building its logistical infrastructure and cloud services that defines the company's core competency and is at the heart of its competitive advantage. In 1997 it opened its first remote distribution center, adding one-click ordering that streamlined the checkout process and minimized the common e-commerce mistakes that were typical of the growing pains of the new digital online market. 1998 marked Amazon's evolution beyond books by adding music and DVDs. To support its expansion in the world of entertainment, Amazon acquired the Internet Movie Database (IMDb) that provided information on popular titles. By the end of the 1990s, Amazon added home-improvement products, software, gift items, and video games to its product offerings. In the early days of the new century, Amazon moved beyond retail by investing heavily in developing its cloud computing infrastructure and capability, which led to the launch of

Amazon Web Services (AWS). Leveraging its new capabilities, Amazon expanded its business to include a host of other product categories such as all types of apparel, office accessories and products, health and personal care items, sporting goods, gourmet food, beauty items and jewelry, toys, and baby gear to name a few. The company also launched the Amazon Prime program and the Kindle e-reader. It also entered the world of entertainment by establishing Amazon Studios, which led to developing original TV shows, comics, and movies. So, as Amazon's evolution was characterized with many twists and turns, it is clear that the evolution was based on factors that were not foreseen at the inception of the company in 1994.

It is important to understand that strategy can emerge differently than intended and still be considered successful. Indeed, in many cases, the success of a strategy may actually depend upon its changing. Henry Mintzberg distinguishes between deliberate and emergent strategies and likens the strategy process to the creation of clay pottery. The strategist, or the potter in Mintzberg's analogy, starts with a set of raw materials, a general idea of where she wants to go and what she wants to accomplish, and a talent for shaping the materials according to her desires. The process itself, however, is more organic than mechanistic as the strategy emerges from the interaction of the strategist's intentions, observations, and experiences. In this sense, strategies are formed in process, as opposed to being formulated a priori.

This metaphor may be useful to some while seeming overly ethereal to others. The point, however, should not be lost. The strategy process, with all of its various components, is meant to be an adaptive mechanism, to keep the organization fit to its environment. Plans should be made and direction should be set. However, those plans should be revisited often, as conditions and competencies change and as feedback is received from the field. New insights should be sought and standing assumptions should be challenged. Simple things, like the definition of the target market, the competitive appeal of the product or service, or the relative strengths and weaknesses of the competition, should be examined regularly, and regular input should be sought and listened to from across the organization. Ralph Waldo Emerson once said that a foolish consistency is the hobgoblin of little minds. Competitive advantage, not consistency, is the object of strategic management. As such, it is important to remember that strategies may often emerge differently but even better than intended.

The Process Is Often Messy

In many ways, models like the one presented in Figure 3.1 do a disservice to students of strategy. The disservice comes in the fact that the actual process of strategy is not nearly so neat and linear as is suggested by this and other similar renderings. Indeed, the actual practice of strategy is considerably messier, with every step in the process affecting every other step. Missions and statements of purpose are often influenced by an awareness of what is possible and popular. Strengths and weaknesses and opportunities and threats are difficult if not impossible to separate and assess independently of one another. Implementation many times is far removed from the more deliberate stages of the process and so often looks more ad hoc and reactive than it does purposeful and strategic. These realities notwithstanding, however, texts like this one continue to present strategy as an orderly and linear series of steps that start at one end and finish at the other, while being governed all the while by a common and overarching logic.

The disconnect between this common depiction of the process and its actual nature is really a matter of perspective. There is an old saying, attributable to Otto von Bismark, that the making of laws, like the making of sausage, is a process best viewed from a distance and by its end result. The same could be said for strategic management. The process is messy and, at times, hard to understand. There are all sorts of fits and starts, attributable to both external and internal causes. It is a very human process and so is subject to all manner of human limitations and biases. Politics, self-interest, misunderstanding, and serendipity all play a role and all influence strategy as it emerges. As a consequence, especially in large firms, it is difficult to pull together and explain all of the various analyses, strategies, and functional efforts that produce a particular set of outcomes. Yet, somehow, at least in firms that perform well, all of this complexity comes together to consistently place on the market products and services that customers value. Thus, the complexity notwithstanding, there are some essential elements of strategic management that, when viewed from a distance, stand out and make a difference to organizational performance. Those essential elements are represented in Figure 3.1.

Each of these tools is an essential component of strategy. Each is necessary, but none alone is sufficient. They all must work in concert and all must point towards and produce some demonstrable effect on customer value. For many organizations, that is where the process breaks down. Thinking through the messiness of implementation during the formulation of strategy is difficult and uncertain. Yet, it is altogether necessary. Revisiting the mission periodically to see whether it still fits the reality of the environment in which the firm is operating is time consuming and tedious. Yet, it must be done if the firm is to avoid stumbling into the future, following without question the path that it is currently on. Taking time to actually listen to and learn from feedback is complicated. Taking sales people away from selling to talk about what they are hearing from customers or pulling consultants off of their projects periodically to have them share with one another some of the new best practices that they are learning often means absorbing real costs or sacrificing real revenues. Yet, how else is the firm to gain information firsthand about the market and the ever-changing opportunities and threats within it?

Recognizing that the strategy process can be a little messy is key to realizing its value. Order and cleanliness, like consistency, can be a hobgoblin in the mind of the strategist. Reality will never look as sterile as the picture in Figure 3.1. The process will never be as orderly as a textbook's table of contents. Yet, it is in learning to use all of these tools and learning to manage the complexity inherent in their use that they become truly valuable.

KEY TERMS

Bargaining power refers to the competitive relationship between suppliers and buyers of any good or service and relates to the ability of either party to exert power and influence over the other. The concept and its application to strategic management will be discussed extensively in Chapter 4.

Deterministic theories of management view a firm's performance as being largely attributable to factors and forces within the environment. The role of management in this view is simply to assess these forces and respond to them appropriately.

Fit is a concept based on the open systems view, where strategic success is linked simultaneously to the strategy, the characteristics of the firm, and the environment. In this view, any combination of strategies, resources, and conditions can yield competitive advantage, when properly aligned.

Imprinting refers to the patterns an organization takes on and repeats over time, without special intent or effort. These patterns may reflect principles of the firm's founders or practices that were instrumental in some early success. Regardless, though, they become part of the routine set of accepted practices or actions within an organization.

Key success factors are the drivers of success within a particular industry, environment, or setting. They are the things that are essential for competitive advantage, in relation to specific sets of customers and specific competitive conditions.

Logical incrementalism is a concept linking the specificity of strategic actions to the certainty of a particular setting. The idea is to set long-term goals in general terms, so as to allow for flexibility and adaptation, but to move forward through incremental and small steps, minimizing commitment and risk and increasing opportunities for learning.

Open systems theory views success as the result of interdependence between the conditions of the environment and the characteristics of the firm. All open systems, whether organizations or organisms, survive by acquiring inputs, performing some value-added transformations on them, and then returning them to the environment in the form of outputs.

Slack resources are resources held by the organization but are in excess of what is needed to satisfy immediate needs. Slack is typically either unabsorbed and available in the form of cash, receivables, or excess credit or absorbed and held in the form of excess capacity, excess inventory, or redundant capabilities.

Voluntaristic theories of management, in contrast to deterministic theories, view a firm's performance as being largely a function of specific actions and resources. The role of management in this view is to leverage unique characteristics and assets, so as to be distinct from the competition.

QUESTIONS FOR REVIEW

1. What does it mean to say that strategic management is "good theory" because it is so practical?
2. What is a mission statement and what two purposes do such statements often serve?
3. Many scholars and managers alike have debated the similarity and distinctions among missions, visions, and statements of purpose. What is the common theme running through all of these various statements?
4. The SWOT framework really consists of two distinct parts; what are they and how does each inform the other?
5. Describe the different forces operating within the macro- and the competitive environments. What value does it add to make the distinction between the two?
6. How does the principle of fit affect strategic management? Does understanding fit appear to make success easier or more difficult to achieve?
7. Is implementation an integral part of the strategic process or simply the execution that comes after the strategy? Whatever your answer, why is this so, and is that how it should be?
8. What is the connection between implementation and those parts of the strategy that the customer sees and the strengths and weaknesses identified through the SWOT analysis?
9. Why are learning, adaptation, and change so important to strategic success? After all, should not good strategy be about precise planning?
10. What is the distinction between intended and realized strategies, and how might a real manager use these concepts to be more successful?

Chapter 4

Analyzing the Environment

Having detailed in the previous chapter the various "tools" of the strategic manager's trade, this chapter looks in detail at one of those tools, the analysis of the environment. In terms of immediacy, the environment is probably the most important component of strategic success. This is because, as many contend, the environment "determines" the success of a company's strategy. This view or belief reflects a deterministic view of strategy (Bourgeois, 1984; Child, 1972).

The academic debate between **determinism**, the view that strategic success is a function of analytical precision and fixed cause and effect relationships, and **voluntarism**, the view that strategic success is a function of creativity, innovation, and the exercise of strategic choice, is not a matter of great practical importance. However, the tension between these two philosophies does reflect a comparable and essential tension between two practical strategic philosophies, proaction and reaction.

A cursory browsing of the day's popular business books will reveal any number of titles dealing with proaction, leadership, taking the initiative, and seizing the moment. However, a relative few are likely to spend much time on the importance of reaction. Indeed, the subject of reaction is far less popular and so often largely ignored. Undoubtedly, there is something satisfying about being first. Especially in business, we tend to celebrate leaders rather than followers. However, the reality is that leading is an imprecise science that often entails significant risk. Sometimes it is better to wait, to allow others to do the basic work of research and development and then to simply react quickly to the emerging changes in the marketplace. Thus, well-timed and appropriate reaction is an important part of strategy. Indeed, in some instances, reaction may be the very key to survival. At the same time, there are instances where being first can yield clear and sustainable advantages. In these cases, a firm would do well to accept the risks and step out ahead of the competition and, sometimes, ahead of the accepted wisdom.

But how is a manager to know the difference? When is it appropriate to act, and when is it is appropriate to react? Answering these questions requires knowing and understanding a great deal about the environment. Unfortunately, most people do environmental analysis only to understand the present. What is the size of the market? What are the attributes of the competition? What are the costs of the raw materials or what is the status of pending regulation? Certainly, these are important questions. However, they are limited in that they look only at static conditions. In essence, questions like this ask, what is the state of things right now? Certainly, the current state of the environment is important. However, good environmental analysis should provide more than just an understanding of the present. Good environmental analysis should also provide insight into how the current environment evolved and how that ongoing evolution affects the future. The philosopher Soren Kierkegaard once said, "life can only be understood backwards, but it must be lived forwards." For strategists, the implication is that the knowledge of how the environment is moving forward is best discerned in understanding the patterns of the past.

Doing good environmental analysis involves following a series of steps. First, the environment must be accurately defined. Many firms have suffered because of poor definition of the environment. The next step involves analysis of the current conditions. This step employs tools such as the PESTEL framework and the "5-Forces" model (Porter, 1980). Like the SWOT analysis, the PESTEL framework and the 5-Forces model are at once simple and yet extremely powerful. A thorough and deep understanding of the PESTEL components and the 5 forces and the factors that govern their interaction can yield substantial insights. The third step in the analysis is to consider how the various forces at work in the environment have been and are continuing to change. Two additional models, both of which will be discussed later, provide further guidance in understanding environmental evolution and the sorts of conditions that will emerge in the future. Finally, there is disruptive change that can occur in a firm's environment, which we will explore in greater depth in Chapter 9.

DEFINING THE BUSINESS AND THE ENVIRONMENT

The process begins with Figure 4.1, which was one of the models presented in Chapter 3. The environment is best thought of as a series of concentric circles. At the center of the rings is the firm itself. This representation reflects the view that

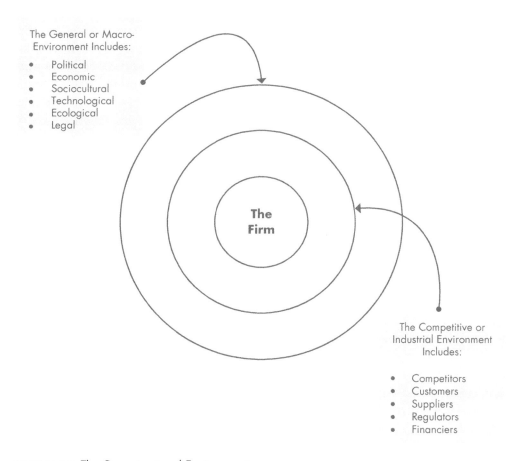

The General or Macro-
Environment Includes:

- Political
- Economic
- Sociocultural
- Technological
- Ecological
- Legal

**The
Firm**

The Competitive or
Industrial Environment
Includes:

- Competitors
- Customers
- Suppliers
- Regulators
- Financiers

FIGURE 4.1 The Organizational Environment

FIGURE 4.2 The Firm as an Open System

organizations are *open systems*. The open systems view holds that firms are inter-active and dynamic systems, embedded within other larger interactive and dynamic systems (Boulding, 1956; von Bertalanffy, 1950). Viewed in this way, a firm looks like a biological organism. Like living organisms, firms engage in three fundamental processes: input, transformation, and output (see Figure 4.2). And like living organisms, firms survive and prosper as they fit themselves into, and interact successfully with, their environments.

THE MACRO-ENVIRONMENT: PESTEL FRAMEWORK

At the most broad and basic level, represented by the outer ring on Figure 4.1, the firm has to fit within the macro-environment in which it operates. If the firm goes against these macro forces, it will find it very difficult, if not impossible, to survive. This is because this environment encompasses the most fundamental aspects of operating a business, from the legal rules and regulations under which the firm is allowed to operate to the cultural values under which the society operates and allows the firm to exist and thrive. An analysis of the macro-environment allows the firm to understand the fundamental opportunities and threats posed by the environment that govern the direct competitive environment in which the firm operates and competes and thus is a key first step in performing a comprehensive environmental analysis before moving to looking specifically at the direct competitive environment through the 5-Forces model.

A useful framework to ensure a comprehensive view of this macro-environment is the PESTEL framework, which divides the environment into six factors: Political, Economic, Sociocultural, Technological, Ecological, and Legal.

Political: The shifting political environment can have an enormous impact on firms. For instance, already in Europe and growing in the U.S., there is political movement towards increasing regulation and taxation on large technology companies, which could result in constraints in their ability to continue to dominate their markets, curtailment of their future growth rates, increases in the amount of taxes they pay, and even the potential breakup of the firms themselves. Stability and predictability of political forces are generally beneficial to companies, and firms often first seek markets where there is political stability. Firms will also actively seek to shape the political environment through lobbying, political contributions, and public relations efforts. Political actions can also directly lead to economic factors that have a substantial impact on companies, for instance, trade wars between nations leading to tariffs and import and export restrictions can have huge impact on firms, particularly those with international supply chains and markets. For example, in the recent trade wars between the U.S. and China, you have seen active lobbying from companies such as Apple to try and gain exemption from tariffs for certain categories of goods which are vital to their supply chain.

Economic: Macroeconomic factors can have a large effect on the head or tail winds affecting all companies. When economic times are good, then it is relatively much easier for a firm to achieve profitability than when economic times are tough, regardless of the resources and capabilities of the firm. Economic cycles affect not only demand for the company's products or services but also many other keys to a firm's operations such as the availability and cost of capital and the ability to hire and retain employees. Other macroeconomic variables such as interest rates, inflation rates, currency exchange rates, and GDP growth rates also shape the economic environment in which the firm exists and competes and, while these factors in some ways are the same for all firms in that they represent overall economic conditions, in other ways they impact firms differently as firms have, for example, different capital structures, reliance on human capital, elasticity of demand, and exposure to international markets.

Sociocultural: Factors such as a country's culture, norms, demographics, religion, and values play an important part in determining the market for a particular product or service. Firms have to pay great attention to these factors or risk rejection in the marketplace. A quick Google search for corporate cultural failures or brand cultural failures produces a vast array of amusing, but tragic, ways in which firms have failed to pay attention to these factors when entering a new market to disastrous results. Even companies that are excellent in many other areas, such as Wal-Mart, can make a cultural misstep when entering new markets and failing to pay sufficient attention to sociocultural factors. When Wal-Mart entered the Japanese market through purchasing a stake in the Seiyu Company and introduced its "everyday low prices" philosophy and slogan, this backfired because in the Japanese culture, customers associated low prices with low quality, turning them off from shopping there.[1]

Technological: Advances in technology can disrupt whole industries, spurring innovation in the creation of new industries and markets along with the disruption of the old. We will look more in depth into the impact of technology in Chapter 9. Often it is very difficult for incumbent firms to shift with new technologies, and the advancements are made by new players into the industry, even when, on the surface, the technology change does not appear that disruptive. For example, the technological shift from videotapes to DVDs allowed the creation of Netflix and a new business model of renting movies via the mail as opposed to retail stores and led to the demise of Blockbuster, which was the dominant force in video rentals. Netflix, though, was able to maneuver through the next, and even bigger, technological shift from physical DVDs to streaming, not only changing the delivery medium of movies but also shifting its business model towards creating its own content. This shift, both in the advent of streaming technology and in Netflix moving from being purely a content deliverer to a deliverer and creator of content, has prompted a further shift in the entertainment industry and the advent of streaming services from content creators such as Disney+.

Ecological: The environmental impact of a company's operations has been slowly rising towards the top of the agenda for boards of directors. Consumers have become increasingly aware of climate change and the impact of the production of goods and services as a contributing factor to the changing climate. Accordingly, consumers have increased their voice and pressure on companies to be proactive in reducing their carbon footprint, and many companies have taken their ecological footprint seriously and have set aggressive targets to reduce their environmental impact. For instance, global consumer products company Unilever has taken a strong position in setting out to decouple its growth from its environmental impact and aligning its corporate mission with the United Nations' Sustainable Development Goals. It has set the goal of halving its environmental footprint in the making and use of their products while improving the health, well-being, and livelihoods of their customers and employees.[2]

Legal: The regulatory framework that a company operates under creates the conditions under which the firm exists. Changes in that framework through regulation and deregulation can have profound effects on individual businesses and entire industries. While we have seen these effects in many long-established industries such as utilities and airlines, this also plays a critical role in the formation of new industries. For example, the relatively new technology of drones and, in particular, their potential for use in commercial delivery, transforming the method of delivery for not only things that we already expect delivered in a few minutes, like pizza, but also allowing the delivery of almost anything that is relatively small and lightweight, promises to solve the so-called "last mile" problem. Taking out the friction and expenses of "the last mile" of delivering to individual homes would be a boon to business and sounds utopian to many. However, the challenge to making this a reality is less of a technological challenge than it is a legal and regulatory challenge.

Developing a regulatory framework that allows drone delivery without causing excessive noise pollution and irritation to many is a current challenge facing law-makers. In October 2019, UPS received Federal Aviation Administration (FAA) approval for drone flights to deliver medical supplies across hospital campuses, opening the door for commercial drone flights.[3]

While a PESTEL analysis at the macro-environmental level provides the firm with a perspective on its basic fit with the environment in which it has to operate, complicating matters is the fact that interaction with the environment is more than just a dyadic exchange with the macro factors. Competitors, suppliers, and customers also affect the conditions under which firms get their inputs and distribute their outputs. Manufacturing facilities, such as paper mills, can have the capability to choose among multiple fuel sources, so suppliers of power are competing with one another for the business of paper mills. When firms have multiple options for their inputs, power shifts towards the buyer and away from the suppliers competing for their business. As the story of International Paper Company's mills and its shift between power sources illustrates, important outputs are subject to competition and demand can affect their price and availability (see Box 4.1: Multi-fuel Paper

Box 4.1
Multi-fuel Paper Mills Have Bargaining Power Over Suppliers

Paper mills use power sources to create heat, which generates the steam and electricity they need to create paper. Traditional paper mills burn two internal sources of power, black liquor and wood chips, as well as outside sources, such as coal and natural gas. *Black liquor* is the carbon-rich residue that is created in the pulp-making process of paper production. Paper mills also use the bark and ground-up wood chips from the logs they buy to create the pulp. While these are both internal sources of power, paper mills also typically rely heavily on outside energy sources, such as coal and natural gas. In addition, paper mills generally purchase a percentage of their wood chips from external suppliers. Paper mills with multiple fuel source options, such as those owned by International Paper Company, can purchase the least expensive power source that is available at a given time. This gives these paper mills a competitive advantage over their more traditional competitors, as well as buyer bargaining power over the various producers of its many options for power sources.

International Paper Company purchases the most inexpensive power sources available to it at the time. This can vary as each supplier increases or decreases its prices. If coal is the cheapest available form of power, these multi-fuel source paper mills can switch from natural gas or wood chips. If natural gas or coal becomes too expensive, the mills can produce power using black liquor or wood chips. This gives International Paper Company leverage over its suppliers, increasing its bargaining power over the various producers of wood chips, coal, natural gas, and electricity compared to manufacturers that cannot switch among multiple sources.

Even with the substantial bargaining power International Paper Company has over its suppliers, it still must function within the constraints of price fluctuations resulting from supply and demand changes. Prices can vary by season, but these multi-fuel source paper mills still have an advantage over manufacturers who do not have the bargaining power that comes from the ability to switch among fuel sources. During hot Southern summers, International Paper Company's mill in Yellow Bluff, Alabama, makes most of its own energy because electricity is more expensive due to the high demand of electricity for air conditioners by local residents. In the winter, the mill burns more coal because winter rains produce damp bark that burns less efficiently. The mill in Alabama generates 40% of the wood chips it burns and purchases the remaining 60% from outside suppliers. The cost of wood chips is low because there is not currently much competition for wood waste in the area. In fact, the plant can produce energy by burning wood chips for two-thirds of the price of the same amount of energy created by burning coal. However, the price of wood chips could increase if biofuel and wood pellet plants move to the region. If wood chips become more expensive, these multi-fuel source power plants still retain some of their bargaining power and will be more cost effective than their more traditional competitors. This bargaining power over its suppliers gives International Paper Company a competitive advantage over its less advanced competitors.

Source: Amy, J. "International Paper spends to cut energy use at paper mills." www.al.com/press-register-business/2011/09/international_paper_spends_to.html

Mills Have Bargaining Power Over Suppliers). Similarly, to have sufficient demand, at a profitable price, the firm's products and services must be seen as being unique and desirable over and above the available options. What that means is that the firm's products and services must either be comparable to but less expensive than the competing alternatives or considered qualitatively better than the competing alternatives. Competitors then threaten the firm's viability by interfering with the relationship that it has with its suppliers (inputs) and its customers (outputs).

Understanding the firm from this perspective means knowing something about the firm itself, as well as about its suppliers, customers, competitors, and the overall context in which all of these various groups interrelate. Thus, Figure 4.1 serves to remind us of two very important points. First, each firm exists within its own unique environment; no two firms, no matter how similar, share exactly the same environment. As a result, good environmental analysis must be done specifically for individual firms and with a specific eye towards the relationship among the firm, its customers, its competitors, and its suppliers. Second, each environment includes the various actors that affect the firm's survival and success. As a result, thorough environmental analysis begins with the identification of these various actors.

Identifying these actors requires understanding what the firm really does. In other words, defining the environment begins with defining the business. Abell (1980) proposes that businesses generally define themselves along one of three dimensions: customer groups, customer functions, or dominant technologies. Some firms, for instance, service particular groups of customers. Wholesale building products firms, for instance, service contractors almost exclusively. They sell many products and provide a host of different services, but they do so specifically for a particular group of customers. Medical supply businesses are another example of this orientation. They carry a range of products and offer a number of different services. Yet, they do this all just for hospitals, medical practices, and outpatient clinics. Other firms satisfy a particular function. Wal-Mart and Target sell to virtually everyone; they do so because they satisfy a function, the supplying of stable goods that are nearly universal. Grocery stores, like Kroger or Albertson's, banks and financial services firms, utility companies and cell phone providers all tend to define themselves in terms of the function that they provide. Finally, some firms define themselves in terms of the technology that they build or employ. Caterpillar, for instance, makes diesel and natural gas engines for all sorts of large industrial machine applications, and General Electric makes turbines for engines and power plants. Anyone who has need of these products or technologies is a potential customer. In that sense, then, it is the technology itself that drives the definition of the business.

With the business defined, two questions arise. First, who are the customers? Second, what other options do these customers have for these products or services? For Caterpillar, the customers are firms in transportation, construction, mining, power generation, and a host of other businesses. The various options for these firms include not just other makers of diesel and natural gas engines but also alternative types of suppliers. For example, a firm that makes no engines at all but rather reconditions older engines would be a potential substitute for and so a competitor to Caterpillar. For a cell phone service provider, like Verizon, the customer includes just about every individual and business interested in mobile communication. The options available to these customers include other cell phone service providers, as well other communication technologies, such as two-way radios, internet-enabled mobile messaging services, and pagers. For a medical supply company, the customers are physician practices, hospitals, and outpatient clinics. The various suppliers to these customers include other specialized supply firms as well as any firm providing the products and services that hospitals and medical practices buy. Indeed, warehouse distributors or large pharmaceutical firms might also offer alternative sources of supply to these customers and so be competitors to specialized medical supply firms.

The common theme across all of these examples is substitutability. Substitutability, in the eye of the customer, is the key to defining a business's competitive environment. Defining the business allows the firm to identify its customer. Identifying the

customer and suppliers of substitute products and services allows the firm to identify its competitive environment. The importance of substitutability goes back to
the open systems view of the firm. Competitors are threats to the firm because they
can disrupt the flow of inputs and outputs into and out of the firm. Who are the
competitors? They are the firms whose products and services lure away customers.
They are the firms whose products and services are the benchmarks, in the mind of
the customer, against which a firm's products and services are compared. Identify
the customer and you will identify this group of firms. Identify this group of firms
and you will identify the competitive environment.

ANALYZING THE COMPETITIVE ENVIRONMENT

The competitive environment, the first circle beyond the firm in Figure 4.1, is the
most immediate and important part of the environment. As such, it is where most
of the time and effort in environmental analysis is spent. It is especially important because the interaction of the actors in the competitive environment directly
affects the *bargaining power* of the firm, in relation to its customers and suppliers.
This can be understood through a simple example. Consider the case of someone
selling a house. As the seller thinks about a price, she considers the attributes of
the property, its size, its age, its condition, and so on. But, more than any of these
issues, she also considers the nature of the market. Is the house in a popular area
or neighborhood? How many other houses are for sale? What is the ratio of buyers
to sellers? How motivated are the sellers to get out and how motivated are buyers
to get in? In popular areas, like resorts or dense downtown districts, properties can
sell at extraordinary premiums even if they are in poor condition. In less attractive,
low-traffic areas, properties can sell at a heavy discount even if they are in excellent
condition. Thus, in pricing her house, our hypothetical seller wants to know her
market. Will she have a large number of bidders? If so, then she can likely ask and
wait for a high price. Or, will she see a relative few bids? If so, then she will likely
have to take whatever price she can get. Are there a large number of comparable
properties on the market? If so, then she may be motivated to get out before the
price declines. Are there a large number of buyers moving into the market? Is so,
then she may be motivated to wait while prices escalate.

This simple example illustrates the importance of bargaining power, and bargaining power relates directly to the economic concept of *elasticity*. Elasticity is about
having options. Do customers have options to the firm's products and services? Can
they afford to "walk away" from the deal? If so, then they have great elasticity and
bargaining power and the burden on the seller is much greater. However, when the
buyer has few options and is unable to walk away, the balance of bargaining power
shifts. In these instances, the burden is on the buyer as the seller can now name the
price and terms.

The concepts of elasticity and bargaining power are powerful and relate directly to competitive advantage, profitability, and overall success. Indeed, because of their importance, these concepts lie at the root of many well-known business practices. ***Branding***, for instance, is a popular term in marketing circles. Branding seeks to promote a high degree of familiarity, recognition, and respect for a particular brand in the mind of the customer. As such, customers will think only of that brand when thinking of a particular product. For example, a customer who wants tennis shoes might think first of the Nike brand name and so seek out only a Nike product, excluding other options. The effect would be to increase Nike's bargaining power by limiting the options, or the perceived options, available to the buyer. By building a strong preference for its brand, Nike is able to affect its bargaining power in relation to its customers, making them less likely to consider the products of other suppliers. As a result, Nike is able to increase its returns.

Other firms may, through regulatory means, try to limit customer options. Cable TV companies, local phone service providers, and power generation firms have all benefited from their status as protected monopolies. While they are subject to considerable regulation and oversight, they are also protected from direct competition. As a result, customers are often left with limited options for cable or power service. In the absence of options, these customers have little or no bargaining power. Indeed, it is to prevent these sorts of suppliers from abusing this bargaining power advantage that these firms and their prices are so carefully regulated. Other firms benefit from legal limitations on competition as well. Companies in the pharmaceutical and biotech businesses often get patents for their products and processes. These patents protect the firms by limiting the ability of competitors to make and sell comparable products. With few if any comparable products available, customers must deal with the patent holder. As a result, the holder of the patent has great bargaining power and great ability to sell more and to sell at a premium price.

Bargaining power relates directly to competitive advantage and is a large part of understanding profitability. Firms with much bargaining power are often able to sell more and to sell at a higher price. Firms with little bargaining power must often work harder to make sales and will often sell less or sell at a lower price. Thus, understanding bargaining power and the various forces that govern it is a key part of environmental analysis.

THE 5-FORCES MODEL

Fortunately, a considerable amount of time and effort has been devoted to understanding bargaining power. From this work has emerged a simple, yet powerful tool, the 5-Forces model (Figure 4.3). Developed by Michael Porter (1980), the 5-Forces model depicts competitiveness or profit potential as resulting from the interaction of 5 forces: the bargaining power of sellers, the bargaining power of buyers, the

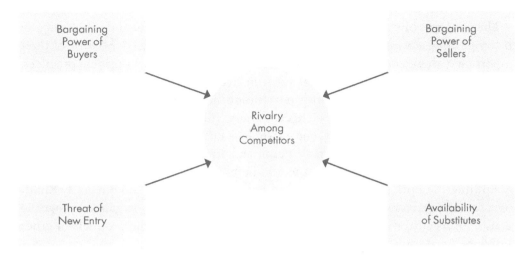

FIGURE 4.3 The Five-Forces Model

availability of substitute products, the threat of new entrants, and the rivalry among existing competitors.

Bargaining Power of the Seller

Bargaining power of the seller relates to the attractiveness and availability of particular products and services in relation to available options. Returning to the earlier example, Nike is considered a maker of reliable, high-quality athletic shoes and apparel. That perception translates into bargaining power for Nike. Customers can pay Nike's price or they can settle for something else, but buying from Nike likely means paying a premium price. Quality then, or perceived quality, produces bargaining power for the seller. Bargaining power for the seller can also relate to the absence of competition. Airline ticket prices are generally higher on routes that are served by only one carrier, for instance (Chen et al., 1992). The importance of the product or service also relates to bargaining power. For example, buyers rarely choose a surgeon based on cost. Because of the importance of the service, customers will generally want the best available provider. To get that provider, they may end up having to wait longer for their procedure, having to pay more for the procedure, or both. Quality, exclusivity, prestige, or importance of the product or service can all shift bargaining power away from the buyer and to the seller by limiting the ability of the customer to walk away and go elsewhere.

Of course, the ultimate example of seller power is a ***monopoly***. Where there is only one provider, the seller can sell at a substantial premium. But monopoly conditions can exist even when no true monopoly is present. As mentioned, there are regulated monopolies, such as cable TV, local telephone service, and residential power distribution. But there are also pseudo-monopolies, conditions where customers feel that they have only one option, even when other options are in fact present. Coke benefits from such an effect in many areas, as some consumers prefer Coke regardless of the presence or price of the various alternatives. In the minds of these customers, Coke has ***monopoly power***, despite the presence of competition. Starbucks benefits from a similar effect. So strong are customers' desires for Starbucks' coffee that they often forgo other coffee options, even if those are more readily available and less expensive. The effect is to give Starbucks monopoly-like power, which translates into tremendous revenue and profits. Micro-monopolies also exist where a customer is limited to one option in a particular circumstance. For instance, Coca-Cola, PepsiCo, Aramark, and Ticketmaster create these micro-monopoly conditions through licensing agreements which give them exclusive rights to sell concessions or tickets at large sporting and entertainment venues, such that consumers in those venues have no alternative brands to choose from in a particular category.

The key to understanding the bargaining power of the seller lies in understanding the needs of the buyer and the available options. When buyers have strong needs but few options, or if they believe that they have few options, the power to bargain or negotiate the terms of the sale shift to the benefit of the seller. Relating this back to the example of our hypothetical home seller, when her home is one of just a few available in an attractive area that is expected only to grow more attractive, she has great power with which to negotiate the sale.

Bargaining Power of the Buyer

Buyers and sellers represent opposing sides of the same relationship. For there to be a buyer, then there must be a seller and for there to be a seller, there must also be a buyer. Thus, when we see bargaining power shifting to the seller, it is necessarily shifting away from the buyer. To understand bargaining power of the buyer, simply think about those forces that affect the power of the seller but think about them in reverse. For example, just as selling a product that is highly important to the buyer will provide the seller with power, so will selling a product that is relatively unimportant translate into power for the buyer. Products like chewing gum, pencils, paper clips, or paper are inexpensive, readily available, and rarely of great and immediate importance. Thus, buyers are rarely in a position of needing them urgently or having to get them from just one supplier. That availability, coupled with a lack of intense need, provides the buyer with great bargaining power.

Buyers can also increase their bargaining power by buying in bulk or by ordering in advance. Both serve as inducements to the seller and so might allow the buyer to negotiate better terms or prices. Having great bargaining power is especially important to firms like Wal-Mart or Target. These firms use their size and volume to negotiate low prices along with favorable payment and shipping terms from their suppliers. Indeed, understanding bargaining power and the importance of volume buying can shed light on the workings of many different industries like groceries, steel, or automobiles. In all of these industries, firms need the ability to negotiate low prices from their suppliers. One way to accomplish that is by being large so that they can buy in bulk.

Buyers can also increase their bargaining power by developing alternate sources of supply. In the earlier example, International Paper Company dramatically increased its bargaining power in relation to paper mills with the capability to run off of multiple fuel sources. Similarly, for firms like Dell, Lenovo, and HP, having the option of using AMD processors increases their bargaining power in relation to Intel. Many firms actively seek out and cultivate new sources of supply, not necessarily because they are unhappy with their current providers but because doing so gives then enhanced bargaining power over their providers.

Availability of Substitutes

Bargaining power is all about options. To the extent that buyers have options, they are able to exercise greater elasticity in their purchasing. To the extent that buyers have few options, they are less elastic. In and of itself, elasticity is neither good nor bad. Sellers prefer that their customers come to them first and foremost. Buyers prefer a range of options and the ability to select from among multiple suppliers. Understanding the dynamics of elasticity though is important to both buyers and sellers, as both seek to get the best deal and to maximize their returns. Thus, the availability of substitutes is a key component of bargaining power.

The problem is that substitutability lies in the eye of the beholder. Are Coke and Pepsi substitutes? That depends upon who you ask. Some would say absolutely; others would not think of drinking anything other than their favorite. Is a Surface Pro a substitute for an iPad? Again, it depends upon the user. Some would say yes, the devices are similar technologically and provide similar functionality. Others though would disagree and say that the two products are wholly different. Thus, just because two products "look" alike does not mean that they are truly substitutable. Indeed, substitutes need not look like the product or service that they are substituting. Natural gas is a substitute for electricity, ceramic tile and hardwood can substitute for carpet, and the internet has proven to be an effective substitute for newspapers and magazines. Substitutability lies in the eye of the one doing the substituting. That is why it is so important to look at competition as being any force that disrupts the relationship between the firm and its customers and suppliers.

Of course, there is one potential substitute for just about every product or service. That substitute is the option of walking away and buying nothing at all. Staying home is a substitute activity to going out for a movie or dinner. Keeping an automobile one more year is a substitute to buying a new one. Driving is a substitute for flying, and making coffee at home is a substitute for purchasing from Starbucks. Understanding substitutability requires getting inside the mind of the customer and asking, what options does he or she have? What alternatives does the customer consider in the decision to purchase or not to purchase? As that customer sees more alternatives, as he or she identifies more products or services that will substitute, so will his or her bargaining power increase.

Threat of New Entrants

New entrants, or the threat of new entrants, play an interesting role in effecting bargaining power. New entrants to an industry can offer alternatives to customers, reducing the bargaining power of the sellers. The emergence of new entrants into the entertainment distribution industry, for instance, had a substantial impact on the bargaining relationship between cable or satellite companies and their customers. The entrance of Hulu, Netflix, Amazon, YouTube, and even Facebook among others dramatically altered the notion of traditional television entertainment, setting in motion a series of events that would reshape the entire industry. Cable companies and satellite TV companies, such as DirecTV and Dish Network, have seen a substantial erosion of their customer base as consumers "cut the cord" on traditional television distribution. This is a prime example of how new entrants can have a profound impact on both buyers and sellers.

The effect of new entrants can be felt even before entry occurs. Indeed, the mere threat of new entrants can be a powerful force. Economics tells us that new entrants are encouraged by the prospect of profitability. During the 1990s, when fuel was cheap, Mercedes, BMW, Acura, and Nissan all entered the SUV market. The attraction for these firms was the profit that other firms like GM and Ford were at the time making off of these vehicles. A multitude of "reality" television shows followed the initial success of shows like *Survivor* and *The Bachelor*, endeavoring to capitalize and make money off of this trend in the viewing market. The potential for profit provides an incentive to new entrants. Those new entrants, in turn, provide options to customers, increasing their bargaining power and reducing the profitability of the sellers.

As a consequence, firms will often try to deter new entry by making the market appear less attractive. This is called ***contrived deterrence***, and it affects the bargaining relationship between buyers and sellers. To deter new entrants, a firm may build overcapacity and, in so doing, reduce its own profit. If that overcapacity deters new entrants, however, it may well be worth the cost. A firm may intentionally sell below the highest possible price that it could charge. Coca-Cola does this in many places. While it could likely reap higher profits from those who strongly prefer it, raising prices could open the door for Pepsi, or for some other drink maker, to gain market share. Thus, Coke leaves its prices below full potential to deter the competition.

As these examples illustrate, where there is the potential for new entry, there is increased bargaining power for the buyer and decreased bargaining power for the seller. Alternatively, where there is little potential for new entry, there is decreased bargaining power for the buyer and increased bargaining power for the seller. Thus, in analyzing the environment, it is important to assess the potential for entry. When is it difficult for new firms to enter the market? It is difficult when there is some legal or structural impediment. Patents and copyrights are legal barriers to entry. Licensed monopolies, such as exist in retail electrical power and some other utilities, are all barriers to entry. **Switching costs**, the cost to the buyer to change from one provider to another, can be a barrier to entry. Brand preferences, shared usage, network connectivity, and distribution channel saturation can all be barriers to entry and so forces that can deter a competitor from entering. That deterrence translates into increased bargaining power for the seller.

The key to understanding the threat of new entry is remembering that new entrants represent potential new alternatives, new options that increase the bargaining power of the buyer. Thus, industries lacking the sorts of barriers discussed earlier are unable to prevent or deter new entry and so will likely see bargaining power gravitate towards the buyers and away from the sellers.

Rivalry Among Competitors

The last of the forces is rivalry among the existing competitors. Even in those instances where there is little threat of new entry, existing firms may still compete fiercely by offering substitute products, by offering inducements for customers to switch suppliers, and by working to convince customers that their products or services are better than the available options. This sort of competition, called rivalry, impacts bargaining power directly, shifting it away from the sellers and to the buyers. In the context of this model, then, rivalry always refers to competition that results in some form of price competition between rivals, lowering the profitability of the industry as a whole as buyers benefit from the competitive rivalry within the industry.

But what leads to rivalry? Essentially, rivalry reflects the balance of supply and demand. When there is more demand than supply, rivalry will be relatively low because firms can grow by selling to new customers. On the other hand, when there is more supply than demand, rivalry will be relatively high because firms can only grow by inducing customers to switch from one provider to another.

Thus, mature markets, where sales growth is slow or nonexistent, generally have higher rivalry than growing markets. Mature markets, with stagnant or slow-growing demand, are typically populated with large firms, with substantial capacity. Such firms often have low marginal costs and so great incentive to increase volume. Such increases, however, come at the expense of competitors who retaliate in their own defense. Substitutability is often high in mature markets, as customers frequently see little meaningful distinction among the products and services of the leading firms. Moreover, many of those firms have invested heavily in the specialized plant and equipment necessary to compete effectively. Those investments become exit barriers, locking the firm into the particular business, despite its marginal profitability. Indeed, firms in mature markets, where high exit barriers exist, will sometimes find it necessary to operate at a loss simply to create positive cash flow. Recall that firms can operate at a loss for so long as marginal revenues are higher than marginal costs. Such firms can continue to generate positive cash flow by slowly cannibalizing the value of their assets. High levels of investment in fixed and specialized assets then often create exit barriers and low marginal costs, both of which lead to intensified rivalry.

Taken together, these 5 forces can provide an excellent picture of the competitive conditions within a firm's environment. Where customers feel that they have options and where firms are motivated to increase volume, the exercise of elasticity will lead to lower prices, provide inducements for the buyers, or both. Where customers do not perceive that they have options and where firms are less motivated to increase volume, there will be less elasticity and so higher prices, lower inducements for customers, or both. Notice then that competitiveness also relates directly to profit potential. Where there is greater competitiveness, the potential for profit will be low. Where there is little competitiveness, the potential for profit will be higher.

The implication of all this is clear; firms should carve out a market space that is defensible, where competition will be low and where customers will have little opportunity to exercise elasticity. This implication, however, is just the tip of the iceberg. Indeed, many have criticized this model by asserting that it offers little more than this simple prescription to find non-competitive positions within the environment. The problem with that is that ongoing change in the environment makes such spaces very rare and such prescriptions worth little. There are few niches that are not subject to competition over time and few positions that can be defended indefinitely. Thus, the 5-Forces model is often criticized for not being sufficiently dynamic. Such criticisms, though, fail to comprehend the full potential of the model. Indeed, understanding the 5 forces and understanding how they change over time can provide powerful insights into the nature of market evolution and environmental opportunities and threats. Thus, the next section extends the concepts of bargaining power and competitiveness by exploring how they change over time.

COMPETITIVENESS AND THE LIFECYCLE MODEL

Figure 4.4 will be familiar to most students of business. It is sometimes called the industry or product lifecycle, as it depicts the common pattern by which the market for given products evolves and changes over time. To appreciate its utility, it is important to understand some of the model's basic features. First, there are two axes; the horizontal axis is time and the vertical axis is sales volume. Second, the function itself is a curve, upward sloping in the beginning, flat or nearly flat at the top, and then tapering off at the end. Finally, this curve is typically illustrated as being divided into stages. Some schemes will use 4 stages, others will use 5. However, the progression of stages always follows the same basic pattern. First, there is an initial, start-up phase, during which time the new product is introduced. Second, there is a growth phase, where product/industry standards begin to emerge, standardization in manufacturing and delivery begins to proliferate, and acceptance and demand grow. Then, there is some sort of maturation period, where supply catches up with demand, where overcapacity begins to emerge, and where the growth in sales volumes begins to flatten. Ultimately, there is some period beyond maturation, where growth becomes negative and volume actually declines. Over the course of this lifecycle, both sales and profitability follow a predictable pattern. In the figure, the solid top line is sales and the dashed bottom line is profitability.

Understanding this basic pattern of relationships provides a powerful tool for analyzing environments. Indeed, combining this model, and an awareness of the changing dynamics that it represents, with the 5-Forces model outlined earlier can provide a vivid picture of emerging opportunities, potential threats, and the

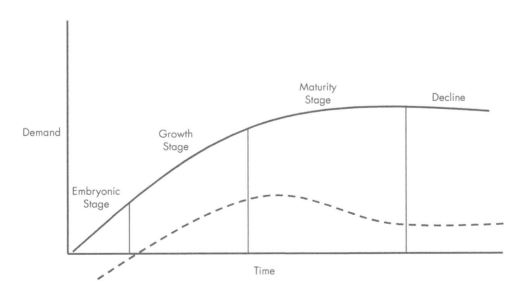

FIGURE 4.4 The Product/Industry Lifecycle

evolution of environmental conditions over time. Thus, rather than think of these two models as distinct analytical tools, it is better to see them as providing different but complementary pieces of information that, when combined, provide a more complete picture of the environment, how it has evolved, and how it is evolving.

To illustrate, consider any new product or industry. In its infancy, it would be described as being in the embryonic or introductory stage of development. Typically, in very new environments, there is very little bargaining power on the part of the sellers. After all, the customers must be convinced of the product's utility and value. They must be sold on the fact that this new product is worth the investment in effort, time, and money. Given this position of general indifference, customers will have substantial bargaining power. They may try the product or not but most will generally require some sort of inducement before buying. Sellers, as a consequence, will generally have to offer some sort of promotion if they are to increase their sales volume. Given little knowledge and understanding of the product, substitutability is hard to measure. Some will see no need for the product at all while others will see it as a one-of-a-kind solution. Still, given the newness and the variety of forms in which the product or service may come, the availability of substitutes will be difficult to determine. The threat of new entry will still depend on a number of things like the accessibility of the technology and requisite resources. At the same time, it is difficult to determine exactly what constitutes new entry at this stage, as industry standards have yet to clearly emerge and potential substitutes have yet to materialize. Many firms, with many somewhat similar products, may be undertaking similar developmental activities simultaneously. Thus, other firms might have already "entered" but simply have not yet been recognized. Finally, given this lack of clarity about the product, the general indifference on the part of customers, and the potential variety in product features and service models, there is not likely to be great rivalry among competitors.

However, as the products gain acceptance and become more popular in the marketplace, these conditions begin to change. First, as the customers perceive value in the new products and services, bargaining power begins to shift away from the buyers and towards the sellers. Whereas they had formerly been indifferent, customers now demand the product. As the product proliferates, it gains further acceptance and so creates more demand. This acceptance and rapid growth in demand leads to an imbalance of demand and supply, with more of the product being demanded than can be supplied, which increases bargaining power for the sellers and decreases bargaining power for the buyers. Of course, one reason that sales of the product are growing and one reason that bargaining power increasingly favors the sellers is that customers have few available substitutes. Even if many firms are making and selling the product, there may be few available given the high demand. Such an imbalance of supply and demand, however, will inevitably attract new entrants, who seek to satisfy the unsatisfied demand. Indeed, even in cases where the technology is proprietary or where there are physical or legal barriers to direct competition, competitors will try to adapt and imitate elements of the new product so as to capture some of the demand.

Finally, in the face of this growth, rivalry among the competitors will generally be low. With more demand than they can satisfy, firms are not likely to offer inducements to attract new customers, nor will they likely target one another's customers and prompt any sort of competitive retaliation. Instead, during these periods of rapid growth, firms typically concentrate on expanding their own capacity to meet the unsatisfied demand and working to position themselves as a desirable brand.

So long as there is more demand than supply, there is easy money to be made. However, the prospect of those "easy" profits will continue to attract competitors and continue to provide an incentive for firms to increase capacity. Thus, inevitably, supply catches up with demand and a balance, or equilibrium, is reestablished. It is at this point on the curve that sales begin to flatten, that sales growth actually declines, and the industry begins to mature.

That maturation brings with it some new challenges. As supply catches up with demand, sales growth slows. Slowed sales growth prompts efforts at innovation in terms of product features, marketing efforts, packaging and delivery services, and so on. These efforts are aimed at stimulating demand so that it returns to the growth seen in previous periods. However, these new efforts cost money, and these new expenses often reduce overall profitability. Thus, as sales growth slows, maintaining volume becomes increasingly expensive. In addition, as firms seek to stimulate demand, they will begin to target the customers of their competition. Whereas previously there was sufficient demand for the suppliers to grow their sales without having to compete head to head, slowing demand prompts direct competition. Such competition leads to rivalry, increased perceptions of substitutability, and decreased bargaining power for the sellers. As a consequence, profit margins begin to decline. As profits decline, efficiency becomes increasingly important. Customers, who are now very familiar with the product, will have several options for obtaining it. As such, they will have more bargaining power than in previous periods. As they demand lower prices, better services, quicker delivery times, and more features, they put downward pressure on the profits of the suppliers. As a result, these firms must become more efficient and find ways to reduce their costs, sell more products, or eliminate some competition. In light of the pressures associated with this stage, it is common to see some firms succeed, while others fail.

Thus, this stage of the cycle is often called the shake-out or consolidation stage, because it is during this time that the number of firms declines, while the remaining firms grow through the consolidation of the industry's demand. It is important to note that the forces underlying this process are the same 5 forces discussed earlier. Changes in supply, demand, and the nature of the marketplace cause fundamental shifts in the balance of bargaining power between buyers and sellers. In the face of the resulting decline in sales and profits, some firms fail while others sell out to their more successful competitors. The result, though, is the consolidation of the demand and assets into the hands of a smaller set of larger competitors. As illustrated by the case of the banking industry (see Box 4.2: Consolidation in the Banking Industry), consolidation produces an industry with fewer but larger firms.

Box 4.2
Consolidation in the Banking Industry

In 1980, there were 14,434 U.S. FDIC-insured commercial banks. By 2000, that number had fallen to 8,315 and by 2017 it was down to only 4,918. During this same period, the total assets of those banks increased 900%, from $1.8 trillion in 1980, to $6.2 trillion in 2000, to $16.2 trillion in 2017. No doubt by the end of 2020, the number of banks will be even lower and yet the average value of the assets held by each of those banks will be much larger. What accounts for this pattern? Consolidation. Indeed, over the past 30 years, the banking industry has undergone dramatic consolidation.

Much of this consolidation occurred, and is continuing to occur, within three waves. The first major wave was in the late 1980s and early 1990s. During this time, the banking industry came under tremendous competitive pressure from a variety of external sources, such as non-bank financial institutions, as well as from internal sources, such as other banks seeking to expand. As a result, many poorly performing banks closed and were merged into healthier banks, and many healthy banks became aggressive in seeking opportunities to acquire former competitors for the sake of ensuring their own survival. The second wave occurred around 1997, in response to the Riegle-Neal Act, which allowed direct interstate banking. This second wave, however, was somewhat different than the first in that it was marked by healthy banks acquiring other healthy banks. Moreover, while the number of mergers that occurred in this second wave was smaller, the size of the institutions merging was much larger. Indeed, in 1998 alone there were 34 mergers in which both partners had assets of over $1 billion. As the statistics show, as a result of this consolidation, there are fewer banks than there were 25 years ago, but those banks that remain are much larger and generally healthier. The third wave occurred and is still occurring as a result of the financial crisis and economic decline that began in late 2007.

Experts in the industry attribute the success of these mergers to three underlying economic causes. First, with an increase in scale economies, as banks have grown larger, their average cost per unit has declined. Doubling the size of a bank's loan portfolio, for instance, rarely necessitates doubling the size of the loan department staff. Thus, as revenues increase more rapidly than costs per unit, financial performance improves. Second, with an increase in economies of scope, larger banks can often offer a wider range of products and services at lower marginal costs than smaller banks. Third, by merging with other banks, a bank is able to spread its portfolio of loans and deposits over a larger geographic area, thereby reducing its exposure to regional financial shocks. In so doing, the bank can lower its cost of capital and further leverage the sale and scope economies of size.

Where will this trend lead? How large can banks get before their size and complexity overwhelm the benefits of scale and scope economies? Certainly, the turmoil that began in 2007 has caused banks to reconsider their strategies carefully. However, even that turmoil has led to further consolidation, as poor performers like Washington Mutual and Wachovia faded out of existence and were absorbed into healthier rivals like Wells Fargo and Bank of America. Thus, as long as the benefits of consolidation continue to outweigh the costs, we can expect the trend to continue.

Source: "Banking Consolidation." 2004, Federal Reserve Bank of San Francisco Economic Letter. June 18, 2004.
Federal Deposition Insurance Corporation: U.S. Commercial Banks Report.

An industry that has substantially consolidated is said to be mature. Those firms that survive the consolidation are typically large, efficient, and able to operate on slim profit margins. Because of their size and level of investment, they typically have high barriers to exit and lower marginal costs. Customers in these mature industries are generally well informed about and somewhat elastic with respect to the products or services. Thus, mature markets are generally very competitive such that it is difficult for firms to maintain high profit margins.

There is, however, opportunity in mature markets. As industries consolidate, the number of suppliers declines, which eliminates some competition. Indeed, many firms will acquire their competitors as a part of this process for the express purpose of limiting competition (see Box 4.3: Kroger Acquires 15 Harris Teeter Stores). Moreover, the surviving firms, being larger, generally have greater bargaining power over their suppliers. That bargaining power and scale may translate into lower costs and greater operational efficiency. Given the size of the firms in mature markets and the modest opportunities for growth and profitability, there is generally little threat of entry from new firms.

Box 4.3
Kroger Acquires 15 Harris Teeter Stores

On June 25, 2001, Kroger announced that they would be purchasing 15 Harris Teeter supermarkets, all of which were located in the region of north Georgia, in and around Atlanta. These stores were to be added to Kroger's 107 stores in the same region. Initially, the purchase was publicized by Kroger as a growth opportunity and employees of the Harris Teeter stores were assured that they would be afforded the chance to continue their service under the Kroger brand.

It was later announced however that Kroger would be closing 6 of the newly purchased stores, mostly because of their close proximity to existing Kroger stores. The remaining Harris Teeters from the purchase would either be remodeled and renamed as stores in the Kroger chain, or the land would be sold for non-grocery use.

The growing #2 supermarket in the Atlanta region, Publix, had been buying stores such as Harris Teeter in order to increase their market share. While some see the purchase as Kroger as removing Harris Teeter from the Atlanta market, it also serves the defensive purpose of preventing Publix from acquiring these same locations. Kroger and Publix continue to remain the top two grocers in the metropolitan Atlanta region and continue to fight each other for competitive advantage.

Source: DeGross, Maria. "Kroger knocks Harris Teeter out of Atlanta."
Atlanta Journal-Constitution, June 26, 2001.

Ultimately, as industries continue to evolve, they may become so consolidated, efficient, and competitive that it becomes virtually impossible to make profits. That was the case for that segment of the airline industry populated by the major carriers like United, Delta, American, and USAir in the early to mid 2000s. Substitutability had become so easy, imitation was so quick, fixed costs were so high, marginal costs were so low, and barriers to exit were so high that there was virtually no opportunity for sustainable profit. Such industries are said to be *empty core* markets or industries (Button, 2002). Empty core markets exist where substitutability is so easy and the bargaining power of the sellers is so low that there is little prospect for sustainable profit (Sjostrom, 1993). With many options, a high degree of substitutability, low switching costs, and ample inducements for switching, customers have great power. Such conditions, however, are not sustainable over the long term, as they lead to persistent under-supply and, ultimately, to some sort of radical change in industry structure. Indeed, such a radical change did ultimately occur in the airline industry. And, during the past decade, virtually all of the major carriers went through chapter 11 bankruptcy. The resulting restructuring produced a radical transformation of the industry, the expansion of international routes, increased alliances allowing the carriers to share revenue, a reduction in fleet sizes, and the outsourcing of commuter flights. It also led to the elimination of older, less fuel-efficient planes, which were replaced with newer, lighter, and more fuel-efficient planes. All of these changes produced a significant shift in bargaining power, away from the customers and back to the carriers. As a result, the financial performance of the major carriers has improved significantly.

The lifecycle model suggests that beyond this point of maturity industries begin to decline. However, it is really more accurate to say that they change. Indeed, the processes of maturation, consolidation, and competitiveness create pressures on firms to find better ways to supply their customers. Those pressures will frequently lead to greater standardization in products and processes and greater homogenization of customer services and inducements. While focusing on standardization and homogenization increases efficiency and reduces cost, it also alienates those customers who value more personalized service and greater product customization. These customers are left with few good options. As a result, they become pools of unsatisfied demand or what are sometimes called *market niches*. These niches are small pockets of inelastic customers, who want something different than what is valued by the majority of the market. Because of their inelasticity, these niches represent opportunities for new and innovative suppliers with new technologies and operating models. These new suppliers create new products and services that have the potential to become new "industries" and the cycle begins again.

ONGOING EVOLUTION IN THE ENVIRONMENT

Figure 4.5 is offered to depict the process by which markets evolve from start-up to growth, through maturity and decline, and into other new start-ups again. The figure is a model of *punctuated equilibrium*. Punctuated equilibrium is a concept advanced first in paleobiology (Eldredge & Gould, 1972), to explain the irregular but ongoing and continuous nature of biological evolution. However, it can also explain other types of evolutionary dynamics as well (Gersick, 1991).

For our purposes, it is helpful to think of the total evolutionary model as a series of sequential product lifecycles. Each grows and evolves according to the principles outlined earlier. Each follows a recognized series of steps, with direct implication for the nature of the bargaining power and competitive forces affecting buyers, suppliers, and customers. However, over time, these very forces produce fundamental changes that trigger innovations and the emergence of new technologies, products, and processes. Those innovations in technologies, products, and services initiate again the cycle of industry emergence, development, and maturity. Thus, over time, industries appear to evolve, changing form through iterative periods of predictable, regular, and incremental change and brief, tumultuous, and radical change (Cheah, 1990; Nelson & Winter, 1973; Tushman & Anderson, 1986).

The process has been referred to as *creative destruction* (Abernathy & Clark, 1985). The term creative destruction was introduced by Joseph Schumpeter (1942) and is generally associated with entrepreneurship and technological innovation. However, its implications are much broader. Industries are constantly changing in response to stimuli that are themselves constantly changing. Customers are constantly "demanding" more or demanding to pay less. As they consider new and different options, so do they create opportunities for new suppliers.

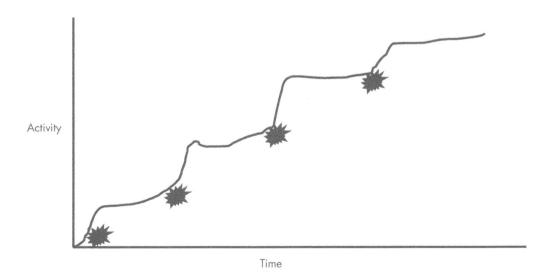

FIGURE 4.5 Environmental Evolution and Punctuated Equilibrium

At the same time, individuals, firms, and other entities like universities are constantly creating new products and technologies. Some of these find acceptance; others do not. But they all represent the potential to satisfy some customers somewhere. Personal computers, for example, were not created in response to customer demand but emerged through the work of inventors who were convinced that a new technology was possible. Radial tires, digital music, microwave ovens all emerged not in response to demand but from the research and development activities of suppliers who foresaw opportunities in the new technologies. As these technologies spawned new products and services, the industry and the environment changed, creating new opportunities, new options, and new competitive pressures. As Steve Jobs' career illustrates (see Box 4.4: Steve Jobs' Visionary Innovations),

---

Box 4.4
Steve Jobs' Visionary Innovations

In 1976, Steve Jobs and Steve Wozniak started Apple computers from the Jobs family garage. Unlike many products, personal computers were not created as a result of customer demand, and in fact everyday consumers had to be convinced that they needed a PC. Instead, PCs were developed by individuals who believed that this ground-breaking technology was possible. Jobs and Wozniak are recognized for revolutionizing the computer industry by developing Apple computers, which were smaller, reasonably priced, and intuitive, making them accessible to more customers.

Steve Jobs is known as an innovator of the people because he seemed to have a keen sense of what customers wanted, and those are the products he developed. Apple has created revolutionary products, such as the iPod and iPhone, which became industry-wide benchmarks by being creative, aesthetically pleasing, reliable, and user-friendly. Apple's innovations dictated the evolution of existing technologies, such as MP3 players, cell phones, and personal computers.

However, Steve Jobs seemed to not only have an understanding of what customers wanted, he also seemed to understand what customers *should* want. Through his leadership, Apple has become well known for pioneering products, such as the iPad, which were not in demand. Previous tablet computers failed to gain popularity in the late 1990s because they were heavy and had poor software and few applications. In 2010, the iPad became the first easily portable tablet computer to hit the market. The iPad was an instant hit, with over 7 million selling in its first year. In 2012, Apple sold its 100 millionth iPad, yet the success of this radical new innovation doesn't stop there. Just like so many Apple products have done, the creation of the iPad initiated a wave of technological innovation by its competitors' efforts to create comparable products.

Steve Jobs' reputation as a visionary innovator lives on even after his death in 2011. His company, Apple, is still known for developing ground-breaking products technologies that are not responding to customer demand, yet that are wildly popular and even spawn new industries.

Sources: "Steve Jobs.biography." 2013. Biography.com
www.biography.com/people/steve-jobs-9354805

new products are often developed before there is any demand for them. And yet, these products can spawn whole new industries. In essence, these products fill a vacuum before the customer even recognizes that a vacuum exists; put differently, they actually create the demand that they are meant to satisfy. Apple's radical new innovations fit this pattern of creative destruction.

Thus, there is a constant ferment of new products and services, fueled by the continuous opportunity for new profits, generated by the insatiable appetite of customer demand. These ongoing and continuous forces interact over the range of the product/industry lifecycle, favoring evolutionary and adaptive changes at some points and radical and revolutionary changes at others.

As mentioned, the airline industry just passed an inflection point. After a dramatic period of bankruptcy, consolidation, and reorganization, the industry is now more profitable than at most any time in its history. But this is just the most recent of several punctuations for the airline industry. To illustrate, consider this brief history. Though the Wright brothers made their historic flight in 1903, commercial air travel did not become a really plausible option for nearly 30 years. Indeed, the early development of the industry was funded by the government, which saw military potential in the technology. In 1927, however, Charles Lindberg captured the imagination of the American population with his flight across the Atlantic. Moreover, in 1925, the U.S. government began allowing mail to be carried by air. In the years that followed, several companies formed to capitalize on the new opportunity. Among these were the early ancestors of American Airlines, Pan American Airlines (Pan Am), United Airlines, and Boeing. Initially, these carriers saw passengers merely as a source of supplemental revenue on top of what they earned carrying mail.

As the number of carriers and the number of flights increased, so too did the quality of the service improve, so too did the reputation for reliability and safety improve, and so too did the overall demand grow. That growing demand represented an opportunity for new entrants and established competitors alike. Thus, new capital flowed into the industry, and revenues and profits grew. With increasing revenues and profits and with increasing prospects for future opportunities, the investment in new technologies grew as well. Such investment was also fueled by World War II and the military advantages brought by flight. All of this led to improvements in aircraft size, speed, and efficiency. The "stressed-skin" construction design, pressurized passenger cabins, the turboprop, and the jet engine were all a part of this ongoing technological evolution and escalation. Each new technology produced a revolution in competitive interaction and opportunity, offering customers more and longer routes, faster flying times, greater flying service, comfort, and lower prices.

Of course, while this all was transpiring within the U.S., a parallel cycle was developing in Europe. In Germany, France, and England, commercial air travel began in the 1920s. As it evolved and grew, so too did the investments in technology, equipment and infrastructure, enabling the industry to expand and grow at a rate comparable to that in the U.S. Moreover, as the industry was expanding throughout the world, so too was the influence of government regulation. In the U.S., for instance, the creation of the Civil Aeronautics Authority, in 1938, and the Federal Aviation Administration, in 1958, led to standardized industry practices, enhanced public confidence, and created slower but more uniform and controlled growth.

Finally, with the deregulation of the U.S. industry in the 1970s and 1980s, the expansion of worldwide route systems, the growth of large international carriers, and the increased use of various partnering arrangements among carriers, the industry underwent another dramatic reorganization, with many carriers and service providers exiting the business either through failure or acquisition. Today, the industry both in the U.S. and elsewhere is represented largely by two types of firms, either large, so-called "major" carriers, flying diverse fleets over complex "hub and spoke," transcontinental route systems, or smaller, regional, "discount" carriers, flying smaller fleets on "point-to-point" routes within limited regions.

What this history depicts is a cycle of ongoing evolution with periodic revolution. There have been several periods of initiation and start-up, where new norms and practices have emerged in response to some radical change. There have been several periods of growth, where new investment flowed in and where revenues and profits rose. There have also been just as many periods of shake-out and consolidation, followed by periods of stabilization and maturity. Each sequence can be viewed in terms of a single lifecycle. However, together, they can all be seen as part of a larger punctuated evolutionary process. With each new revolution, the process of creative destruction removed the old status quo and initiated a new period of emergence and growth, reinvigorating the lifecycle of the industry.

What Figure 4.5 depicts then is a series of connected and sequential lifecycles. It shows that industries are constantly changing. Sometimes those changes are incremental and evolutionary; sometimes they are radical and revolutionary. Sometimes the changes produce opportunities for new growth and new profits; other times they produce greater competition and reduced profitability. Thus, it is important for anyone who does industry analysis to look past the immediate conditions and consider how those conditions came about and how they might portend changes for the future.

For example, in the early 2000s, competition in the airline industry had eroded virtually all of the profitability for the major carriers. Even in such an unattractive climate, though, there were still new carriers emerging who are willing to try new operating models and to work in new areas. The low profitability of the industry left large numbers of underutilized aircraft, offering further opportunity for innovative new entrants. And many of the industry's best customers were alienated by the declining quality and reliability that characterized those carriers that were under the most financial distress. Those customers and their frustration provided the strongest incentive for new innovation.

When taken together, this idea of punctuated equilibrium, combined with these other concepts and models, provides a solid foundation from which to view industry evolution and from which to conduct industry analysis. Environments and industries are constantly in motion. New products and services are constantly emerging, built on the newest technologies and designed to take advantage of current conditions and preferences. As they create superior value, the best providers derive competitive advantage and earn profits. But like gravity, the forces of competition exert an inevitable and unavoidable pull on those profits. New technologies spring up and new competitors emerge. Customers look for better deals, demanding more for less, which provides opportunities for imitation and refinement of existing products and services. Opportunity and the potential for profit attract new entrants and substitute products. The result is increased competition; marginal performers are shaken out and their assets and customers are consolidated into the remaining firms, who gain the **economies of scale** and **economies of scope** with which to better compete.

Paradoxically, as those firms grow increasingly large, increasingly efficient, and standardized, as necessary to meet growing demand, the most demanding customers are driven away. These customers are alienated by the emerging status quo and so begin to search for new and better options. When those buyers meet new and innovative suppliers, the seeds of creative destruction are sown and new industries begin to emerge. As industries emerge, the cycle begins again. In some cases, these cycles are very long; in others, they are very short. However, the process and the forces that drive them are always the same. Thus, by understanding these basic forces and understanding the nature of how they interact and what they cause, students and analysts alike can begin to truly discern what an environment is like, how it evolved into its present state, and where it is likely heading.

CONCLUDING THOUGHTS AND CAVEATS

This material is meant as a general framework, a guide for interpreting and analyzing the environment. It would be a mistake to think that every industry evolves in exactly the same way or to think that competitors, customers, and suppliers are always going to be easy to identify and evaluate. Like the strategy process itself, environmental analysis can be messy and irregular. Information is often unclear and ambiguous; the various actors are hard to identify, and the pace of events is hard to predict. Rather than making environmental analysis less important, though, this complexity and ambiguity makes all the more important the use of some accepted frameworks and principles. The concepts presented here provide some order to the otherwise complex and almost chaotic events of most environments. Thus, it is important that they be understood generally and that they are seen as a structure of common relationships but that they are applied individually to specific situations. Every environment is unique, but all environments share some common features, follow some general rules, and fit into some common patterns. This framework and these models then provide an outline for understanding those common attributes. These final points then are meant to highlight some special circumstances and illustrate some special issues related to the application of these models.

Hypercompetition

Hypercompetition is a term made popular by Richard D'Aveni in a book published in 1994. In it, D'Aveni describes how the evolutionary cycle in many industries, from emergence to maturity and again to reemergence, has accelerated to the point that these various stages are almost indistinguishable. Indeed, in the early 1990s, many speculated that hypercompetition was a fundamentally different sort of competitive dynamic than had been seen before. In this new dynamic, the old rules of competition and evolution no longer applied, and concepts like lifecycles and bargaining power were outdated and obsolete. As a consequence, the process of strategy making was somehow fundamentally different as well. Strategy was less about competition than about creation and less about analysis than about innovation. Such thinking, however, proved to be an artifact of the time. As events eventually showed, the basics of competitive dynamics and the economic realities of strategic competition have not changed in any fundamental way. Basic forces like supply, demand, and bargaining power continue to drive the evolution of the environment and the profitability of industries and firms.

D'Aveni's observations remain valid and important though. The pace of evolution in many industries and in the environment overall is accelerating to a point that it appears "hyper" in relation to historical norms. What is important to remember though is that this acceleration is constant. In other words, the pace of change in the marketplace is always increasing. It is the idea that there are historical "norms" that is flawed. The speed of innovation, the pace with which competition reacts, and the intensity of market forces are all greater now than they were at the turn of the century. And, they will be even greater still as we move further into the future. One of the many challenges of doing environmental analysis is accepting that the pace of the overall process is constantly accelerating. There will always be new and exciting events emerging; there will always be a sense that the pace of change is increasing and that things were simpler and slower in the past. Thus, it is important not to fall into the trap of viewing the environment in terms of discreet, categorical periods, like yesterday and today. Conceptualizing in simple categories like past, present, and future or thinking in terms of simple labels, like the industrial age and the information age, can be misleading and cause misunderstanding. While thinking in such terms is certainly easy and fine for casual conversation, it is important that we view the environment in terms of continuous and ongoing evolution, revolution, and change.

Industry Definition

Industry definition is a key element of environmental analysis. Yet, the process of identifying and defining an industry is highly problematic. The North American Industry Classification Systems (NAICS) and its forerunner, the Standard Industrial Classification (SIC) system, both provide numerical indexing schemes for categorizing firms into industries. Yet, while both systems give the appearance of within-group similarity and between-group discrimination, neither delivers such precision practically.

The NAICS, the more recent of the two, was developed in 1997 through a cooperative effort of the U.S., Mexican, and Canadian governments. The NAICS uses a 6-digit index to capture similarity on products and services as well as on the processes used to produce those products and services. For example, the NAICS code 51 is for the business sector entitled "information." That sector contains sub-sector code 513, which is "broadcasting and telecommunication." Code 513 contains industry group 5133 "telecommunications," which contains industry 51332, "wireless telecommunications (except satellite)." The system is reviewed every 5 years to maintain its relevance and to adapt as necessary to emerging business categories.

But even with a system like this, there remains room for confusion. For example, NAICS industry number 722211, defined as "limited-service restaurants," includes pizza delivery shops, delicatessens, and carry-out and fast food restaurants. While grouping these firms may seem logical, when viewed in an abstract sense, it probably does not make much sense practically. Would the owner of a McDonalds franchise limit an analysis of his or her competitors to just these sorts of firms, or would he or she want to also include some full-service establishments as well? Many convenience stores, supermarkets, and gas stations offer prepared food for carry-out. Should these firms be considered part of the same industry? How should location factor in? The NAICS includes firms in Mexico, Canada, and the United States. Is a delicatessen in Brooklyn, New York, in the same industry as another delicatessen in Boca Raton, Florida? Are they competing against one another? The problem is that the term industry has become clouded and confused by a number of overlapping and conflicting definitions.

For describing similar types of firms, engaged in similar types of business, and using similar technologies and operating models, a system like the NAICS can be a useful tool. Also, for benchmarking performance levels, capital structures, or operating norms, the NAICS can be an efficient means for identifying appropriate referents. However, for doing actual strategic analysis on specific firms, a much more precise picture of the competitive landscape is needed. That is why it is important to start the analysis with a definition of the firm and its customers. Identifying the competition involves identifying those products and services that customers see as substitutes. For a McDonald's franchisee, this may include convenience stores near his or her locations. For a Brooklyn delicatessen, it may include full-service restaurants in the vicinity but would probably not include a deli in Florida. Doing the sort of good environmental analysis that can lay the groundwork for good strategy development requires understanding the competitive environment in a way that goes beyond broad and general categories. It means understanding those forces that actually affect the relationship between the firm and the customers it is trying to reach.

Locus of Competition

The final comment then relates to the **locus of competition**. To understand this point, consider an old saying from politics. Thomas (Tip) O'Neill, Jr., a former congressman from the state of Massachusetts and long-time speaker of the U.S. House of Representatives, coined the phrase "all politics is local." The phrase illustrates two important points. First, people vote on issues that are important to them personally and directly. Second, they only vote for those who are running in their particular districts or precincts. Thus, a Massachusetts congressman who is unpopular with voters in every other state could still be very successful if he was responsive to the needs of the voters in his district. O'Neill learned this lesson following the only electoral loss of his career, a race for a seat on the City Council of Cambridge, Massachusetts. In this losing effort, O'Neill campaigned hard and gained considerable popularity across the various precincts of Cambridge, but he took for granted the voters in his own backyard and, as a result, lost the election (O'Neill & Hymel, 1994).

Business students and managers alike often make the same mistake when doing environmental analysis. They collect and analyze aggregated data representing broad categories of businesses, trends, and preferences. But in so doing, they often overlook the specific nuances and details that affect their business directly. As Tip O'Neill reminds us, *all competition is local*. In this context, that means that competition occurs in the minds and hearts of individual customers. Customers cannot consider products and services that are beyond their reach or about which they have never heard. Even when using the internet, customers are concerned only with those products and services that fall within their field of vision and to which they have some access. Moreover, they are motivated only by those products and services that appeal to them directly.

Wal-Mart, for instance, competes in a global environment, but that environment is itself a collection of many different locations, each with its own unique set of competitive opportunities and threats. Consequently, even though Wal-Mart delivers on its promise of low prices, prices for the same item may vary from one Wal-Mart store to another depending on the nature of local competition. Delta is a worldwide carrier of airline passengers, but its competition occurs on each route, with whatever competitors are present to provide customers with alternative choices. Ford's success is a function of how many people find its products appealing, relative to the alternatives available, at the time of purchase.

The important thing to remember is that aggregate data are the result of many individual actions. However, individual actions are not the result of aggregate data. Thus, it is important not to focus just on data that are accessible, easy to gather, and easy to manage. So, abstracting too far from the reality of competition can lead to poor analysis. Dell looked only at other PC makers and so missed the emergence of the tablet and mobile devices. Coke looked just at Pepsi and the other soft-drink makers and so overlooked the emergence of non-carbonated drinks like Gatorade, Snapple, and Sobe, which were all acquired by PepsiCo, and only later did Coca-Cola begin venturing deeply into the non-carbonated segment with acquisitions of brands such as Vitamin Water and Honest Tea. Major recording labels focused just on one another and so overlooked the technological revolution that would spawn the iPod and the iTunes store and a whole new industry of digital music delivery systems. Ford, GM, Toyota, and Hyundai compete against one another but all also understand that the greatest, long-term competitive threat is self-driving car technology and the massive restructuring it will cause across the industry.

All competition is local and occurs around specific transactions between specific buyers and specific sellers. Understanding the environment means understanding the context in which these individual transactions take place.

KEY TERMS

Bargaining power refers to the competitive dynamics that exist between suppliers and buyers within industries. The buyers' ability to bargain for better terms by playing competitors against one another depends on a number of factors, including the importance of the buyers' purchases. Suppliers, on the other hand, may threaten to raise prices or reduce quality, but may only do so when the conditions mirror those that give power to buyers.

Branding represents one of the primary mechanisms by which firms differentiate their products and services.

Contrived deterrence describes those investments made by incumbent firms that discourage new entrants from opting to compete. Incumbents' investments in excess capacity, altering cost structures, product differentiation, and vertical integration can all increase barriers to entry and may also have an effect on smaller existing competitors.

Creative destruction, a term coined in 1942 by economist Joseph Schumpeter, describes the process whereby the economic structure of industries is revolutionized from within—old structures become replaced by new ones. For management, the concept suggests that only those firms that can respond to dynamic capital markets and relax their conventional notions of control and decision making can maintain superior long-term returns.

Determinism is the view that firm performance is largely attributable to factors in the external environment. The influence of external factors, such as industry attributes, was popularized by Michael Porter (1980) and is consistent with the so-called industrial organization (IO) model of economics.

Economies of scale describe a measure of economic growth wherein the average per-unit costs associated with the production, marketing, or distribution of a product/service decreases as the number of units increases.

Economies of scope occur when the average total cost of production decreases as the number of different goods/services produced increases.

Elasticity refers to a measure of the rate of response of quantity demanded resulting from a change in price, with all other factors held constant. For products with high elasticity, a price increase will result in a decrease in revenue since the revenue lost from decreasing quantity demanded outweighs revenue gains from the price increase.

Empty core markets exist when there is no sustainable, equilibrium, market-clearing price. That condition exists where capacity exceeds the quantity demanded at the price equal to the minimum average cost.

Monopoly describes a market condition whereby one firm is the only firm that produces (or provides an overwhelming majority of) a certain good. In such conditions, the demand curve for the firm is identical to the market demand curve.

Monopoly firms will produce a quantity at the level where marginal costs equal marginal revenue. The ability to do this and the degree to which a seller has the ability to set the market price for a certain good is referred to as monopoly power.

A niche market is a focused, tangible segment of the general market that receives no or limited service from existing mainstream providers. Such narrow market segments, which tend to be either undetected or omitted by potential competitors, can be attractive targets for focused differentiators.

Open systems—A perspective that, when applied to organizations, views success and survivability as a result of the interdependence between the conditions of the environment and the characteristics of the organization. By acquiring inputs, performing some value-added transformation upon them, and generating outputs, open systems are capable of sustaining themselves.

Punctuated equilibrium—A view describing organizations and industries as evolving through relatively long periods of stable and incremental change punctuated by relatively short periods of radical and fundamental change. These changes disrupt the established patterns of activity and provide the basis for new equilibrium periods.

Switching costs—The costs incurred when customers change from one supplier or market to another. These costs are a key factor in determining the bargaining power of suppliers/buyers. When switching costs are high/low, bargaining power of suppliers is high/low, and bargaining power of buyers is low/high.

Voluntarism, in contrast to *determinism*, is the view that firm performance is primarily linked to firm-specific factors and actions voluntarily taken by specific firms. This view has been recently adopted by the resource-based view (RBV), in which differences between firms' resources best explain competitive advantage.

QUESTIONS FOR REVIEW

1. Why is the definition of the business so important to environmental analysis? What are some key dimensions along which a business should be defined?
2. What is an open system, and why is an understanding of open systems important to strategic management and success?
3. Describe the 5-Forces model and its various dimensions. What do these forces point to collectively?
4. How can the lifecycle model be useful in environmental analysis? How might the various components of the 5 forces change the range of an industry's lifecycle?
5. Explain the cycle by which industries grow, mature, decline, and then grow again. What are some evolutionary principles that aid in understanding this pattern?
6. What does it mean to say that all competition is local? What implication does this have for competitive advantage, strategic management, and firm performance?
7. Why is it important to define carefully the environment before conducting environmental analysis? To be most effective in the strategic process, how should the environment be defined?
8. Define elasticity. What forces impact elasticity, and why is this economic force so important to strategic management?

NOTES

1   www.mbaskool.com/fun-corner/popular/12291-top-brand-failures-due-to-differences-in-culture.html?start=2
2   www.unilever.com/sustainable-living/our-strategy/un-sustainable-development-goals/
3   https://www.faa.gov/uas/advanced_operations/package_delivery_drone/

Chapter 5

Organizational Strengths and Weaknesses

Analyzing a Firm's Capabilities and Resources

HARLEY-DAVIDSON

Is there a more recognizable symbol of the American spirit of freedom and independence than the unmistakable brand of Harley-Davidson? Rarely has one brand elevated its relationship with consumers to that of a lifestyle in itself. However, this motorcycle manufacturer managed to grow from a company that started in a small wooden shed to one that celebrated its 100th anniversary in 2003 with a nationwide ride that attracted huge corporate sponsors, well-known entertainment personalities, and people from all over the world.

Harley-Davidson began in 1903 as the dream of schoolyard pals William S. Harley and Arthur Davidson. A 10 × 15-foot wooden shed served as the first factory, and the only thing that distinguished this shack from any other tool shed was the name "Harley-Davidson Motor Company" scrawled across the door. Later that year, the first dealer opened in Chicago, Illinois, and by 1908 Harley-Davidson had incorporated.

The world-famous bar and shield logo was used for the first time in 1910 and was registered as a trademark. In 1912, Harley-Davidson made company history when it sold its first exports in Japan, marking the company's first international sales. The company's formal entry into motorcycle racing came in 1914 and it earned the nickname "the Wrecking Crew" due to its dominance of the sport.

Harley-Davidson became the world's largest motorcycle manufacturer in 1920 and its products could be purchased at over 2,000 dealers in 67 countries. The company's dominance of the industry continued into the next decade, and by 1931 the only other competition in the U.S. market came from Indian Motorcycles. Harley would later help to create its own competition by licensing blueprints, tools, and other equipment to the Sankyo Company in Japan. This would launch the Japanese motorcycle industry.

In 1969, Harley-Davidson merged with American Machine and Foundry Co. (AMF). AMF was a sporting good and leisure product company that did not fit especially well with the Harley-Davidson product and brand. Indeed, in 1981, 13 members of senior management orchestrated a leveraged buyout and took control of the company from AMF. By this time, however, the once proud organization had acquired a reputation for low quality and fallen out of favor with consumers. Smaller, more reliable bikes, primarily from Japan, now dominated the industry. Under the new management, however, quality became the theme and a complete turnaround was initiated. The rallying cry for Harley-Davison became "The Eagle Soars Alone." Over the next few years, many technological and production innovations helped to restore quality and the image of the company. The company also realized that when people bought a Harley, they were buying more than just a bike; they were buying an image, a lifestyle. This led to a greater effort in brand extension and a widening of the product line.

In 1986, for the first time since the merger with AMF, the company returned to the public stock market. The same year, the company expanded its portfolio with the acquisition of Holiday Rambler Corporation, a producer of motor homes. The next major acquisition would come in 1992 with the purchase of a minority interest in Buell Motorcycle Company. Buell provided the company with a smaller racing-style compliment to the company's now traditional large cruiser. A 90th anniversary party took place in 1993 and attracted over 100,000 riders to celebrate in a parade of the legendary machines.

Since the year 2000, Harley-Davidson has held roughly 27% of the North American motorcycle market, and its share in the heavyweight bike segment has been even higher. Beyond just market share, Harley-Davidson was generating increasing profits, peaking at over $1 billion in 2006. While the recession caused by the financial crisis from late 2007 hurt the sales of motorcycles worldwide, throwing Harley-Davidson into a loss-making year in 2009 when they lost $55 million, they have since been recovering, recording profits of $845 million in 2014 before dipping again. The Harley-Davidson brand is a symbol of resurgence and strength and a great example of how a company develops and exploits resources and capabilities to sustain itself over a long period of time.

INTRODUCTION TO ORGANIZATIONAL ANALYSIS

Strategic management is about creating and sustaining competitive advantage. Competitive advantage emerges when a firm creates value for its customers, some of which it captures and extracts in the form of profits. What that means is that for competitive advantage to be realized there must be a seller, a buyer, and an exchange that both find valuable. To better appreciate this, it is important to understand three related concepts, **use value**, **exchange value**, and **consumer surplus** (Bowman & Ambrosini, 2000; Priem, 2007). Use value is the subjective valuation of a product or service by a particular customer. In essence, use value is what the product or service is actually "worth" to a particular buyer. Exchange value, on the other hand, is the actual price at which an exchange takes place. The difference between these two values is called consumer surplus. Consumer surplus is the net value the customer derives from the purchase, over and above the price and other costs paid. Figure 5.1, which was also presented in the first chapter, illustrates the relationship among these values.

It is important to remember that consumers spend their money where they believe they can derive the greatest satisfaction (Bach et al., 1987; Bowman & Ambrosini, 2000). Customers choose to purchase from firm A, rather than from firm B, because there is some reason for them to do so. Firm A then is in a competitively advantageous position and that position translates into profitable transactions and ultimately earnings. As discussed in previous chapters, a portion of that

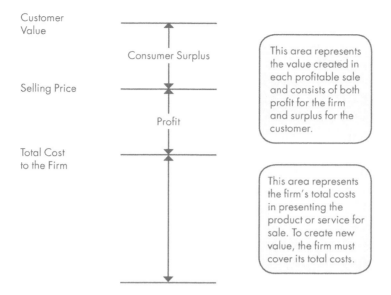

Customer
Value

Consumer Surplus

This area represents
the value created in
each profitable sale
and consists of both
profit for the firm
and surplus for the
customer.

Selling Price

Profit

Total Cost
to the Firm

This area represents
the firm's total costs
in presenting the
product or service for
sale. To create new
value, the firm must
cover its total costs.

FIGURE 5.1 Competitive Advantage as Value to the Customer

advantage is attributable to the nature of the demand and to the options that the customer has available. Thus, a portion of the advantage is attributable to the nature of the environment. But there is also a part of the advantage that is attributable to the firm itself. For instance, why would customers buy from firm A at all? What is it that makes firm A more attractive than firm B or some other substitute supplier? Customers buy from firm A because they derive greater consumer surplus from the purchase than they would from some other action. Thus, based upon Figure 5.1, firm A provides the buyer with greater use value, a more favorable exchange value, or the best combination of both.

But how is firm A able to do this? How does it create better use value, or how is it able to provide a more favorable exchange value? What is it about Firm A that makes it more attractive than any of the various alternatives? These questions relate to the organizational side of strategic analysis and to what is commonly called the **resource-based view** (RBV) of the firm (Wernerfelt, 1984; Peteraf, 1993; Barney, 1991).

As explained in Chapter 1, strategy and strategic success are best understood as resulting from an interaction between the firm and its environment. Recall that the SWOT analysis, one of the basic tools of the strategic manager's trade, is simply a framework for assessing the external forces of the environment and the internal capabilities of the firm. On the external side, industry structure, competitive dynamics, bargaining power, and the evolving nature of supply and demand are the major parts of the story. However, they do not explain it all. To completely understand competitive advantage, we must also understand the internal side, how the firm creates value in the eyes of the customer and how it emerges from the ferment of environmental options to appear uniquely attractive to customers. Understanding these issues requires knowing something about the firm's capabilities and resources, hence the resource-based view of the firm.

The story of Harley-Davidson illustrates the value of the resource-based view very well. Harley-Davidson is known best for motorcycles, and most of its various products in some way or another capitalize on the image created by its motorcycles. However, the motorcycle industry is very competitive. Indeed, some of the other best-known makers of motorcycles, firms like Triumph and BMW, have found it difficult if not impossible to compete effectively in the face of competition from the likes of Honda, Kawasaki, and Yamaha. Indeed, an analysis of that environment might well lead one to conclude that, because of high bargaining power of the buyers and the substantial availability of high-quality substitute products, profitability in the motorcycle industry would be all but impossible to achieve and sustain. Yet, Harley-Davidson has managed not only to compete but to thrive in this otherwise competitive environment. How has Harley-Davidson managed this?

In short, Harley-Davidson has managed to develop and leverage a set of unique and valuable resources, which make its products uniquely and especially attractive even in relation to other high-quality competitors. For example, Harley-Davidson has a unique history. It is one of the oldest and largest motorcycle makers in the world. Yet, it is uniquely American, having been founded in Milwaukee, Wisconsin, and having supported the U.S. war efforts through the First and Second World Wars. Following the 1969 film *Easy Rider*, Harley-Davidson became inextricably linked to the tumultuous period of cultural upheaval that was the 1960s and 1970s. Finally, the company itself became a symbol of the American entrepreneurial spirit during the management-led buy-back from AMF in 1981. In many ways, the history of Harley-Davidson is the history of the U.S. motorcycle industry. Indeed, in the early 1980s, following the recapitalization, the company's slogan was "The Eagle Soars Alone." By illustrating its story of success with an eagle, Harley-Davidson further linked its reputation to this symbol of American culture.

But there is more to this story than mere symbolism. Harley-Davidson also works diligently to foster the belief that its motorcycles are more than simply modes of transportation. Rather, they are a part of a culture of freedom and independence. To ride a Harley-Davidson is to enter a lifestyle of genuine expression and non-conformity. Harley owners are members of a unique and exclusive group. To promote this shared identity, Harley-Davidson developed, in 1983, the Harley Owners Group (H.O.G.). The website for the group states that it is "more than 900,000 people around the world united by a common passion: making the Harley-Davidson dream a way of life." By connecting with its customers at a level beyond their simple need for transportation, Harley-Davidson is able to enrich and add value to the ownership experience. Beyond even this cultural heritage and name recognition, however, Harley-Davidson builds high-quality motorcycles that look stylish and that perform well. Indeed, following the recapitalization in 1981, Harley-Davidson undertook a program of quality improvement and innovation. As a result, Harley-Davidson products are considered among the highest quality and most innovative in the industry. Moreover, Harley-Davidson makes and sells a range of well-designed and appealing accessories that feature the Harley-Davidson brand name and logo.

These various strengths, capabilities, and resources combine to give Harley-Davidson extraordinarily high use value among many customers. With such high use value, Harley-Davidson is able to charge prices or exchange values that are not only higher than its costs but that are also higher than most other motorcycle manufacturers. As a result, Harley-Davidson is able to generate a substantial surplus for its customers while also generating substantial profits and returns to its shareholders. In essence, then, because of the way Harley-Davidson combines and utilizes its resources, in this particular environment, it is able to generate competitive advantage.

THE RESOURCE-BASED VIEW

The earlier example illustrates the importance of organizational resources to strategic management. Firms are constantly seeking to gain advantage and to translate that advantage into profits. In a practical sense, that means appearing more attractive than any of the other options in the eyes of their customers and thereby getting customers to spend money for their products and services. This basic contest, between rival firms for individual transactions, lies at the very heart of strategy because it is the ability to win these basic contests, over and over again, which drives a firm's performance and ultimately determines its success. To win these basic contests, a firm must make deliberate decisions about the procurement, development, and deployment of its assets and resources. Those firms, like Harley-Davidson, that marshal and use their resources wisely will generate greater use value, provide a more favorable exchange value, or offer greater consumer surplus by providing customers better combinations of both. Those firms will then earn a measure of competitive advantage and the opportunity for profit that goes along with it.

But what sorts of resources can provide that advantage? What sorts of resources make a firm more attractive than its rivals to a prospective customer? The RBV holds that competitive advantage accrues to specific types of resources, those that meet 5 criteria, (1) value, (2) rarity, (3) inimitability, (4) non-substitutability, and (5) appropriability. As firms control resources that meet these 5 criteria, they are able to provide greater consumer surplus either through creating better use value, providing better exchange value, or both. As a result, they are able to generate more and more profitable transactions, which lead to better performance.

Value

What are valuable resources? Valuable resources are resources that consumers desire or resources that give a firm the ability to produce products and services that consumers want. A good location for a hotel, for instance, could be a valuable resource as it provides customers with convenience or allows them to be near some desirable attraction. A good credit rating is a resource that a firm could draw upon in deploying capital expenditures such as building efficient facilities or acquiring choice locations. A key technology could be a valuable resource in that it enables the delivery of customer service in a more efficient or more satisfying manner. The ability to provide an ever more sophisticated online service, for example, is a valuable resource for many banks that results in a substantial amount of business.

It is important to understand that valuable resources are those that lead to profit-rendering transactions. As such, they can be both **tangible resources**, as in the fleet of tractors and trailers used by a trucking company, or **intangible resources**, as in the reputation for expertise held by a surgical care center. Valuable resources are responsible for the products and services that customers find desirable and worthwhile. Thus, analyzing the resources of an organization often involves looking beyond the obvious and most visible aspects of a firm and discerning the underlying and embedded causes of the visible effects. Wal-Mart, for example, is valued because of its huge selection and low costs. However, underlying the products and locations that customers see is a vast network of infrastructure dedicated to the efficient procurement of goods and movement of inventory, as necessary to produce the product variety and low prices. Coca-Cola also has a powerful competitive advantage, attributable to both intangible resources such as its reputation, brand recognition, and place in the memory of so many of its customers, as well as tangible resources such as its distribution capabilities, its shelf-space in supermarkets, the locations of its vending machines, and its contracts with venues. As with Wal-Mart though, these sorts of valuable resources, both tangible and intangible, are embedded in the structures, systems, and histories of the firms.

Rarity

The desirability of a resource, however, is insufficient to assure competitive advantage. If every firm had the buying power and logistical capabilities of Wal-Mart, consumers would not find Wal-Mart uniquely attractive. If every soft drink enjoyed the same name recognition and brand loyalty as Coca-Cola, then the value of those resources would quickly diminish. Consider the fact that many other motorcycle makers produce models that mimic the style and look of Harley-Davidson, yet these motorcycles are not Harleys and so do not hold the same degree of attractiveness for consumers. Similarly, Google has become synonymous with search to the point of becoming a verb, so this brand awareness makes it difficult for other search engines to compete with Google even if their search capabilities are similar. The desirability or value of a resource then is only one of the criteria which must be met for competitive advantage to emerge and to be sustained. In addition, resources must also be rare. Value and rarity together provide great opportunity for competitive advantage and profit as they give the seller a unique ability to supply some desired product or service.

Like value, however, the antecedents of rarity are not always obvious. Take, for example, the Starbucks coffee shop in downtown Athens, Georgia. In the middle of a bustling college town, one would expect to find many similar shops. Indeed, within walking distance of this Starbucks are no fewer than three other gourmet coffee shops, offering coffee, lattes, pastries, and a host of other related products around the clock. How could this Starbucks location or any of the other competitors hope to gain an advantage? The answer lies in understanding that, despite their various similarities, these stores are nevertheless not exactly the same. Each offers a slightly different location, a slightly different set of surroundings and features; each has different personnel, different histories, different reputations, and a historically different clientele. At various times and for different segments of the market, each may appear to offer a uniquely different combination of products and services, a uniquely rare bundle of resources.

What specifically are these rare resources? The answer to that question lies in the eyes of any customer who values one of these stores over the others. Some may prefer Starbucks, owing to its national presence, familiarity, and reputation. Others may prefer a locally owned shop for the very opposite reason, because it is not a large national chain. Still others may see subtle differences in the locations, depending on which is the most convenient for them. Thus, even in the face of apparent similarity, there are still nuances of dissimilarity that can make one or the other location appear rare and unique. In assessing rareness then, it is important to look beyond the surface, to the many attributes on which firms' resources can and do differ. Indeed, it is often in these subtle differences that the greatest opportunity lies.

Inimitability

Any resource that is valuable and rare can provide opportunities for competitive advantage and profit. However, such advantages and profits will dissipate quickly if those resources are effectively imitated. IBM once held a commanding competitive advantage in the personal computer business. Its name recognition and reputation, combined with its ability to make reliable PCs, represented a rare and valuable combination of resources that IBM leveraged into substantial profits. However, as those profits attracted competitors and as those competitors sought to imitate IBM's designs and reliability, the uniqueness of the IBM machines began to decline. With its uniqueness effectively imitated and the value of its product diffused among a host of imitators, IBM's competitive advantage began to erode and its profits began to fall. Ultimately, IBM exited the computer hardware business altogether, selling it to Lenovo of China. Thus, as computer hardware became increasingly homogenous, the ability to appear unique declined and the opportunities for competitive advantage and profitability declined as well.

Interestingly, one of the precipitating factors of this homogeneity was the use of common components in the computers themselves. The central processors were almost all made by the same two manufacturers, Intel and AMD. The operating system was made by Microsoft. The disk drives were typically made by a handful of firms like Maxtor, Seagate Technology, and Western Digital. Memory was typically supplied by firms like Kingston Technology or Samsung Electronics. In an effort to be efficient and to reduce their costs, many computer manufacturers became little more than assemblers of these common components. As a result, the unique and rare value of their resources and products declined. Thus, even though the production and product costs of these firms declined, the common availability of these easily substitutable products enabled buyers to bid down the price, increasing their own surplus but reducing dramatically the profits to the firm.

One lesson then that students and business leaders alike should bear in mind, given this example, is that **diffusion** of a core capability can undermine competitive advantage. Many firms are all too willing to outsource key elements of their processes or products in the interests of lowering costs. However, while the cost savings from such outsourcing can be appealing, it is important to think about the long-term implications and about the potential for imitation of the firm's basic competitive advantage generating resources.

As was the case with value and rareness, the determination of inimitability is subtle and obscured by a range of overlapping issues. For example, Sam's Cola, the private label soda of Wal-Mart's Sam's Club is an imitation of Coca-Cola. But is it an effective imitation? Well, that depends upon who you ask and how you measure effectiveness. Surely it is very similar in terms of composition, packaging, and taste. Yet, there is more to Coca-Cola than merely the taste or packaging. Thus, the attempted imitation has had limited success among those consumers who see high use value in Coca-Cola. However, among consumers who see little difference in the use value of different sodas, Sam's Cola has been an effective imitation.

TiVo introduced the world to digital video recorders (DVRs), which transformed the way consumers watched television, allowing for much simpler time-shifting of programming and pausing live TV. Indeed, just as Google has become a verb in the world of internet search ("Wait a second while I google that . . ."), so TiVo briefly became used as a verb to record and watch television. However, while TiVo sought to build a brand to become synonymous with recording television programming and built partnerships with companies such as DirecTV in the U.S. and British Sky

Broadcasting (Sky) in the U.K., the underlying hardware for the device was built on readily available components, and the software was readily imitable. Other companies, including the cable providers and even DirecTV and Sky, began to build their own DVRs and TiVo's market share declined rapidly.

Understanding what is or is not likely to be effectively imitated means understanding the nature of the value that the product or service provides. In the case of Coca-Cola, that value comes largely from the brand, its reputation, and familiarity. Those sorts of resources are hard to imitate. TiVo, on the other hand, though innovative in developing the DVR, did so using components that any rival could also buy, and once the idea of the DVR was in the public domain, the idea was easily imitable. While TiVo tried to develop a brand and succeeded to some degree, this brand did not engender a level of loyalty sufficient to protect it from functionally equivalent competitors in the same way that a long-established brand such as Coca-Cola could do. Thus, as firms are able to develop, control, and sustain their hold on resources that are both valuable and rare, they are able to sustain their competitive advantage.

Non-Substitutability

Imitating a valuable and rare resource can be difficult. Thus, rather than trying to imitate it directly, it can make sense sometimes to simply substitute it with some equivalent resource or product. The ease of substitutability then is another criteria on which competitive advantage depends. Resources that are easily substituted cannot provide sustained competitive advantage because, once substituted, they lose some of their value.

Apple computers were an early pioneer in the business of personal computers and personal computer software. Indeed, most customers considered Apple's products to be superior to the competition. Thus, those products, and the resources which created them, were valuable and rare. They were also difficult to imitate, as Apple safeguarded the source code of its operating system as well as keeping many of the engineering details of its hardware proprietary. From the perspective of Apple's management, maintaining control over their rare and valuable resources was a wise move, designed to prolong Apple's competitive advantage. However, it provided an opportunity for competitors to develop products, specifically the Microsoft/Intel-based personal computers pioneered by IBM but imitated by many others which, while different from Apple's, performed many of the same functions and so became effective substitutes. As those substitutes grew in popularity, Apple's competitive advantage declined to the point that Apple was almost eliminated from the industry. So just as IBM lost advantage in PCs due to imitability, as a result the PC industry as a whole grew and became an effective substitute for Apple's own personal computers, reducing Apple's competitive advantage.

The same substitution effect can be observed in the landline telephone business, where the proliferation of cell phones and voice-over-internet technology has reduced the demand for traditional landline services dramatically, or in the steel business, where the emergence of recycling mills and composite materials have cut into the competitive advantage of the integrated mills, which produced steel from raw ore. The ability to substitute the value-generating function of a resource reduces its value and its ability to sustain a competitive advantage.

Appropriability

The final criterion for a resource to be a source of competitive advantage for a firm has less to do with how that resource sets the company apart from others in the marketplace and more to do with the firm's ability to obtain the financial benefit from the resource. Appropriability is the ability of the firm to extract value from that resource versus the value being extracted by someone else. As we examined earlier, we have seen how IBM lost its advantage in the PC business because of imitability. The use of standard parts to produce the PC led to the ability of other manufacturers to imitate the PC and take market share away from IBM. The use of generic parts meant that IBM and other competitors were only able to create value by virtue of putting the parts together to assemble a computer which created value of more than the sum of the parts for the consumer. Some of these parts were themselves subject to intense competition and became essentially generic parts whereby a computer manufacturer could choose a variety of different suppliers for the part, reducing the ability of those part manufacturers to extract, or appropriate, value from the part. However, two companies, Microsoft and Intel, were able to appropriate much of the profitability, or value, from the PC industry. Microsoft, as the only supplier of the necessary operating system to allow PC software to be usable on the PC was able to appropriate a great deal of the value of the PC for themselves, to the extent that it became one of the most valuable companies in the world. Intel, as a supplier of the key hardware component of the PC was able to appropriate a great deal of value itself, although it was subject to competition from AMD. Intel, by creating the Intel Inside campaign which drove consumer demand for Intel-branded chips over AMD in their PCs, was able to appropriate more value from the PC industry. Hence, Microsoft and Intel were able to appropriate more value from the PC industry than the PC manufacturers themselves, even though they were a supplier to the industry rather than a direct player themselves.

The resource-based view of strategy then views competitive advantage as arising from the differing capabilities that firms have, as a result of their differing resources (see Table 5.1). As a result of those differing resources and capabilities, some firms are simply known for and identified by specific capabilities, like Amazon with its 2-day Prime shipping or Volvo with its reputation for car safety. Because

Table 5.1
Resources, Capabilities, and Competitive Advantage

Sustainable Competitive Advantage Emerges From Resources That Are:

Valuable	Valuable resources are used by firms to create products and services that customers find desirable. They allow firms to exploit opportunities and to respond to threats.
Rare	Resources that are rare are held by just a very few. As such, when valuable resources are also rare, they are likely to be in great demand.
Inimitable	Inimitability simply means difficult, costly, or impossible to imitate or develop. Resources that are inimitable are not likely to lose their value through diffusion.
Non-substitutable	Resources that have no obvious or direct equivalents are difficult or costly to substitute.
Appropriable	The ability of the firm to extract the value that its resource creates.

Valuable, rare, inimitable, non-substitutable, and appropriable resources give rise to competencies that are valuable to customers and distinct to particular organizations. These distinctive competencies form the basis of an organization's competitive advantage.

of their resource endowments and capabilities, some firms are simply able to offer things that few competitors can match, like JPMorgan Chase with its network of over 18,000 ATMs or Halliburton with its worldwide logistics capabilities. These capabilities, and the resources which underlie them, provide firms with **distinctive competencies**. The ability of those competencies to generate value for customers, while remaining distinct to the firms that possess them, is a key to competitive advantage and profit.

THE VALUE CHAIN

A tool for further understanding and decomposing the value generating activities and resources of an organization is the **value chain**. Porter (1985) devised the value chain as a means of illustrating the various categories of value-adding activities that organizations perform; each category represents a potential source of competitive advantage. Like many of the other models in the field of strategic management, the value chain is based on a simple but powerful and broadly applicable idea; specifically, that the value that customers see and the value that leads to profits results from a series of distinct but interconnected activities. Consider, for example, this textbook and think about what went into getting it into the hands of the customers. First, there had to be authors, who actually wrote the content. But content, in and of itself, is insufficient to constitute a book that provides value to a consumer. There also had to be a publisher, who provided editorial services and converted the raw content into the printed and bound volume that would be sold. But to sell the book, there also had to be a sales force, combined with a marketing effort, to promote the book and to make the users aware of its existence and attributes. Even with the book selected and ordered, there was still need for logistical support to move the books in the proper numbers from publication, to warehouse, to booksellers, and ultimately into the hands of the consumers. Thus, even in this simple example, we can see a chain of value-adding events that begins with the collection of inbound materials, moves through some process of refinement and operations, into sales and marketing, and ultimately to those who actually buy the product itself, the customers. These various types of activities are called the **primary value generating** activities of the value chain (see Figure 5.2).

Primary activities are those that contribute directly to the creation, manufacture, marketing, sales, and service of products and services. In that regard, the primary activities of a firm's value chain correspond closely with what are called in accounting **direct costs**. Direct costs are defined as that portion of total cost that is directly expended in providing a product or service for sale. Direct costs can be traced directly to units of the product or service and include such things as raw materials, labor, and inventory. In the textbook example earlier, the costs of the content; of the editorial services; of the materials; of the binding, packaging, and shipping; and of the sales and marketing are all costs directly attributable to the total cost of each individual textbook. Thus, one way to think about the primary activities in a value chain is as those activities through which the firm incurs direct costs.

Of course, thinking about it this way makes it clear to see that it takes more than just the primary activities to run a firm and to produce and sell a product. Thus, the

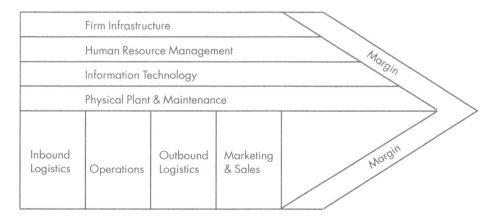

FIGURE 5.2 The Value Chain

value chain also illustrates the **support activities**, as they are called, which maintain the firm and provide the necessary infrastructure. Just as the primary activities are related to direct costs, so are the support activities related to **indirect costs**, which are that portion of total cost indirectly expended in providing a product or service for sale. Indirect costs cannot be traced to a given unit in any simple or transparent way and include things like utilities, physical plant and maintenance expenses, human resource administration, and IT infrastructure. These sorts of costs and the activities that they support are essential to a firm's overall operation and may often be at the very heart of a firm's competitive advantage.

Returning again to the textbook example, consider that the publisher, in this case, Routledge, has made substantial investments in technology over the years. That technology enables many of the processes required to edit and print a textbook. However, few of those costs relate exclusively to this or any other product. There are also substantial costs associated with the selection, training, and compensating of the Routledge employees. These costs include administration of the retirement and health insurance plans, as well as the recruitment and retention of talent. There are costs associated with the firm's infrastructure, its buildings, the maintenance of its equipment and grounds, and the taxes on its property. All of these various costs must be paid for the firm to continue to operate. However, none of these activities or costs are immediately obvious in terms of the textbook's competitive advantage. Yet, all of them are essential to putting the book on the market and delivering it at a profitable price.

The value chain then can serve two important functions in analyzing the capabilities and competitive advantage of an organization. First, it can serve as a valuable reminder of the various categories of value-adding functions in which firms engage. Where customers see superior use value and where firms are able to capture a profitable exchange value, the sources of that value can be traced to some combination of activities depicted in the value chain. Second, the value chain can serve as a tool for analysis, for identifying the key success factors for competitive advantage within a particular industry, and for finding areas of strength and weakness within the firm. As identified in the previous chapter, key success factors are simply those parts of the value chain that are essential for profitable competition within a given industry. By matching the firm's strengths and weaknesses against these key factors of success, a firm can be assessed in terms of its resource and capability strengths and weaknesses.

ANALYSIS OF RESOURCES AND CAPABILITIES

While the value chain is grounded in economic theory, its application is really just an exercise in deductive reasoning. The idea is simple, to cultivate and leverage those resources and competencies that correspond to the conditions of the industry and environment. Practically, this is done by starting with information from the environmental analysis, as described in Chapter 4. Based on that analysis, a good strategist will then "assign" values to the various activities within the value chain. So, staying with the textbook example, we could assess the competitive nature of the textbook industry and the emerging trends within the textbook publishing environment. Based on that information, we could assess each of the primary and support activities within the value chain, in an effort to discern which are most important and which are likely to contribute the most to competitive advantage (see Box 5.1: Resource-Based/Value Chain Analysis in the Textbook Industry).

Box 5.1
Resource-Based/Value Chain Analysis in the Textbook Industry

This is an example of how the two concepts illustrated in this chapter, the resource-based framework and the value chain, can be used to analyze an industry's key success factors and an organization's strengths and weaknesses.

The analysis should begin with an assessment of the environment and industry, as was described in Chapter 4. That process starts with the identification of the competitive environment. Once identified, the competitive environment can be assessed in terms of its growth stage (Figure 4.4) and the forces which affect bargaining power (Figure 4.3). The next step is to assess the various general macro-environmental trends affecting the industry. These sorts of trends include things like changes in technology and their effect on publishing, changes in demographics and their effect on demand, changes in copyright law nationally and internationally, and the effect of those changes on supply and demand.

The point of the environmental analysis is twofold. First, it is important to understand the opportunities and threats, the supply and demand, the growth, competition, and profitability prospects for the industry. Second, the environmental analysis is a key input to the next step in the strategy process, the analysis of the organization's resources and competencies, its strengths and weaknesses. The reason that the environmental analysis must precede the organizational analysis is that resources and capabilities are neither important nor unimportant, intrinsically. Their value comes from their use within a specific context. Thus, it is essential to understand that context fully, before undertaking an assessment of the firm's resources.

With the environmental analysis completed, the organizational analysis begins with the primary activities of the value chain. Each activity is evaluated and given a score. In this example, the scores range from 10, which means the activity is a supremely important key factor of success, to 1, which means that the activity is a relatively unimportant factor for success. The scores for each activity are subjective and based upon the judgments of the person doing the analysis, in relation to two key issues: first, the environmental analysis and the industry's key success factors and, second, their rating in terms of the 4 criteria from the resource-based framework. Capabilities and resources that are valuable and that are also rare, difficult to imitate, and hard to substitute are especially important. For the industry in this example, an assessment of the primary value chain activities might look like this:

TABLE 5.2 Assessing Key Resources and Value-Added Functions

Functions/ Resources	Value	Rareness	Inimitability	Substitutability	Rating
Inbound Logistics	High	Very high	Very high	Modest	9
Operations	Modest	Low	Modest	Modest	5
Outbound Logistics	Modest	Low	Low	Modest	4
Sales and Marketing	High	High	Modest	Low	8
Service	Modest	Modest	Modest	Low	6
Firm Infrastructure	High	Low	Modest	Low	5
HR Management	High	Modest	Modest	Low	8
Technology	Very high	Low	Low	Modest	5
Physical Plant	Low	Low	Low	High	3

THE PRIMARY FUNCTIONS

Inbound Logistics: Score—9

Value:	high
Rareness	very high
Inimitability	very high
Substitutability	modest

The score is based on the fact that content, organization, and author reputation are among the principal selling points of a text. Moreover, because the author is contractually bound to the publisher, the relationship is both rare and difficult to imitate. Of course, substitutability is somewhat lower because a publishing company can only sign a limited number of authors, leaving others available to sign elsewhere. Nevertheless, this function is a key point of value creation in this value chain and is likely to be based upon some persistently valuable resources. As such, it receives a high score in terms of its importance to overall competitive advantage.

Operations: Score—5

Value	modest
Rareness	low
Inimitability	modest
Substitutability	modest

The score for this set of functions is lower for two reasons. First, most of these activities are invisible to the customers and have little impact on their purchase criteria. Things like graphics quality, appearance, and even cost may matter to some final users. But final users typically are not the ones who make the purchase decisions. To the instructors who do, those sorts of issues are generally secondary. More importantly, even if those issues were key to the adoption and purchase decision, it is not clear that a firm could gain competitive advantage based upon them. The reason is that the technologies and talents that contribute to operations are not especially rare. Many firms have access to the same publishing technologies. And, where they do not have access, they may be able to find comparable technologies or people who could provide substitute functions. Thus, this set of value-adding functions receives a relatively low score in terms of contribution to competitive advantage.

Outbound Logistics: Score—4

Value	modest
Rareness	low
Inimitability	low
Substitutability	modest

The score for outbound logistics follows much the same thought process of the operations functions. While all of the various activities that go into outbound logistics, things like shipping, warehousing, inventory, and order management, are important, few really contribute in an affirmative way to the buying decision or to the margin on the product. We might say that the outbound logistics are necessary but not sufficient for the product to achieve competitive advantage. Moreover, many of the sorts of capabilities needed for high-quality outbound logistics are widely accessible through vendors who specialize in logistics management. While it is difficult to substitute outbound logistics, there are numerous paths and providers who offer a range of options from which to choose in getting goods and services to the customer. Thus, this set of value-adding functions receives a relatively low score in terms of its importance to competitive advantage.

Marketing and Sales: Score—8

Value	high
Rareness	high
Inimitability	modest
Substitutability	low

Perhaps as important as the content is the sales and marketing effort that promotes it. Here again, the contribution of this function to the competitive advantage of the text is substantial. Given the nature of the customer, the product must be promoted to get it into the hands of the instructors who are in a position to select it. Without such an effort, even good content may go unnoticed (the better mousetrap fallacy). Moreover, the resources necessary for good sales and marketing take time to develop and are difficult to substitute. They may be imitated though as sales personnel and marketing expertise can be acquired. Still, on balance, this value-added function contributes substantially to competitive advantage and is built upon resources that can make that advantage sustainable. Thus, this set of functions receives a relatively high score.

Service: Score—6

Value	modest
Rareness	modest
Inimitability	modest
Substitutability	low

While not an obvious source of competitive advantage, service after the sale is important in this business because of the high potential for repeat business. Instructors who use and become comfortable with a text are likely to continue using it. Thus, it falls to the service function to gather their feedback, to incorporate it into future editions, and to adjust as necessary to shifts in demand. While most firms endeavor to provide the same sorts of services, there are few ways to substitute this basic function. Thus, substitutability is low but inimitability and rareness are no more than modest. On balance, then, this set of functions receives a score somewhere near the midpoint of the range.

THE SUPPORT FUNCTIONS

Just as the assessment of the primary functions depends upon the environmental analysis, so does the assessment of the support functions depend upon the analysis of the primary functions. Having assessed the primary functions, managers and analysts can assess the support functions, looking again for the key factors that will determine competitive advantage in this particular industry. For the industry in this example, that assessment might look like this:

Firm Infrastructure: Score—5

Value	high
Rareness	low
Inimitability	modest
Substitutability	low

In an industry with low margins and relatively high fixed costs, firm infrastructure—things like the IT network, the managerial decision processes, and the organizational structure—could be the difference between profitability and loss. Thus, an efficient organization, with few layers between the inbound logistics and the sales, marketing, and service functions, could be a key to competitive advantage and profitability. Of course, given the consolidation in this industry and the familiarity of the competitors, the chances are good that such efficient practices are imitated whenever they are observed. As such, they are not likely to be rare. Thus, this group of support functions rates in the middle of the range.

Human Resource Management: Score—8

> Value high
> Rareness modest
> Inimitability modest
> Substitutability low

Recall that the key sources of competitive advantage in this industry are inbound logistics, sales and marketing, and service. In some way or another then, competitive advantage rests on the ability of the people in the field to form and maintain relationships with potential authors and customers. From the perspective of the authors and customers, those relationships are with the people from the firm, more so than with the firm itself. That means that the HR function is very valuable as it is this function which selects, socializes, and trains these individuals. Perhaps even more importantly, it is this function which retains them and so preserves the rareness and inimitability of the resource. Thus, it is seen as a key source of potential advantage.

Technology Development: Score—5

> Value very high
> Rareness low
> Inimitability low
> Substitutability modest

This particular industry has seen a dramatic revolution in technology in previous decades. From simple printing and binding, the technological requirements have advanced to electronic distribution, custom publishing, publishing on demand, and the integration of online materials. Thus, the value of this function in support of the primary functions is undeniable. Unfortunately, the majority of the technological tools that are used are available on the open market. Moreover, even when firms do innovate, they often must make their innovations public, on their website or as a part of their marketing, and so accessible to their competitors. Thus, as important as this function is, its rareness, inimitability, and substitutability make it an unlikely source of sustained competitive advantage. Thus, it receives a modest score.

Physical Plant and Maintenance: Score—3

Value low
Rareness low
Inimitability low
Substitutability high

This final support function is a classic example of a function that must be done but that will likely provide little if any direct and affirmative contribution to competitive advantage. Moreover, the resources at use in this function are highly substitutable and accessible. Thus, this set of support functions receives a low score.

For this hypothetical firm in the textbook publishing business then, the final assessment of key success factors and resources would be:

Primary Activities

Inbound Logistics: 9
Operations: 4
Outbound Logistics: 4
Sales and Marketing: 8
Service: 6

Support Activities

Firm Infrastructure: 5
Human Resource Management: 8
Technology Development: 5
Physical Plant and Maintenance: 3

ASSESSING THE GAPS

For each of these categories, the firm could now be assessed in relation to industry leaders or other "state-of-the-art" benchmarks. Using the same scoring system, a manager or an analyst might ask, how strong is this firm's human resource function? Given that this function was rated an 8 in the first step of the analysis, it would be important that the firm rate highly on it. If it does, then there would be a match between a particular strength of the firm and an opportunity within the environment. If there is a gap, such that the firm is well below where it needs to be, then the analysis would have identified a weakness in the firm's resource and competency profile. Alternatively, where there are gaps in the other direction, for instance, if the firm had a score of 8 on physical plant or on operations, then the analysis would have identified an opportunity for costs savings or for the redirection of some resources.

This analysis can also be used to identify activities that should or at least can be effectively outsourced. Clearly operations, outbound logistics, and infrastructure functions could be outsourced with no great loss to competitive advantage. However, other key functions, such as inbound logistics, sales and marketing, or human resources management, that lie very near the source of the firm's competitive advantage, should not be outsourced.

As the example illustrates, the inbound logistics function is very important. Indeed, without the right content, content that will be attractive to and valued by the market, competitive advantage will be difficult to achieve. Moreover, in addition to being valuable, content providers are also rare and hard to imitate, in that once signed to a particular publisher, they are committed to that publisher exclusively and so unable to provide content for others. Thus, the inbound logistics function is a key success factor in this industry and a key source of competitive advantage.

The next function is operations, which in this industry includes graphics, type-setting, printing, and binding. However, it also includes such things as online distribution, indexing, and editorial value added. These functions are an important contribution to the final product. However, they cannot make up for deficiencies in other areas nor are they likely to be unique to any one firm, as they are often based on broadly available technologies and on know-how that can be acquired on the market. Thus, although important, their importance to competitive advantage is somewhat lower.

Outbound logistics are similar in that they are an essential function but not a function that contributes tremendously and uniquely to competitive advantage. Naturally, books have to be shipped on time and must be inventoried and tracked appropriately. However, such logistical functions rarely add much value to the text-book over and above other textbooks. Moreover, these sorts of abilities and functions are also generally characteristic of many firms. Granted, a publisher that is frequently late with shipments, that makes mistakes in order quantities, or that fails to bill for its shipments accurately will not generate much competitive advantage. However, among all the publishers that do all these things at least somewhat well and reliably, the key determinants of competitive advantage will not relate to these functions. Thus, again, while important, outbound logistics are necessary, but not sufficient, to deliver competitive advantage.

Sales and marketing, however, are tremendously important. The instructors who select textbooks and the students who read them are busy and distracted, with very little time to peruse the market of its various offerings and select the one that suits them best. Thus, they rely heavily on the sales force, on the pre-publication marketing, and on the reputation of the publisher. Indeed, there have been many good textbooks, authored by outstanding experts in their fields, which have failed to gain acceptance in the marketplace because of poor sales and marketing. Not only is this function valuable, it is also rare and unique. An established relationship and a good reputation are key elements of an effective sales and marketing effort. However, building a strong reputation and developing those trusted relationships takes great time and effort, and once established, they represent competencies that are difficult to imitate. Thus, a competency in sales and marketing can be a key source of competitive advantage.

Finally, service after the sale is modestly important. Upon using a textbook, customers may want to feedback information, to see some changes in the content, to see the content arranged differently, or to have some additional supplemental material. They may ask for the ability to customize the content or to have some different delivery media. The ability to gather this input and to respond effectively to it is part of the service function and is potentially important to the ongoing competitive advantage of the text. However, it would probably not be as important as the inbound logistics or the original sales and marketing functions.

As illustrated in the example, the same analysis could be performed on the support functions, in light of the assessment of these key primary functions. Some of the support functions will represent essential activities that must be emphasized, so as to maintain the working of the key primary activities. Others are perhaps less central to the competitive advantage of the firm and so are probably less important to emphasize. What is important though is that all of these assessments be done based upon the environmental analysis. Looking at the competitive structure of the industry and the position of the firm, considering the pace of technological change and of changing demographics, and understanding how quickly innovations diffuse and how rapidly successful practices are copied, what are the key determinants of the success, the key competencies that a firm must possess? The value chain and the resource-based framework can be used to make these assessments.

The next step is to evaluate the firm in relation to those key competencies. That involves asking, in relation to others in the industry and in relation to the state of the art in each function, how well does your firm stack up? Given the example provided, that comparison can be done using the same simple scores. A gap between an importance score of 8 and a firm score of 5 would suggest the need to invest more heavily in the development of that activity. At the same time, an importance score of 3 combined with a firm score of 8 might suggest either the prospect for some cost savings through the elimination of some resources, an opportunity to reallocate some resources from a less important function to a more important one, or an opportunity for new business through the provision of this activity for other firms.

SUMMARY

This chapter, on organizational capability and resource analysis, follows the previous one on environmental and industrial analysis because that is the flow of the logic in the strategic process. Competitive advantage emerges as organizations **fit** themselves into their environments. Recall that the concept of fit was introduced in Chapter 3 and was defined as the alignment of the organization's resources, its strengths and weaknesses, with the nature of the opportunities and threats within its environment. Assessing fit then requires first understanding the nature of the environment both as it exists presently and as it is likely to exist in the future. The next step then is to evaluate the organization in terms of its capabilities and resources. The object of that analysis is to determine how the organization's profile of strengths and weaknesses fit what is or what will be required.

To facilitate and guide that analysis, strategic management offers two simple yet powerful concepts. The first is the resource-based view of the firm; the second is the value chain. Both were explained and an example of how they should be integrated within a single analysis was offered. From the perspective of the resourced-based view, competitive advantage and profitability rest upon the development and use of resources that are valuable, rare, inimitable, and non-substitutable. From the perspective of the value chain, competitive advantage is attributable to a sequence of value-generating activities that can be decomposed and assessed in their constituent parts. By combining the two models, we can get a sense of which capabilities contribute the most to competitive advantage and what sorts of resources underlie those capabilities.

It is important to keep in mind though that resources and the competencies that they enable are valuable only when applied in the appropriate context. Indeed, some of the earliest strategy literature emphasized the importance of strengths and weaknesses that were appropriate to the extant opportunities and threats in the environment (Andrews, 1971). Thus, from this early literature, we derived the SWOT analysis. That framework and analysis are the basis for this chapter and the one before it. In analyzing the environment, as described in Chapter 4, we get a systematic and sophisticated understanding of the opportunities and threats, both presently and into the future. In analyzing the firm, in terms of its value chain and resources, we get a sense of the strengths and weaknesses within the context in which the firm operates. Combining the two perspectives, the external and the internal, provides a powerful lens through which to see and assess the firm, its strategy, its competitive advantage, and its prospects going forward.

CONCLUDING THOUGHTS AND CAVEATS

The Fallacy of the Better Mousetrap

Customers can only value that which they can see and evaluate. In other words, the only products or services that can compete for a customer's business are those to which he or she has access. This is an important caveat, as many have fallen victim to the "better mousetrap" fallacy. The better mousetrap fallacy had its origins in a quote from Ralph Waldo Emerson in 1871. Emerson is reported to have said, "if a man can write a better book, preach a better sermon, or make a better mousetrap than his neighbor, though he builds his house in the woods, the world will make a beaten path to his door." While there is an appealing and equitable logic to this suggestion, research in the field of entrepreneurship underscores the reality that a better mousetrap, a better invention, a better technology, a better product, or a better service will not necessarily make a better and more profitable business. Indeed, Timmons (1999) explains that profits reflect timely interactions between the products and services that customers find attractive and a host of other contextual circumstances that make those products and services valuable and difficult for other firms to imitate. Thus, even a truly better mousetrap might be ignored if it is never noticed by the market or if it is improperly marketed to consumers who do not have mouse problems! Going a step further, it is important to remember that resources themselves are not valuable intrinsically. Their value derives from their use and the contextual conditions in which they are employed.

Consider Dyson, a company based in the United Kingdom, which is known for its vacuum cleaners, hand dryers, and fans. Dyson has a solid reputation in these categories with excellent, high-quality, superior products. All of these products are based on a core competency in electric motors, and they have shown a consistent track record of developing and building high-quality, powerful, quiet, and efficient electric motors. This competency has resulted in a powerful competitive advantage for Dyson in these categories. Recently, Dyson announced that it is developing a range of electric cars to compete with the likes of Tesla. In doing so it is seeking to translate that core competence in electric motors to an entirely new category with a new scale of engine. The question, though, that will only be answered in the marketplace is not just whether Dyson can develop a superior electric motor to power a car, but whether the brand reputation for innovative, well-designed, efficient electric motor–powered products can stretch from vacuum cleaners to cars. Does the consumer who has a Dyson vacuum cleaner or fan in their home want a car that has the same brand as their vacuum cleaner?

As this example illustrates, resources do not exist in a vacuum (pun intended!), nor are they valuable in and of themselves. Rather, they are valuable in specific contexts, under specific conditions, and in specific combinations. Resource-based analysis then should never be done in a general and abstract way. Doing so reduces the whole process to a quest for the "holy grail." Indeed, many managers, students, and academics alike have misunderstood this very point and so have reduced organizational analysis to a futile search for resources that are intrinsically valuable, without comparable alternatives, and that are completely inimitable and non-substitutable. Such resources are illusory. Thus, analyses of that sort are doomed to frustrate and fail.

Real and specific resources should be assessed in relation to real and specific contextual conditions, just as competitive advantage should be assessed at the moment of the transaction. What is it that customers find valuable, and why do they see greater value in transacting with one particular firm than with any other? From there, work backwards to the resources that enable the transaction to take place, in the context that the customer is able to consider. Doing this will make the assessments of strengths and weaknesses, and of resources and value chains, much more practical and relevant to the process of strategic management.

The Ongoing Nature of Sustainability

Just as context and conditions are important, so too do those things change. As a result, resources that are valuable and rare today may be less so tomorrow, and resources that seem to have no value today might be very valuable in the future. This is an especially important caveat as it relates to the sustainability of competitive advantage. Sustained competitive advantage is built upon resources that are valuable, rare, inimitable, non-substitutable, and appropriable. However, over the long term, few resources retain their value and few will remain highly rare if they are highly valued. Moreover, most resources can be imitated or substituted, given sufficient time and motivation on the part of competitors. Indeed, economics teaches us that the presence and use of highly valued resources creates a strong incentive for imitation and substitution. Indeed, even Coca-Cola, the venerable leader of the carbonated soft drink industry, has seen its competitive advantage erode as consumers have increasingly embraced non-cola substitutes such as bottled water, sports drinks, and fruit juices.

What then becomes of the pursuit of sustainable competitive advantage; is any competitive advantage truly sustainable? The answer to that question is that it is all a matter of perspective. Sustaining an advantage, even for a short time, is still an important achievement, as it allows the firm to reap greater profits and to realize greater returns. At the same time, no competitive advantage is sustainable indefinitely. History teaches that even the Roman Empire collapsed eventually, despite its unrivaled hegemony in military, political, and economic power. Indeed, a study of more recent industrial history would show that many firms, such as GE, Xerox, Kmart, Sears, Yahoo, and McDonalds, all enjoyed tremendous competitive advantage at one time or another. Yet, they all have seen some or all of that competitive advantage erode as technology and demographic patterns change, as consumer tastes evolve, and as competition adapts.

Similarly, some resources have retained their value for many generations. Diamonds, for example, have been considered a precious stone for centuries. Thus, the ability to control that resource has afforded a few firms the opportunity for substantial competitive advantage. The De Beers Group, for example, has been in operation since 1888 and, in its early years, controlled nearly 90% of the diamond market. However, even De Beers has seen some of its market power and leadership erode. As noted on the De Beers website, the emergence of competition has led to a decline in market share, to the point that De Beers has chosen to shift its strategy away from a "supply-driven" approach to focus more on customer service and retail distribution.

Sustainability of competitive advantage then is a fluid and continuously moving target. Firms pursue it daily, yet they never achieve it fully, as each day the challenge is renewed. By way of analogy, if the pursuit of sustained competitive advantage can be compared to a race, then it is a race that is run on a treadmill. While we can generally see those firms who are in the lead, their ability to sustain that lead depends upon their ability to continue working harder than the firms behind them. As a firm's competitive advantage persists, so is it sustained. The longer a competitive advantage can be sustained, the more profit the firm can realize from it. However, for the same reasons that there are no perpetual motion machines, there is no competitive advantage that is sustainable absolutely. With time, the friction of the market, the drag of competitive rivalry, and the burden of constantly changing tastes and technology will undermine any competitive advantage, offering opportunity to new rivals and prompting in market leaders an incentive for adaptation and change.

Ambiguity and Social Complexity

As Barney notes, "firms cannot purchase sustained competitive advantage on open markets" (1991). Indeed, the relationship between competitive advantage and the resources that underlie it is quite often complex and difficult to discern, embedded in human interactions, historical endowments, and networks of tacit knowledge. Thus, achieving competitive advantage is not as simple as many would make it out to be. Rather, the link between any particular resource and competitive advantage is said to be causally ambiguous and socially complex. Thus, the process of gathering resources and creating from them competitive advantage is an imperfect one that cannot be reduced to a simple and generalizable formula.

Causal ambiguity exists when the connections between a firm's resources and its competitive advantage are not well understood. Under such conditions, it is difficult to know which resources produce which outcomes. As a result, the process of resource acquisition and development becomes much more imprecise, uncertain, and expensive. For example, consider a situation where comparable firms, located in close proximity to one another and offering similar products and services, do not perform equally well. As with the coffee shop example earlier in this chapter, there are a variety of small differences between the firms that could account for the performance differences. But which differences, in particular, are the most important? The locations are not exactly the same. The employees are different and the products and services have some modest variations. The management of the firms is different and so the personality of the stores themselves may also be somewhat different. However, even though these differences are observable, it is difficult to know just how each impacts performance or even whether any of those observable difference contribute to the performance differences. Thus, the link between the various resources of these shops and competitive advantage is ambiguous.

Causal ambiguity also makes it difficult for one firm to simply imitate the success of another. As illustrated in the example of Harley-Davidson, there is more to competitive advantage than just the ability to build high-quality and stylistically attractive motorcycles. There is also more to the competitive advantage of Harley-Davidson than just the image, the history, or the Harley Owners Group. While all of these various attributes contribute to the overall advantage, it is difficult to know just which is the most important and which contributes most to competitive advantage. As a result, it is difficult to imitate the competitive advantage by simply imitating the resources.

The same sorts of principles and effects also apply to social complexity. Social complexity simply means beyond the ability of most to understand or influence. Competitive advantage is generally embedded in bundles of resources that connect to one another and to the people and operations of a firm in complex ways. As a result, competitive advantage is rarely attributable to any single, solitary resource or ability. The best example of this is that of a sports team with the best and highest-paid athletes. Such teams do not always win championships. Indeed, it is very often the case that such teams perform below expectations. Producing a championship team involves more than simply hiring the best players or paying the highest salaries. There is also chemistry, the togetherness and coordination of the team, the attitudes and atmosphere in the clubhouse, and the willingness to play within the system. None of these alone is sufficient to assure a winning team, yet all of them are necessary.

In the same way, competitive advantage depends upon a complex interaction of resources and conditions. Southwest Airlines, for example, is a very successful passenger airline in an industry where many firms are struggling to survive. What is the key to Southwest's competitive advantage? Certainly a number of different factors contribute to it. Southwest has a unique and attractive culture that creates a pleasant environment for employees and customers. Southwest has limited variety in its inventory of aircraft, which saves on maintenance costs. The route structure at Southwest is designed to serve popular cities but to avoid direct competition with the major carriers and the expensive fees of the major airports. This route system has very few interconnecting flights. As a result, passengers and their luggage travel "point-to-point," meaning fewer lost bags, fewer missed flights, and fewer system-wide delays. Finally, the employees at Southwest are encouraged to have fun and are given considerable discretion in making each flight an enjoyable experience for their customers. All of these things together interact to create the competitive advantage that Southwest enjoys. While any single part of their resource configuration might be enviable and even valuable by itself, the competitive advantage is the result of them all, working in conjunction with one another in a complex web of interacting forces.

Thus, as Barney points out, competitive advantage is not a commodity that can be bought and sold. Rather, it must be crafted, cultivated, and maintained. It must be developed with forethought, insight, and patience as the relationships between causes and effects will often be ambiguous and the benefits and capabilities of resources will often be embedded within networks of social interactions. In short, the resource-based view, indeed, the organizational side of strategic analysis, is more than a simple recipe for gaining competitive advantage. Instead, it is a tool for understanding how competitive advantage works, where competitive advantage comes from, and under what conditions competitive advantage can be sustained.

KEY TERMS

Consumer surplus is the difference between the use value and the exchange value. In essence, it is the difference between what the customer must pay and what the he or she is ultimately willing to pay. Thus, customers seek to maximize consumer surplus and consumer surplus is directly related to perceptions of overall value for the money.

Diffusion describes the process by which innovations are adopted and spread by firms and individuals other than the original innovator. The process was formally identified in 1962 by Everett Rodgers, who noted that diffusion occurs at different rates over the course of an innovation's introduction.

Direct costs are the costs incurred by the primary activities. They are called direct because they represent activities that contribute directly to the firm's revenue generating activities.

Distinctive competencies are capabilities that firms have that exceed the capabilities of their competitors. A unique location, a strong reputation, or key technology could all be examples of competencies that would be distinct to a particular firm.

Exchange value is the price paid by the customer and realized by the producer. It is the value at which the purchase or the exchange takes place.

Fit is the term used to describe the relationship between the firm's environment and its resource endowments and configuration. When a firm's resources and its various strengths and weaknesses align well with the competitive conditions of the environment, its various opportunities, and threats, that firm is said to be well "fit" to its environment. As a result, that firm should perform well.

Indirect costs are costs that relate to the support functions. They are labeled as indirect because they represent activities that contribute indirectly to the revenue generating functions of the firm.

Intangible resources are those that cannot be seen and measured in an objective fashion. Reputation, culture, or visionary leadership are all intangible resources, not immediately obvious nor easily measured or replicated, but still very important to organizational performance.

Primary value-generating activities are those activities within the value chain that contribute directly to the products and services that customers see and buy. In the most common depiction of the value chain, the primary activities are inbound logistics, operations, outbound logistics, sales, and service.

Resource-based view is attributed originally to Penrose (1959), Wernerfelt (1984), and Barney (1991) and holds that competitive advantages reflect resource asymmetries among firms. Sustained competitive advantage occurs where firms have superior resources that are somehow protected from diffusion within the environment.

Support activities are those activities in the value chain that do not contribute directly to revenue but rather contribute indirectly by supporting those functions, such as operations, sales, or service, that do contribute directly to revenue.

Tangible resources are those that can be seen and measured in an objective fashion. Locations, facilities, technologies, and finances are all examples of tangible, measurable resources.

Use value relates to the qualities of the product or service, as perceived by the customers and in relation to their needs. These customer judgments about the value, attractiveness, and desirability are subjective and bound to the context in which they occur.

The **value chain** is a framework for illustrating the sequential activities in which firms engage to create value for the customers. The value chain was made popular by Michael Porter (1985). However, it is a common and highly generalizable framework that applies in a multitude of settings.

QUESTIONS FOR REVIEW

1. What is the key to Harley-Davidson's competitive advantage? Can the success of this firm be attributed to any one resource, capability, or attribute?
2. How is organizational analysis different from environmental analysis (discussed in Chapter 4)? What do the differences in these two important analyses imply about strategy and competitive advantage?
3. What is the resource-based view of strategy and competitive advantage? What are its principal tenets and contributions?

4. Describe the value chain in general and then in terms of a specific firm. Can you articulate the functions in a practical way and explain how each contributes to competitive advantage and strategic success?

5. Describe the steps in the resource-based/value chain analysis. How does this analysis reflect the same basic principles as the SWOT framework discussed in Chapter 3?

6. Fit, among the environment, the strategy, and the firm, is a major driver of strategic success and has been an important concept throughout this text. How does the resource-based/value chain analysis use the concept of fit to produce better strategy?

7. What is the fallacy of the "better mousetrap" mentioned in this chapter, and why is it such a pervasive and vexing problem?

8. Define the terms causal ambiguity and social complexity, as they relate to the resource-based view and competitive advantage. Why are these theoretical concepts of substantial importance to practicing managers?

Chapter 6

Strategies for Competitive Advantage

HOME DEPOT AND LOWE'S

Home Depot opened its first store in Atlanta in 1978 before expanding from Georgia into Florida and from there into the rest of the United States. Framed around the concept of the "built from scratch" warehouse, Home Depot was quickly embraced by building contractors, a segment of the overall market that was predominantly male. So successful was the concept that it quickly eliminated most traditional hardware and building supply stores from the markets Home Depot chose to enter. These smaller regional and local home improvement stores were simply unable to compete with Home Depot's low prices, massive inventory, and broader selection of goods. As Home Depot developed its many "do-it-yourself" learning programs and cultivated its brand identity, smaller chains such as Ace Hardware, West Building Supplies, True Value, and Hechinger began to shrink or disappear.

North Carolina–based Lowe's began to respond to the new competitive threat of the Home Depot warehouse stores in the early 1990s, converting the majority of its retail centers into a similar warehouse format. Lowe's, however, chose to differentiate themselves from the Home Depot model by moving away from the rugged contractor look, choosing instead to market more to the female segment of the home improvement market. As a result, Lowe's concentrated on nicer looking stores, with higher-end products, while still managing to maintain similarly low prices and high levels of inventory and selection.

Lowe's identified this opportunity through market research, which showed that the majority of home improvement decisions were made by women. Thus, Lowe's designed its stores with less clutter, more spacious aisles, and redecoration centers that focused on kitchen and bathroom design. In essence, Lowe's devised a strategy that was a refined version of Home Depot's. And that strategy appealed to many, both women and men, who wanted large selection and low price, but who found Home Depot too unfriendly.

Despite this competition from Lowe's, however, Home Depot has maintained its status as the market leader in the home improvement industry, with $108.2 billion in revenues in 2018, compared to $71.3 billion for Lowe's. Both chains are avid sponsors of NASCAR, and Home Depot has entered into a sponsorship contract with ESPN in an effort to attract middle-aged men and to cultivate the 18- to 25-year-old college male market. However, recognizing Lowe's greater appeal to female consumers, Home Depot stores began to mimic the openness and cleanness of Lowe's and the differences in appearance between the two stores began to shrink.

THE NATURE OF COMPETITIVE ADVANTAGE

The previous chapters discussed competitive advantage in terms of either its antecedents or its effects. Competitive advantage is the object of strategy and of strategic effort. It arises amidst environmental conditions where the bargaining power of customers and suppliers is limited and where options for product substitution are rare. It emerges from resources that are valuable, rare, inimitable, non-substitutable, and appropriable, and it can be sustained only for so long as those resources can be maintained and protected. It relates to customer satisfaction and perceptions of value, as firms with a competitive advantage are seen as the most attractive option, among all the various and available alternatives, by their customers. Finally, competitive advantage leads directly to performance, in terms of sales, in terms of profits, and ultimately in terms of firm value. But what exactly is competitive advantage? That is the topic that this chapter will address.

To understand competitive advantage, it is important to recall some basics. First, it is important to understand that competitive advantage emerges in the transactions between buyers and sellers. Firms can hold rare and potentially valuable resources or they can occupy valuable and protected market space. However, none of that matters in any tangible way until customers act and transactions take place. Thus, while it is necessary to understand the environment and the firm's resources as the sources of competitive advantage, it is just as important to remember that these things are not the competitive advantage itself. Instead, the competitive advantage is the reason that a purchase is actually made. At the most basic level, competitive advantage is the answer to the question, "Why does a customer choose the products or services of firm A over those of firm B?" Thus, competitive advantage is really evidenced only when there are profitable transactions because it is in those transactions that customers reveal their judgments about the relative value of various products and services competing for their attention and preference. So, when a customer buys a Honda CRV, rather than a Toyota RAV-4, it is because the Honda offered some superior value to that particular customer. Equally, when a different customer buys a Toyota RAV-4 instead of a Honda CRV, that customer found superior value in Toyota rather than in Honda. When a firm contracts with Dell, rather than with Lenovo, as its computer vendor, it is because that firm, as the buyer, perceives an advantage in dealing with Dell. When a client chooses to retain a particular law firm, rather than one of that firm's competitors, it is because that client perceives superior value in transacting with that vendor, as opposed to another. Competitive advantage then is the reason that a firm succeeds over its rivals in a particular competitive episode.

Competitive Advantage as an Interaction

Competitive advantage occurs because a particular firm has some specific value-generating capability that other competing firms do not possess or cannot immediately replicate or substitute with an alternative. While this statement is a brief summary of the **resource-based view**, as discussed in Chapter 5, it also carries implications that go beyond the obvious relationships to firm resources. For example, what makes a capability or a resource valuable? The most immediate and tangible demonstration of value is the price a buyer is willing and able to pay. Thus, to say that a firm has some value-generating capability implies that it can produce goods or services that someone is willing to buy. Assessments of a firm's value-generating capacity then must take into simultaneous account both the resources and capabilities of that firm as well as the valuation of those resources and capabilities by the buyers.

Buyers however, do not exist in a vacuum; buyers have alternatives, either to purchase elsewhere or to not purchase at all. Moreover, buyers' valuations of any firm's products and services will reflect, at least in some measure, the attractiveness of the alternatives available. Where there are few attractive alternatives, customers may value a given firm's products more. Where there are numerous attractive alternatives, customers will value a firm's products less. This focus on the context in which buyers make determinations of value is the focus of the **industrial economic view**, which was discussed in Chapter 4. As explained in that chapter, competitive advantage can be viewed as arising from conditions where the options and the bargaining power of buyers is limited by the desirability of the product or service and by the absence of suitable alternatives.

Competitive advantage then reflects the intersection of two sets of interdependent forces. On one side of the equation are the contextual forces of the competitive landscape. These are the conditions like the bargaining power of the sellers and buyers, the availability and attractiveness of the various alternatives, the willingness of competitors to offer inducements, and the ability of customers to search for alternatives. On the other side of the equation are the capabilities of the firm, which must be able to generate value in the eyes of the customers and which must generate that value in a unique fashion if they are to be valued above the alternatives. Understanding competitive advantage then requires understanding that all transactions occur at the intersection of these two sets of forces and that it is through these transactions that competitive advantage emerges.

The Transaction-Based View

What was just described can be called a transaction-based view of competitive advantage. Transactions are the building blocks of competitive advantage and of firm performance. At one point or another, all of the effects of strategic management are manifested in the stream of transactions among a firm, its customers, and its suppliers. As such, transactions represent key linking pins between goals and objectives, the competitive environment, a firm's resources and capabilities, and a firm's performance (Hofer & Schendel, 1978).

Viewing competitive advantage as this key linking event, reflecting the intersection of customer perceptions of value, firm resources and capabilities, and resulting firm performance, can have a number of benefits. Foremost among those is focusing the attention of management in the proper place. Whereas every firm needs profits to survive, profits are still a reflection of other, more basic realities, such as favorable competitive conditions or the presence of valuable and rare capabilities. Thus, focusing on profits, rather than on the things that lead to profits, can be a mistake. Sales growth is another goal of many firms. Yet, sales growth too is a reflection of other things like the stage of environmental development, a superior resource position, or a temporary imbalance between demand and supply. Thus, sales growth is also the result of other more basic forces on which managers can and should focus. As discussed in Chapter 2, a variety of different financial measures can be used to assess a firm's success. However, those measures themselves all reflect the basic underlying cause of performance, competitive advantage. Thus, strategic managers would do well to focus on competitive advantage, its development, and its maintenance. If they are able to do that and do it well, then the chances are good that financial performance will follow.

Viewing competitive advantage at the transaction level can also serve to keep management hungry and vibrant. Competitive advantage is not a designation of superiority. As the opening case of this chapter illustrates, a firm can have competitive advantage and then lose it, through the actions of competitors, through the changing tastes of customers, or through simple evolution of the environment. Even in those instances where one firm seems to be better positioned, or simply better managed than another, its advantage is still a temporal achievement, earned one transaction and one customer at a time. Because the tangible benefits of competitive advantage are realized one transaction at a time, viewing competitive advantage as an ongoing and continuous pursuit can serve to keep management focused and motivated. Indeed, no advantage is ever fully safe or assured and as strong as a firm's advantage may be, there are always opportunities to build more.

In a transaction-based view, competitive advantage is less about the firm and its attributes than it is a reflection of a variety of interacting forces. To really understand this, it might be helpful to think in terms of a sports metaphor. As discussed in Chapter 1, such metaphors can be misleading and should be used with caution. In this instance, however, the shortcomings of the sports metaphor actually illustrate well the true nature of competitive advantage. As mentioned in Chapter 1, success in business is often related to one team besting another in some field of competition. Thus, competitive advantage is often equated with winning. Yet, it is important to note that one win does not make a winning season; a team can win one game and still lose the next. But because no team can win a championship without winning multiple individual games, each individual game is a stepping stone to a winning season. In the same way, no firm can perform well without earning multiple, profitable transactions. And, by winning multiple competitive contests, over and over again, a firm ultimately outperforms its rivals. Winning then is an episodic event that occurs one transaction at a time. Performance, on the other hand, is measured both in terms of single competitive episodes and as the aggregate result of many such episodes.

It is also true in sports that games can be won by underdogs, teams with less talent, or teams with some apparent disadvantage in terms of setting or competitive position. As the old saying goes, that is why they play the games, because the team that is thought to be the best does not always win. In business, the same is true; competitive advantage is decided in the marketplace, in the midst of the competitive interaction among firms, as customers evaluate their options and make their decisions. And, as in sports, the underdogs can and often do win. Consider that Lowe's was, and may still be, an underdog to Home Depot. Home Depot is larger, with more stores, more extensive financial resources, and greater name recognition. But not every transaction a consumer makes in regards to home improvement goes to Home Depot. Some go to Lowe's, and some go to other vendors. Interestingly, Wal-Mart was once an underdog to Kmart, with little name recognition, little purchasing power, fewer locations, and few resources to throw behind market research and development. Fortunately for the underdogs, customers do not make decisions based on analysts' assessments or on measures of aggregate market strength. Rather, customers' decisions reflect their own individual values and judgments, along with the variety of options available to them. As a result, what appears to be an advantage on paper can often fail to translate into an advantage in the marketplace. Indeed, even firms that appear to be tiny, insignificant underdogs, such as DuckDuckGo, in competing with Google in internet searches, can still find a way to be effective competitors in reality and find a competitive advantage by becoming the choice of some customers.

Thus, it is both important and helpful to view competitive advantage at the transaction level, where the actual competition takes place, and to then view firm performance as reflecting that ongoing stream of competitive events. Adopting this perspective allows us to see clearly three fundamental attributes of competitive advantage. The first is that competitive advantage is a reflection of value and that value is determined by the customer. Firms cannot determine for themselves the value of their own resources and capabilities, products, and services; those determinations must come from the marketplace and from the collective actions of consumers. The second is that determinations of value are context-specific. Customers do not exist in a vacuum, and their determinations of value involve more than just the products and services in question. Past experience, competitive options, economic conditions, and temporary fads and fashions can all affect the context in which a customer assesses her options and makes decisions to buy. Finally, competitive advantage is episodically specific. In other words, competitive advantage occurs in specific competitive episodes, where the specific desires and tastes of buyers and the particular capabilities and resources of sellers meet, amidst the ferment of contextual forces described earlier in the text. As any of these conditions, whether specific to the buyer, the seller, or the context, change, so too is the nature of the competitive advantage likely to change.

Value Is Determined by the Customer

As discussed in the previous chapter, the resource-based view holds that competitive advantage emerges from resources that are valuable, rare, inimitable and difficult to substitute and from which the firm can appropriate the value created. However, value is a function of **scarcity**. Scarcity simply means an insufficient supply to meet the existing demand. When something is scarce, there is not enough of it to go around. What is important to note about scarcity then is that it reflects information about both supply and demand. Valuable resources must be scarce resources. Thus, valuable resources must also be resources that are demanded and demanded in meaningful amounts. Resources then can not be intrinsically valuable; rather, their value reflects their desirability and their availability, in combination. The same is also true for products and services; they are not intrinsically valuable. Rather, the value of any product or service reflects the willingness of customers to pay for them.

If there is a weakness in the resource-based view, it is this apparent **tautology** (Priem & Butler, 2001). Specifically, competitive advantage is thought to be a reflection of resource value. However, it is the ability of any resource to produce profitable transactions that makes it valuable in the first place. Thus, while the value of a resource is what leads to competitive advantage, it is also the ability of that resource to generate competitive advantage that makes it valuable. As a result, it is impossible to identify reliably valuable resources a priori because value is not intrinsic to the resource but is manifested only through the resource's use. As a practical matter, then, value is determined by the customer, as it is customers who decide what is valuable to them and so what they will use and buy.

While fine-grained definitional issues like this are of more interest to researchers than they are to managers, the point is an important one, nevertheless. Specifically, the pursuit of competitive advantage is about generating value for customers, not about the pursuit of special and uniquely valuable resources, products, or services. Indeed, the challenge is to acquire and utilize resources that will create products and services which customers will value and for which they will pay.

What makes that so especially challenging is that customer tastes vary and change such that creating value for them is like hitting a moving target. Creating value is challenging because a host of other competitors are all seeking to do the same thing and are often seeking to do it in the same way. On top of that, selling products or services inevitably involves making at least some part of them available for observation, inspection, and refinement. In creating competitive advantage for themselves, firms often must provide for their competitors the very example by which those competitors will challenge them. Creating value is a challenge because much of the money and effort associated with product and service development must be invested prior to the introduction to the market. The pursuit of competitive advantage then is an ongoing effort of trial and error, learning and adaptation, where customers are ultimately the arbiters of success, choosing which products, which services, and which resources are, in fact, the most valuable and which firms will have the greatest competitive advantage as a result.

Determinations of Value Are Context-Specific

It is the reality of these shifting conditions that makes this second tenet so important. Customers reveal their determinations of value and their judgments about competitive advantage in their purchases. However, those purchases are influenced by more than just the dyadic interaction of the attributes of the product or service and the attributes of the customers. They are also influenced by the conditions in which those interactions take place. Economists note that **demand curves**, the mathematical functions illustrating the dynamic relationship between consumption and price, shift frequently in response to such things as changes in customer tastes, changes in overall economic conditions, and the availability of substitutes. Shifts in the demand curve reflect a fundamental change in the value that customers see in a particular product or service.

For example, Figure 6.1 provides an illustration of a demand curve, showing the relationship between the price and quantity of jet skis, with 2-cycle engines, purchased in a particular region of the country during a given season. In the first instance, the prices range from $6,000 to $10,000 and the level of consumption varies between 10,000 and 15,000 units. Of course, the price and consumption levels reflect other sorts of differences as well. The more expensive units may be the ones with the larger engines, more advanced instrumentation, or a better brand name. Similarly, the less expensive units may be the "starter" models, with fewer features, smaller engines, or shorter warranties. The aggregate of these differences

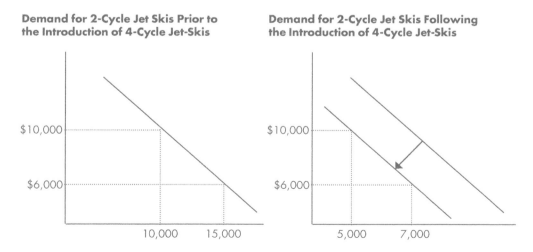

Demand for 2-Cycle Jet Skis Prior to the Introduction of 4-Cycle Jet-Skis

Demand for 2-Cycle Jet Skis Following the Introduction of 4-Cycle Jet-Skis

FIGURE 6.1 Changes in Context/Changes in Demand

though is the demand curve illustrated. Given the income level of the consumers, the costs of the suppliers, and the relative supply and demand, this curve illustrates the collective valuation of the products by the market and prices that customers are willing to pay.

Consider though how that function changed shape with the introduction of 4-cycle jet skis. These newer machines were, in the eyes of most users, technologically superior to the older ones. They were larger and quieter, with lower emissions, better gas mileage, and more power. As a result, many of those buyers and potential buyers who had formerly purchased, or formerly wanted to purchase, the 2-cycle machines no longer valued them at the same level. Thus, the new demand function shows lower overall demand, ranging between 4,000 and 7,000 units, even though the prices across all the various models remained essentially the same. In essence, a technological change had shifted the demand curve, altering the nature of the relationship between the buyers and the sellers of the 2-cycle machines. What is important to notice though is that this shift was completely **exogenous** to the relationship between the buyers and the sellers. In other words, it came from outside of the bargaining relationship itself and thus was simply a part of the context.

This sort of contextual force influences the nature of competitive advantage by influencing the value that customers place on particular products or services. Consider the most obvious case from the previous example; those firms that introduced the 4-cycle machines would find their competitive advantage strengthened. Those firms that were late in introducing 4-cycle machines would see their competitive advantages eroded. However, it is possible to take this example one step further and to imagine the reaction of the firms whose advantage eroded. Having seen the demand for their products erode and having seen the value of their products reduced in the eyes of the customers, these firms would want naturally to invest their own efforts in imitating the innovations of their competitors by introducing their own 4-cycle machines. This sort of ebb and flow, between buyers and sellers and across competitors, reflects the ongoing ferment of the environment, discussed in Chapter 4. New competitors, new technologies, new products and services, changes in consumer tastes or in societal fashions, shifts in demographic patterns, and changes in the economy all affect the context within which customers evaluate and value various products and services. As a result, all of these sorts of changes affect competitive advantage.

Underscoring further the points in Chapter 4, that is why it is so important to approach environmental analysis from a dynamic perspective. Indeed, if there is a weakness in the way that environmental analysis is typically understood, it is the failure to take into account the dynamic and ongoing nature of change. Context matters to competitive advantage, and context is always evolving and changing. The bargaining power of the buyers and sellers, which is driven by how badly either group needs or wants a specific transaction, affects the value that customers place on a given product or service. Thus, shifts in any of the conditions that affect bargaining power will affect competitive advantage. The level of rivalry among competitors, which is driven by the relative level of supply and demand and the willingness of competitors to target one another's customers, will affect the value that customers place on a given product or service and so will affect competitive advantage. Even the ease with which new firms can enter the industry affects competitive advantage by imposing a time limit on the exclusivity of a firm's offerings.

Value Is Episodically Specific

Because competitive advantage occurs at the intersection of two sets of dynamic forces, each occurrence is episodically specific. In other words, it is possible that competitive advantage can occur in a particular instance that a firm can produce a valued and rare product or service that has no immediate substitute and that attracts the value and demand of customers but that then does not occur again. So, in each competitive episode, the battle for competitive advantage is renewed. In each instance, customers are presented with potentially new and different sets of options from which they must choose. And in each instance, firms are revising their offerings, developing and acquiring new resources and new capabilities, imitating one another's successes, and learning from the successes and failures of previous episodes. As a consequence, every competitive episode is essentially unique because with each iteration some of the variables on either side of the equation change, even if only modestly.

What this means is that no competitive advantage is safe. Moreover, no disadvantage is insurmountable. Nokia and Ericsson came from positions of relative obscurity to take much of the cell phone market from Motorola. Yet neither firm was, in turn, able to prevent the rapid growth and success of LG, Samsung, and Apple. Even Microsoft, with its enormous cache of talent, money, and will, could not prevent the rise of Linux as a competing and often favored product. The reason is that each competitive episode occurs as specific customers, with specific needs, go into the marketplace in search of the best value from their perspective. As they do, they encounter unique and finite sets of options, products, and services with specific attributes and features, at specific prices and terms, offering a particular level of value to particular customers. Customers then choose the option that, to them, appears to offer the greatest value, the greatest surplus, and the greatest advantage. That chosen supplier then, in the mind of that customer and in economic fact, was competitively advantageous. In a real and tangible sense, that firm had a competitive advantage over its rivals and that firm realized the benefits of that advantage by making a sale that its competitors did not. However, the advantage exists only for so long as that set of conditions exist. Any change, on the part of the customer, on the part of the firm, or on the part of the exogenous context, can affect that advantage and so can have real and tangible affects on the performance of the competing firms.

Understanding and learning to manage the episodic nature of competitive advantage is the heart of what is called the **dynamic capabilities** perspective. More will be said about this view of competitive advantage in the final section of this chapter. For now though, it is enough to simply know that competitive advantage emerges through the interaction of two dynamic forces. As a consequence, competitive advantage itself is highly dynamic and subject to change. The pursuit of competitive advantage then is an ever-changing, ever-adapting, and continuously ongoing challenge.

DIFFERENT TYPES OF COMPETITIVE ADVANTAGE

Traditionally, scholars in the field of strategic management have distinguished among different paths to achieving competitive advantage. For example, Michael Porter (1980) outlined three fundamental approaches to competitive advantage: *focus*, *low cost*, and *differentiation*. Inasmuch as every firm seeks competitive advantage and because competitive advantage is achieved through one of these basic means, these three approaches were labeled, and are still referred to as, **generic strategies**. Viewing these three generic strategies through the lens of the transaction-based view provides some new insights to the actual nature of these strategies and the types of competitive advantages to which they lead. Viewing these generic strategy types from a transactions-based perspective can also provide practical guidance as to how competitive advantage can actually be achieved and sustained.

Focus

To begin, it is important to remember that, in every purchase, customers, acting rationally, to the best of their ability, and in their own best interests, seek the best value. As defined earlier in the text, the best value simply means the greatest level of consumer surplus. Where the use value of a product or service is sufficiently high, even a high price can yield high consumer surplus. At the same time, even if use value is low, a sufficiently low price can still yield high consumer surplus. Thus, value to the customer should not be perceived as being analogous to any particular level of quality or any particular level of price. Instead, value to the customer is the difference between overall use value and the total cost of the transaction to the customer. Total value to the customer then is synonymous with consumer surplus, and consumer surplus is a reflection of both the levels of use value and the cost of the transaction. Given this, we can effectively categorize the type of competitive advantage by the way in which a firm seeks to increase consumer surplus. First, firms can work to increase use value for the customer.

Where use value for a firm's products and services is sufficiently high, firms can make profitable transactions even when their costs are high. Alternatively, firms can work to reduce their costs. In reducing their costs, firms gain the ability to make profitable transactions even when the use value of their products or services is not especially high.

More will be said about each of these conditions in a moment. For now though, what is important to notice is that both sets of conditions are specific to a particular subset of the overall demand. In the first case, creating high use value requires targeting and segmenting a particular set of preferences, specific to a particular set of customers. Returning to the jet ski example, not everyone has need or desire for a jet ski. Moreover, even among those who do, different buyers will be attracted to different things. Some will value speed; others may value reliability. Some may want styling or the ability to carry more passengers. The point though is that creating high use value for any of these groups requires focusing on the preferences that they value. In the same way, firms that seek competitive advantage by seeking to reduce their costs must still be the most attractive option relative to the available alternatives. Thus, these firms must provide value to these customers, not by focusing on their specific tastes and preferences but by becoming the best choice within the context of the options available. In both instances, then, the pursuit of competitive advantage requires an element of focus. Focus then is less a generic strategy itself, or even less a source of competitive advantage, than it is a characteristic of every strategy that leads to competitive advantage.

Every successful strategy has some measure of focus. That focus will either be on the unique preferences of a specific group of customers or it will be on a specific space within a market where a firm believes its products and services appear as the best option among many alternatives. Thus, as illustrated in Figure 6.2, focus transcends the other two types of competitive advantage. The challenge is to match that degree of focus appropriately to the segment of the market and to the type of competitive advantage that is being pursued.

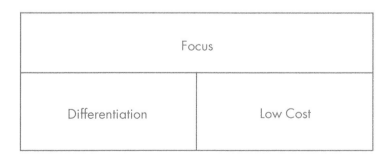

FIGURE 6.2 Porter's 3 Generic Strategies and Types of Competitive Advantage

Differentiation

Specific levels of focus correspond to particular approaches to competitive advantage. As mentioned earlier, one path to competitive advantage is through increasing use value. By focusing on use value, a firm can increase the desirability of its products and services, even when the prices of those products or services are high. Consider the example of Breitling watches. Breitlings are designed to appeal to a particular group of customers, those with some affinity for, or connection to, aviation. Breitlings are styled in a particular way so as to appeal to those customers. They are messaged in a particular fashion, again to catch the eye of those particular customers. And they are marketed through their affiliation to prominent individuals and organizations connected to flying. Thus, they are watches that are made for and sold to a particular group of individuals who value this particular styling and this particular appeal.

At the same time, this relatively small, relatively homogeneous, and relatively wealthy group of individuals has few options for this type of watch. There are few other watch makers who have the same sort of styling and offerings. More importantly, there are few other watch makers who have invested the necessary time and effort to cultivate a reputation as the preferred maker of aviation watches. Thus, there are few, if any, other watch makers who can offer the level of use value to customers who value this sort of watch as Breitling. Indeed, as Breitling stimulates interest with its advertising and as customers become attracted to this type of watch and so begin considering their options for buying one, they will often find that Breitling is one of only a very few alternatives. As a result, those buyers are likely to be highly **inelastic**.

Understanding differentiation-based competitive advantage requires understanding elasticity. As it was described in Chapter 4, elasticity is simply the sensitivity of demand to the cost of acquisition. These customers have very little bargaining power, see very few substitutes, and are not likely to be swayed by new or alternative products. For these customers, there is one preferred option and one preferred supplier. That supplier can then be thought of as having **monopoly power** over those particular buyers. For example, consider that different people have different soft drink preferences. Some prefer Coke strongly, some prefer Pepsi strongly, and still others prefer different sorts of drinks altogether or indeed may have no preference. However, for those who prefer Coke strongly, differences in price or in packaging, advertising, or placement will make little difference. Accordingly, these customers are not likely to care about taste test results or about which drink is winning the battle for market share. They simply know that they prefer Coke. So, for them, there is no competition between the two. Coke is the monopoly provider, de facto. These buyers are inelastic, unwilling to consider other options, unwilling to substitute any other product for their favorite, and unwilling to entertain competition for their purchases.

As illustrated in Figure 6.3, that sort of inelasticity enables those firms that supply these preferred products and services to charge premium prices. Breitling watches

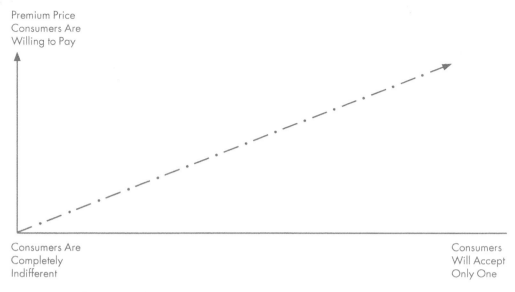

Premium Price
Consumers Are
Willing to Pay

Consumers Are
Completely
Indifferent

Consumers
Will Accept
Only One

FIGURE 6.3 Elasticity and Price

are much more expensive than the average watch, and Coke is more expensive than any number of other no-name-brand sodas. Yet, because of their inelasticity, customers are willing to pay premium prices for these products. Or, they are willing to expend more time and energy in the search for them. Indeed, not only are they willing to pay more but customers actually prefer to pay the premium prices for these products so as to get the higher use value and so obtain what for them is actually a higher consumer surplus. This strategy of differentiation then is one that seeks to create competitive advantage through the cultivation of preferences that lead to inelasticity and to monopoly power for the specific provider.

As with all things, however, this is easier said than done. Developing that sense of preference requires finding and focusing on a particular segment of the market. It requires understanding the preferences and desires of that group of buyers sufficiently well to create for them the sort of products and services that they will value highly. It requires creating a sense of exclusivity, where those customers will see the particular firm as the one best option for this purchase, to the exclusion of other alternatives and potential substitutes, even when those other alternatives and substitutes are less expensive. It requires the creation and delivery of products and services that are in fact of sufficient quality to make good on the appeal of the image and the advertising. Finally, it requires being able to price these products at a point that is sufficiently high to provide a good return, despite the costs of development, marketing, and placement, but that is not so high that it creates an incentive for customers to begin considering other options. Differentiation then is a strategy that necessitates higher costs but that still yields high margins, by creating higher use value for the customer.

Low Cost

The explanation of differentiation-based competitive advantage reflecting customer inelasticity begs the question, what sort of competitive advantage reflects customer elasticity? The answer, not surprisingly, is low cost–based competitive advantage. Understanding this type of competitive advantage requires imagining those instances where customers see no discernable difference in a desired product or service. In essence, they are indifferent among the various alternative providers and substitute products. This indifference gives these customers great bargaining power. They can play one provider against another; they can also simply walk away and purchase some substitute product or service instead. Because customers are indifferent, the product or service in question becomes a **commodity**. When customers see very few differences in the use value derived from any particular provider, they maximize their consumer surplus by purchasing at the lowest cost.

It is important to note, however, that low cost means more than simply low price. This oversimplification has led to great misunderstanding of low cost competitive advantage and the sort of strategic actions that a company can take to achieve it. For example, consider that most consumers view gasoline as a commodity; most see few if any real differences in the use value derived from various providers of gasoline. As such, most consumers buy based upon the lowest price. No one, however, would drive across the country to save a $1 a gallon, nor would many be willing to drive across town to save $.20 per gallon. Rather, customers place some value on their time and on the energy and effort required to make the purchase. The total cost of the acquisition then involves the price, the search time, as well as a number of other factors. In purchasing a new piece of machinery or in buying a new computer system, a procurement officer might consider the reliability and the cost of the repairs, along with the initial out-of-pocket costs of the hardware. This perceived **total cost of ownership** is the figure that is most relevant to low-cost competitive advantage. Low-cost competitive advantage then is achieved by offering the lowest cost of ownership to customers who see identical or nearly identical use values across the range of comparable products or services.

As with differentiation, achieving competitive advantage in this fashion is easier said than done. Indeed, achieving low-cost competitive advantage is a challenge because, by its very nature, it involves creating value for customers who are largely indifferent and **elastic** and so have substantial bargaining power. The challenge is to be the best option to those customers, despite their willingness to consider other options. Wal-Mart, for instance, is considered by many to represent the state of the art in low-cost competitive advantage. Everything that Wal-Mart does is designed around the elasticity of their buyers. Wal-Mart's prices are very low. If they are not the absolute lowest on all the items they carry, Wal-Mart is certainly very near the lowest. Wal-Mart also carries an enormous inventory. While most, if not all of the things, that Wal-Mart sells are available elsewhere, from other providers, few if any of those providers carry the full variety of things that Wal-Mart carries. Finally, Wal-Mart stores are virtually everywhere. With over 5,000 locations, a Wal-Mart is within easy reach for the vast majority of consumers throughout the U.S. Thus, because their inventory is so vast, because their prices are so low, and because their locations are typically so convenient, Wal-Mart is the lowest-cost option for most consumers. Indeed, rather than drive around, searching for and comparing prices on a wide range of different items, most consumers simply choose to buy from Wal-Mart. They do so because the convenience of knowing that Wal-Mart will have what they want and will have it at or near the lowest available price provides the lowest overall transaction cost.

A number of things about this example are worth noting, however. First, it is important to note that none of this happens by accident. Wal-Mart has deliberately set out to be the most rational choice of elastic consumers. Thus, they have invested enormous amounts of resources in the development of systems for managing their vast stocks of inventory. They have matched that system to a network of stores that serve as both customer outlets as well as market research centers, gathering data on what customers do and do not value. They have deliberately sought to position their stores in the path of customers and in such a way as to facilitate convenience and ease. Wal-Mart has then aggressively cultivated the message that they are, at once, the best one-stop shop, with the easiest access, the widest array of options, and the lowest prices. Thus, they have deliberately set out to become the best option for customers who are highly elastic and so willing to consider options.

The second observation from this example is an extension of the first; specifically, because Wal-Mart knows that their customers are elastic, they also appreciate that those customers are willing to seek out and consider better options. Indeed, Wal-Mart's customers were once customers of Kmart, Walgreens, Sears, and others. Yet, it was their elasticity that brought them to Wal-Mart. Because Wal-Mart offered them a better deal, in the form of a lower overall cost of acquisition and ownership, these customers left these other suppliers and came to Wal-Mart. By their very nature, then, these customers could just as easily move away from Wal-Mart, if and when a better, lower-cost option becomes available. Sustaining their advantage then requires that Wal-Mart be relentless. They must understand that customers come to Wal-Mart not because of high use value but because Wal-Mart provides the common level of use value at the lowest possible cost. Thus, Wal-Mart can provide the most consumer surplus only for so long as they remain the lowest-cost alternative.

The low-cost strategy then seeks competitive advantage by being the lowest-cost option to elastic customers. Even where the use value associated with a particular seller is no greater than the use value associated with any other seller, a firm can still gain competitive advantage by offering the lowest cost of ownership, thereby maximizing consumer surplus to the buyer. Such a strategy will necessarily involve very low margins and so necessitate that the firm have very low costs.

Moreover, achieving and sustaining this sort of competitive advantage is a relentless challenge. Success with a low-cost strategy involves becoming the best option for customers who are elastic and largely indifferent across the range of sellers. These customers have little if any true loyalty and will be willing to move around in search of the best options. Thus, keeping them satisfied requires persistence and ongoing effort.

DIFFERENTIATION, LOW COST, AND PERFORMANCE

Both differentiation and low cost can lead to competitive advantage and financial success. Of course, which of these two basic strategies is most effective depends upon the nature of the environment and the resources and capabilities of the firm. Moreover, because of the various and fundamental differences in these two strategies and these two types of competitive advantage, each will produce different sets of operational imperatives and different patterns of financial success.

To appreciate this, compare two firms like Target and Nordstrom. Both are performing well, with growing revenues and profits. However, these firms are pursuing somewhat different strategies and different types of competitive advantage. Nordstrom's competitive advantage is built largely on differentiation, with high-quality, designer merchandise, upscale locations, and top-notch service. Nordstrom seeks to cultivate bargaining power over its buyers by being a destination of choice that is valued despite the presence of alternative providers offering lower prices. On the other hand, Target has a competitive advantage oriented more towards low cost. With a much larger inventory and much greater variety in that inventory, Target seeks to appeal more broadly to elastic customers as the best choice for a range of staple items. It is important to note that while Nordstrom is not the most highly differentiated provider in its industry and while Target is not the lowest-cost of all providers, the distance between them and the implications of their different strategies is still evident in a comparison of some financial and operational data.

Target is clearly much larger than Nordstrom, reflecting Target's broader focus and appeal. At the same time, sales per square foot for Target is lower than it is for Nordstrom. Coupled with the fact that Target's inventory turns over more quickly, these differences reflect the fact that Nordstrom charges substantially higher prices and likely carries substantially more customized and expensive inventory. It is also interesting to compare the two companies on selling, general, and administrative (SGA) expenses as a proportion of sales. For Target, SGA expenses are 20.9% of sales; for Nordstrom they are 31.4% of sales (2018 figures). Thus, Target is able to leverage greater sales volume off of its overhead than Nordstrom. Yet, in terms of profitability, as a percentage of sales, Nordstrom produces a pre-tax margin of 4.7%, which is more than Target's 3.9%.

Table 6.1
Nordstrom and Target: Comparing Low-Cost and Differentiation Strategies

Nordstrom (Fiscal 2018)	Target (Fiscal 2018)
$837m (profit) / $15,480m (sales) = 4.7% (profit margin)	$2,937m (profit) / $74,433m (sales) = 3.9% (profit margin)
Store sales per square foot = $509	Store sales per square foot = $310
SGA % of sales = 31.4%	SGA % of sales = 20.9%
Inventory turnover = 5.13 ×	Inventory turnover = 5.61 ×
(sq. ft.) 80,171 × 379 (stores) = 30,385,000 sq. ft.	(sq. ft.) 129,924 × 1,844 (stores) = 239,581,000 sq. ft.

This simple comparison illustrates how both strategies, differentiation and low cost, can be successful but for different reasons. Low cost necessitates a relentless focus on efficiency, standardization, high volume, and low average costs. It is no accident then that Target has high inventory turns. Target strives to increase the efficiency in its supply chain and to move items into and out of the system quickly so as not to incur unnecessary costs. It is no accident that Target has enormous square footage, with over 1,800 locations averaging 130,000 square feet. With the purchasing power of its enormous scale, the variety of products in its inventory, and the ability to move those products quickly and efficiently through its supply chain and stores, Target is able to appeal to a vast market of elastic customers. As a result, Target has sales of over $74 billion and net profits of over $2.9 billion.

Nordstrom, on the other hand, employs a different strategy, reflecting a focus on a different sort of competitive advantage. Its products are much more specialized, and its services are much more personal. As a result, its customers are less elastic. However, Nordstrom also recognizes that its more customized and expensive offerings will appeal to fewer people. Thus, it has fewer locations, 379 stores averaging 80,000 square feet, and lower overall sales volume of just under $15.5 billion and net profits of $564 million. However, because of its higher prices, Nordstrom has higher sales per square foot and a higher gross profit margin. But premium prices and higher margins reflect operational realities that cost real money. As necessary to provide top-level service, Nordstrom devotes a higher percentage of its revenues to administration and overhead. It also devotes greater energy and resources to acquiring and carrying the right types of inventory to appeal to the preferences and tastes of its customers. Thus, Nordstrom's inventory moves somewhat more slowly than the inventory at Target.

Competitive advantage, then, can be thought of in terms of differentiation and low cost, focused on a specific space in the market. Low cost is generally focused broadly but need not always be so, provided customers are only considering options within a limited range. The important thing to remember about low cost–based competitive advantage though is that it seeks to capitalize on customer elasticity. Because these customers have high bargaining power, this strategy must offer a low cost of ownership. That entails operational efficiency and the ability to reduce prices while offering convenience and ease. Differentiation, on the other hand, is often associated with a narrower scope. However, the breadth of the market is less the issue than the ability to make that market inelastic. To reduce elasticity, and so reduce customer bargaining power, it is necessary to appeal to customer preferences in a way that cannot be easily imitated. That will often require higher costs and a willingness to sacrifice some volume. However, this strategy will generally produce higher prices and higher margins.

SOME FINAL CAVEATS

Simple Supply and Demand?

It is important to note that strategic management and the pursuit of competitive advantage are practical and tangible efforts. While much of this chapter has focused on economic principles, strategic management is more than simple supply and demand. Rather, strategic management is about managing the firm over the landscape described by economic theory. The distinction between simply allowing the invisible hand of economic logic to determine performance and purposefully exercising strategic choice and control over the firm is the issue of determinism and voluntarism, discussed in Chapter 4. As mentioned then, it is a distinction that often means more to theorists and researchers than it does to practicing managers. It would be a mistake, however, to overlook the issue altogether because strategic success requires managing the interplay between these two sets of forces.

Certainly, the deterministic, economic realities of the firm's environment are key factors. Understanding bargaining power, substitutability, barriers to entry, and elasticity are essential to formulating and implementing good strategy. But just as important is understanding that none of these conditions are fully fixed. Through purposeful strategic actions, firms can create inelasticity, despite the availability of substitute products. Coffee, for example, is a commodity, available in any number of places. Yet, Starbucks has been successful in differentiating itself and earning good margins in a market that would have been labeled as unattractive by many. Through purposeful strategic action, firms can find attractive spaces even in markets that are highly competitive and where the bargaining power of the customer is extremely high. Southwest Airlines, for example, has been very successful in an industry with high customer bargaining power and high elasticity. Southwest has done this by serving markets that were underserved by the major carriers and by flying direct routes to these less crowded destinations. Interestingly, Wal-Mart employed a similar strategy for many of its early years, choosing to avoid direct competition with Kmart and Sears by locating in small, rural markets, considered too out of the way to be served by these larger retailers. Moreover, even where there is great substitutability, such that customers are elastic and sellers have little bargaining power, there is still room for growth and profit. By catering to the motivations of elastic customers and capitalizing on the substitutability of their products and services, firms in commodity-driven industries like Wal-Mart, BP, Cemex, and Georgia-Pacific have enjoyed great success.

The opportunity and the challenge of strategic management is that there are always possibilities. But those possibilities emerge from the economic landscape. Thus, the pursuit of competitive advantage involves the development and implementation of strategies that leverage a firm's resources in unique and creative ways, so as to create value for customers who live in and are influenced by the constellation of forces in the environment.

Monopoly, Limits to Competition, and Competitive Advantage

In many ways, strategic management can be seen as a process of cultivating small, pseudo-monopolies. Recall that a monopoly is simply a situation where there is only one supplier. Where there is only one supplier, there is no competition and so few limits on profitability. Of course, even monopoly profits are limited by the resource constraints of the buyers. Still, where there is no competition, profits are certainly easier to achieve and sustain. Thus, strategic management can be viewed as a process where firms seek to attract customers and to limit competition, in effect creating for themselves monopoly-like conditions. Indeed, the different types of competitive advantage discussed earlier can be seen as different paths to monopoly power. With monopoly power, firms can charge prices over their costs because of the inelasticity of their buyers. Firms do this by positioning their products and services so that they represent the highest available level of consumer surplus to their customers.

For example, say that you wanted to fly from London, England, to Perth, Australia. While any number of carriers may be able to get you from London to Perth via different parts of the world, your only option for a direct flight is with Qantas Airways. This gives Qantas some degree of monopoly power over people wanting to fly between these two cities and allows them to charge a premium price over other carriers who must have at least one stop with a total journey time that is at least 2.5 hours longer. While some people may choose to save some money by flying with another carrier, they are trading off their time and the inconvenience of changing planes in a third country, not to mention the risk of a missed connection. These costs, while not monetary, factor into the consumer surplus calculation by consumers and allows Qantas to charge a monopoly premium to those consumers who are willing to pay extra to avoid these non-monetary costs. Thus, to these consumers, Qantas, despite having a higher price, has a lower overall cost to the alternatives.

There are also instances though where monopoly power is less a function of limitation than it is a function of choice. Consider tennis rackets, which are very important to people who play tennis seriously. There are literally dozens of makers of rackets, each with their own models and designs. Yet, most serious tennis players have their favorites. Some prefer Wilson, while others prefer Babolat, Head, or Yonex. And all of these brands, along with others as well, have been used by top-ranked professionals in winning grand slam events. So, it would be difficult to argue that any specific make or model is truly superior to the others. Yet, many tennis players choose to buy only their favorites. In so doing, they maximize their own consumer surplus by buying the brand of racket that gives them the greatest use value, price notwithstanding. However, note that in so doing they are themselves limiting competition and ceding monopoly power to their preferred supplier.

These two cases illustrate competitive advantages resulting first from a low cost–based and second from a differentiation-based strategy. In the first case, the intent is to gain a measure of power over elastic consumers by limiting the range of competitors available for consumers to consider. That monopoly power then yields above-market prices and margins because the monopoly providers are the ones that offer the lowest overall cost of ownership, even if that cost is not entirely monetary. In the second case, the intent is to gain a measure of power by making the consumers less elastic and thereby limit the range of options that they will consider. This monopoly power yields above-market prices and margins because customers see higher use value in the particular brand of the specific providers.

Stuck in the Middle

In articulating the three generic strategies outlined earlier, it was Porter's contention that no firm could succeed for long in a position that was in between the most differentiated provider and the lowest-cost provider. Such firms were said to be "stuck in the middle" and so at a persistent disadvantage to both those who were more differentiated and so offered greater use value and those who had lower costs and so were able to offer lower prices. While subsequent research has provided more insight into this issue (Hill, 1988), there remains considerable misunderstanding of what it means to be stuck in the middle and whether or not firms can be successful when so positioned.

To help understand this issue, it is important to remember two key principles. First, all competition is local. This principle has been discussed previously, but it bears repeating. It is relevant because determining whether a firm is stuck in the middle requires determining first the nature of the competition. To be stuck in the middle, in the way that Porter describes, a firm must be "stuck" between other real competitors, operating within the same space and competing for the same customers. Otherwise, the designation has no real meaning. Herein lies part of the misunderstanding: simply because a firm is not the lowest-cost provider everywhere does not mean that it cannot be the lowest-cost provider for some group of customers and for some subset of the market. In the same way, just because a firm is not the most differentiated among all providers does not mean that it is not the most differentiated for some group of customers or some subset of the market. Thus, firms that are neither the most differentiated nor the lowest-cost providers, in general, may still hold strong competitive advantages by being the most differentiated or the lowest-cost providers within specific markets or for specific customers. For example, going back to our tennis racket example, Wilson need not have the lowest costs or the highest degree of differentiation among all tennis racket manufacturers. They simply must be either the lowest-cost or the most differentiated to that subset of customers who are able and likely to consider them. Further, the basis for that differentiation may vary by consumer. For instance, some consumers may focus on the design of the racket, others on how the racket feels in their hand or their experience when trying it out, and others because it is the racket brand used by Roger Federer, who is their favorite player.

The second principle to remember is that all purchases reflect the desire by consumers to increase their surplus, which is a function of both use value and total cost. Thus, every purchase reflects a trade-off of sorts between high use value and high costs and low use value and low costs. Every strategy then reflects some combination of differentiation and low cost. Indeed, there are no purely low-cost strategies. Even among low-cost providers, there is typically some effort made at adding value, to provide some qualitative differentiation to the product and to reduce elasticity of the buyers. Similarly, there are no purely differentiation strategies. Even the most differentiated provider must acknowledge that customer resources are finite and so, at some point, must make some effort to acknowledge the importance of cost.

It can be helpful to think of these two strategies as combinations of two basic types of effort. Such a combination is best represented by the concept of a **production possibilities frontier**. A production possibilities frontier is illustrated in Figure 6.4. In the illustration, a firm can choose either to focus exclusively on differentiation or exclusively on low cost. A firm at position A on the curve might be Breitling. As described earlier, a firm like Breitling serves inelastic customers with strong preferences and little sensitivity to cost. On the other hand, firms at position X on the curve focus almost exclusively on costs. A firm like Wal-Mart serves highly

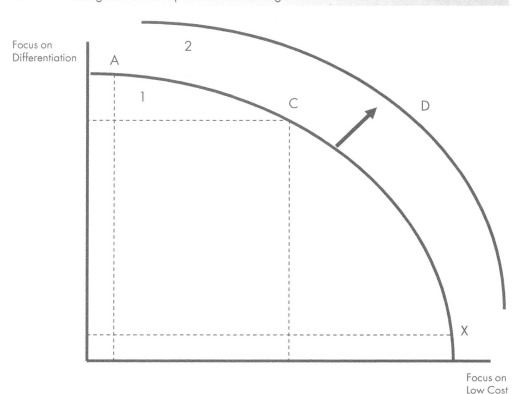

FIGURE 6.4 Combination Strategies Illustrated by the Production Possibilities Frontier

elastic customers, with products and services that are substitutable and easily imitated and that offer few if any opportunities for premium pricing.

Yet, it is important to note that this curve represents a continuum, where firms can choose to focus almost entirely on differentiation or almost entirely on low cost or to trade off some focus on one for the other. Thus, a firm might choose to compete mostly on differentiation but to also make some effort to reduce costs. Because resources are finite, specific, and limited, it is not possible to focus entirely on differentiation, while also working to reduce costs. Thus, emphasizing low cost means moving to the right along the curve. The amount of movement reflects the amount of emphasis. Nevertheless, to one degree or another, differentiated producers do this all the time, offering incentives or offering discounts for their products and services or by offering special financing, extended warranties, or additional services at no extra cost. Efforts such as these represent attempts to mitigate the full cost of the product's or service's premium price. As a result, they represent combinations of differentiation and low-cost strategies (Wright et al., 1991).

In the same way, a firm that is focused almost exclusively on low cost may choose to add some features to its product or some additional services to its delivery. For example, gas stations along interstate highways serve highly elastic customers and so must be focused intently on low-cost strategies. However, by also offering attractive facilities, clean restrooms, and a brighter, more accessible atmosphere, they may entice customers into shopping on more than just cost, in effect, making those customers less elastic. Such a strategy would represent some movement along the curve away from and somewhat to the left of the X position. Such a strategy would also be a combination of low-cost and differentiation elements.

One final implication of the production possibilities frontier is the impact on strategies when the curve shifts. Shifts in the production possibilities frontier reflect the impact of new technologies, new inputs, and new methodologies. Dell, for instance, assembles PCs, using many of the same components as other manufacturers, such as HP or Lenovo. However, Dell introduced a different production model, incorporating online order taking, inventory and parts delivery, manufacturing, and shipping. The result was a process that produced machines of equal or superior quality, with a higher degree of customization, at greater speeds and lower costs. In essence, Dell's innovation shifted the production possibilities curve, leaving Dell, represented at position D on curve 2, at a persistent advantage to any firm still on curve 1. At the same level of low cost, Dell could provide more differentiation and at the same level of differentiation, Dell could provide lower costs.

Viewing strategies as particular combinations of low-cost and differentiation elements allows us to see a near-infinite number of positions along the continuum between a pure low-cost and a pure differentiation focus. As a result, it is possible to position firms, in relation to one another, along this continuum. Nordstrom, for instance, is more focused on differentiation than is Target, and that difference showed up in the financial comparisons done earlier. Nordstrom, however, is probably still somewhat less focused on differentiation than a store such as Bergdorf Goodman. At the same time, just because Target is focused more on low cost than it is on differentiation, it is probably still more focused on differentiation than a firm like Wal-Mart and certainly more focused on differentiation than a firm like Dollar General. Thus, every firm's strategy can be seen as a combination of low-cost and differentiation elements. Which combination ultimately yields competitive advantage though is a function of how that strategy fits within the specific contours of the environment in which the firm is competing.

The Dynamic Capabilities Perspective

Until now, we have not discussed directly the dynamic capabilities view of competitive advantage. However, it is very important to understand that competitive advantage is not static. Firms do not simply acquire competitive advantage and then never lose it, nor do attractive positions in an industry remain attractive indefinitely. Rather, maintaining competitive advantage requires managing a dynamic process, where demand is constantly shifting and adapting, where competitors are moving into and out of different markets, imitating one another and innovating themselves, thereby creating and refining new alternatives from which customers can choose. It is also important to remember that while all of this activity is in reaction to changes or expected changes in the environment, so too does this activity cause change in the environment.

For example, when Home Depot introduced the super store concept to the building supply business, it did more than simply create an advantage for itself. It also demonstrated for its various competitors, including Lowe's, a concept that they could replicate. It created in the mind of customers the expectation that building supply products could be inexpensive and accessible, and it created for investors the expectation that sustained returns of 15% to 20% were possible in an industry that heretofore had been considered mature and stagnant. As a result of this innovation, the landscape of that particular environment changed forever. Whole new categories of customers were drawn into the market and competition was initiated on a new and higher plane. Models of store location, store design, and store operation changed dramatically, necessitating innovations in managing supplies and suppliers. Human resource practices changed as needed to provide better service and better education. And all of these things contributed to earnings that attracted investors and competitors alike.

Thus, as Home Depot was innovating in an effort to build its competitive advantage, so too was it contributing to a set of evolutionary forces that would make that competitive advantage increasingly difficult to sustain. Indeed, you could say that in developing its own competitive advantage and in cultivating its own successful strategy, Home Depot was sowing the seeds of its future competitive challenges. This apparent paradox will be discussed in greater detail in Chapter 8. For now, though, it should serve to illustrate the importance of the dynamic capabilities perspective in envisioning, developing, and sustaining competitive advantage.

KEY TERMS

Commodities are goods of value and uniform quality that are produced by multiple suppliers, such that buyers see the goods from the various suppliers as being interchangeable.

Demand curves are a graphical representation of a mathematical function, describing the relationship between the price of a commodity and the quantity demanded at that price.

The dynamic capabilities view, as articulated by Teece et al. (1997), is the ability to develop and sustain competitive advantage reflects the ability to renew competencies so as to achieve congruence with a rapidly changing environment.

Elastic is condition whereby a certain percentage change in the cost of a good results in a more than equal percentage change in the demand for that same good.

Exogenous comes from the Greek words "exo" meaning outside and "genes" meaning production. An exogenous change is a change in the state of a system from factors external to the model and not explained by the model.

Generic strategies is a term coined by Michael Porter (1980), describing three basic approaches to achieving competitive advantage: "cost leadership," "differentiation," and "focus."

The industrial economic view is the explanation of competitive advantage provided by the field of industrial organization (IO) economics. IO economics studies the strategic behavior of firms and the structure of competitive markets. Industrial organization economics is often referred to as the economics of imperfect competition.

Inelastic is a condition whereby a certain percentage change in the cost of a good results in a less than equal percentage change in the demand for that same good.

Monopoly power is the ability to charge above marginal costs, even in the presence of competition. Suppliers with monopoly power can behave as if they were monopolies because of the inelasticity of the demand for their products and services.

Production possibilities frontier is the term used to describe a graphical depiction of the different combinations of goods that a rational producer can make with certain fixed amounts of resources.

The resource-based view is attributed originally to Penrose (1959), Wernerfelt (1984), and Barney (1991) and holds that competitive advantages reflect resource asymmetries among firms. Sustained competitive advantage occurs where firms have superior resources that are somehow protected from diffusion within the environment.

Scarcity, in economic terms, is defined as not having sufficient resources, goods, or services to fulfill the extant demand. By implication, then, scarcity implies that wants and needs cannot be satisfied simultaneously, which means that trade-offs must be made.

Tautology is a self-evident, true statement with multiple parts that is true regardless of the truth of the parts. For example, the statement "either all sheep are white or not all of them are" is a self-evident truth.

Total cost of ownership is a term originally developed by the Gartner group. It reflects all the various direct and indirect cost related to purchasing an asset. Total cost of ownership includes not only the purchase price but all other aspects in the further use, such as installation, training, and maintenance.

QUESTIONS FOR REVIEW

1. How would you describe the competitive nature of the home improvement industry? Does either Home Depot or Lowe's have a discernable competitive advantage? If not, does it mean that neither firm has an advantage?
2. What does it mean to say that competitive advantage occurs at the intersection of the industrial economic and resource-based views? Are these theoretical perspectives at odds with one another or are they complementary?
3. If resources, products, and services are not valuable intrinsically, what gives them value?
4. How is scarcity distinct from value, and why is scarcity so important to competitive advantage?
5. How can competitive advantage ever be sustained if it occurs only in specific episodes?
6. Explain the relationship between low-cost and differentiation-based strategies and the economic concept of elasticity.
7. What does it mean to be "stuck in the middle"? Why is that position so disadvantaged, and when might combinations of low cost and differentiation be indicators of a superior strategy?
8. What are dynamic capabilities, and does this view of strategy and competitive advantage differ from the industrial economic and resource-based view?

Chapter 7

Corporate and Multi-Business Unit Strategy

GOOGLE AND THE FORMATION OF ALPHABET INC.

On August 10, 2015, Google Inc. announced the creation of a new public holding company by the name of Alphabet Inc. The announcement was made by CEO Larry Page via a post on Google's official blog site. The new company serves as a holding company taking over the Google subsidiaries, thus allowing Google to maintain a sharp focus on its core internet business, Google Maps, YouTube, Chrome, and Android. In the new structure, long-time lieutenant and product chief Sundar Pichai took over as Google CEO, while founders Page and Sergey Brin ran the parent company Alphabet. Some of the key companies that fall under the Alphabet umbrella include in-house incubator X, life-extension project Calico, a drone delivery venture called Wing, as well as their self-driving vehicle venture, Waymo.

HISTORY AND THE TRANSITION FROM GOOGLE TO ALPHABET INC.

Google started out in the late 1990s primarily focused on internet searches. In 1999 it was processing 500,000 searches per day. With the explosive growth of the internet at the turn of the century, by 2004 Google would process 200 million searches a day. This explosive growth in demand for internet searches continued such that by the end of 2017 Google was processing approximately 3.5 billion searches per day. The company's name became synonymous with internet searches such that it entered the dictionary as a verb: **"to google something"** became a common expression for searching the internet. The company's initial public offering (IPO) in 2004 raised $1.66 billion and in 2006 Google joined the S&P 500.

As noted earlier, in 2015, Google underwent a corporate restructuring and became a subsidiary of Alphabet, the parent holding company. Google retained its core internet businesses such as internet search, advertising, apps, maps, Android mobile operating systems, and YouTube. Separate Google ventures such as the life-extension project Calico, home-related products Nest and the internal incubator X became separate companies under the Alphabet portfolio of companies. Google's former CEO and founder Larry Page became CEO of Alphabet. Sergey Brin, the other Google founder, became Alphabet's president, while Sundar Pichai, senior vice president of products, became Google's new CEO. The primary reason for creating the parent company Alphabet was to enable research and growth into new innovative ideas, products, and services such as life sciences (that works on products such as a glucose-sensing contact lens) and artificial intelligence (AI) technology that are beyond Google's core internet business. This allows the company to develop speculative technology that one day may become a core part of their business, without distracting from the current core mission related to search and organizing the world's information.

As Alphabet CEO Larry Page put it:

> This new structure will allow us to keep tremendous focus on the extraor-
> dinary opportunities we have inside of Google. Sergey and I are seriously
> in the business of starting new things. Alphabet will also include our X
> lab, which incubates new efforts like Wing, our drone delivery effort.
> We are also stoked about growing our investment arms, Ventures and
> Capital, as part of this new structure. The whole point is that Alphabet
> companies should have independence and develop their own brands.

Alphabet Inc. replaced Google Inc. as the publicly traded entity in which Google
became a wholly owned subsidiary of Alphabet. Currently there are two classes of
shares traded on NASDAQ as GOOGL and GOOG. At the end of 2018, Alphabet
Inc. market capitalization was over $780 billion, and it surpassed the $1 trillion
mark for the first time on January 16, 2020, becoming only the fourth company to
reach this milestone.

INTRODUCTION

To this point in the text, the discussion of strategic management has focused on
what is called **business-level strategy**. Business-level strategy is the pursuit of competitive advantage by a single business within a specific competitive environment.
Business-level strategy is associated with firms operating in single industries and
serving single market segments. Business-level strategy then can be thought of as
the answer to the question, how will a firm compete against its rivals in a given
industry or a particular market? Competitive advantage, as discussed in the previous chapters, emerges from this sort of single business competition.

However, as illustrated in the Alphabet example, some businesses compete in
more than one product market, with multiple and different business units, each of
which operates within its own industry, with its own customers, competitors, and
market dynamics. Honda, for example, makes automobiles and so competes with
firms like Toyota, Ford, and Hyundai. But Honda also makes lawnmowers and so
competes with firms like Murray, Toro, and John Deere. Honda makes jet skis and
so competes with other firms like Bombardier and Yamaha. And, of course, Honda
began by making motorcycles and so competes with firms like Yamaha, Kawasaki,
BMW, and Harley-Davidson. Honda thus competes in a variety of different industries, in a variety of different markets, and with a range of different competitors.

Moreover, each of the different **business units**, as they are frequently called, in
firms like Honda or Alphabet may operate somewhat independently of the others.
Indeed, it is possible that a firm could hold a strong competitive advantage in one
or more business units, while having little or no competitive advantage in some

others. For example, consider Microsoft and its efforts to compete in the mobile phone business. As early as 1996, Microsoft unveiled its first mobile device prototype, Windows CE, which entered a market for handheld devices dominated at the time by Palm. After several iterations, in 2000, Microsoft launched Pocket PC 2000, later renamed Windows Mobile, which enjoyed some success. However, after the launch of Apple's iPhone in 2007 and Google's Android OS in 2008, Microsoft consistently struggled for market share in the single digits, even with the launch of its new Windows Phone platform in 2010. After developing a long-term partnership with Nokia, once the market leader in handset manufacturing and one of the only manufacturers to develop phones for the Windows Phone, Microsoft bought Nokia for $7.6 billion in a deal that closed in April 2014 amidst rumors that even Nokia was developing Android phones. The purchase, which was one of outgoing CEO Steve Ballmer's last big moves, and one that Microsoft hoped would allow them to gain traction in the mobile phone market, turned quickly into an unmitigated disaster. Microsoft's share of the mobile phone market continued to decline to virtual insignificance, and merely a year after the acquisition, Microsoft wrote off almost the entire purchase price of Nokia. In May 2016, just over 2 years after its purchase, Microsoft sold Nokia for a mere $350 million.

Like Microsoft, Toyota is well known for its primary business, automobiles. As one of the largest car makers in the world and with 2017 revenues of $248 billion, Toyota is often seen primarily as a car maker. However, through its various subsidiary business units, Toyota is also involved in housing, financial services, energy, web-based solutions (e-Toyota), marine, biotechnology, and agriculture. Of course, Toyota's competitive position is much stronger in automobiles than in any of these other businesses. Presumably, though, Toyota's management would not be in these other businesses if it did not think that, at some point and in some way, they would benefit the company as a whole. Similarly, Microsoft believed that their powerful brand name, their dominant market presence in the PC software world, and their "success formula" would transfer to mobile phones, but instead, Apple and Google are the dominant players in mobile phones, and Microsoft has exited the business.

CORPORATE-LEVEL STRATEGY

Corporate-level strategy is about the different businesses a firm chooses to enter and the intentions of the firm in entering those businesses. Thus, while business-level strategy answered the question, how does a firm compete in its business, corporate-level strategy answers the question, in what businesses will the firm compete? The distinction is subtle but also important, for a number of reasons. First, each business and each business environment is unique. Microsoft's knowledge and brand, which it uses to great advantage in the PC software business, did not necessarily translate into competitive advantage in the mobile phone business. Similarly,

Toyota's reputation and position in the automobile business may not be of significance in the financial services business.

The distinction is also important because competition in many industries will sometimes involve investments in others. More will be said about this later. Consider though that Unilever produces a host of different food and non-food items, such as Breyers and Ben & Jerry's ice cream, Lipton teas, Dove skincare products, Lifebuoy soap, Surf detergent, Axe men's personal care products, and Vaseline among many others. Unilever's products are sold primarily through large grocery store chains like Kroger and Publix as well as other "big-box" retailers like Wal-Mart and Target. Because of their size and reach, these large retailers enjoy tremendous bargaining power, which they use to extract favorable prices, delivery, and payment terms from their vendors. Indeed, given their market presence and scale, these retailers can often name their price, leaving vendors little recourse. A firm like Unilever, however, will have substantial bargaining power of its own. With the large number of products and brands it controls, Unilever has substantial bargaining power, which it can use to resist pressure, to improve the placement of its own brands on the store shelves, and to leverage acceptance of its new products. Unilever then gains a benefit from its **diversification** over and above the performance of its individual products and brands. In other words, Unilever could gain market power through its diversification, and it could use that power to strengthen its competitive advantage and financial performance, even if some of its individual products and brands were not themselves profitable.

Corporate-level strategy then involves choosing and managing all of the various business units in which a firm competes in such a way that the strength of the whole firm is maximized. This may involve entering markets and industries that are substantially different from the firm's core business. It may involve entering businesses that have yet to show their full potential or that might seem unattractive on their own. It may involve exiting businesses or redirecting investments as necessary to move the firm away from stagnant industries into newer growth opportunities. It may involve any number of such decisions in combination. However, it will always involve viewing the firm as a whole and viewing its different business units as investments with the potential to value both directly and indirectly.

Corporate Strategy and Portfolio Management

In many ways, managing corporate strategy is like managing an investment portfolio. Indeed, one of the earliest and most influential models of corporate strategy, the Boston Consulting Group (BCG) matrix, suggested just that. As illustrated in Figure 7.1, the BCG matrix is a 4-quadrant framework, with 2 dimensions on which business units were evaluated. These 2 dimensions are the growth rate of the business itself and the relative position of the business within its market or industry.

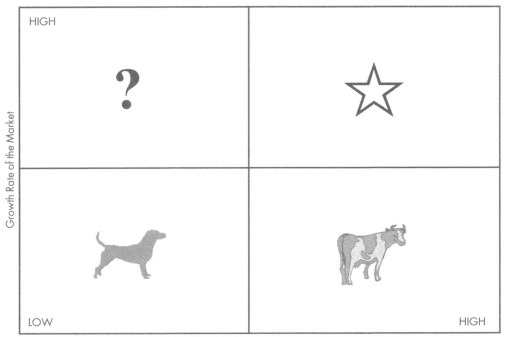

FIGURE 7.1 The BCG Matrix

Each business unit is evaluated on these 2 dimensions and positioned in one of the quadrants on the 2 × 2 matrix. The position of a business unit within the matrix then determines its strategic purpose and direction.

Business units that were slow growing were considered either "dogs" to be liquidated if they had a weak market position or "cash cows" to be used as a source of investment capital if their market position was strong. Neither of these conditions warranted additional investment, however, because of their poor growth expectations. At the same time, businesses that were growing rapidly were considered either "stars" or "question marks." Both of these types of businesses required substantial investment, owing to their high growth rate. However, stars also had strong market positions and offered relatively certain and strong returns. On the other hand, question marks were much more speculative and risky, while still being quite expensive. Without significant improvements in their market position, question marks could not be sustained for long. With improvements in their market position, however, question marks became stars.

Although significantly oversimplified, this model was both powerful and important in that it integrated the underlying principles of business strategy into a framework that could be used to assess multi-business unit firms. The performance of each business unit was a reflection both of the attractiveness of its market and its performance in that market. At the same time, there was more to the performance of a whole corporation than just the strength of its units. A firm could not have just stars in its portfolio of business units because stars required investment and so consumed capital. Stars needed to be supported by cash cows, which also played a key role in the overall portfolio by generating the money for further investment. Moreover, because the growth rate of stars would inevitably decline, firms would constantly be seeking new stars through their investments in question marks. Of course, as the new stars emerged and as the growth rate of older stars declined, those older stars became cash cows. Ultimately as the cash cows became less attractive, they were liquidated and their resources plowed back into the development of new markets and businesses. This framework then offered a picture of how multiple business units could work together to maximize the long-term performance of the firm. In so doing, it illustrated how the value of the corporate whole could be enhanced through specific combinations of very different types of business units.

While our understanding of corporate strategy, along with the sophistication of how it is analyzed, has evolved substantially from the BCG matrix, the underlying principle remains the same. Corporate strategy focuses on maximizing the value of the entire firm by managing which businesses a firm will be in and how those different business units will work in combination. Much like the management of an investment portfolio, corporate strategy focuses on the value of the whole, as a result of the performance and interaction of the various pieces. Business units, like individual investments, can be especially strong performers or they can be not so strong performers. In either case, though, unit-level performance is secondary to the contribution of the business unit to the overall portfolio. Corporate strategy then seeks to produce a more valuable corporation, where the value of the whole is greater than the summed value of the individual parts.

The Challenge of Corporate Strategy

To illustrate the fundamental challenge of corporate strategy, the challenge of making the value of the whole worth more than the summed value of the parts, consider the following figures. The first figure illustrates three businesses, businesses A, B, and C. Each business pursues its competitive advantage in its own competitive environment and through its own strategy. As such, each business is successful or not based upon the success of its strategy and the strength of its competitive advantage. As a result of that success, each business has some quantifiable value.

As discussed in Chapter 2, a common way to estimate that value is with a **net present value** (NPV). Recall that the NPV of a business is a function of 4 factors. The first is the future cash flow that the business is expected to produce. Whether the business is a going concern or a new start-up, there is an expectation that it will produce tangible and real earnings at some point. That stream of earnings or cash inflows can be reduced to a present value based upon their **time value**. Thus, assessing the NPV requires knowing the time horizon over which any cash flows will be realized. The third factor is the risks and opportunity costs associated with those cash flows; cash flows that are risky have a lower present value than cash flows that are more secure. With those variables, the amount of future cash flows, the time horizon over which the cash flows are realized, and the risk level, the present value of the future earnings can be calculated.

Each of these businesses then represents a stream of future earnings and so has some quantifiable present value. That present value is the minimum amount the owners would be willing to accept in selling the businesses. Similarly, a buyer would not want to pay more than the present value, unless he saw some opportunity to increase those future earnings. For example, suppose that business A has a present value of $1 million. If that fact was well known and generally accepted, then no buyer would pay more than $1 million for the business unless he or she had some expectation that future earnings would increase. At the same time, if the seller also anticipated that future earnings would increase, then he would be unlikely to sell at a price below the present value based upon the expectation of the increased future earnings. The final factor then in calculating the net present value is the amount invested. Investing too much, even in a good business with strong and secure future earnings, can still yield a poor net present value. Similarly, investing in a business with poor earnings and poor prospects might still yield a good return, if the purchase price is sufficiently low or if the future cash flows can somehow be increased.

Viewing an acquisition as an investment opportunity, it is easy to see that positive NPV investments are those where the present value acquired is greater than the value invested. The challenge then is to either find firms that are undervalued or to increase the earnings of an acquired firm above the value on which the acquisition value was based; therein lies both the challenge and the opportunity of corporate strategy.

To illustrate, consider that each business in Figure 7.2 has a present value based upon its expected future earnings. Acquiring these businesses would require paying an amount equal to or greater than their present value. The summed value of the three businesses then would be Σ (PVBA + PVBB + PVBC). Of course, making the acquisition would itself involve some additional costs for things like due diligence, processing fees, and legal and investment banking services. Moreover, in publicly traded firms there is often a premium of as much as 30% associated with the acquisition itself (Jensen & Ruback, 1983). Some of that premium simply reflects a natural market dynamic, where the actions of the acquiring firm bid up the price of the target. However, there is an additional explanation for this purchasing premium, involving the information asymmetry between the buyer and the seller. Essentially, sellers typically know more about their own firms than do buyers. Therefore sellers have a truer picture of the real value of the firm and will

Value = (npvBA + npvBB + npvBC)

FIGURE 7.2 Valuing Multiple Business Units

only sell if the price meets or exceeds this figure. Thus, it is far more likely that a buyer will overpay than underpay. In addition, acquiring firms often feel pressured to complete an acquisition once it is announced and initiated. Thus, as the price of the target escalates, many acquiring firms will continue with the deal and overpay for the acquisition. Even vaunted investors like Warren Buffett can succumb to overpaying for an acquisition.

For all of these various reasons, though, acquisitions generally involve the buyer paying at least a price equal to the target firm's present value, along with an additional premium over and above that value (Nielsen & Melicher, 1973; Rosen, 2006). Moreover, once a new business is acquired, there are additional ongoing costs associated with its management. Those ongoing administrative costs will vary, depending upon the degree to which the acquired businesses are integrated into the corporate whole. However, even in cases where there is little or no operational integration, some new administrative costs must result. There will be costs associated with reconciling and reporting the financial activity of the firms. There will also be costs associated with any corporate-level management, salary, benefits, real estate, and so on. Even where there is very little corporate staff or infrastructure, there will still be some new administrative costs associated with the common ownership of the businesses.

But what is especially important to note is that all of these additional costs must be paid out of the earning streams of the combined businesses. In other words, earnings will still come into the firm through only one source, the activities of the individual businesses. This means that the present value of the combined whole can be represented by the expression Σ (PVBA + PVBB + PVBC) − (AQC + ADC), where AQC is total of the acquisition costs and ADC is the total of the new administrative costs.

In comparing the two figures, it is easy to see and understand why the value of the whole corporation must be lower than the summed value of the individual business units. That value must be lower because the earnings from the business

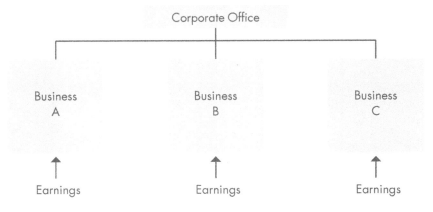

$$Value = (npvBA + npvBB + npvBC) - (aqc + adm)$$

FIGURE 7.3 Valuing the Corporate Whole

units remain the same, while the costs are increased. As a result, the value of the whole will be lower than the summed value of the individual parts. The only way that the value of the whole could be greater than the sum of the individual units is if the combination of those units somehow increased the net of their present values. Consequently, for corporate strategy to be successful, the value of the whole has to be worth more than the sum of the individual parts. The earnings and net value of the business units must somehow be increased as a result of their involvement in the larger corporation.

That is the fundamental challenge of corporate strategy: to enter and manage businesses that are made more valuable through their inclusion in the corporation. Simply entering new businesses, whether successful or not, will not create new value. In November 2006, Google acquired YouTube for $1.65 billion. At that time, Google was widely criticized because detractors did not see YouTube as a revenue-generating business model. Hence, the YouTube acquisition as a stand-alone business was not a lucrative proposition. However, by integrating YouTube with Google and bringing to bear Google's expertise in search and advertising, YouTube was propelled into both the dominant online video platform and a highly lucrative business based on an advertising model. Indeed, in 2018, the financial website *The Street* hailed Google's acquisition of YouTube as "one of the smartest big tech acquisitions in history" and estimated YouTube's stand-alone value at over $100 billion.

Simply doing business in new industries, whether attractive or not, will not create new value. Rather, entering a new business or industry will most often consume value by imposing new costs. Success in corporate strategy then is elusive; indeed, research has shown that many more efforts at diversification fail than succeed (Porter, 1987).

It is important to note as well that the challenge of corporate strategy transcends the **mode of entry** into the new business or businesses. In the preceding example, the corporate parent diversified into businesses A, B, and C by acquiring them. Suppose, however, that the parent started these companies from scratch. Would the calculation of success be any different? The answer is probably not. Even had the new businesses in this example grown organically, the challenge would remain basically unchanged. The parent would still have to invest an amount near or equal to the present value of the new businesses' resources and assets. In addition, the parent company would still likely have a variety of new costs, associated with corporate overhead that would have to be paid out of the earnings of the business units. Thus, the corporate whole would have to add value over and above the expected value of the new businesses individually. Otherwise, the value of the corporate whole would still be lower than the summed values of the individual business units.

Because the parent or diversifying firm will generally pay the full present value of any business or asset that it acquires, and because that parent will almost always impose some new costs on that business or asset, the only way the parent company can be successful is by adding value that was not reflected in that original price. The challenge of corporate strategy then is to take a business or asset with some known value and to strengthen its earning ability, so as to make it more valuable as a part of the corporate whole than it was operating independently. The result is a corporate whole that is worth more than the sum of its individual parts, an effect known as **synergy**.

Synergy is simply the additive effect whereby two things, with some known value, become more valuable through their combination than they were independently. Honda, for example, likely derives some synergy from being in both the motorcycle and the automobile business. Certainly, the reputations of the two business units affect one another. Moreover, it is likely that some of the technologies of the two business units inform the others. The business units may also coordinate the sourcing of raw materials and so gain bargaining leverage over the vendors. Certainly, the corporation as a whole represents a stronger, safer bet to the investment community, which enables a lower cost of capital at the corporate level than could be obtained at the level of the individual business units. Synergy then may come from any number of different interrelationships among the value chains of a firm's business units. What will always be true though is that synergy will provide those businesses some ability to do things that they simply could not do if they were stand-alone businesses and not a part of the larger corporation.

Corporate Strategy and Competitive Advantage

While competitive advantage is generally considered a business-level phenomenon, it is important to note the connection among synergy, competitive advantage, and corporate-level strategy. A successful corporate strategy increases the net value of its business units. As a practical matter, this means increasing the net earnings of the business units over time. As discussed in previous chapters, earnings relate directly to competitive advantage. So, a successful corporate strategy really strengthens the net competitive advantage of the business units. In other words, corporate strategy employs all the resources of the organization in such a way that that the net competitive advantage of the whole is maximized.

In his classic 1987 article, Michael Porter described the true test of corporate strategy as being whether it produces an organization that is better off than it would have been otherwise as independent businesses. As illustrated in the previous example, being better off simply means that the business units are worth more together than they are independently. But, how does corporate strategy make a diverse set of business units better off than they would have been otherwise? How does a firm use corporate strategy to strengthen the competitive advantage of its business units? Porter describes 4 common approaches: portfolio management, restructuring, transferring skills, and sharing activities.

Portfolio Management

The portfolio approach to corporate strategy is often associated with the **conglomerate** organizational model. Richard Rumelt (1974) defined conglomerate firms as companies that diversified into multiple unrelated businesses through the acquisition of large numbers of business units. The conglomerate approach was to acquire solid and well-run companies, in attractive industries, and to then allow those businesses to continue operating autonomously. Because the business units were independent, there was little need for corporate-level management, beyond shared services like legal, finance, and executive-level planning. Strategic and operational management of the businesses was handled at the business level, by the business-level managers, who were evaluated based upon business unit success. In this respect, each business unit was its own **profit center**, responsible for its own revenues, costs, and profits. And the corporate whole prospered as the business units prospered. The key to this strategy then was the identification and acquisition of strong and well-managed business units and the provision of basic services that would allow these business units to operate more efficiently. What synergy there was in this model resulted from the sharing of corporate overhead, the access to lower cost capital, and the superior knowledge of the restructuring management.

The BCG matrix, described earlier in the chapter, grew out of this concept of corporate strategy. The corporation viewed the group of business units as a portfolio of varied investments. Corporate management then allocated capital across the investments based upon their various growth and performance expectations. This created an internal capital market where management had access to better information than other private investors about the companies in its investment portfolio. Similarly, the business unit managers had better communication with and participation from their investors. The result was a more efficient capital market, with lower transaction costs and better information. Because of the greater information symmetry and because of the opportunity for the investors to be more involved in their investments, conglomerates were thought to be better at allocating capital than the public market. Moreover, because the corporation represented a market unto itself, with multiple and diverse sources of cash flow, it was seen as being less risky than any single business organization.

In addition to the lower cost of capital, corporate management also provided oversight and counsel to the business unit managers, along with administrative support in the areas of human resource management, accounting, and infrastructure. Across these various functions and areas, the conglomerate model sought to build synergy by offering the business units the freedom to focus only on their key value-adding operations. Being able to off-load a measure of their administrative overhead onto the corporation and gaining the freedom to focus just on their own products, services, customers, and competitors helped to make these individual businesses more profitable. Thus, the portfolio concept was and still is a basis for a successful corporate strategy. Indeed, Warren Buffett's Berkshire Hathaway and Sir Richard Branson's Virgin Group Ltd. could be described as successful conglomerates, operating in a range of dramatically different industries, with largely autonomous business units and synergy that comes only through subtle interventions by corporate headquarters.

Overall, though, the portfolio approach has proven problematic more often than not. The reason is that while the various benefits seem logical and reasonable in concept, they are actually quite difficult to achieve in practice. For example, while administrative areas like human resources and accounting may seem reasonable areas in which to consolidate, these functions often work very differently in different types of industries and firms. Thus, conglomerates that became too diverse or involved in too many dissimilar industries often found that the expected cost savings failed to materialize. Corporations can end up adding costs at the corporate level without reducing them adequately at the business level. Being involved in too many dissimilar businesses can also reduce the value of the counsel and advice that corporate management provides. Corporate-level managers often find that they simply lack sufficient expertise to add value in the broad variety of businesses in which they are diversified. Even in the area of financial synergy, expected benefits often fail to materialize. The lower risk associated with having multiple sources of cash flow, for example, offers little to stockholders that they cannot achieve by simply diversifying their own investment portfolios. Moreover, while an internal capital market may provide for better information, it is also subject to greater bias. Corporate managers can be slow to recognize their own mistakes or biased in their assessment of their own portfolios. As such, they may be slow to sell underperforming businesses or be influenced by considerations other than just the economic performance of their units. Thus, the efficient flow of capital across the business units can be hindered by a host of different human biases, conflicting motivations, and political interests.

Thus, despite some apparent advantages, the portfolio concept of corporate strategy has been shown to be workable only in rare instances. Indeed, the stock market is so skeptical of the conglomerate approach to corporate strategy that the stock value of an acquiring firm frequently declines upon the announcement of an unrelated acquisition (Berger & Ofek, 1995; Servaes, 1996). The challenge then for the portfolio manager is to actually achieve the expected financial and administrative synergies that were foreseen at the time of the decision to diversity. Without those synergies, the corporation will inevitably impose new costs and impediments without creating new revenues or savings. The result of this will be a corporation that is worth less than the sum of its parts.

Restructuring

The second approach described by Porter is **restructuring**. In some ways, this model is the antithesis of the traditional approach to corporate strategy. Whereas corporate strategy determines what businesses a firm should be in, the restructuring approach looks ahead to the firm getting out of its businesses. Perhaps the single biggest key to success in the restructuring approach is the spread between the cost of the acquisition and the price of the sale, along with the earnings that can be achieved in the interim. To facilitate those earnings and so to increase the value of the acquired business, the corporation restructures the business in an effort to make it worth more than it was worth before the acquisition. The synergy in this approach comes from combining the undervalued assets of the business unit with the managerial expertise and resources of the corporation.

There are 3 key requirements for making this strategy work: the ability to spot undervalued opportunities, the expertise to reorganize the business unit's assets and activities as necessary to unlock that unrecognized potential, and the discipline to see each investment as a means to an end and so to sell it and extract its newly increased value. Of course, developing these skills is easier said than done. After all, what company would not want to find that proverbial diamond in the rough? Most every manager would like to buy an undervalued company at a discounted price, make some changes in that company's operating model and management, and then sell the investment at a premium. However, recognizing those opportunities in time to capitalize on them before their value becomes public knowledge and so apparent to everyone is difficult.

Take the example of Patriarch Partners LLC, which is a company that acquires failing or distressed companies, restructures them, and increases their value. The company was founded by a New York–based businesswoman, Lynn Tilton, in 2000. Since then, Ms. Tilton and Patriarch Partners have invested in and restructured more than 240 companies which, combined, employ over 700,000 people, with revenues in excess of $100 billion. Patriarch Partners focuses on the acquisition and restructuring of iconic, but distressed American brands across a variety of industries, encompassing such diverse firms as Rand McNally, Spiegel catalogs, MD Helicopters, and Stila Cosmetics.

Box 7.1
Corporate Raiders

The term corporate raider became well known during the 1970s and 1980s and was made infamous through the actions of swashbuckling investors like Robert Campeau, Carl Ichan, and Robert Maxwell (Close, 2013). It was the practice of such raiders to buy a controlling interest in struggling companies, hold them, and then sell off the assets or business units of those firms at a profit. They would move quickly, often buying a company from its stockholders against the will of management and then dissolving the company by liquidating its assets. The practice was often cast in a negative light as a number of different raiders went after several well-known organizations like Revlon and Disney.

While this developed a rather negative reputation for corporate raiders, they serve a valuable function in the market. In more recent times, that reputation has become more positive. As we mentioned in the text, Patriarch Partners LLC acquires troubled and devalued companies, takes them over, and orchestrates a turnaround for profit. Through their multiple investment funds, the company invests in companies in a multitude of industries. One of the companies under Patriarch Partners' management is a very well-known American brand that has a long history and is synonymous with maps and travel: Rand McNally.

Rand McNally, the country's top seller of road maps and regional atlases, was founded in 1856 by a printer named William Rand. The company's other namesake, Andrew McNally, joined the firm about 4 years before the duo published their first railroad map in 1872. However, the company filed for bankruptcy in 2003. In the next few years, the company's ownership changed multiple times to private equity investors such as Los Angeles–based Leonard Green & Partners L.P. In 2008, Patriarch Partners LLC, previously an investor in Rand McNally, became the sole owner of the privately held company. Patriarch Partners' motive to take full ownership of the company was a belief that Rand McNally had been hampered by the absence of capital to grow and advance its technology but was a well-recognized brand name with great potential.

Patriarch Partners allowed the business to invest significantly in product development so it can rebuild on 160 years of history and restore its value and reputation. In 2015, CEO Steve Fletcher, who took over as CEO in December 2013, said that he "wanted to restore Rand McNally to its former glory." The company developed a commercial transportation business model, moving into full fleet management solutions. Rand McNally was the first to offer a single box, in-cab, mobile communication system for fleets. Most recently, Rand McNally has launched a suite of electronic logging devices just as the federal government mandates such systems in all large trucks and buses. Following this success, Rand McNally has moved into consumer electronics. Leveraging years within the commercial transportation sector, Rand McNally brought its award-winning navigation to the consumer markets with vehicle-specific GPS and GPS tablets. Going forward, Rand McNally is poised to expand its footprint, launching innovative connected car product devices and accessories. Current financials are not published due to being a privately held company, but there are significant developments which should lead to value creation and thus potential for a handsome return for Patriarch Partners, if and when they sell the company.

In general, the goal of buying undervalued companies and restructuring them is to "buy low and sell high." Any firm like Patriarch Partners that hopes to follow this corporate strategy must have a well-developed sensitivity to market opportunities. They must be able to discern environmental change and to envision the impact of that change on the affected industries and companies. This sort of opportunity recognition though is an inexact science. Still, restructuring is a corporate strategy that has proven viable for some firms over the years, and indeed it is the core focus of many private equity companies.

Another of the keys to success is timing. As industries go through their typical evolutionary cycles, there are certain points in the cycle where the opportunity for restructuring is greater than others. As industries advance in their maturity, for instance, some of the firms that were formerly successful in an industry will inevitably face decline. Firms and industries in this condition can seem to be ripe for restructuring. Rand McNally, once a market leader in maps and travel publications and an American brand icon, fell into bankruptcy in the early 2000s, with the advent of GPS undermining the need for printed maps. Over a number of years in limbo and changing ownerships, it was acquired by Patriarch Partners, which has focused them on developing GPS and fleet management devices for trucking companies as well as specialized GPS devices for categories like RVs. With this strategy, over time, the result is a company that is operationally very different, but connected to its original heritage, and one that is much more valuable than the one originally acquired. This approach to corporate strategy then can be successful, for those with the right skills, resources, and good timing.

Transferring Skills

Whereas the previous approaches focused on the relationship between the corporation and the business units, the final two focus more on the relationships among the business units themselves. To understand these two approaches, it is helpful to reflect back on the value chain (Chapter 5) and recall that the value chain provides a graphical depiction of the various activities in which a firm engages to earn a profit. Each of these activities should be viewed as a potential source of competitive advantage. Amazon, for example, has unique and substantial capabilities in the area of logistics. Those capabilities enable Amazon to manage more inventory at a lower cost than any of its competitors and do it for both themselves and the thousands of independent vendors who use Amazon as their retail and fulfillment platform. A significant measure of Amazon's competitive advantage then can be traced back to its strength in logistics. Transferring skills is an approach to corporate strategy where different business units leverage a single area of strength. That single area of strength becomes the source of synergy to the corporation, enhancing the competitive advantage of the individual business units and making them more formidable competitors in their respective industries and markets.

For example, as mentioned previously, Honda competes in the automobile business, in the motorcycle business, and in the personal watercraft business, among others. What is common across these business units though is Honda's competency in the area of engineering and internal combustion engine design. Honda is able to transfer this skill effectively across all of the businesses, making them all stronger competitors. Disney competes in a host of different businesses and industries, from theme parks, to movies, to television, and retail merchandise. Most all of these businesses though draw value in some way from Disney's creativity and strength in character and story development. Even among business units that seem unrelated, there is an opportunity for synergy and the sharing of valuable resources and skills. Berkshire Hathaway, for example, competes in a wide range of businesses both related and unrelated from insurance to utilities and energy to building materials and products. Although these businesses are all very different, Berkshire Hathaway is able to leverage its competencies in human capital management, capital budgeting, and strategy across them all, to the benefit of the corporate whole.

In terms of the hypothetical firms depicted in Figures 7.1 and 7.2, the sharing of skills can be seen as enhancing the competitive advantage of the business units, enabling them to compete more effectively in their own industries. As a result of this resource sharing, the combined value of the corporate whole is greater than the summed value of the business units, had they continued to operate independently. Corporate strategy then may add value by capitalizing on the lateral connections across the business units. These connections may reflect the relatedness of the products and services, as in the case of Honda, or they may not, as in the case of GE. In every case, though, the objective is to increase the competitive advantage and earnings of the entire corporation by sharing the skills of some units with the others.

Sharing Activities

The final corporate strategy builds on the same concept as the previous one but takes the idea an additional step further. Rather than simply transfer competencies from one business unit to the others, sharing activities involves two or more business units actually linking their value chains together and sharing a common set of resources. The advantage of this sort of sharing is that it provides scale economies in the shared activity. For two automotive brands under Tata Motors, Land Rover and Jaguar's shared dealership model is a good example of sharing resources. The Jaguar/Land Rover dealership layout houses both brands under one roof. This shared arrangement allows both brands to showcase a wide range of vehicles ranging from sports cars to premium luxury sedans to high-end sport utility vehicles under one roof. The combined or shared space (in this example's case, a vehicle dealership) facilitates reducing the cost associated with running the dealership such as supply chain, vehicle platforms, shared showrooms, parts storage, administrative space, as well as common overhead expenses like utilities and insurance. In so doing, the overall cost is reduced, increasing the overall profitability. In the United States, Jaguar/Land Rover have over 150 shared dealerships.

Activity sharing often takes the form of administrative or "backroom" consolidation. A highly diversified firm, with a variety of unrelated business units, may still share common legal resources, common human resource management resources, or common insurance resources. In 2011 The Coca-Cola Company completed the acquisition of Honest Tea, the leading bottled organic tea company, giving the world's largest soft-drinks maker a stronger position in the bottled tea space. In so doing, Coca-Cola was able to leverage its extensive logistics and distribution infrastructure to streamline Honest Tea operations. This was not the first time that Coca-Cola entered a new space through acquisition and leveraged its resources and logistics infrastructure to create value. In 2007, The Coca-Cola Company acquired Vitaminwater for $4.2 billion in cash. In addition to the extensive distribution networks, Coca-Cola also leverages other significant capabilities to adapt to the acquired subsidiaries and create synergy such as product innovation, marketing, and R&D. In both cases, Coca-Cola was able to eliminate some costs of the new subsidiaries while expanding their reach through access to the Coca-Cola distribution system, thereby helping to create new value for the corporation. Firms that acquire new units may choose to consolidate their advertising expenses by using a single provider, thereby taking advantage of their increased bargaining power. In the same way, a firm may decide to consolidate its purchasing function in an effort to get better prices or terms from vendors. In any of these cases, the focus of activity sharing is to increase resource utilization and so reduce the cost of the activity to the business units involved. The result is greater earnings for the businesses and for the corporation as a whole.

SUMMARY

Corporate-level strategy can best be thought of as the strategy for dealing with multiple business units. As reviewed in the preceding chapters, the strategy at the business unit–level deals with how to compete in a particular business and business environment. Corporate-level strategy, on the other hand, deals with the value of the corporate whole. The ultimate challenge of corporate level strategy is to satisfy what Porter (1987) called the "better off" test. In other words, the corporate strategy must somehow create new value, through its multiple businesses and business units, for the strategy itself to be successful.

While simple in concept, this better off test has proven to be a very high standard in practice. Indeed, corporate strategy and diversification seem to fail as often as they succeed. The reason for this has to do with the economic realities of corporate strategy. As explained in the chapter, adding business units, whether through organic growth or acquisition, imposes new costs and new pressures. With all else being equal, business units would run more efficiently and more profitably without these new costs and pressures. Thus, with all else being the same, combining business units and imposing new costs and pressures necessarily creates some new inefficiencies and burdens. The key to success then comes in the things that the corporation does that are not the same. Creating an internal capital market that can allocate resources more efficiently and with better information and insight can lower the overall cost of capital and make the business units more profitable. Combining resources or linking value chain activities across the business units so that they are more competitive in their various industries can make the business units more profitable. Even sharing expertise within the corporation such that underperforming business units can be restructured and turned into sources of greater profit can increase the value of the corporate whole. These various different types of activities are all sources of synergy, which is the key to success in corporate strategy.

FINAL CAVEATS

Related and Unrelated Diversification

In 1974, Richard Rumelt published what is still considered by many the seminal work on diversification and corporate-level strategy. In it, Rumelt provided a framework for categorizing different types of diversification. Using three values, the specialization ratio, the related ratio, and the vertical ratio, Rumelt's framework placed firms into one of 9 categories: single business, dominant-vertical, dominant-unrelated, dominant-constrained, dominant-linked, related-constrained, related-linked, unrelated business, and conglomerate. Over the years, this elaborate framework has been abbreviated into two simple categories, related and unrelated diversification. Textbooks, articles in the popular press, even comments by business managers often contain references to related and unrelated diversifications. Along with those references are implicit judgments about the value of each such that related diversification is generally considered to be better than unrelated diversification. There are a number of reasons for this, some of which are sound and others of which are not.

Perhaps the biggest contributor to this view is the past experiences of conglomerate diversifiers. As described earlier in the chapter, conglomerate diversification typically offered fewer obvious opportunities for synergy because few if any linkages were attempted across the value chains of the different business units. Rather, the principal source of value add from conglomerates was thought to be cash flow stability, the reduction of financial risk, and the associated reduction in cost of capital. That benefit, however, offered little in the way of new value to shareholders, who could diversify their own risks themselves and do it with few, if any, transaction costs. Thus, most conglomerate diversifiers failed to produce the synergy or new value needed to sustain the organization. Beyond this, though, there is also a bias against unrelated diversification related to the results of Rumelt's study. Rumelt found that, generally, related diversification produced better results than other types. He speculated that this may have to do with the ability of related diversifiers to transfer managerial expertise or to share various assets and skills. Because of their similarity, related diversifiers were simply able to achieve synergy more readily than unrelated diversifiers.

While the contribution of Rumelt's work is undeniable and while the common view of related and unrelated diversification may be grounded in his findings, it is important to note that related diversifiers do not always succeed and that unrelated diversifiers do not always fail. Rather, in every case, the success of a diversification is a function of the synergy that the firm is able to realize. As illustrated through Figures 7.2 and 7.3 and as explained throughout the chapter, diversification success is really about the creation of new competitive advantage and new profitability at the business unit level. There are certainly instances where this occurs in related diversification. However, there are also many examples of it occurring in unrelated businesses as well. The key in each case is the ability to share some resource, skill, or activity along the value chain, so that the net earnings of the business units are increased. While the possibilities for this sort of sharing may be more readily apparent and more easily achieved in related firms, they exist nevertheless in unrelated ones as well.

Market Selection

As discussed throughout the chapter, the key to successful corporate strategy is the creation of new value through the interaction of the corporation and its business units. A successful corporate strategy produces an organization that is worth more than the sum of its parts. But what of firms with unsuccessful corporate strategies; can a corporation be worth less than the sum of its parts? The answer is yes, a firm can indeed be worth less than the summed value of its business units. When diversification imposes new costs over and above the new earnings generated by the business units, the value of the firm as a whole will necessarily decline. Firms that find themselves in that position will often become targets of an acquisition, in a process that looks very much like a market form of natural selection (Hughes & Singh, 1987). Market selection refers to the tendency of the market to penalize inefficiency and the underutilization of valuable assets. In such cases, the market actually provides an incentive for firms that are worth less than the sum of their parts to be purchased, broken apart, and reorganized into a more efficient and more valuable form.

One mechanism by which this selection process can occur is the **hostile take-over**, and the principal actor in such takeovers is often called a **corporate raider** (see Box 7.1: Corporate Raiders). Unfortunately, the term corporate raider has become a pejorative, as hostile takeovers have been linked to a narrative of profiteering, downsizing, asset stripping, and the elimination of jobs. In reality, though, corporate raiders often fulfill an important function, identifying poorly managed firms and then facilitating the reallocation of underperforming assets to more productive and valuable uses.

Indeed, the incentive for a corporate raider is the value that can be realized through the elimination of inefficiency. Typically, a raider will spot a corporation that is not creating new value. Because the corporation is failing to create value in excess of the costs it is imposing, it is necessarily worth less than the summed value of its individual business units. A raider then can buy the corporation at its fair market value and break it apart, selling off its various business units individually, and still realize a substantial gain. Of course, the loser in this transaction is typically the corporate management and staff. With the business units all sold, there is no longer any need for corporate administration. Thus, corporate management generally resists these sorts of takeovers, arguing that the value of the business units will not be greater than the value of the corporate whole. And sometimes they are right. However, the mere threat of a takeover is often enough to motivate management to be diligent regarding synergy and value. Stockholders simply will not long tolerate a firm whose efforts at diversification are costing more than they earn. Thus, the process of market selection is, over time, an effective judge of corporate strategic success.

The M-Form Organizational Structure

One of the most vexing issues in corporate strategy is the dual responsibility it creates for the business units and the business unit managers. On the one hand, the business units must add to the value of the corporate whole. Some units will do this directly, through the revenues and profits they create, while others will do it indirectly, through their relationship to the other units. Within Disney, for instance, there are individual business units competing in the theme park, movie, and television industries. The strategies of these businesses are simple enough to understand and evaluate, and the performance of each is simple enough to measure in relation to its competitors. But how should these revenue-producing business units be compared with Disney's more creative, non-revenue-producing business units? The creative arm of Disney, known for years as the "Imagineering" group, sells its products primarily to the other Disney divisions, enabling their competitiveness but generating little outside revenue and earning no direct income on its own. Moreover, the various units within Disney support one another through co-branding of the characters and stories and through shared promotion of many of the firm's products. While this sort of activity and resource sharing is good for synergy, it is not always good for the performance of the business units themselves. Thus, there is an inevitable tension between the demands of the corporate-level strategy and the pressures of the business-level strategy.

It is probably unrealistic to think that these tensions can ever be fully resolved, even with the best strategy, management, and accounting methods. Business unit managers are most easily evaluated on the performance of their units. So, they understandably want to be as successful as possible competing within their own industries. However, operating as if they were single businesses may not be what is best for the corporation as a whole. For example, Sharp Corporation is one of the leading manufacturers of LCD screens, and it sells those screens to many different consumer and commercial electronics manufacturers. Sharp also produces consumer electronics, such as cell phones. Suppose that the Sharp Smart Homes division management that produces cell phones believed that they could maximize the performance of their business unit by purchasing its LCD screens from Japan Display, another LCD screen manufacturer, instead of Sharp's own Advanced Display Systems division. Even if such a move were to benefit the Sharp Smart Homes division, it would hurt Sharp Corporation as a whole. Thus, the business units within larger corporations must be managed to serve two masters. They must try to compete effectively within their industries, as a function of their business unit strategy, while also serving the greater interests of the corporate whole. To facilitate this, business units are often managed in a semi-autonomous fashion, operating independently, within the constraints and mandates of the larger corporate strategy. The structural mechanism that facilitates this state of semi-autonomy is called the "M-form" organization.

The M-form is a label given to the structure of many multi-divisional corporations (Williamson, 1975). An M-form structure, illustrated in Figure 7.2, has a headquarters and then a series of semi-autonomous business units. Each of these business units operates under the mandate of the larger corporate strategy, sharing resources as required, for instance, to benefit the corporate whole but also with its own management and its own strategy competing within its own industry. Georgia-Pacific, for example, has several separate divisions: building products, pulp and paper, even real estate management and development. Each of these business units has a dual charge: to add value to the corporate whole and to compete effectively within its industry.

To facilitate this dual responsibility, corporate strategy and structure must provide a number of infrastructural support mechanisms. Most significant among these is an accounting and compensation system that effectively tracks the real value added by the business units to the corporate whole, independent of the individual business unit's profits. Such contributions may come through the sharing of a resource, such as the brand name of another unit, or the transfer of a skill, as would be the case where one unit provided engineering expertise to another. Regardless of how the value is added, the challenge is to account for it accurately so that its contribution can be effectively measured and incentivized. In the absence of such mechanisms, business unit managers have little incentive to support the corporate strategy. Indeed, they may find that in trying to create synergy they actually hinder the performance of their units. As such, they may choose not to pursue synergy. The M-form then is an important tool in helping firms to manage both the vertical and the horizontal relationships required for an effective corporate strategy.

Organizational Culture

One of the frustrating realities of corporate strategy is that synergy is much easier to envision than to realize. Indeed, in case after case, firms believe that they can diversify and create new value, only to find that the envisioned synergy never materializes and the corporation consumes more value than it creates. While this occurs for a number of reasons, one of the main reasons is that the corporation cannot get the business units to change as necessary to fulfill their new roles. One of the main culprits in this common problem is the culture clash of the organizations.

In 2011, Google acquired Motorola for $12.5 billion. Two years later, they ended up selling it to Lenovo, less some of the patents and its research facility, for $2.9 billion. So, even a savvy and innovative company like Google, who saw its value skyrocket and made a number of successful acquisitions over the years, can also fall in the trap of a failed acquisition. Now is it reasonable to state that Google forked out the $12.5 billion because they had expectations that adding Motorola to their portfolio would add value to the company as a whole by catapulting them to a competitive position in the mobile phone market that was dominated by Apple and Samsung. Their expectation was that the overall value of the combined company, by integrating Google's Android operating system with Motorola's advanced hardware, should be higher than the sum of the companies individually, which, as already discussed, is the key metric for successful mergers and acquisitions. That, of course, is predicated on achieving synergies; sharing resources; and optimization of systems, capabilities, and personnel. But in this case, Google was not successful in assimilating Motorola into the Google universe and thus was not able to reap the expected value. Instead of the envisioned combination, they both continued to work on somewhat separate tracks. At the time, Google's Android OS already had huge market share. So the acquisition of Motorola was to combine this with world-class mobile devices and further propel Google into a leadership position in the mobile phone market. Unfortunately, Motorola was plagued with underwhelming phones and the inability to upgrade older Motorola phones already in consumers' hands to Google's latest Android OS. Google also contributed to the failure of the acquisition by supplying the market with Nexus brand phones, partnering with other "competitors" to manufacture these devices for them such as Samsung and LG. Google's backing of Motorola's Moto X line was lackluster at best, and the brand failed to gain widespread attraction and pose a real challenge to the market leaders, Apple's iPhone and Samsung's Galaxy. In fact, the Moto X was launched without the latest version of Android software; thus, it was unable to demonstrate Google's latest technology.

So, what could have gone so wrong such to cause this failure and subsequent significant loss? The Google/Motorola failure points to a crucial aspect of strategy: cultural fit. In this case, there was no strategic alignment between both companies to enable the synergy and reap the "best of both worlds" value. Google represented the Silicon Valley successful high-tech company, out-of-the-box thinking, innovative, exciting and cutting edge, while Motorola represented a deep and proud pioneering history and heritage, which is a completely different culture and mindset. So, both companies had very different styles, cultures, and ways of doing things. Moreover, Motorola employees were treated as "second-class citizens" in the Google hierarchy. They did not technically work for Google, but instead for "Motorola, a Google company"! There was no cultural fit and Google was not able (or did not attempt) to bridge the cultural gap and absorb Motorola's employees as Google employees and indoctrinate them into the "Google culture." Having these types of barriers and a resultant "us versus them" mentality between employees of both companies further deepens the cultural divide, and that is a recipe for disaster.

These "soft" things such as a company culture and "fit" are often not handled as top priorities in mergers and acquisitions and are relegated to lower levels of management to implement the integration of the two companies. Too often, in fact, they are considered just the mundane work of implementation, barely worthy of the attention of upper management, whose time is best spent on more important issues like financing or market positioning. However, as the old saying goes, the devil is in the details, and these sorts of cultural details can be the essence of strategic success. Without synergy, acquisitions fail to bring value. And, without some means of bridging the cultural divide between the combined organizational units, there is likely to be very little synergy.

Multi-Point Competition

Because a corporation consists of multiple business units, which compete in different competitive environments, it stands to reason that some corporations will have business units that compete in multiple yet similar business units. Indeed, this is actually quite common and for understandable reasons.

Consider that a business unit that is part of a larger corporation and that derives synergy from the corporation will likely have a substantial competitive advantage over any single business competitor. Think about just four firms: Microsoft, Apple,

Google, and Amazon. Each of these firms comes from a different starting core focus and are thought of primarily in different markets—Microsoft in operating system and business software, Apple in computers and phones, Google in search and advertising, and Amazon in retail. So, in this sense, they might not be immediately seen as competitors. However, they also overlap and compete fiercely in many different categories. Amazon, Microsoft, and Google are the three major competitors in cloud services. Apple, Microsoft, and Google compete in internet browsers. Microsoft has sought to compete with Google in search, and Amazon is now also competing in advertising with Google. Apple and Google compete in cell phones with the iPhone iOS and Android and their respective application stores dominating the mobile phone landscape. These two also have rival digital payment services. Apple, Microsoft, and Amazon compete in tablet devices. Microsoft also produces Office software that is critical to the wide acceptance of Apple's computers. Apple and Amazon compete in music streaming services. And all 4 compete in natural language artificial intelligence devices: Microsoft with Cortana, Apple with Siri, Google with Google assistant, and Amazon with Alexa. The fact that each of these firms has multiple business areas that provide them with advantages and synergies across domains not only allows them to compete with each other to a more or less effective degree in each domain but gives all of them advantages in every domain over other companies that are seeking to compete in just a single domain.

Multi-point competition is a complex but fascinating phenomenon that has been the subject of considerable academic research (Baum & Korn, 1996; Gimeno & Woo, 1996). One interesting observation from this research is a phenomenon called ***mutual forbearance*** (Karnani & Wernerfelt, 1985). Mutual forbearance occurs when firms, competing in multiple different markets, choose to compete less vigorously as a result of their broad interdependence. Increasing aggressiveness in one market could lead to increased competitive intensity across the full range of the different markets and product lines. As a result, the firms will often choose to forebear one another, rather than risk intensified competition that could hurt them all. The logic for this forbearance reflects a sort of competitive parity, where corporations have so much exposure and so much to risk across the breadth of their multiple business units that they choose to accommodate rather than to provoke their competitors.

Multi-point competition can also lead a corporation to remain in a business or an industry long after the attractiveness of that industry has faded. It may also lead a corporation to enter a business, less attractive than its own, as a way to defend against a potential competitor. Certainly, as business has grown increasingly global, there are more and more instances where firms bump into one another, through different product or geographic units. Thus, the strategist will want to be cognizant of the full range of implications of his or her strategic initiatives. What may seem a good idea for a business unit may well produce problems for the corporation. And what the corporation needs may not always be in the best interest of the business unit.

KEY TERMS

Business-level strategy is that part of a firm's strategy that focuses on how a single business or a single business unit will compete in its industry or business environment.

Conglomerate refers to a corporation that is highly diversified and involved in a number of unrelated businesses.

Corporate raider refers to a person who purchases or attempts to purchase a controlling interest in a company against the wishes of the current management. The raider will often then sell off the assets of the company and generate a substantial profit.

Diversification is a strategy for expanding organizational scope or reducing organizational risk by adding additional products, services, locations, or customers to a company's existing portfolio of offerings.

A **golden parachute** is a clause in an executive's contract specifying that he/she will receive large benefits in the event the company is acquired and the executive is terminated. These benefits can take the form of severance pay, bonuses, stock options, or some combination thereof.

Hostile takeover refers to a change in ownership that occurs against the wishes of the target company's management and board of directors.

Mode of entry refers to the way a firm enters a new country or place or business. For example, a firm can enter by exporting, licensing, joint venture, or direct investment.

Mutual forbearance is said to occur when rival firms engage in tacitly collusive or non-competitive actions across a range of common market interactions because of their mutual interdependence.

Net present value is the current value of an investment's future net cash flows, discounted by the effects of time and risk, minus the initial investment. A positive NPV suggests a good investment.

Poison pill refers to any tactic by a company designed to avoid a hostile takeover. For example, a firm may issue preferred stock, giving existing shareholders the right to redeem shares at a premium after a takeover.

Profit center refers to a business unit or department, within a larger corporation, that is treated as a distinct entity, with its own revenues, expenses, and profit.

Restructuring is the process of changing the way in which a firm is organized or arranged. This type of action is usually required when there are significant problems which are causing some financial harm and putting the overall business in jeopardy.

Strategic business units or SBUs are distinct and semi-autonomous units within a larger corporation. These units will often operate in their own industry, with their own business-level strategy and with full responsibility for their own revenues, costs, and profits.

Synergy refers to situations where different units cooperate to produce more than could be produced otherwise. Stated simply, synergy is said to occur when the whole is greater than the sum of the parts.

Time value refers to the current value of a sum of money to be received or paid at some time in the future, adjusted either for the growth that will occur through earnings or the discount taken to reflect opportunity costs.

QUESTIONS FOR REVIEW

1. What advantages and disadvantages can you see for Google transforming itself into Alphabet? Why did they make this transition?
2. What is the difference between corporate-level strategy and business-level strategy? What is the practical value in distinguishing between these two levels of the strategic process?
3. How is corporate strategy like managing a portfolio of stocks, bonds, and other investments? How is it different?
4. Research suggests that most corporate strategies fail to achieve the value that they were intended to produce. Why is success in corporate strategy so difficult and elusive?
5. Describe the 4 approaches to corporate strategy described in the chapter. What are the differences and similarities across these general approaches?
6. What is synergy, and how does it contribute to competitive advantage?
7. How does corporate strategy accentuate the value, rareness, inimitability, and sustainability of the firm's resources?
8. What is market selection and what are the positive and negative connotations associated with it?
9. Define multi-point competition. Why does it exist and how does it affect the strategies and competitive dynamics of the firms involved?

Chapter 8

Implementation, Adaptation, and Learning

BILLIONS SERVED

If good strategy is reflected in performance and performance over time, then few firms have had a better strategy over the years than McDonalds. The modern day company took shape in 1954 when Ray Croc teamed up with brothers Dick and

Mac McDonald to open the first location of the famous golden arches. By 1958, McDonalds had sold its 100 millionth hamburger. The stock went public in 1965, selling for $22.50 per share; by this time, there were over 500 locations across the U.S. Since those early years, McDonalds has grown and profited steadily, providing solid value for its customers, substantial wealth for its owners, and a wide variety of employment opportunities for it managers and employees. By 2019 McDonalds had nearly 38,000 locations in 120 countries worldwide, with system-wide revenues of over $86 billion and earnings of over $5.9 billion. Indeed, with over 767 million shares outstanding, McDonalds stock price ended 2018 at $177.57 per share. An investor who purchased 100 shares of the original offering in 1965 would have seen that investment increase to 74,360 shares, worth more than $12 million, by 2018. That investor would have also received dividends, which have been paid continuously since 1976. And this example applies only to investments in McDonalds corporate; many thousands of other investors became millionaires by investing in independent McDonalds franchises.

Yet, despite all of this long-term success, the ride has been bumpy, prompting speculation at different times that the firm's best days were in the past. For example, there have been any number of competitors who appeared for a time to be better positioned to the changing tastes and fashions of the day. Such was the case when Wendy's began offering a drive-through option or when Burger King began offering limited made-to-order service. More recently, competitors like Chick-fil-A, Subway, and Chipotle have promoted their products as healthy alternatives to the traditional offerings at McDonalds. And there have been a variety of other unorthodox challenges as well, such as when McDonalds came under fire from consumer groups for preparing food in advance and then packaging it in non-recyclable polystyrene containers. A similarly unusual challenge arose when Morgan Spurlock released the movie *Super Size Me*, criticizing McDonalds for its portion sizes, as well as for the high levels of fat and sodium in its products. McDonalds even suffered losses when episodes of food contamination struck other chains, such as Jack in the Box in 1993, creating a perception that hamburgers were unsafe.

And there were still other challenges as well. When Starbucks began offering greater variety in its food selections across its 11,000 stores, there was concern that McDonalds would suffer as consumers chose to move upscale for their breakfasts and midday snacks. Finally, rapid growth among independent "fast casual" restaurants has caused concern among investors that traditional, quick serve restaurants are becoming dinosaurs, with little growth potential and little upside for those seeking competitive returns.

Despite all of these different and various challenges, McDonalds continues to thrive. Indeed, one could be reminded of the famous quote, often attributed to Mark Twain, "the reports of my death have been greatly exaggerated." Competitors and activists, analysts, and professors have all reasoned at one time or another that McDonald's strategy was misaligned and out of touch with the environment, leading to speculation that its success was nearing an end. Yet, McDonalds continues to innovate and to maintain its position as the leader in the quick serve restaurant market, continuing to expand, continuing to deliver good value to its customers, and continuing to grow and profit as a result.

While this example may offer a number of significant lessons, perhaps none is more important than this: *strategy is ultimately about what you do to create value for your customers*. Competitors, activists, analysts, and the like are all important at some point. However, firms that stay connected to their customers, that continue to offer products and services that their customers value, and that do so at a profitable price will maintain their competitive advantage and as a result, continue to perform well. Recall from Chapter 1 that strategy may at times appear to be part plan, ploy, pattern, position, and perspective. However, what makes all of these facets of strategy meaningful is their link, whether immediate or eventual, to action. A ploy, for instance, would have little value if there were not some action implied, so as to misdirect the competition. Similarly, plans are important because of their implication for action; otherwise, they become little more than sources of frustration and cynicism. Strategy then is ultimately about action, about doing things that create value and so enable competitive advantage. Moreover, because the things that create value and enable competitive advantage will change along with the environment, so too must a firm's actions change as necessary to stay fit to the environment.

Those two issues, fit and change, are the subjects of this chapter. Moreover, throughout the discussion of fit and change, a parallel and important distinction will become salient. That distinction is between the long term and the short term and the different types of thinking and actions that good strategists will use to prepare for and perform well in both. For now, it is enough to understand that a short-term focus will often be at odds with a longer-term focus. In the same way, long-term thinking will often conflict with shorter-term realities. Thus, there is an inevitable tension between the two, just as there will an inevitable tension between the principles of fit and change. One is about immediacy and efficiency; the other is about flexibility and the creation of options. However, both are essential to success over time.

IMPLEMENTATION

As discussed in Chapter 3, implementation is an integral part of strategic management and is defined as the deployment and operation of organizational structures, facilities, human resources, and support systems as necessary to bring a strategy to fruition. The guiding principle of strategy implementation goes back to the work of Alfred Chandler (1962) and the idea that structure should follow strategy. Structure, in this sense, means all of the systems, processes, and functions of the organization. Structures take shape according to the design of strategy. Put simply, if strategy is the plan then implementation is the execution.

This distinction between planning and execution or between what theorists typically call formulation and implementation is both intuitive and seductively simple. It stands to reason that some planning should precede action and that resource deployments should be guided by some deliberate purpose. Over the years, though, implementation has come to be seen by students and practitioners as being less and less "strategic." Scholars spend much more time researching the analytical and creative aspects of formulation than the nuts and bolts of implementation. New managers are often encouraged by senior executives to think big and to think long term and so not to confuse strategy with tactics. The unfortunate result of this is that both students and managers often view implementation as less meaningful; implementation is what comes after strategy making and is the work of others, somewhere lower in the organization.

The reality though is that formulation and implementation are intertwined in a very complex way. Each impacts the other and each exerts great influence over the performance of the firm. Consider that a well-formulated strategy should specify what a firm intends to do and how it intends to do it. However, if that is all there is then nothing ever actually happens. Something tangible must occur; some action must be taken, someone must do something for the intentions of a strategy to become a reality and so have their intended effects on customers, competitors, and competitive advantage. Implementation is that something; thus, implementation is a key to strategic success.

In an insightful article, Mintzberg (1987) described strategy using the metaphor of a potter and a lump of clay. As Mintzberg explained, the potter starts with a plan for what the clay will become. Of course, the clay is unaffected by the plans. Rather, it is the actions of the potter that shape the clay. Just as importantly, those actions also lead the potter to adjust her plans. If the clay has a flaw or if some accident leads to a surprise discovery, the potter may reconsider her plans and undertake something different than what she intended originally. By illustration, Mintzberg makes the point that there is always an initial plan, what we would call the formal strategy. Nevertheless, the reality of the outcome emerges from a process of doing and learning. The clay is shaped by the potter but the potter also responds to the clay, acting to convert her plans into reality and learning how best to achieve her objectives, given the details of the situation as they unfold.

While a bit esoteric, this picture is still closer to the reality than most textbook depictions of formulation and implementation. Indeed, the illustration makes especially clear two important points. First, implementation requires some action or some change of assets from one purpose or state to another. Plans aside, the potter only gets the outcomes she wants by getting her hands dirty; it is action then that converts plans to reality. Second, strategy is simply a means to an end; it is not an end unto itself. No one should be surprised when the strategy changes, most especially the strategist. Rather, good strategists expect it. It has been reported that Mike Tyson, the famous and former world champion boxer once said, "Everyone has a plan until they get hit." His quote reflects the famous insight offered by Prussian General Helmuth von Moltke, who observed that no battle plan survives contact with the enemy. No one can anticipate every contingency and every change in circumstance. Instead, good strategists must prepare to respond as needed as the situation changes.

Thus, if strategic management is all about performance, then good strategists should be obsessed with implementation. Implementation is how plans are converted to reality and how firms interact with the environment so as to learn about new opportunities and threats. Going back to the example, McDonald's has created a record of sustained success by doing things that actually deliver value to its customers, that lower costs for its franchisees, and that drive traffic to its stores. Most of these things resulted from learning, either from customers or competitors. That learning then had to be converted into the sorts of action that produced real and tangible results. Redesigning facilities and menus to compete with new entrants are real actions requiring specific and new investments and changes in procedures. The initiative to build and market the McCafe offerings in the restaurants required layout and pricing changes, new marketing campaigns, and the addition of new equipment. Over time there have been many such changes, some of which resulted from creativity and innovation, some of which were simply responses to the marketplace. All of the changes though required some new or different action, yet all were driven by the desire to build and sustain competitive advantage.

Another Level of Fit

As discussed in Chapter 3, success is a reflection of fit. In that context, fit meant alignment or congruence between the competitive environment and the strategy. For example, Ryanair is a discount airline, with a fleet of more than 450 aircraft, flying more than 2,400 flights a day to 83 different locations in Europe and North Africa. With high consumer satisfaction, steadily increasing traffic, and a history of strong profitability, Ryanair's strategy of being the lowest-cost and most reliable discount carrier in Europe seems to be working well. It works though because it fits the environment. That Ryanair is successful tells us for instance that there is a portion of the market for air travel that is highly elastic. It also tells us that there is a substantial and underserved group of travelers who were either unwilling or able to fly with other non-discount carriers. Ryanair charges for things like luggage, priority boarding, and refreshments in flight. That passenger traffic remains strong despite these charges suggests that most customers are willing to accept them, provided that the savings are passed back in the form of low ticket prices. For now, at least, the success of Ryanair in this market and at this time is undeniable. And that success is the best evidence of the fit between the strategy and the environment.

But there is another level of fit. Here, the idea is the same but the pieces are different. This second tier is the fit between strategy and all of the elements of the organization's structure and operations. Different strategies require different types of organizational structure and action. It was in observing the relationship between how strategies evolved and how that evolution necessitated changes in structure that Chandler (1962) reasoned that structure followed strategy. Other early organizational theorists like Lawrence and Lorsch (1967) and Burns and Stalker (1961) drew similar conclusions from their own observations. Organizations that performed well over time were organized and operated in ways that were fit to their strategies. The notion of fit then applies at two levels: the environment, and the strategy first, but also at the level of the strategy and the firm's operations. Incongruence anywhere along the chain threatens the ability of a firm to deliver the value that customers want. Thus, incongruence anywhere along this chain threatens performance.

In the abstract language of theory, this notion seems more complicated than it need be. So, to illustrate by example, return to the case of Ryanair. Ryanair's strategy of low cost and reliability is well formulated and fit to its environment. Thus, to succeed, Ryanair needs to implement its strategy as designed; in essence, it needs to convert its plans into reality. The question is, how?

Using the example, it is clear that one imperative of this low-cost, high-accessibility strategy is a route structure that facilitates high load factors and short turnaround times. Over its history, Ryanair has built a route structure precisely for those purposes. It serves major cities or population centers with heavy traffic and little surplus capacity. This facilitates full planes, which lowers cost per unit. Moreover, the route and ticketing system operates mostly on a point-to-point, single-segment basis. There are few connecting flights and baggage is priced per segment; this reduces the opportunity and the company's responsibility for missed connections. Planes are loaded at the point of origin and unloaded at the destination, with little accounting for connections. This simplifies the scheduling and servicing on the ground, lowering administrative costs, reducing risk and increasing reliability. It also facilitates faster turnaround by reducing system-wide delays, allowing the planes to spend more time in the air, making more trips per day, than the competition. This increases asset utilization, further enabling lower ticket prices.

Ryanair is decidedly no frills; snacks and beverages are sold, not given away, and unless a customer pays extra for premium seating, there are no classes of service. This minimizes time at the gate, facilitating reliability and asset utilization. The limited cabin service also fits with the many short and intermediate haul flights in the route system. The fleet consists only of variants of the Boeing 737. While this plane is efficient for short- and medium-range routes, the real advantage comes in having only one type of aircraft; there is only one set of maintenance routines, mechanics, and tools needed. There is also only one procedure for servicing the aircraft at the gate. Again, this facilitates lower costs, quicker turns, and greater reliability. Ryanair uses discount prices to actively encourage online booking and check-in, so as to reduce staffing and administrative costs.

Even its indirect activities reflect its strategy. In the case of marketing, for instance, Ryanair attracts customers by positioning itself as an alternative to the more established, major carriers like British Airways or Lufthansa. To build awareness and position itself as the counter to these established carriers, Ryanair uses quirky and unorthodox advertising, at times courting trouble for its racy and offbeat campaigns. But this approach facilitates the purpose, leveraging an unorthodox strategy while building an "us against them" reputation. Finally, even its employment practices reinforce the unique and low-cost strategy. Ryanair builds performance incentives into its salary structure, encouraging its employees to find new savings and efficiencies. It also uses its strategy in recruiting in an effort to attract workers suited to the culture, thereby reducing the costs associated with staffing.

When considered in detail, it is easy to see why Ryanair is successful. Its strategy is well fit to its position in the marketplace. Beyond that, though, the organization itself is well fit to the strategy. Where that sort of multi-level fit exists, good performance follows. It is important to remember two things though. First, the principle of fit goes both ways. While effective for this strategy and context, these structures and practices would work less well elsewhere. Indeed, the very same structures and practices would likely be less effective if employed by Lufthansa, because Lufthansa's strategy and competitive market are fundamentally different. Second, implementation works through a combination of elements. There is no single part of Ryanair's implementation that carries the load, no single facet of the operation that is by itself the key to competitive advantage. This echoes the point made in Chapter 5 that competitive advantage emerges from a complex sequence of actions and events.

McKinsey 7-S Model

Notwithstanding that complexity, though, the example serves to illustrate the importance of fit between strategy and the various levers of implementation. Figure 8.1 is meant to reinforce the point again. Figure 8.1 depicts the McKinsey 7-S model. Developed in the late 1970s by a group of consultants at McKinsey & Co. (Peters et al.,1980; Pascale & Athos, 1981), the 7-S model is ultimately a depiction of how an organization works. The categories represent the various facets of a firm that are likely to affect its performance. The model also serves to remind us that all of these 7 factors are connected to one another, either through direct causal linkages or through indirect consequences. And so the model illustrates how performance is attributable to more than just a good strategy, more than just good human resource practices or good logistics. Rather, performance results from all of these things, working together in combination, to produce value for the customer.

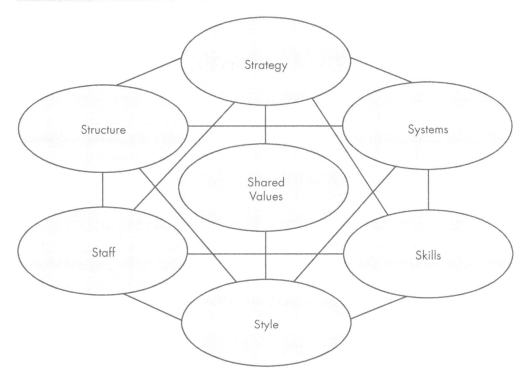

FIGURE 8.1 The McKinsey 7-S Model

While robust in its implications, the model is too often dismissed for its simplicity. In reality, it is a powerful analytical guide that can help to diagnose dysfunction in a firm or to design structures and practices to complement a strategy. Its use involves some intuition and judgment and can at times seem tedious and unstructured. It involves working through a variety of linkages which are often straightforward and intuitive in isolation but that can yield indirect effects that are subtle and highly complex. Overlooking these indirect effects can lead managers to decisions about structures or systems that seem reasonable and appropriate at a high level but that can produce unintended and indirect effects detrimental to success.

Such was the case at Wells Fargo, which was fined $185 million in 2016 and which paid nearly $3 billion to settle various civil and criminal charges through 2018 (Tayan, 2019). What led to these enormous fines and judgments, and what was at the root of the problem for Wells Fargo? Well, like most complex stories, this one had complex origins. In the early 2000s, Wells Fargo was among the larger and stronger banks in the country. Following its acquisition of Wachovia in 2008, Wells Fargo became the 3rd largest bank in the U.S. With assets of nearly $1.4 trillion, Wells Fargo was a leader in retail and investment banking, insurance, and commercial and consumer finance services, with more than 9,000 offices and 12,000 ATMs.

In the years following the acquisition, and with the banking industry emerging from the financial crisis, Wells Fargo grew rapidly and earnings soared from $7.9 billion in 2009 to more than $21 billion in 2014. Along with the strong financial performance, the stock price soared as well, from $18.50 per share in 2009 to $58 per share in 2015.

Behind the success was an aggressive company culture that set ambitious targets and that emphasized business development and sales. Given the context, all of that seemed rather appropriate. After all, the market was ripe with opportunity; asset prices were down and the markets were looking for strong leadership following the crash and subsequent downturn in 2008 and 2009. Debt levels were down nationwide and, as the economy began to recover, there was capacity to borrow and grow. So, a bank with a strong balance sheet, with a broadly diversified product portfolio, and with a newly expanded market following a major acquisition should have been in a position to capitalize on the timing and the opportunity by moving quickly and aggressively to sell new business and grow. And so, Wells Fargo set aggressive sales targets for the people in its divisions, including retail banking. Management focused increasingly on cross-selling of products and translated its goals into various incentives and sanctions for meeting or failing to meet the targets. Meanwhile, the company's culture was something of an echo chamber. Wells Fargo was decentralized and often listed among Gallup's list of "great places to work." Senior management consisted of long-time insiders, with the CEOs various direct reports averaging more than 25 years of Wells Fargo experience. The team had confidence in one another and in the practices of the various operating units.

On the surface, all of this seemed quite reasonable and consistent with the bank's overall strategy. The unintended consequence though was the practice of opening accounts in customer names without those customers' knowledge. This practice allowed the employees and managers to receive incentive payments, often as high as 20% of their salaries, and to generate the required number of cross-sold products, including mortgages, consumer loans, credit card applications, and deposit accounts. That fueled growth and added to the database of customer information, which allowed the bank to better asses risk exposure and build on the broad portfolio of the bank's products. Moreover, because of the decentralized and trusting culture, initial hints and rumors about the problem were largely ignored. Senior management considered the stories to be isolated and so tried to wall off the issue by firing a small number of directly implicated employees and then "circling the wagons" in an effort to protect the brand.

As history shows, however, the scandal was much broader and more systemic than originally understood. Ultimately, more than 5,200 employees were fired and $5.2 million in fees were returned to customers who had been fraudulently charged; investigations showed that more than 3.5 million accounts had been created without customer knowledge or approval. But the real damage came to the bank's reputation and structure. As noted, regulatory fines and lawsuit settlements cost the bank billions. CEO John Stumpf was forced to resign and to forfeit $41 million outstanding deferred compensation. The head of retail banking, Carrie Tolstedt, was fired for cause and the bank revoked over $47 million in planned compensation as part of her retirement. Congress held public hearings into the case, and over the course of the long, slow investigation, the stock price fell by roughly 20%, from a high of nearly $58 in 2015 to a low of $44 in late 2016.

What this example illustrates is how even good strategy, when matched to the wrong set of organizational systems, practices, and process, can produce bad results. Indeed, Wells Fargo gave every indication of a well-run organization, with a strong culture, with reliable systems and practices, and with a management team committed to doing the right thing for the customers, the bank, and one another. The problem though was not in the various components of strategy implementation; rather, it was in the interrelationships of those components and the unexpected consequences that they produced. The example then serves as a reminder that the 7-S model should be applied in a thorough and detailed way, with full consideration given to the realities of each relationship, direct and indirect.

It should also be acknowledged that while the model is powerful in its implications, there is nothing magical about the actual items. Indeed, the number of items and the items themselves were likely chosen intentionally to create the alliteration, which helped to make the model familiar and easily remembered. These items though are just broad categories of the types of functions and actions that occur in almost every organization. There is certainly some overlap between them and certainly different terms that would work better for different organizations. What is important though is that the model represents a robust representation of the activities, characteristics, and functions that are necessary for strategy to become reality.

Structure, for instance, refers to the way work is organized and the way that products, processes, and information flow through the firm. For Ryanair, structure includes things like the route system, the terminals and ground infrastructure, and the aircraft inventory. Systems include things like the online reservation system; the flight operations system, which manages the planes and routing; and the procurement systems that deliver fuel to the planes and that schedule the flight crews and maintenance. Staff includes the people from the managers, to the pilots, to the baggage handlers, while skills include all the abilities of those people, the attributes that go into their selection and training, and the institutional memory of how things get done. Every strategy requires certain skills for its effective implementation and those skills are a reflection of the people the firm hires, as well as the training and development it provides. Style refers to the personality of the organization. Every firm has a personality. Ryanair has a very clear style that reinforces its strategy and that is recognizable to customers. Moreover, it is a style that should be cultivated intentionally and deliberately as necessary to support the strategy and the other elements of the model. The final element is shared values. Shared values are also called culture and are simply the core of what the people in the firm believe. An often-heard quote, of unclear origin, is that culture is simply the sum of "how we do things around here." At Ryanair, there is a strong shared value of low cost; of being distinct from other, more traditional carriers; and of making air travel a fun and easy experience. To create value for customers, given the choices, alternatives, and expectations created by the environment, and to produce good performance, these 7 elements must complement one another as well as the strategy.

As a result, whether building new strategy, optimizing existing strategy, or diagnosing poor performance, the 7-S model can provide a clear and cohesive guide. A good strategist will review continuously the linkages and relationships depicted in the model, in an effort to improve, to identify potential problems, or to work through the implications of changes in strategy. For McDonalds, the strategy has always been to be the option of first choice for consumers searching for a quick and inexpensive and yet reliably tasty meal. To facilitate that strategy, there must be the right locations, the right menu, and the right procurement and preparation procedures all matched to the right marketing, financial, and HR systems. As the environment changes and as customer tastes change along with it, so must the menu change as well. Changing the menu though will necessitate changes in procurement and preparation procedures, as well as in the marketing and store layout. When all of these parts work together, good performance follows. Conversely, when performance is poor the cause can usually be traced to some inconsistency or lack of fit in what the firm seeks to do and what it is actually doing.

In concluding the discussion of fit and of the 7-S model, then, two issues need to be reinforced and especially well understood. The first is that many of the important determinants of performance are subtle and indirect, embedded in the various linkages among the elements of the model. Thus, 7-S analysis can be complex and even tedious, requiring detailed evaluation, imagination, and expert judgment.

Blockbuster video was once a stalwart of growth and earnings, with more than 9,000 retail locations worldwide, millions of customers, 84,000 employees, and a massive library of videos. It was founded in 1985 and by 1994 was valued at $8.4 billion. Yet, despite the strength of its brand and market position, Blockbuster began to fade; growth had peaked, the brand was growing stale, and earnings began to decline. By 2010, the company could no longer service its billion-dollar debt and so filed for bankruptcy. By 2011, the brand, along with the thousands of stores, was largely gone. Many attribute the failure of Blockbuster to the rise of Netflix and the failure of Blockbuster to capitalize on the emergence of streaming video. But such observations miss the point. Given its strong position, its experience and connections in the video industry, and its awareness of the emerging new technologies and competitors, the real question is why Blockbuster failed to adapt. Why didn't they simply invest when Netflix CEO Reed Hastings offered the opportunity? Why didn't they foresee a backlash from the market when late fees reached nearly 20% of total revenues?

The answer is that the real problems are never quite the result of just one or two elements working in isolation. Blockbuster certainly wanted to maintain a dominant position in the market. However, simply launching an on-demand video service might not have been sufficient to make that desire a reality. Other issues would have to be addressed as well. For example, what would the company do with all those retail locations and the associated leases? What about the videos themselves, along with the infrastructure dedicated to housing and shipping them, as well as the implications to the company's balance sheet should they change their asset mix suddenly? While they knew how to market and price video rentals, how would that model work for streaming video content? Was top management sufficiently well prepared and connected that it could solve the marketing problems, along with the licensing questions of streaming video content quickly? The chances are good that multiple roadblocks and shortfalls in numerous areas throughout the organization undermined Blockbuster's strategy and success. Thus, just as competitive advantage is embedded in a complex and interacting set of resources and actions, so does effective implementation depend upon a combination of events and factors. The challenge then is to understand all of those linkages and their implications and to use that understanding to create a firm that can deliver on the promise of its strategy.

The second thing to remember then is that because of all this complexity, fit can always be improved. Just as competitive advantage can always be strengthened, so too can the various connections across the firm be strengthened. Indeed, one way to put relentless pressure on the competition is by continuously tightening the fit among the elements of the 7-S model. Ryanair is constantly looking for ways to make its operations more efficient, so that it can further lower ticket prices or provide better service. Understanding that its market is highly elastic, Ryanair understands that its customers will continue to buy only for so long as Ryanair continues to be the lowest-cost alternative. Thus, it is always interested in ways to turn planes quicker, to move passengers and luggage more efficiently, and to reduce the overhead associated with technology, HR, and infrastructure. Thus, it is constantly reviewing the elements of the 7-S model, looking for new opportunities to reduce costs, to increase speed and reliability, and to better support the strategy through tightening the fit inside the organization.

SHORT-TERM FIT, LONG-TERM FLEXIBILITY

As with most things, though, it is never quite as simple as even this. Indeed, there are subtle trade-offs and hidden consequences in this principle of fit that have vexed managers and academics for years. As recounted earlier in the text, history is full of examples where firms that once held dominant positions in their industries and that once performed well above the average somehow managed to slip and lose their advantages to unforeseen or upstart competitors. These firms often were the best positioned, with the best fit both internally and externally. Yet, their competition found a way to overtake them, to lure away their customers and, in some cases, like Blockbuster, to drive them out of business. Given this, it has been argued that strategic success is somehow paradoxical and difficult if not impossible to sustain over time (Amason & Mooney, 2008; Miller, 1992).

The idea that performance is somehow paradoxical was introduced in Chapter 2. However, a full discussion of the topic has waited until now because the issues are most clear when viewed in the context of implementation. The connection among these issues, strategy implementation, and the paradoxical nature of performance mirrors the relationship between short-term and long-term thinking. Often, doing what is necessary for the short term means sacrificing some flexibility in the long term. Alternatively, building for the long term may involve forgoing some benefits in the short term. A good example of this is research and development spending. Most investments in R&D constitute expenses in the current period, yet the benefits of those expenses are not likely to be realized until much later. And those future benefits are speculative, involving some risk and uncertainty. Indeed, research shows that R&D spending does not guarantee future profitability (Foster, 2003). Given the delay and the uncertainty in the benefits, it stands to reason that financial pressure would often lead to reduced R&D spending (Demirag, 1995). Managers facing intense competition or serious financial distress will find it difficult to justify speculative expenses like R&D and so often pare them back, to conserve cash and address more immediate problems.

Of course, such decisions, while potentially necessary in the short term, may have dire consequences in the longer term. Indeed, *The Wall Street Journal* reports how many executives in 2009 struggled to maintain R&D investments, fearful that cutting research and development would leave them with obsolete products or technologies and poorly positioned to compete in the future. History shows that many major innovations, things like the iPod and iTunes, or like the composite turbine blades in the GE90 turbofan engine, resulted from research and development that occurred during economic downturns. Given the lesson of examples such as these, many consultants and academics have advised that firms should be most aggressive during periods of economic distress, to seize the initiative and outmaneuver the competition (Rhoades & Stelter, 2009). Such advice, though, while easy to give can be difficult to take when sales are dropping, cash flow is tight, and the future is uncertain. After all, investing for the long term makes little sense if you cannot survive past the short term.

Thus, the conundrum between maximizing returns based upon current resources and capabilities and creating value for the future by investing in new resources and capabilities is a familiar one. It is also a problem with no simple solution. Certainly, there are anecdotes where speculative investments, made against a backdrop of pressing and immediate needs, produced great innovation and success. But such investments involve great uncertainty which can place a firm at risk. On the other hand, there are just as many stories of firms that missed opportunities by playing it safe. Worried about cash flow and profits, managers stood pat, only to later watch as competitors overtook their market with new products and services. So, there is no formula, no rule by which managers can know exactly how to balance these two imperatives. Nevertheless, they both must be served; firms must do what is necessary to profit and thrive in the short term. However, they must also invest in new resources and capabilities if they hope to survive in the long term.

The Paradox of Success

The dilemma maps onto two specific challenges in strategy implementation. The first is to make sure the organization fits the strategy as it exists in the current competitive environment. As discussed and illustrated earlier, that involves aligning the elements of the 7-S model, both to the strategy and to one another. But more than just that, it also involves continuously fine-tuning and refining the alignment, looking for opportunities to improve, to tighten the fit, and to strengthen the competitive advantage of the firm. The second challenge though is to look beyond the current strategy and the current environment in an effort to build new capabilities and new strategies for the future. As discussed in Chapter 4, environmental change is inevitable. Thus, all firms must change too by developing new assets, new resources, and new capabilities if they hope to sustain a competitive advantage over time.

But there is a problem: these two processes, strengthening fit in the present and developing new capabilities for the future, are largely at odds with one another. Tightening the fit between the current strategy and the various parts of the organization requires eliminating unnecessary effort, reinforcing successful routines and practices, and the relentless pursuit of efficiency and consistency. Strengthening fit means identifying and reinforcing the practices that contribute to competitive advantage, while eliminating virtually everything else. Unfortunately, though, building new capabilities requires a different type of effort altogether. Building new capabilities requires experimenting with new, unfamiliar, and often unproven practices. It requires speculative investment in the development of new ideas and novel resources that may one day prove valuable but that is likely to provide little immediate benefit.

The challenge of improving fit involves a short-term focus and an immediate set of imperatives and rewards. Increasing efficiency and consistency in structures and systems can yield all sorts of benefits in areas like the costs of current products and services, the speed of moving products to market, and the ability to measure and respond to customer feedback. These are the sorts of benefits seen in the example of Ryanair. Meanwhile, cultivating future resources and capabilities involves a longer-term focus and a less tangible set of imperatives and rewards. Environmental change is uncertain. Thus, managers are unsure which capabilities to develop or which resources to acquire or divest; this was the challenge faced by Blockbuster. New products and services can fail to achieve all that was hoped and new technologies can fail to deliver all that was envisioned. Building for the future then will involve investing in some hits and some misses. Across a range of speculative initiatives, some will succeed while others will not. Of course, finding those winning new products, services, or technologies will mean enduring the losses and frustrations associated with some failures. While necessary for innovation and development, those losses will place a real drag on short-term fit and efficiency. Speculative and uncertain investments in the future will divert energy and effort away from the current competitive advantage, hampering competitiveness and fit in the present, as well as earnings and stock performance. However, while eliminating speculative and uncertain initiatives can improve short-term fit and performance, it can also leave the firm unable to adapt and respond to the future.

Exacerbating the problem is a subtle dynamic known as **path dependence** (Nelson & Winter, 1982). The basic idea of path dependence is simple: current decisions reflect decisions made in the past. The idea is illustrated in a quote by Winston Churchill, who once observed "we shape our buildings, thereafter they shape us." The point is simple and powerful; a building's design and construction reflect the intentions of its builders. The size, layout, shape, even the placement and orientation reflect the purposes for which the building was built. Once constructed, though, the building becomes a fixture that must be accommodated by the future plans of others. In essence, once built, the building begins to shape the actions of those in and around it. The builders then establish a path that is followed long after the actual design and construction are forgotten.

Translating this pattern to human behavior, it is understandable that people capitalize on experience and familiarity, to economize on effort and reduce uncertainty and risk, by following established patterns and precedents. A number of psychological and organizational processes, like **problemistic search**, **satisficing**, **filtering**, and **framing** (Cyert & March, 1963; Dutton et al., 1983) combine to produce this tendency. But the pattern will often produce suboptimal decisions and ultimately poor performance. Beyond this, though, what is so vexing is that path dependence often masquerades as sensible and reasonable, even strategic and data-driven decision making. Indeed, in the normal course of managing it makes good sense to follow established precedents, to rely on proven practices, and to stick to familiar frameworks. By so doing, we reduce uncertainty, increase efficiency, and promote reliability and consistency. However, this sort of thinking increases path dependence, reinforcing the status quo and limiting the consideration of options and alternatives.

Paradoxically, then, managers can seek to maximize fit and efficiency, doing what seems right at each and every step and making decisions based on the best examples and data available in the context of the current strategy and environment. And yet, in so doing, they can create and reinforce a process that, over time, will produce suboptimal decisions that can leave them unable to effectively compete in the future. This phenomenon has contributed to a number of surprising missteps by well-known firms. Microsoft, for example, despite its great technical expertise and overwhelming financial strength, has a history of missing opportunities identified by its competitors.

Consider the fact that Microsoft dominated the computer software business for two decades. It produced extraordinary levels of value and cash flow and so it could afford the absolute best in engineering talent and in research and development facilities. It could build and test prototypes on an almost unlimited scale, acquire most any new technology it deemed worthy, and push new products through the distribution channels better than virtually any competitor. Yet Microsoft, despite beginning to develop many of the technologies we see today, missed multiple opportunities to capitalize on their dominant resources. Think Kindle or iPad; Microsoft built a prototype e-reader in 1998 but decided not to market it. Or consider Internet Explorer, even with its strong legacy position and built-in familiarity by being pre-installed on Windows machines, IE lost market share to Firefox and Chrome. Moving away from computers, take the market for smartwatches, which is now dominated by Apple and Samsung; Microsoft developed a smartwatch product called the SPOT (smart personal objects technology) in 2002, but discontinued the initiative in 2009. How much market share, market opportunity, and market value could Microsoft have generated had it stuck with these investments or had it foreseen their application and attractiveness?

The pattern though is less about reluctance on the part of Microsoft than it is about the success of a business model based mostly on preloaded operating systems and applications. This business model has served Microsoft so well over the years that is has become central to its strategy and culture. In essence, Microsoft's past decisions and practices constrained its vision, its actions, and its perception of the environment. Now, think for a moment about how pervasive this phenomenon really is. As described earlier, it is the same pattern that led Blockbuster to reject an opportunity to partner with the upstart Netflix on streaming video.

Indeed, the effects of this phenomenon echo throughout the history of many leading companies. Dell computers was something of an upstart in the mid 1980s, but with the growing accessibility of the internet and desire for many to buy direct online, Dell created a new business model and by 2008 dominated the industry, with nearly 25% of the market. A decade later, though, Dell's market share is roughly 17% worldwide; more troubling though is that the market for personal computers overall is shrinking. Competition has cut into profitability, and Dell has few strong entrants in the market for mobile devices. Sony is another example. Throughout the 1980s and 1990s, the Sony Walkman was as ubiquitous as the iPad is today. Over the 30-year period in which it was marketed, Sony sold more than

400 million Walkmans; the name itself was even included in the *Oxford English Dictionary*. By 2011, though, the Walkman was gone and the market had shifted completely. Newer technologies and products, made and marketed by firms like LG, Samsung, and Apple, had become the industry standards and Sony had shifted its focus to gaming and movies.

The pattern is pervasive and can be seen in a variety of different examples. Industry leaders like RIM (creator of the Blackberry), Toys "R" Us, and Yahoo! missed opportunities in technology, product, and market, that were seized by new competitors with names like Apple, Walmart, Amazon, Facebook, and Google. Firms like Ryanair and Southwest gained their footholds because established incumbents like Lufthansa, American, and British Airways chose to reduce their coverage areas, leaving underserved gaps in the market. And dozens of beverages, with names like LaCroix, Topo Chico, Sparkling Ice, and Zevia have emerged as consumer tastes have evolved away from the traditional sodas that dominated the market for years.

Of course, change is constant and inevitable, but that is not really the lesson. Rather, the lesson is that, often, the leading firms actually create the gaps and opportunities that give rise to their competitors, by doing things like increasing operational efficiency, consolidating market share, and pricing to increase margins and maximize returns. As the earlier examples illustrate, well-managed and successful firms often make conscious and rational decisions to tighten fit and to leverage their strong positions in an effort to reinforce an existing competitive advantage. In so doing, however, these firms overlook new and emerging products, technologies, and business models that may later prove a substantial threat.

Such is the case in the music industry where the RIAA (Recording Industry Association of America) has spent years fighting to protect their revenues and profits from the threat posed by online music downloading. While some of these downloads may be illegitimate and even illegal, no one can deny that the technology that made them possible has revolutionized the way consumers think about and acquire music. Moreover, it is all but certain that whatever the future of the industry may be, the trend is towards reduced market power and lower revenues and profits for the major recording labels like EMI, Sony, and Warner. It also seems clear that, barring some significant change of heart and strategy, these incumbent firms are not likely to be the ones to transform the marketplace and lead the industry into the future by capitalizing on the new and revolutionary technologies.

Exploitation Versus Experimentation

This tendency for strong and established firms to look inward and focus on ways to strengthen their current advantage while failing to develop new products and processes for the future was noted by scholars (Hedberg et al., 1976). It has often been called the **curse of incumbency**. Incumbent firms are typically larger and more bureaucratic than their smaller and more entrepreneurial competitors. As a result, they may be slower and less flexible, with more vested in the continuation of the status quo than newer rivals. Larger and more successful will naturally have an **inertia** that smaller, newer, and less successful firms do not have. While providing some advantages, the size and tradition of these large incumbents can also prove to be a liability over time, as they can often restrict creativity and the creation of new options.

One way that size and tradition limit creativity and flexibility is by influencing the way that managers frame and make decisions. Indeed, researchers have noted how success can create a sense of creeping defensiveness in the minds of top managers (Amason & Mooney, 2008; Fredrickson & Iaquinto, 1989). To understand this tendency, consider this principle; the more successful a strategy is, the less attractive any alternative strategy will appear in comparison to it. The analogy of picking low-hanging fruit is appropriate here. It is quite natural that so long as there is low-hanging fruit available, no one will want to invest additional energy trying to pick the harder-to-reach fruit at the top of the tree. Rather, a sensible person would make that extra effort only after the easily picked fruit has been taken. Managers often view alternatives to a successful strategy in much the same way. The current strategy is familiar, well understood, and easily implemented. Any alternative to that current strategy will be more difficult, involving change, additional effort, and the risk of failure. So as long as that current strategy is successful, there is a tendency to continue exploiting it, rather than exert time and effort looking for something else. Over time, as new alternatives emerge in the form of new products, markets, technologies, and business models, managers will begin to view those alternatives as threats to the status quo, rather than as opportunities for learning, innovation, and change.

This phenomenon relates to **prospect theory** (Kahneman & Tversky, 1979), which deals with decision making and risk, and the effects of context on the evaluation of alternatives. At the heart of prospect theory is an S-shaped value function (see Figure 8.2). This function depicts the values associated with all the potential outcomes to a decision, ranging from large losses to large gains. The first and most important thing to note about the function is that it is not linear. As discussed in Chapter 2, while outcomes are typically quantified in standardized units (such as U.S. dollars for instance), the actual values associated with different outcomes can be quite different. For example, a firm like Johnson & Johnson, that is accustomed to profits in the hundreds of millions of dollars, would be disappointed in an annual profit of a mere $1 million. Yet, some other firm, with a small operation or a history of losses, might be thrilled with a profit of $1 million. Thus, where the firm starts affects how it values the outcomes. This starting point is the reference point on the figure. This reference point moves based upon historical precedent and future aspirations. The higher the reference point, the more difficult it is to have outcomes that feel like gains and the easier it is to have outcomes that feel like losses. In the

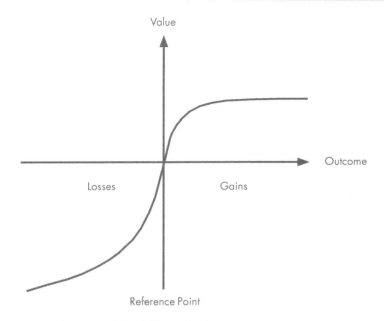

Value

Outcome

Losses

Gains

Reference Point

FIGURE 8.2 Prospect Theory and the S-Shaped Value

world of sports, for instance, teams that are used to winning, like the New York Yankees, have little patience for even modest performance. Because the reference point is so high, anything short of winning the pennant feels like a disappointment.

The second important characteristic of the value function is its asymmetric S-shape. This shape suggests two things. The first is that beyond some point, marginal gains and losses become increasingly less important. For example, in the early years, each new location was very important to McDonalds, affecting growth and profitability significantly. As McDonalds grew large and successful, though, the value of each additional new store grew increasingly small. In the same way, losses can seem devastating at first. When a firm fails to meet sales or earnings projections for instance, analysts and investors react quickly and negatively, selling the stock and depressing the price. Over time, though, as the firm continues to sustain losses, the effect diminishes; losses cease to be a surprise and come to be expected. At that point, the value or significance of each marginal dollar lost is low.

The second important implication is that, near the center, where the outcomes are nearest to the reference point, people will work harder to avoid a loss than to achieve a gain of similar size. Kahneman and Tversky (1979) confirmed this across a large number of observations and experiments. In case after case, the research revealed a tendency to safeguard against losses before pursuing gains. What this showed was that for a manager near his or her reference point, if given a choice between making $750,000 but potentially losing $500,000, versus making only $250,000 but potentially losing nothing, managers will frequently choose to make less if that choice also shelters them against the loss. In essence, most managers will work harder to avoid a loss of some amount than they will work to achieve a gain of the same amount. The only time that is not true is when they are so far below the reference point that additional losses seem unimportant. At that point, there is an incentive to risk even a great deal, in an effort to produce even a small turnaround in performance.

Taking together the effects of incumbency with the tendencies illustrated by prospect theory, it is easy to see why success can be so difficult to sustain. Indeed, it may well be that as firms become established, large, and successful they are, without knowing it, also sowing the seeds of their own demise. Firms and managers can grow dependent on the strategies and practices that produced their success. In so doing, they can fail to invest in the necessary experimentation, fail to take the chances needed to learn new things, and fail to notice when events create new opportunities. As a result, history shows that the most successful firms are often the least likely to undertake novel courses of action, to create and introduce radical innovations, and to engage in the sort of creative destruction of the status quo that can create new competitive advantage and spawn new industries (Ghemewat, 1991; Schumpeter, 1942).

This pattern has been called the paradox of success (Miller, 1992). It is subtle, embedded deeply in the process of strategy implementation, and of tremendous importance to the ability of a firm to sustain its competitive advantage. It is pervasive in the sense that it reflects subtle natural tendencies, shared by virtually all managers and firms. Finally, it is an ongoing conundrum with no simple solution. There is no formula a manager can apply to know exactly how much emphasis to place on fit and the exploitation of the current competitive advantage versus how much to place on innovation and experimentation, as necessary to develop potential advantages for the future. Rather, managers must simply sort this out, day by day, doing what is necessary for the short term to sustain success and provide resources, while also investing those resources for the long term, in an effort to prepare for change before it is thrust upon them.

When Less Is More

In their article on the paradoxical tendency for successful firms to stagnate over time, Hedberg et al. (1976) offer suggestions on how the pattern can be broken. Their advice is both counterintuitive and somewhat esoteric. Yet it is also highly valuable for what it illustrates and quite practical when fully understood. The crux of the advice is this: do only what is necessary for the short term to gain competitive advantage and to maintain success. Any additional effort, beyond what is minimally necessary for ongoing survival, should be directed towards the future and towards the cultivation of new alternatives, options, and ideas. Hedberg et al. (1976) offer six specific prescriptions, designed to prevent the paradoxical tendency outlined earlier. These prescriptions are outlined below.

The first is for *minimal consensus* on the part of the firm's decision makers. Contrary to common and conventional wisdom, firms can suffer from too much consensus. Managers can become too insular and distant. They can restrict the flow of information and limit the sources from which they receive information. In so doing, they may sharpen their focus, reduce their disagreements, and maximize their own efficiency. However, without knowing it, they may also be cutting off the very sources of creativity and insight that will stimulate innovation and new ideas. While some minimal level of consensus among the managers and key decision makers is necessary, the idea that cooperation is synonymous with consensus is counterproductive and dangerous, providing the illusion of satisfaction and success in the short term but stifling initiative and opportunities for learning in the future.

The second prescription is for *minimal contentment*. As with the others, this one may seem counterintuitive and unnatural. Managers spend their careers trying to provide stability for their firm and its constituents. And most stakeholders, including employees, suppliers, and owners desire some level of satisfaction and contentment. What possible advantage could there be in fomenting discontent or promoting the idea that true satisfaction rests upon minimal contentment? To understand this, it is important to understand problemistic search. The term was introduced earlier and is defined at the end of the chapter. It applies in this context because the search for alternatives is typically motivated by discontent. When a gap exists between the current and the desired state, when there is pressure to improve upon current performance, or when there is a sense of restlessness and uneasiness with the status quo, decision makers are motivated to take risks and make the efforts necessary to learn. Where there is too much contentment and too much comfort, there is little incentive to change.

Great champions in sports, people like Tiger Woods, Serena Williams, Roger Federer, Tom Brady, and Lebron James, often cite the key role of hunger in sustaining their motivation. That intrinsic desire to improve and excel is especially important when there is no obvious or immediate threat from the competition. Without it, complacency begins to emerge and the firm loses its edge. So, there is an advantage to never being fully content and to constantly pushing for more and better results.

The third prescription is for *minimal affluence*. Firms and managers are typically judged on their financial success. So, as affluence rises, discontent will typically decline. With affluence comes the ability to build **slack resources**. Slack resources enable a firm to better absorb mistakes and to better insulate itself against shocks from the environment. Firms with deep pockets of slack resources have a buffer that can be used to absorb mistakes and to mitigate the effects of oversights. Those deep pockets protect a firm from immediate threat and provide the luxury of time when responding to change. As a direct result, affluence can have the unintended effect of making a firm less aware of its surroundings. With the accumulated cushion of strong affluence, changes in the competitive landscape will arouse little urgency. Early signs of dissatisfaction among the customer base may be met with little more than a shrug, while promising new products and technologies get lost amidst the bureaucratic shuffle.

Of course, some affluence is necessary. Firms must have resources to operate in the present and to invest in the future. Affluence can buy the best talent, the best technologies, and the best locations. Affluence can enable rational and reasoned decision making, supported by all the research and data necessary for an informed decision. Experimentation and learning both cost money and so affluence can provide for both, while also offering greater margin for error. Affluence then is a good and important resource. The danger is too much affluence. As odd as it may seem, too much affluence in the short term can hinder the cultivation of wealth in the longer term. Thus, managers must decide how much affluence is absolutely necessary and then keep no more than just that.

The next prescription is for a firm and its management to have *minimal faith*. Hedberg et al. explain that "an organization should plan its future but not rely on its plans" (1976: 59). This statement can appear at first to be doublespeak, the sort of nonsense that is too often associated with academic impracticality. On closer consideration, though, the point is quite valuable and practical.

Planning is a useful exercise for a number of reasons. It can force management to think rigorously and systematically about the future. It can push managers to consider the cause-and-effect relationships in their industry and the relative importance of various goals and objectives. However, plans can never remove all of the uncertainty from the future. There will always be surprises; events will unfold in a way or at a pace different from what was anticipated, long-held assumptions will prove faulty and new revelations will emerge that change the landscape on which the plans were based. Thus, too much planning or planning in too much detail can be counterproductive. Much like the hypothetical building in the Churchill quote, plans can take on a life all their own. Shaped in one set of circumstances and for one reality, they end up shaping behavior in another.

It is better, then, that managers plan but do so only minimally. Set direction, articulate goals, provide the guiding principles as well as the ongoing support and attention, but otherwise allow the details to evolve over time. This is another application of the **logical incrementalism** philosophy discussed in Chapter 3. Planning is an important process, but if the plans are articulated in too much detail and if they are held to too rigidly, the plans can be like a straightjacket, restricting flexibility and limiting the ability of the firm to respond and adapt as the changing circumstances warrant.

The fifth prescription is for *minimal consistency*. Of course, this suggests that there will be some inconsistency. While unorthodox, it is nevertheless quite logical in the context of strategic management, because the environment is by its nature inconsistent. To maintain the sort of fit described in Chapter 1, a firm must adapt constantly and accordingly. It must reassess its market, its competitors, its resources, and its business model regularly. It must search out new technologies and products and it must listen to its customers, anticipating their motivations and adapting in response. With the ferment of new competitors, innovations, products, services, and technologies, and with the continuous evolution in customer tastes, preferences, and patterns, change in the environment is constant. Thus, firms are under continuous pressure to keep up by changing themselves as well.

Change though can be difficult and uncomfortable. It can increase uncertainty and reduce efficiency; it can undermine the value of existing resources and it can dilute focus and energy. In short, change can make a firm appear inconsistent. But consider the alternative: when a firm fails to change, pressure from the environment builds up. This pressure may build slowly, so that it is barely perceptible or it may build quickly. Ultimately though, the pressure from the environment will force a change by the firm. The only question is whether the firm will be able to survive that change and respond. As noted earlier, often the answer is no because the change is simply too dramatic and unfamiliar.

The sixth and final prescription is for *minimal rationality*. Rationality is defined by Allison as "not just intelligent behavior, but behavior motivated by a conscious calculation of advantages, a calculation that is based on an explicit and internally consistent value system" (1971: 13). While scholars and managers have long realized that the sort of rationality described in this definition is unrealistic in practice, it nevertheless remains an ideal in the minds of many. Specialization and the division of labor are rational practices, designed to limit redundancy and increase asset and knowledge utilization. Lines of authority are made clear to minimize conflict and to reduce the likelihood of miscommunication. Objectivity is emphasized and hard data are valued over intuition and subjective judgment. Clear directions are provided and sought so that there will be no misunderstanding of what is to be done and what is being expected. Indeed, professors, managers, consultants, and investors spend much of their time trying to design and enforce greater rationality to produce greater efficiency and better results.

The problem with all of this is that creativity and imagination will often seem less rational than other, more productive options. Thomas A. Edison's famous quote "we now know a thousand ways not to make a light bulb" illustrates this well. To reach his objective, Edison had to endure a long string of failures. While he chose to view these failures in positive terms, they still represented real losses of time, effort, and money at the time they were incurred. Of course, it is now easy to look back, to see this investment in relation to the outcomes and to applaud Edison's determination and vision in making this effort. However, what if he had not succeeded? Indeed, one could hardly blame Edison had he decided that after a mere 900 hundred failures that his time would be better spent on other matters. Moreover, had he quit after 900 attempts, he would have never invented the lightbulb and his efforts, rather than being seen as investments, would have been seen simply as failures.

The true value of creative insight and innovation is rarely obvious to those steeped in the values and practices of the status quo. Indeed, an overly developed sense of rationality can drive these creative energies out of the firm altogether, leaving an organization that may do things right but that may not be doing the right things. This distinction, between doing things right and so being efficient and doing the right things and so being effective, was noted and explained by Peter Drucker (1967). Firms can be well managed, follow the best practices, and apply the best models and so avoid blunders and mistakes. Yet, those same firms can overlook creative alternatives; they can miss key opportunities and forego chances to seize new advantage by focusing too heavily on their own practices, process, and consistency. That is the hazard of rationality and that is why strategists must view it cautiously.

ADAPTATION AND LEARNING

The ultimate goal of these prescriptions is an organization that can learn and adapt, that can redesign itself in an ongoing and continuous way and by so doing stay focused on the bull's-eye of a moving target. Strategy implementation involves building structures, systems, skills, and shared values that complement the strategy. But strategy changes and so must the organization change along with it. Implementation then must also provide for the continuous redesign of the organization, as necessary to stay fit to an ever-changing strategy.

Strategy though does not change for its own sake. Rather, strategy changes to maintain fit with the environment. Fit between the strategy and the environment is the key to competitive advantage. As discussed elsewhere in the text, providing value to customers over and above what is available from other suppliers and from alternate products and services is the essence of competitive advantage and success. To do well and to do well over time, firms must create that sort of value for their customers both in the present and into the future. Implementation then really has two equally vital imperatives. The first is to ensure the creation of value for customers in the present. The second is to enable the sort of learning and adaptation necessary for the creation of that value for customers in the future. It is only through the accomplishment of both that strategy and competitive advantage maintain their currency and relevance in the marketplace over time.

Competitive advantage then is closely related to the processes of adaptation and learning (Duncan, 1974; Fiol & Lyles, 1985). These processes are rarely connected to the nuts and bolts of strategy implementation. Much like the prescriptions outlined earlier, adaptation and learning are often viewed as academic topics of concern to theorists and consultants but of little tangible value to practicing managers. That view, while understandable, is unfortunate. Organizational learning and the adaptation that follows are natural by-products of strategy implementation and essential contributors to competitive advantage and performance. When practiced effectively, strategy implementation should stimulate creativity and innovation. It should provide previews of emerging changes and prepare the firm to adapt. To better visualize this, return to Chapter 3 and Figure 3.1. Virtually all depictions of the strategy process show feedback paths. These loops are meant to symbolize how information on the results of a strategy feeds back to the beginning of the strategy process. Whether called feedback, strategic control, or learning, the effect is the same: to incorporate the best, the most relevant, and the most current information into the formulation of new strategy.

The best source for such current, relevant, and high-quality information is the front line of the firm, where the feedback is the most immediate and tangible. After all, who better to provide input on the current products and services than the customers and those who interact with them most directly? Who better to notice operational shortcomings and to make improvements than those most involved in operations? Who better to spot emerging technologies and competitors than those who are in the marketplace every day? That front line of the firm, where the strategy is converted into action, is also the best place to experiment with alternatives, to try new things, and to refine the current offerings. This process of experimentation is the first step in learning. Creativity is encouraged, innovations in products and processes are attempted, new combinations are tried, and the responses are evaluated. All of the resulting information then feeds back into the crafting and development of new strategy. This approach to implementation enables the firm to learn, in process. It enables ongoing adaptation and evolution, without ever requiring a radical overhaul of the firm's structure and systems. Moreover, it allows this all to happen naturally, on the basis of information that comes to the firm through its normal activities.

But this sort of thing can happen only if the firm is minimally committed to the status quo, willing to reexamine things continuously, able to get outside of itself and so view the world objectively, and then willing to change even before the need for that change becomes urgent. It is this process of continuous learning, adaptation, and change that will emerge from the prescriptions outlined earlier. A firm that can resist the pressure towards excessive rationality, consensus, and consistency can take advantage of the information that flows naturally from its own operations. Once it has satisfied the need for minimal affluence, it can divert resources towards experimentation and innovation, rather than just building slack to buffer the current advantage. By feeding information learned through implementation directly into the strategy-making process, the firm can capitalize on firsthand awareness of the environment. With the ability to experiment and learn in the marketplace, the firm can begin the processes of planning and adaptation before it is forced to change by pressure from the outside. As a result, the firm can understand and be ready for the future before even before that future fully arrives. This is the promise of organizational learning and this is the opportunity of strategy implementation. When done well and when fully integrated throughout the whole of the strategic process, implementation, learning, and adaptation can sow the seeds of truly sustainable competitive advantage.

SUMMARY

This has been a chapter on strategy implementation. Implementation contributes to competitive advantage in two crucial ways. First, it is the process of converting strategic intent into tangible action. Thus, it involves organizing and managing the nuts and bolts of the firm in such a way that the strategy functions as it was intended. Organizational structures and systems, along with processes, practices, style, and culture, all must work together for strategy to create value and produce competitive advantage. Just as strategy must fit the environment, so too must the firm fit the strategy. That internal coherence, among the strategy, structure, systems, skills, staff, style, and shared values of the firm was illustrated with the 7-S model. Each of these elements is important in its own right. However, they are all much more important as part of a larger whole. The fit of that larger whole is essential to the effective implementation of strategy. Strategy that is well fit to the environment and that is supported by coherent alignment of these elements will produce competitive advantage and superior performance. At the same time, where there is little or no competitive advantage and where performance is poor, the cause can be traced to one of two causes, either poor fit between the strategy and the environment or poor alignment between the organization and its strategy. Understanding the 7-S model and learning to apply it to different strategies and organizational configurations then is a key skill for every strategist.

The second way that strategy implementation contributes to competitive advantage is by providing the sensory inputs to the firm. As it implements strategy, learning to create value and refining the processes for delivering it, the firm also gathers information about the environment. This information is immediate and practical and customized to each firm and each environment. In implementing its strategy, McDonalds is perfectly positioned to learn about its customers and to experiment with new products and delivery models. Through implementation, customers and potential customers are engaged as a resource for identifying new opportunities, new competitors, and new technologies. As a firm like Ryanair implements its strategy, it should also be gathering feedback on what works and what fails to work, on what customers like and what they object to, and on what changes are likely as the industry evolves. This information should then be an input for innovation, new product and process development, and the formulation of new strategy. This process of "learning by doing" is designed to keep the firm ahead of changes in its environment, enabling it to learn, adapt, and redesign itself as necessary to sustain competitive advantage.

Unfortunately, this sort of introspective and ongoing redesign is difficult to achieve and manage. As mentioned earlier, it is often at odds with the nuts and bolts of implementation and is most especially challenging in highly competitive environments or in the most successful firms. This is a paradox, plain and simple, that relates directly to the conundrum of long- and short-term thinking. To thrive in the short term, providing the value customers demand while outperforming competitors, firms must use their resources efficiently, tightening the fit between the strategy and the firm and strengthening their own internal alignment so as to eliminate waste and maximize their return on investment. This sort of efficiency, however, leaves little room for creativity, innovation, and novelty. These things, by their very nature, are uncertain, inefficient and speculative. As the quote by Thomas Edison illustrated, the pursuit of creativity and novelty involves certain failure on some things, as needed to learn about others. Even in the best of cases, learning about the future and developing the right products, processes, and strategies for it will involve diverting some resources and some attention away from the present and away from the current competitive advantage.

Resolving this dilemma, and so satisfying simultaneously the demands of both the short and the long term, involves reprogramming the strategy and the strategists. Rather than seeking to maximize internal commitment, consensus, consistency, affluence, rationality, and faith, firms and managers should seek to minimize them. While still doing what is necessary to create value for customers and to develop competitive advantage, firms and managers should also cultivate a healthy sense of insecurity, discontent, and urgency. They should constantly seek better products and processes, constantly challenge their own assumptions and priorities, and constantly try to improve upon the status quo. Rather than defend their own advantages, they should seek to overthrow them before some competitor does. Paradoxically, then, to create the greatest value the firm must be its own fiercest competitor, constantly feeding new information gathered through implementation back into the formulation of better strategy. Fail at this, and the firm will eventually drift out of favor and relevance, losing touch with new customers and being surpassed by newer and more innovative competitors. Succeed in this and the firm will move from strength to strength, maintaining its alignment with the environment and sustaining its competitive advantage.

SOME FINAL THOUGHTS

Dynamic Capabilities

Much of the academic discourse in strategic management over the past two decades has dealt with sustainable competitive advantage. As discussed in Chapter 1, competitive advantage is the object of strategy and the best indicator of enduring firm performance. In every instance and setting, firms should seek to build greater competitive advantage by creating greater value. However, the creation of value and the pursuit of competitive advantage costs money. It involves investment in resources, time, and effort and it involves risk, as these investments are by their very nature speculative and uncertain. Thus, the sustainability of a competitive advantage is important. Advantages that can be sustained provide greater returns, as their benefits persist over longer periods of time. For example, a firm may develop or purchase a technology that can be used to create value in the marketplace. The advantage derived from that technology can be protected with a patent, extending the life and the earning potential of the advantage. Even the patent has a value, directly related to its duration and to the value of the technology it represents. In much the same way, every competitive advantage has a value, directly related to its value and durability. Advantages that cannot be easily imitated or substituted are more valuable than others because they represent returns that can be sustained for longer periods of time.

However, the intensive focus on sustained competitive advantage has led to an unintended and unproductive mindset among students and practicing managers. Specifically, students and managers alike often get caught up in the pursuit of singular, inimitable and non-substitutable resources as necessary to provide a sustainable competitive advantage. Much like 49ers in a modern-day gold rush, there is a perception that by finding the right resources or by staking out the right positions, a firm can gain advantages that can be sustained indefinitely.

While an attractive idea, it is important to understand that these sorts of resources and these sorts of positions are little more than fool's gold. Every resource can be either substituted or imitated with sufficient time and effort, and every advantage will eventually erode, given the continuous drag of competition and market evolution. As a result, sustainability should be seen in continuous, rather than categorical terms. In other words, rather than asking whether an advantage can be sustained, managers should be asking for how long the advantage can be sustained. In essence, managers should ask, what is the window during which the advantage will function and what is the earning potential of the advantage during that time? Moreover, the advantage should be seen in terms of its ability to promote future advantages. Managers should ask themselves whether an advantage will enable the firm to create new options that will facilitate the sort of ongoing redesign discussed earlier. This sort of ongoing process of redesign, as necessary to move the firm from strength to strength and from advantage to advantage, reflects the *dynamic capabilities* of the firm.

Dynamic capabilities are defined as the "ability to integrate, build and reconfigure internal and external competencies to address rapidly changing environments" (Teece et al., 1997: 516). In essence, they are the firm's ability to learn, adapt, and change as necessary to stay fit to the environment, even as the environment changes. These sorts of capabilities are not bound to specific tangible assets nor are they applicable in only particular settings. Rather, they transcend resources and strategies and deal instead with how resources and strategies are used. To return to an issue discussed in Chapter 2, firms have value over and above the value of their assets. Tobin's q was a measure of that value added by management and strategy, over and above the book value of the firm's assets. Dynamic capabilities are analogous to the knowledge, thought processes, and structure that govern how the firm's assets are used and how strategy is applied in the day to day. By way of analogy, if tangible resources and assets are bricks, then dynamic capabilities are the mortar in between. However, this mortar has the special ability to liquefy, harden, and then liquefy again, as necessary meet the changing needs of the environment.

The dynamic capabilities perspective then places less value on the sorts of resources that show up on the balance sheet than it does on how those resources are used and how a firm learns and adapts. The environment is constantly changing and so every advantage is ultimately at risk. The challenge for managers then is not to find that elusive resource that can never be imitated or to develop that strategy that is so unique and powerful that it will never be defeated. Rather, the challenge is to cultivate the sorts of mindsets, processes, and paths that will enable the firm to learn and adapt before change is forced from the outside. Those sorts of capabilities will enable the firm to move from strength to strength, sustaining competitive advantage by changing and creating value by continuously learning, adapting and moving forward.

Real Options

Much of what this chapter has presented in terms of the future value of implementation can be understood in terms of options. Stated simply, an option is the ability to do something in the future. For example, a prospective buyer may purchase an option on a piece of property. The option is not ownership; rather, it is the right to purchase later. For the price of the option, the owner may agree to a purchase price today, even though the sale may not occur until later in time. Or, in return for the option price, the owner might pull the property from the market, agreeing to give the prospective buyer the right to decide on the purchase at some point in the future. In the same way, firms can take options on the future. A firm might obtain a patent on some product or some piece of technology that is yet to be fully developed or commercialized. The product or technology may or may not prove valuable in the marketplace. However, as long as it holds the patent or rights to this product or technology, the firm has the option of moving forward with it. The product or technology may prove very valuable at some point, or it may not. For now, though, just having the option represents some value. Moreover, while it holds that option, the firm is able to refine and improve the product or technology. It is also able to learn about the market, to begin educating potential customers, and to influence the pace at which the process moves forward.

Thus, the value of the option derives from two sources: the actual commercial value of the product or technology in the future and the value of the learning and information that can be acquired as the option is being developed. It has been argued then that the value of any firm is a combination of the value of its current operations and resources, as well as the value of its options on the future (Luehrman, 1998). That future option value can be cultivated and managed, just like the current operations and resources. Given this, the option value of the firm should be an integral part of the firm's strategy. This is what is known as the *real options* view (Scherpereel, 2008). It is an idea that is extremely important to the pursuit of sustained competitive advantage and the long-term performance of the firm (Ferreira et al., 2009).

The real options approach is a little different than the traditional approach to developing and managing strategy. Students and managers are traditionally taught to think about strategic initiatives and the range of strategic alternatives in terms of net present value (see Chapter 2 for a review). Alternatives are assessed in terms of risk and potential cash flow and managers select and invest in those initiatives with the highest net present value. In so doing, though, they also choose not to invest in the others. The real options view changes this approach substantially. Rather than seeking to eliminate potential initiatives, the real options approach suggests keeping the options open until there is better information on which to base a go or no go decision.

Of course, no firm has the resources to invest in everything. Thus, seizing every initiative and trying to fund every potential alternative is simply not possible. Rather, the firm invests modestly in many different projects, thereby purchasing options on those projects into the future. Those options are then managed, just like an investment portfolio. Moreover, as time moves forward, the firm learns about the market for these future options; it also invests in the refinement and development of these emerging products, markets, or technologies. As the firm has better information on the future potential of each option, it can then choose to reallocate its resources, doubling down on the best options and discontinuing or selling the others. The result of all this is a pipeline of projects that move systematically from the farfetched to the probable and from the highly risky to the highly certain.

This pipeline is illustrated well by the initial story on Alphabet (see Chapter 1). Alphabet's Other Bets division was created expressly to identify, nurture, and manage a portfolio of options. Funded largely by out of cash flow created through Google's operations, Other Bets tries to identify emerging new ideas, new technologies, and new opportunities. Many of these will fail, and a few will succeed. But, by engaging them early, Alphabet is able to take an option on a great many bets and to remain involved with them, as the technologies and markets develop. In so doing,

Alphabet is better positioned to adapt and better able to sustain its advantage in the future.

Interestingly, the research on the subject has been promising and suggests that the value of a portfolio of strategic alternatives will be higher over time if a firm adopts this approach than if it selects and cuts too quickly, using just net present value. Of course, both approaches are highly dependent upon the process by which they are managed and the knowledge of those who manage them. The real options approach then is no silver bullet. Adopting this approach can no more guarantee success than can acquiring any particular resource or following any particular strategy. Rather, the value in the real options view comes from its effect on strategic thinking. Recall that the sort of continuous learning and redesign of the firm described earlier requires a reprogramming of the strategists and the strategic process. Adopting a real options approach to strategy development can be a mechanism for accomplishing that sort of reprogramming.

The thinking is that, as managers view their jobs as the creation and management of options to yield an ongoing stream of high value initiatives, so will they internalize the processes of learning and adaptation. In this view, strategy becomes less about analytical precision and efficient execution and more about the ongoing process of continuous evolution and change (Mintzberg, 1987). However, the change is no longer a speculative and clumsy process where managers try to guess about and make bets on the future. Instead, it is a process where the firm, through the cultivation of options and the implementation of its strategy, actually learns its way into the future (McGrath, 1999). When done well, this process yields a continuous stream of competitive advantages, creating an ongoing harvest of value and performance.

Problems With Present Value

Net present value analysis was discussed in Chapter 2 and is a common and widely accepted practice for evaluating performance and for assessing alternative strategies. It uses discounted cash flow to produce standardized values of future events so that those events can be compared to one another directly and assessed in present terms. While a powerful and sound analytical tool, NPV does have a subtle and potential problem.

Recall that NPV works by discounting future cash flow based upon uncertainty and the opportunity cost of the investment capital. This sort of discounting is reasonable and sensible and meant to guard against poor investments. Risky propositions must produce large returns to justify investment, and even good returns may not be sufficient if the capital can be allocated to better purposes. Thus, a good manager will carefully weigh new potential initiatives against the risks and against the opportunity costs. But consider the principle mentioned earlier in the chapter, the more successful any particular strategy is now, the less attractive any alternative will look in comparison to it. Moreover, given that an existing and successful strategy is likely to be well practiced and well understood, the risks associated with any alternative strategy will be higher almost by definition.

As a result, NPV analysis has a built-in bias favoring the status quo in those instances where the status quo is successful. In other words, successful firms that apply NPV analysis to the range of their various strategic alternatives will almost always find that their best course of action is to increase investment in the current strategy, reinforcing their core competencies and buttressing the existing competitive advantage. And the more successful the current strategy, the more this will be the case. As a result, highly successful firms will find it very difficult to try new things, to justify experimentation, and to promote innovation. This is part of the mechanism underlying the curse of incumbency (Chandy & Tellis, 2000) discussed earlier.

Two things about this phenomenon are especially interesting. First, it is interesting how the potential for bias in the use of this analytical tool parallels the effects of prospect theory on decision making. Recall the S-shaped value curve discussed earlier in this chapter and illustrated in Figure 8.2. That portion of the curve above the reference point, in what is called the domain of gains, is flatter than the portion of the curve below the reference point. Thus, marginal gains are less valuable than marginal losses of comparable size. What this means is that decision makers will often work harder to avoid a loss than they will work to achieve a gain of the same amount. Moreover, note that at a point beyond the reference point, the curve flattens almost completely. In this region, the effect of current performance or of the current resource position is so strong that even a large potential gain offers little incentive to change the status quo. While a difficult thing to imagine, history is replete with examples of firms that chose the profitability and security of the status quo over attractive new alternatives. These events are often chalked up to complacency or some sort of fat-cat syndrome, where companies rest on the laurels of past success and executives, blinded by hubris, refuse to acknowledge threats to their hegemony.

But a closer look suggests a more subtle and pervasive problem. The second issue of interest here is whether our analytical methods are reflecting and amplifying our own biases. For instance, it is easy to imagine how NPV analysis might reinforce the effects of prospect theory on decision making. A firm could perform so well that virtually no alternative to the current strategy would appear attractive. If that firm could increase investment in the current strategy, in effect doubling down on its competencies and competitive advantage, no stream of future cash flow from any alternative strategy would produce a positive NPV. The opportunity cost of the capital would simply be too high. It might be then that rather than being complacent fat cats, many executives apply good reasoning and good analysis and choose quite rationally to forego new strategic alternatives because the numbers and the analyses actually favor the status quo. If so, then it is all the more important that students, professors, consultants, and managers work to reprogram themselves and the strategy process. The challenge is to learn to apply the best logic and the best analyses available, while also institutionalizing processes like real option development and the cultivation of dissensus and discontent, as necessary to blunt the effects of subtle biases that can lead to complacency and drift.

A Means to an End

Balancing the short-term demands of fit, efficiency, and performance along with the longer-term need for innovation, adaptation, and learning is a complex and ongoing challenge. It is not the sort of problem that can be easily solved with a simple policy or a single action. Nor is it the sort of issue that can be addressed once and thereafter forgotten. Rather, it requires a different way of thinking, a complete reprogramming of the strategic process and the firm's strategists. Beginning with the mission of the organization and then working through to the strategy and its implementation, resolving this dilemma requires seeing the firm as a means to end, rather than as an end unto itself. But if the firm is merely a means to an end, what is the end that is actually being pursued? To put it succinctly, the end is the creation of value. Firms are to create value for their customers and, in so doing, create value for their owners, employees, and other stakeholders. As explained in Chapter 1, managing the firm's resources to create value is the essence of strategic management and what is expected of good managers. Meeting that expectation though requires seeing the organization and a tool for the creation of value rather than a result unto itself.

Unfortunately seeing the firm as just a tool for the creation of value is easier said than done. Indeed, as Hedberg et al. (1976) describe, firms are often built as monuments to their own greatness and success, with elaborate architecture and structures designed to insulate those on the inside from the outside world. They build slack resources in the form of cash reserves, stock repurchases, redundant capacity, excess infrastructure, and reputation. They then often use that slack to filter information that threatens the status quo, to resist even the most inevitable changes, and to buffer themselves against the very environmental forces that are essential to their success. How many instances have there been where industry leaders acquire potential new competitors, rather than learn from and respond to them? How many firms and industries have lobbied for subsidies or for legislation that would protect and benefit their positions, rather than adapt to inevitably evolving economic forces? It is no secret and no surprise that managers often choose to see the firm as an end rather than a means, and so they work to consolidate their positions, to reduce ambiguity, to promote predictability and clarity, and to provide a large measure of security and consistency for themselves and those around them. This can seem natural and reasonable in the short term.

Unfortunately, though, it is a shortsighted approach. Ultimately, the value of the firm is enhanced when it creates the most value for its customers. Thus, the creation of value both now and into the future is the responsibility of managers in the present. Understanding this, many have begun to focus on sustained competitive advantage as the key to long-term value. But the quest for sustained advantage is complicated by an ever-changing environment, by the changing aspirations of customers, and by an evolving technological landscape. New competitors emerge and old competitors fade away. Customer desires evolve and change as demographics change and as products and services go from being novel to being routine. New technologies are created and new processes emerge, affecting the cost, availability, and attractiveness of all sorts of goods and services. And yet, managers often struggle to find that key inimitable resource or that enduring brand or product feature that cannot be substituted. Such quests are destined for frustration.

Rather, the key to sustainable advantage is the ability to learn and adapt ahead of the demand and the competition. Firms that create an ongoing stream of real options, that build and invest in dynamic capabilities, and that maintain their hunger for new value creation and growth are actually able to create and enjoy multiple temporary advantages. Each periodic advantage reflects the fit among the environment, strategy, and the firm at a specific point in time. Each periodic advantage leads to revenues and profits, which can be invested in the creation of more options and the cultivation of greater dynamic capability. Thus, while the firm is enjoying the benefits of one resource, one position, and one advantage, it is simultaneously investing in the development of resources and positions that may lead to other advantages in the future.

This ongoing process will necessarily involve change on the part of the firm and those within it. A firm may be a leader in an industry for a time, but later sense the need to transition out of that industry and into something else. A firm may enjoy a substantial advantage in one particular environment but later decide that the time is right to evolve into something different. The firm may change its products, technology, people, or strategy. But what does not change, what endures across every form that the company may take, is the pursuit of value. Understanding that, a firm and its managers become better able to implement strategy in the present and better able to learn and adapt as necessary for the future.

KEY TERMS

Curse of incumbency is the term used to describe a group of factors affecting large and established firms. Because of things like size, bureaucracy, and established practices, these types of firms can be rather inflexible and slow in responding to pressure or seizing emerging opportunities.

Filtering is a cognitive process by which individuals organize and attend to information from the environment. Because no one can gather and interpret all the available information, they attend selectively to particular issues, filtering out what is thought to be irrelevant and internalizing that which is thought to be significant.

Framing involves the categorization of complex issues under simple and discrete labels to ease communication and decision making. Two common examples of frames used by managers are opportunity and threat.

Inertia in organizations refers to the tendency for established strategies, practices, and routines to be repeated over and again, such that forces for change are mitigated and the organization continues reliably to move in the same direction and to function in much the same way.

Logical incrementalism is an approach to strategy that involves managing through a series of small changes and adaptations. That the process is logical suggests that there is an underlying consistency or purpose. Managers are explicit on the overarching goals and directions yet leave open the details, allowing them to emerge organically.

Problemistic search refers to the tendency for people to search for solutions only once problems have been identified. Rather than search continuously for opportunities to improve, individuals will typically invest energy in a search for solutions only once some problem has been identified.

Prospect theory was developed by Kahneman and Tversky (1979) and deals with decision making under conditions of uncertainty or risk. The basic premise of prospect theory is that the starting condition, or reference point, of a decision maker influences the valuation of the potential outcomes.

Satisficing is a common occurrence in decision making and refers to the tendency to accept adequate solutions, rather than to continue searching for solutions that could in fact be optimal.

Slack resources are resources held by the organization but that are in excess of what is needed to satisfy immediate needs. Slack is typically either unabsorbed, like cash, receivables, or a line of credit, or absorbed in the form of excess capacity, excess inventory, or redundant capabilities.

QUESTIONS FOR REVIEW

1. What does the example of McDonald's illustrate about the principle of fit and the importance of implementation for long-term performance?

2. What is the distinction between implementation and formulation? What purpose does it serve to make this distinction, and what potential harm can it cause?

3. What is the tension between short-term fit and long-term flexibility? Why does this tension exist, and what sorts of problems can it create?

4. Why is success paradoxical and what forces contribute to this phenomenon?

5. What is the connection between this paradox of success and adaptation and learning? How do adaptation and learning contribute to sustained competitive advantage?

6. What is meant by a real options approach to strategy, and how does this approach resolve the paradox of success and contribute to sustained competitive advantage?

7. How does the use of net present value (NPV) analysis reinforce subtle biases in managerial decision making? What is the danger in relying too heavily on this analytical tool?

8. When done well, strategy implementation should serve two important purposes. What are they and how does each contribute to performance over time?

Chapter 9

Disruptive Megatrends

THE DEMISE OF TOYS "R" US

In the 2017 listing of the Fortune 500, Toys "R" Us was listed at number 244, with sales of $11.54 billion and 64,000 employees. It was its 23rd consecutive year in the Fortune 500. In September of 2017, Toys "R" Us filed for Chapter 11 bankruptcy but continued trading through the holiday season, and finally went into liquidation in March 2018, shuttering all of its approximately 800 U.S. stores and letting go of all employees.

By all accounts, Toys "R" Us began its decline shortly after it first entered the Fortune 500 at number 131 in 1995. In the late 1990s, Toys "R" Us developed an online presence and indeed became one of the early "stars" of online retail. So much so, in fact, that the demand during the 1999 holiday season proved too much for their underdeveloped online logistics that they failed to get orders to customers in time for Christmas, despite customers ordering weeks in advance, resulting in a $350,000 fine from the U.S. Federal Trade Commission. In 2000, following this disaster, Toys "R" Us entered a 10-year agreement with Amazon, paying Amazon $50 million a year and a percentage of sales, to be the exclusive seller of toys and baby products through Amazon, and ceding control of the toysrus.com website to Amazon.

While this was initially successful, the success resulted in Amazon quickly realizing the potential of these categories online and wanting to go beyond Toys "R" Us in growing these categories. By 2003, Amazon was listing other toys and baby products on its site, and in 2004, in failing to reach an agreement over this expansion, Toys "R" Us sued Amazon and in 2006 won the right to rescind its agreement and take back its website. However, by this time, Amazon was far ahead in online retail, and Toys "R" Us, having relied on Amazon for online distribution, had no capabilities in the digital sphere. In the meantime, in 2005, Toys "R" Us was purchased in a leveraged buyout which left them with a $400 million-a-year debt servicing cost on some $5 billion in debt, leaving little ability to reinvest in their stores let alone their online capability, and so were never able to successfully develop its online business. As such, Toys "R" Us was overtaken on the brick-and-mortar side of the business by other big-box retailers like Wal-Mart and Target, and trounced online by Amazon in a decade-long decline before its eventual demise.

The Toys "R" Us story is a cautionary tale of how even the largest, most dominant firms can soon be extinguished when there are large, disruptive changes in their environment, such as, in Toys "R" Us' case, the advent of the internet and online retail. However, Toys "R" Us is by no means an isolated example. While we commonly hear of the vulnerability of start-ups and small businesses to failure, even the largest companies, those that might have taken decades or even a century or more to build, are not immune to failure. If we look at the Fortune 500, representing the largest 500 public companies in the United States by revenues, we see not only a rapid pace by which companies fall off this list, but that the pace of this disruption is accelerating over time. Figure 9.1 shows different cohorts of the Fortune 500, beginning with the original cohort, those firms that were on the Fortune 500 when *Fortune* first published its list in 1955. If we track across the line to the point where 250 companies of that cohort are left—where half of the original cohort has disappeared from

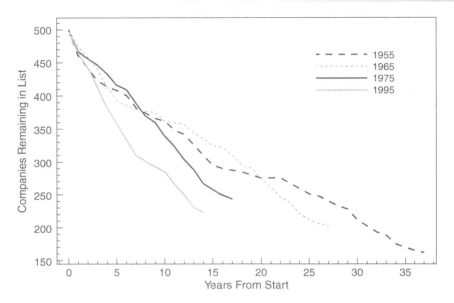

FIGURE 9.1 Disruption in the Fortune 500

Source: www.kauffman.org/-/media/kauffman_org/research-reports-and-covers/2012/06/fortune_500_turnover.pdf

the list, we see that it took 25 years, or until 1980, for half of the 1955 cohort to fall off the list.

If we look at the 1965 cohort, the Fortune 500 listed in 1965, we see that it took 22 years, or until 1987, for half of them to fall off the list. For the 1975 cohort, it took 16 years, and for the 1995 cohort, it took a mere 12 years, until 2007, for half of these companies to drop off the list. Think about that for a second. The Fortune 500 represents the largest, most established companies in the United States, many of which have taken many decades to build. Within 12 years, half of them fall off the list, many disappearing altogether. Going forward, looking at today's Fortune 500, in perhaps a decade half of them will fall away. That represents a tremendous amount of disruption for even the biggest companies. In other words, no business is immune to these disruptive forces. To drive the point home, let's look at some of the household names from 20 years ago that were among the Fortune 500. Toys "R" Us has already been mentioned. But what about Compaq Computer, Silicon Graphics, Lehman Brothers, Mays Department Stores, Continental Airlines, Circuit City, Wachovia, MCI WorldCom, and Bethlehem Steel? These were all household names at the turn of the millennium and coming from many different industries from technology to finance to retail to heavy industry. All are now consigned to the history books as all were unable to shift and adapt to major changes in their environments and competitive landscapes.

In broad terms, we have seen three highly disruptive megatrends that, over the time since *Fortune* magazine has been publishing the Fortune 500, have been the primary cause for much of this disruption: globalization, the internet and, more recently, mobile devices.

Globalization

In 1941, in the midst of World War II, Robert Woodruff, then Chairman and CEO of The Coca-Cola Company, famously declared that any person in uniform should be able to get a bottle of Coke for 5 cents, wherever they were and whatever it cost the company. In order to fulfill this promise, Coca-Cola worked with the U.S. military to establish 64 bottling plants around the world and served 5 billion bottles of Coca-Cola to servicemen and women. While prior to the war, Coca-Cola had already been one of the pioneers of globalization, this war effort propelled its capacity to new heights and, at the close of hostilities, it was positioned to be one of the world's first truly global companies. Since WWII, globalization has happened across industries to the point that, now, nearly all companies are subject to global competition and face competitors from many different countries. This rise in global competition has had profound effects on many industries, particularly in the manufacturing sector, causing much of the disruption we have seen in those early Fortune 500 cohorts. For example, Bethlehem Steel ranked number 12 on Fortune's inaugural Fortune 500 list in 1955 and provided the steel for iconic structures such as the Empire State Building, the Chrysler Building, Rockefeller Center, Madison Square Garden, and the Golden Gate Bridge. In this golden age for Bethlehem Steel in the 1930s, 40s, and 50s, they faced little to no competition from overseas steel companies. However, by the 1970s, cheaper imported steel began to appear in the market, and new technologies for steel making such as continuous casting and mini-mills allowed smaller entrants to compete with, and even undercut, the large integrated mills like those of Bethlehem Steel, and the decline of Bethlehem Steel began. (See story from *Wired* magazine about Bethlehem Steel's decline in Box 9.1.)

Internet

While the rise of the internet—with its origins in the late 1960s with the creation of the Advanced Research Projects Agency Network, or ARPANET, to the addition of an internet protocol in the 1970s, and the invention of the World Wide Web in 1990, to where it is today—has created enormous opportunities and spawned some of the largest firms that exist today, such as Google and Amazon, it also created disruption for many industries and individual companies. A prime example of

Box 9.1
Wired **Magazine Story: Meltdown**

On October 15, Big Steel became a museum—as in Smithsonian. A case study on the effects of globalization.

On a chilly winter morning in the Lehigh Valley in eastern Pennsylvania, the buildings of the Bethlehem Steel plant loom out of the fog like the ruins of an abandoned civilization. The five towering blast furnaces, which produced more than 8,000 tons of molten iron a day back in the 1960s, turned cold in 1995. Sunlight filters weakly through the tall windows of the No. 2 Machine Shop, a hall a third of a mile long that used to be the largest machine shop in the world.

The fall of Bethlehem Steel, which declared bankruptcy on October 15, has become a parable of industrial decline. At its core, however, the story of Bethlehem is simply that of the double-edged nature of global trade: the inevitable transformation of America even as American companies transform the world, the imperialist invaded. Like U.S. Steel and LTV, Bethlehem couldn't adapt to a new environment of cheap foreign steel and modern technologies. Saddled by corporate arrogance, outmoded factories, and swollen labor costs—and "protected" by backward-looking bureaucrats—an American icon couldn't compete.

Although U.S. demand for steel continues to grow at close to 40% a year, the domestic industry has lost some 350,000 jobs since 1979, and 27 companies have filed for bankruptcy since 1998 (including 12 in 2001 alone). Scrambling U.S. steelmakers invested almost $50 billion during the past 20 years to build new plants and modernize old ones, but that hasn't been enough. The Asian economic crisis of 1998 sent a cascade of excess steel to American shores, and the strength of the dollar made those imports too cheap to resist. More recently, new producers such as Ukraine, India, and China—now the world's largest—further swamped the market. There's something on the order of 230 million tons of excess steelmaking capacity in the world, a glut that has driven prices even lower. Now Big Steel accounts for just 42% of U.S. steel consumption, while a nimbler breed of mini-mills supplies 36% and foreign companies the remaining 22%.

Meanwhile, the Bethlehem plant is slated for a very postindustrial rebirth as Bethlehem Works, an entertainment and commercial complex. In a move fraught with symbolism, the vast machine shop of this monument to 20th-century manufacturing will become the home of the National Museum of Industrial History, an affiliate of the Smithsonian.

Source: *Wired* Magazine 2/1/02. www.wired.com/2002/02/steel/

this is the rapid decline of the newspaper industry in the United States. From 1985 to 2018, paid circulation of daily newspapers declined from 62.7 million to 28.5 million, and the pace of decline has increased since the financial crisis of 2008–09. Indeed, from 2004 to 2018, 1,810 newspapers went out of existence, either closing completely or merging into another newspaper. Even *The New York Times*, one of the most well-known and influential newspapers in the country, has seen its advertising revenues drop from $2.15 billion in 2006 to $558 million in 2018.[1] Many industries, while not facing the same degree of decline as the newspaper industry, have seen disruption to the way in which business is done and have struggled to adapt to the rise of the internet, particularly as it relates to access to information. Take the example of retail and the example of Toys "R" Us at the beginning of this chapter.

Mobile Devices

More recently has been the rise of mobile devices, the start of which is marked by the introduction of the Apple iPhone in 2007. Smartphones have completely changed the way we live our lives: the way we shop, the way we communicate, how we get information, how we bank and engage in financial transactions, how we consume media, and numerous other ways. In 2019, the average smartphone user in the United States spent 3 hours and 43 minutes per day using their mobile devices.[2] And while 71% of the total U.S. population own smartphones, that increases to well over 90% in the 18- to 49-year-old age bracket.[3] Because these devices have changed the way consumers behave, and the expectations they have for instant access to information, as well as goods and services, this has impacted consumer-facing businesses of all kinds, but particularly in the retail sector.

The ability to comparison shop in-store by using smartphones to compare the price of an item in store to that same item at any number of online and brick-and-mortar stores has led to what has become known as "showrooming" where online retailers benefit from the customer's ability to look at and try out an item in store, but then purchase from an online retailer who doesn't have the overhead associated with the retail locations. This has forced stores like Best Buy to not only offer a price match guarantee but also add additional services like Geek Squad to entice people to purchase from the store. This combination of additional services, plus the overhead of the physical stores, plus the need to price match online retailers has hurt the ability of many retailers to compete, resulting in the shuttering of stores and even whole shopping malls. Indeed, in Best Buy's own category of consumer electronics, there was a net closure of 6,425 consumer electronics retail stores in the U.S. in the decade from 2007 to 2017.[4] On a more positive note, for those stores that embraced the power of the smartphone to entice people into the store and make their purchase in store, there have been gains to be made. For instance, the most used digital payments app is not Apple Pay or Google Pay, but the Starbucks app, with 23.4 million users in 2018, compared to 22 million for Apple Pay and 11.1 million for Google Pay.[5] For Starbucks, mobile payments now account for about 30% of their total sales and helped drive an 11% revenue increase in the third quarter of 2018.[6]

But while these forces have been highly disruptive across industries, resulting in the demise of some of the great firms of the past, they have also created opportunities for new firms to emerge to become the household names of today. Take firms like Amazon, Facebook, Alphabet (Google), Netflix, Tesla, and Salesforce.com, all household names that 20 years or so ago were either tiny start-ups or perhaps not even in the imaginations of their founders. And it isn't just technology firms that were created by the opportunities provided by these disruptive forces; firms such as Steel Dynamics and LifePoint Health are also firms that now appear in the Fortune 500 that didn't even exist 20 years ago.

So, these disruptive forces, or megatrends as we might call them, are behind what Joseph Schumpeter labeled as far back as the 1940s as "creative destruction": waves or forces of destruction for some firms that equally provide opportunities for new firms to emerge and prosper. If globalization, the internet, and mobile devices have been the primary disruptive forces of the most recent decades, what will be the disruptive forces of the coming decades? And, importantly, how do firms prepare for both the disruption to their current operations and the opportunities provided by these new megatrends? These questions are the focus of this chapter.

Before we delve into looking at these future megatrends and their likely impact, it is important to note that this is not just an academic exercise. Major disruptive forces that are on the horizon can usually be seen in advance, and hence prepared for, even if their precise manifestation is unclear. The rapid emergence of the COVID-19 pandemic that spread across the world with devastating speed in 2020 demonstrates how large, global, forces can create massive disruption to societies and businesses. While the occurrence of this pandemic came as a surprise to most, the threat of such a global pandemic was on the radar of many governments and organizations and indeed was spoken about in public forums as a serious potential threat by prominent figures such as President Barack Obama and Bill Gates. Yet, despite these warnings, and previous deadly virus outbreaks such as SARS and Ebola, most people and businesses gave this potential disruptor little thought until the world came to a screeching halt in the spring of 2020. The foresight to be aware of coming global shifts and the ability to prepare your company to be resilient to, and aligned with, the disruptive force is key to the ability to sustain competitive advantage over the long term.

Most of the large consulting firms such as McKinsey & Co, PwC, and Deloitte, among others, have major practice areas devoted to examining these future disruptive forces and the challenges and opportunities they present to their clients. While each of these firms has a slightly different viewpoint on which megatrends are important and perspective on the impacts of each, the variation of viewpoints is less important than the fact that there are major changes on the horizon. These changes will impact society and business and businesses, if they are to continue to thrive, and even survive, cannot ignore but need to think about and build their businesses to be resilient to the disruption they will bring and build capabilities to take advantage of the opportunities afforded by these trends. So, while there are certainly other major trends out there, we have chosen in this chapter to highlight eight potentially disruptive megatrends that firms need to be concerned about going forward: changing demographics; climate change; big data, fast data; rapid urbanization; social commerce; technology advances; blockchain; and energy generation and storage. While, for any given firm, some of these will be more applicable than others, an awareness and understanding of these trends is of paramount importance to every firm.

Changing Demographics

There are large shifts happening globally in demographic change. In most developed economies, we are seeing a declining birthrate, with people having children later in life and having fewer of them. At the same time, we are seeing increased longevity, with some demographers predicting that the life expectancy of children born today in many developed economies may exceed 100 years. This combination of factors is also leading to rapidly aging societies, with the proportion of people aged 65 or older expected to reach over 20% by 2040 in the United States from 13% in 2010 as the baby boom generation moves into retirement.[7] China, meanwhile, starting at a similar position with 12% of its population older than age 65 in 2010, will surpass Japan as the world's most aged society by 2030 and have over 30% of its population older than 65 by 2050. This brings all sorts of challenges at the societal level in terms of supporting retirements and healthcare systems, but also for businesses it brings challenges and opportunities internally in terms of the dynamics of a multi-generational workforce and a shift in the demographics of their customer base. In their book, *The 100-Year Life*, Lynda Gratton and Andrew Scott foresee a major shift in how people think about their lives and the interplay among work, leisure, and learning, with the traditional "3-stage" life of learning, working, and retiring being replaced by multiple stages where people take a more portfolio approach to their life and intermingle multiple periods of work, leisure, and learning over their extended life course. If this prediction is correct, then this implies a major shift for every business in how they think about and manage their workforce, as well as disrupting markets in everything from housing to financial services.

At the same time, in emerging markets we are seeing a very different demographic pattern taking shape, with high birthrates and declining death rates across much of the developing world. This is leading to a population explosion in those countries and a very young population. There is huge potential for what is known as the " demographic dividend" in these countries whereby there exists a very young, healthy workforce with few elderly dependents, giving the opportunity for huge economic growth. But the emergence of this demographic dividend is dependent on stable, effective governance at the country level, investment in educating the young population, and economic opportunity sufficient to employ the rapidly growing workforce.

The combination of a shrinking working population and increasing aging population in the developed economies together with a booming, younger workforce in developing economies poses great challenges and opportunities to governments and businesses, but both overcoming those challenges and taking advantages of those opportunities provided by these fundamental demographic shifts will require major shifts in thinking and the location of economic activity.

Climate Change

While there are different political views on climate change, its existence, causes, and effects, what is not disputable is the empirical evidence of increasing numbers of disruptive weather events. The National Oceanic and Atmospheric Administration (NOAA), the government agency that tracks natural disasters, keeps count of those weather events that cause more than $1 billion of damage. In the 1980s, the United States experienced 28 such events, costing a total of $172 billion (in inflation adjusted dollars) and resulting in 2,808 deaths. In the 2010s there were 119 such events, costing $807 billion in damage and resulting in 5,217 deaths. The total cost of billion-dollar-plus weather events in the United States from 2000 to 2019 totaled $1.317 trillion and resulted in 8,268 deaths. Table 9.1 shows decade by decade how the number of these devastating events, and the costs associated with them, both in terms of dollars and lives, has escalated dramatically since the 1980s.

Table 9.1
Billion-Dollar Weather Events in the United States

Decade	# of events	Total $ cost (billion)	# of deaths
1980s	28	172.4	2,808
1990s	52	268.8	2,173
2000s	59	509.8	3,051
2010s	119	807.3	5,217

Source: National Oceanic and Atmospheric Administration: National Centers for Environmental Information www.ncdc.noaa.gov/billions/summary-stats

Already the effects of these increasingly frequent and severe weather events are being felt, not only by society and especially the impacted areas but also by businesses. Businesses may be severely impacted whether or not they are directly hit by the weather event. For those that are hit directly, there is obvious potential for destruction of company facilities and operations. But more than this, there is also likely devastation to the homes of employees and local customers and suppliers. But even if the facilities of the company are not directly affected, weather events in other parts of the country, or even the world, can have severe impacts on supply chains, disrupting the company's ability to conduct business.

Big Data, Fast Data

The statistics on how fast we are generating and accumulating data are staggering and only accelerating. In 2010, Eric Schmidt, Executive Chairman of Google noted that "From the dawn of civilization until 2003, humankind generated five exabytes of data (5 billion gigabytes). Now we produce five exabytes every two days . . . and the pace is accelerating." In fact, it is accelerating so fast that by 2015, Forbes estimated that the amount of data we have will rise from 4.4 zettabytes in 2015 to 44 zettabytes, or 44 trillion gigabytes, by 2020. However, despite this astounding rise in the accumulation of data, what is more compelling is that less than 0.5% of all data is ever analyzed and used.

While most people and businesses have been aware of the rise of big data for quite some time, what will drive the profound impact of this megatrend is not only the increasing ability to analyze this data but the ability to do so in real time. As the tools to gather and analyze data in real time become more widespread, the business applications, in everything from marketing to supply chain, from finance to manufacturing, fast data will profoundly change the way business is done and how competitive advantage is generated and sustained.

The challenges for businesses around big data and fast data are numerous. In most industries, we will see a divergence between companies that are able to collect and analyze data effectively and those that can't. The effective use of data will become one of the fundamental generators—and destroyers—of competitive advantage. Ownership and access to data will become critical. This could give advantages to industry incumbents who have access to data; otherwise, these firms could be disrupted by new firms, or firms outside the industry who are able to access and analyze data finding new sources of competitive advantage and undermining established patterns of behavior.

While the rise of big data and fast data will create myriad opportunities for companies that can take advantage of using data effectively, the big challenge that comes with this critical data is security. Cybersecurity is going to be more and more critical as businesses rely more and more on the use of data as a source of competitive advantage. We are already seeing the catastrophic impacts of large data breaches, but even these major events that are made public are only the tip of the iceberg. The rise of ransomware hacks and other malicious attacks on a company's critical data infrastructure is perhaps one of the most critical challenges facing many companies today and will only continue to become more important.

Rapid Urbanization

World Bank data show a steady rise in the proportion of the world's population who live in urban centers, rising from 36.5% in 1970 to 41.1% in 1985 to 46.5% in 2000 to 53.8% in 2015. By 2030, this is likely to be more than two-thirds of the world's population. In the United States, while this growth flatlined from 1970 to 1990 as many cities experienced social problems and economic flight, urbanization has resumed its march such that by 2015, 81.6% of the population lived in urban areas.

The rapid urbanization that is happening poses both challenges and opportunities. Contrary to the expectations of many, urban living can be much more efficient from a sustainability perspective, reducing per capita carbon emissions and lessening the impact on the environment. At the same time, dense populations can pose a challenge to infrastructure, particularly in older cities that were not designed for the volume of people living in them.

A higher proportion of people living in urban centers also attracts resources, stimulates innovation, and facilitates the development of creative industries. At the same time, this also begets the potential to increase the divisions between rural and urban populations. Even within cities, we are seeing the effect of an increasing wealth divide where some cities essentially become accessible only to the wealthy to actually live in, with service providers having to live outside the city and commute in as the ratio of real estate cost to average wage escalates to seemingly unsustainable levels.

This rapid urbanization provides opportunities to business, with dense markets, increased flow of resources into cities, and opportunities to create innovation centers. At the same time, with increased abilities to communicate, and the easy access driven by close proximity, the development of peer-to-peer platforms allows the sharing economy to flourish and potentially disrupt more and more established incumbents in many industries, as we have already seen, for example, in the hospitality (Airbnb) and urban transportation (Uber, Lyft, and others) industries.

Social Commerce

While we have already seen the impact of Uber, Airbnb, BlaBlaCar and others, we are only at the tip of the iceberg in terms of the potential for peer-to-peer platforms to disrupt industries, particularly in the consumer-facing space. The rise of the internet, social media, smartphones, and app stores have created the ability for consumers to procure the goods and services they need and want from other consumers rather than from established companies. But the real behavioral shift that has occurred is a complete change in the basis of trust which facilitates these transactions. In previous generations, trust was institutionalized—we trusted institutions, both because of the consistency of institutions and the ability for recourse should things not turn out as promised. Now, however, we are trusting individuals that we have no direct past history with. While we grew up with the notion of not getting into cars with strangers, if we request that car through an app, and it shows up with a "U" sticker on it, we happily get in. We previously relied on reviews from trusted sources before making major purchases. Now we rely on the views of strangers. This has also given rise to the age of social influencers, not just the celebrity endorsements of the past coming from established celebrities from the worlds of entertainment and sport, but ordinary people from all walks of life who become influential using the power of social media. At the same time as the rise in our trust of other individuals through electronic ratings, our trust in institutions has declined. A glance at the Gallup polls across various types of institutions over recent decades shows a dramatic fall in the public's trust in institutions such as Congress and the presidency, banks, big business, newspapers, television news, public schools, and the church. This dramatic fall in the public trust in institutions that were the pillars of society, and the shift to trust in individuals through peer-to-peer exchanges, represents a remarkable shift that has huge implications in most consumer-facing industries.

The rise of peer-to-peer platforms, and the shift in trust that has developed alongside it, has prompted a range of differing responses from incumbent companies in those industries. Some have tried to resist through direct action, such as striking taxi drivers in cities such as London and Paris in response to the disruption of Uber. Some have sought to influence changes in laws to protect their turf, such as the hotel industry lobbying to restrict the scope of Airbnb through clamping down on an individual's ability to rent out their property on a short-term basis. Still others have sought to embrace the sharing economy notions of peer-to-peer platforms by introducing or acquiring sharing platforms and infrastructure, such as BMW's ReachNow car-sharing initiative, or car-rental company Avis' acquisition of Zipcar, or Marriott's Homes and Villas, a curated selection of private homes and villas offered through a Marriott platform.

Technology Advances

The scope of this megatrend is vast. Technological change is impacting every industry, and some of those technological advances will completely disrupt particular fields or industries. However, there are several technological advancements that will have profound impact across many sectors. Two of these, and they are related, are the Internet of Things and artificial intelligence.

Much of the hype around the Internet of Things has focused on household applications, or "smart home" applications, and these applications will have a great impact not only on how people manage their households and, indeed, live their lives but also how companies market, sell, and deliver products and services. However, less attention so far has been paid to how the Internet of Things transforms business applications, which could have a far greater overall economic impact. The Internet of Things will impact every industry from farming to advanced manufacturing. This innovation will transform how businesses manage and control supply chains, how they add value through producing goods and services, and how those products and services are delivered. The boundaries between the firm and its suppliers and customers become more fluid as data are generated by suppliers and customers and used by the firm, and vice versa, resulting in smoother, more timely, and more tailored transactions.

Artificial intelligence is rapidly evolving and is poised to disrupt a number of industries and occupations. While in the past, technological advances have more often disrupted blue-collar workers and have, for the most part, enhanced the productivity of professional workers, artificial intelligence has the potential to decimate some professions and severely disrupt others, even those that have been immune from disruption, or even enhanced, by prior technological change. Occupations from financial advisors to doctors, marketers to educators, all face either a dramatic shift in the way they operate or face extinction altogether. These occupations and their respective industries, financial services, healthcare, education, and almost any knowledge-intensive industry, face major challenges but also equally major opportunities with the emergence of artificial intelligence.

While artificial intelligence may disrupt some by replacing human expertise in terms of diagnosing a disease, creating a financial plan, pinpointing a market opportunity, or communicating knowledge, those who can embrace these advances and adapt to and unlock the potential of artificial intelligence in their field will be able to provide a quantum leap in the level of service to their customers and generate great gains in competitive advantage over their less adaptable competitors. As virtual agents replace the diagnostic elements of these knowledge-intensive professions and industry roles, this enables these professionals and their organizations to utilize that diagnostic capability and translate it into more effective action.

Blockchain

The most well-known blockchain application currently is the cryptocurrency Bitcoin. The terminologies and concepts behind how Bitcoins are created, or "mined," the anonymous nature of the creator(s) of the platform, and the volatility of the exchange rate between Bitcoins and established national currencies make many people distrustful and suspicious of the value of the Bitcoin currency and blockchain in general. However, despite this perception, the underlying technology on which Bitcoin is built, the blockchain, has vast potential to disrupt the way transactions happen and how we verify information, and accordingly, how we trust that what individuals and organizations claim is true is verified as being true.

The concept of the blockchain is a peer-to-peer decentralized database that stores an encrypted registry of assets and transactions, creating the potential for an ultra-secure, highly versatile way of verifying ownership, transactions, and other information that requires independent verification. The possible applications of blockchain are numerous and may fundamentally alter how a large portion of business transactions occur. This would, for example, enable consumers to verify supply chains of components used in the production of the goods they purchase, in turn enabling companies to verifiably demonstrate ethical supply chains and business practices to their customers. It would enable food producers to show fair-trade or organic ingredients and enable consumers to know the origin of their food. Beyond supply chain applications, it can enable distributed cloud storage; decentralized exchanges that facilitate transactions without an intermediary institution; the managing of digital identity, which reduces the possibility of fraud and identity theft; as well as enabling applications such as digital voting, smart contracts that self-execute under predetermined conditions, and many other applications. In short, the development of the blockchain will revolutionize transactions, enabling even the smallest transactions—like the purchasing of a song on a digital music service, to be easily recorded and verified.

While the blockchain may give greater security for transactions—reducing one of the biggest threats to business today—the flip side to the verifiability of every transaction and data about that transaction is that consumers will demand greater transparency from companies as to their supply chains and hold them to higher standards of ethical practices within supply chains that they may not directly control.

As the transition to blockchain occurs, there is the real possibility that consumers will adopt this technology for transactions faster than many incumbent businesses will. If this is the case, then transactions may shift away from such businesses at a rapid pace, causing shifts in the market dynamics of many industries.

Energy Generation and Storage

Electricity is the energy powering modern society. One of the major security threats to nations today, particularly the U.S., is the vulnerability of the power grid, particularly given the aging and fragile infrastructure on which it rests. Any major, prolonged outage has the potential to bring down the communications infrastructure on which society and commerce depend.

The prospect of efficient, scalable, and affordable energy storage would be a game changer. The ability to disaggregate the storage of energy, which would also facilitate the disaggregation of the production of energy, would both reduce the vulnerability of society to the prospect of the power grid going down and allow for scalable micro-generation of power in the face of ever increasing energy demand. Scalable, efficient storage would also unleash the potential for the growth of renewable energy, enabling the balancing of supply and demand from erratic renewable energy sources such as wind and solar.

More efficient energy storage also opens up new possibilities in mobile applications, from increasing the practicality of electric cars and other transportation systems, to facilitating mobile businesses.

While breakthroughs in energy generation and storage will have obvious, but huge, disruptive impacts on the traditional energy businesses and ripple effects on other sectors such as automotive, the promise of disruptive change in energy generation and storage provides opportunities for many other sectors that are otherwise constrained by the portability of power.

While we have outlined eight potential megatrends, as we noted earlier before describing them, this is not an exhaustive list. Indeed, the very nature of change implies that there will be other major trends that continue to emerge, and so being aware of the emergence of trends, and their implications, is an important part of strategy in that it enables firms to continually test and refine their sources of competitive advantage and build resilience into their strategy. One important variable to consider is that megatrends, and the disruption they cause, emerge at different speeds, and they can manifest themselves in short, but devastatingly disruptive events, such as the severe, billion-dollar weather events that are a symptom of climate change, or more of a slow-moving continuous force, such as the evolution of demographic change. With the force and momentum of megatrends, while some companies may be effective at prolonging their decline through various resistance tactics, despite being against the overall direction of the megatrend, particularly for those slower-moving megatrends, generally speaking, the exploration and embracing of business strategies that align with the direction of the megatrend are more likely to be successful over the long term. But how, to what extent, and at what speed companies make this transition are key factors in future success. Much of this future success in the midst of disruptive change revolves around the strategic creation of real options, as discussed in Chapter 8, that align with the forces of the megatrend. But in order to do this, companies need to be intentional about the investment in such real options. This intentionality begins with a well-developed concept in strategy, that of scenario planning.

SCENARIO PLANNING

Scenario planning, which was first used in the military, came to prominence in a business setting in the early 1970s when Royal Dutch Shell's use of the technique helped them navigate through the 1973 Oil Crisis and the formation of OPEC, which fundamentally changed the oil market. While the technique of scenario planning has gone in and out of favor over the years, Royal Dutch Shell remains a big proponent and continues to build and refine scenarios. Those firms that dismiss scenario planning often rely more on conventional forecasting techniques in their future planning. The fundamental difference between scenario planning and traditional forecasting is that forecasting is projecting forward from current and historical data to arrive at forecasts for the future, whereas scenario planning is completely future-oriented, looking at different possibilities for how the future might evolve without respect to the limitations of what has occurred in the past or what current data might suggest. Consequently, both techniques are useful in different circumstances.

Conventional forecasting is extremely helpful in relatively benign environments where tomorrow looks much like today or where future events are relatively predictable and not subject to outside shocks, or at least not to shocks which haven't been seen before, and can therefore be anticipated. Scenario planning, on the other hand, gives a much wider range of potential future outcomes, which allows for disruptive events to occur in the future. While this technique gives rise to multiple potential scenarios, and, by virtue of the uncertainty inherent in these less certain futures, their usefulness lies in enabling the organization to prepare to be resilient to different future outcomes rather than predicting with greater confidence at the outset the specific future direction that the firm should pursue. Accordingly, firms may often use both techniques in parallel, using forecasting for more immediate short- to medium-term planning and scenario planning for a longer time horizon. As such, scenario planning becomes the most appropriate and useful tool when thinking about disruptive megatrends that lie on the horizon.

BUILDING SCENARIOS

Scenarios are descriptions of a future state and tell a story about what the world will look like under that scenario. Given the broad nature of a future context, in order to be useful, it is important to develop scenarios with the particular organization in mind to be able to curtail the description to those dimensions that are at least potentially relevant to the organization. However, the other side of this coin is that there are many dimensions that could have secondary effects on the organization, and, as the future may look very different from the present as these scenarios play out, it is also important that the organization is conceptualized appropriately.

Accordingly, the first step in a scenario-building exercise is for managers to define their organization conceptually. For example, take Ford Motor Company. If they were to conceptualize themselves narrowly as an automobile company, particularly one based on the internal combustion engine, then there may be may future scenarios where it becomes difficult to exist. However, by conceptualizing themselves more broadly as a transportation company, Ford allows itself to think more expansively about different modes of transportation, such as electric and self-driving vehicles, as well as other modes of transportation, particularly in urban settings, such as electric scooters. Indeed, using this type of thinking, Ford purchased electric scooter-sharing company Spin in 2018 to enable them to explore this type of alternative urban transportation. In 2017, Ford also purchased a majority stake in Argo AI, which is developing autonomous self-driving vehicles. These investments are a reflection of a broader concept of the organization and provide real options that enable the development of capabilities and resources that are outside the current core competence of the firm.

Once the organization has conceptualized itself in a way that allows them to adapt to different future scenarios while retaining the core essence of the business, they can begin to build scenarios based on combinations of the different megatrends. While there are different ways to do this, a typical procedure might be as described in Box 9.2.

Box 9.2
Scenario Planning Steps

Step 1: Decide on the relevant megatrends. As more megatrends are added to a scenario, the scenario becomes exponentially more complex. Most firms will therefore decide to limit the number of megatrends considered in building a scenario. Additionally, there are likely to be some megatrends that are more relevant to the organization than others, allowing the organization to pare down to a small handful of the most relevant megatrends.

Step 2: Using the PESTEL framework described in Chapter 4, **pick out the most relevant dimensions, or factors, of the future state**. These factors are those that have a meaningful impact on the firm's future strategy and might vary due to the impact of the megatrend.

Step 3: Combinations of the factors under different states lead to independent scenarios. The strategist's task is to **build a picture or story of what the future looks like** under that combination of factors.

Step 4: Scenarios are examined from the point of view of the various stakeholders of the organization (customers, suppliers, employees, etc.) to determine how their engagement with the organization might change.

Step 5: The organization's **current strategy is viewed in light of each scenario** to determine whether the current strategy is viable or resilient to each individual scenario. This enables the organization to see where its vulnerabilities lie in relation to the potential impacts of the combinations of the megatrends.

Step 6: The organization develops strategies for **building resources and capabilities to overcome these vulnerabilities**. These are often relatively small investments that allow the company to begin to develop capabilities in areas that could occur in the future that would be critical to succeeding in that future environment. Ford's purchase of the electric scooter-sharing company Spin is an example of such an investment. These investments are monitored both for their ability to develop capabilities as well as how the megatrends are developing over time and whether the scenario where those capabilities are critical are emerging.

Step 7: The environment is tracked to see the trends that are developing which will indicate which scenarios are on track to emerge and which are becoming more distant possibilities. Key metrics of the various factors are developed to track the progress towards different scenarios.

Step 8: There is a **periodic revisiting of the scenario planning exercise** to revisit the scenarios based on progress in the key metrics to cull some scenarios that are no longer consistent with the way the megatrends are developing and developing new ones based on these developing trends.

The key diagnostic that scenario planning facilitates is the resilience of the organization's current strategy to future scenarios. While there may be some aspects of the current strategy that may fit with, and even thrive in, some of the future scenarios, most likely this exercise will point to ways in which these changes in the firm's environment, caused by the megatrends and embodied in the scenarios, would lead to the firm's extinction or, at the very least, a poor fit with the new state of the world. The firm then needs to use these scenarios to conceptualize what the organization might look like in order to fit with the different scenarios and the changes that this would entail to the organization's strategy and the capabilities and resources that would need to be developed in order to make that strategy happen.

As an example of how an organization might do this, let us revisit the example of Alphabet with which we opened Chapter 7. There we described the change in corporate structure and name from Google to Alphabet. This enabled the creation of an umbrella holding company, Alphabet, with two main units under this umbrella: Google and "Other Bets." Other Bets allows Alphabet to develop technologies and capabilities which are unrelated, or perhaps distantly related, to the core business, Google. The primary vehicle for developing what Alphabet calls "Moonshots" is a division called "X." Moonshots are based on how Alphabet conceptualizes the big problems of the world and what the future could look like—essentially their scenarios. But instead of just building scenarios of how the future might look, Alphabet is actively trying to shape that future through its innovation. These Moonshots are relatively small investments in technologies that, while perhaps unrelated or distantly related to the current Google core of the company, have the potential to become large businesses, and part of their core, in the future. But importantly, for a company on the scale of Alphabet, such Moonshots need to address big problems, or the resulting technologies and businesses that might come out of a successful Moonshot won't be large enough to become a new core of the business. As X describes on its website:

> X is a diverse group of inventors and entrepreneurs who build and launch technologies that aim to improve the lives of millions, even billions, of people. Our goal: 10× impact on the world's most intractable problems, not just a 10% improvement. We approach projects that have the aspiration and riskiness of research with the speed and ambition of a start-up.[8]

Once the Moonshot is developed to the point where it looks like it has the potential to move towards becoming a viable business, it is spun out of X into its own company under the Alphabet umbrella. Such spinouts to date include Waymo (autonomous self-driving vehicles), Chronicle (cybersecurity), Verily (life sciences), Wing (delivery drones), Makani (energy kites), and Loon (internet via hot-air balloons).

It is instructive to examine X's process for developing innovation in a systematic way as other organizations seek to use the scenario planning process to place their own Moonshot bets in developing the capabilities to allow their strategy to fit with future scenarios. The leader of the X division, or "Captain of Moonshots, X" as his title reads, the aptly named Astro Teller describes the key ingredients to developing a systemized process, or "moonshot factory," that is overtly focused on developing innovations that will lead to future revenues and profits.[9] Such a disciplined, systemized creative process requires:

- Solving a problem that affects millions or billions of people.
- Having a chance of being achievable in 5 to 10 years.
- Finding the sweet spot between high risk and idealistic versus a safe bet and pragmatic.
- Being "responsibly irresponsible"—setting out to make mistakes, seeking out "frequent, messy, instructive failure" that directs future investigation.
- Learning cheaply and quickly what doesn't work.
- Being in love with the problem, not the technology.
- Employing and engaging people who are "T" shaped—people with enormous intellectual flexibility combined with a deep expertise in a particular area.
- Creating a small core project team, supplemented with a structure of shared experts who move across teams and shared resources. X has what they term a "Design Kitchen" where teams can engage in design sprints and rapid prototyping of ideas and, importantly, conduct a failure analysis.
- Having clear budgets and criteria for continuing projects. This may be in terms of how the world is moving towards or away from particular scenarios, but it also needs to have a hard-nosed business viability component. X has a 3-stage

rapid evaluation process to weed out impractical ideas early. The first lasts a few weeks, where the project team gets a few thousand dollars to understand the biggest risks in the project. Second is a more extended trial where they continue to take on the hardest and riskiest element of the project or technology, develop prototypes, and try to prove that the idea would work in the real world. Finally, if the idea survives the first two stages, it goes to the X-Foundry where a small team has about a year to learn whether the idea can potentially be turned into a product and business that can make money in a reasonable amount of time.

- Actively killing off ideas. Part of the evaluation process described earlier is about creating a high bar for projects to move on and receive more investment. But even when projects continue, they have to be constantly evaluated, and the organization needs to be willing to kill off the project if it becomes clear that it won't turn into a viable business within the 5- to 10-year window that X projects are aimed at. One recent project that X killed off was called Foghorn, in which they had successfully produced a carbon-neutral fuel from seawater. However, they could not see how this technology could, within the 5- to 10-year window, get to a point of being price-competitive with gasoline, and so the kill signals, or metrics of success for the project, indicated that the project needed to be killed and walked away from.

- Graduating projects into real businesses. Once X has a project that is ready to launch products or scale operations, then they are ready to be spun out of X, freeing X's resources to focus on new projects and allowing the projects to turn into fully fledged businesses under the Alphabet umbrella. These graduations are celebrated with great fanfare.

While Alphabet's process may not fit every business, it provides a model of how companies can approach turning scenario planning into an actionable strategy to address disruptive change in the organization's environment driven by these emerging megatrends. Regardless of the process adopted, as evidenced at the beginning of this chapter by the accelerating pace of disruption even among the largest companies, it is critical that an organization has an intentional process in place to address this future disruption. In the end, without such a process, as this book has been all about, sustaining competitive advantage over the long term is a futile hope.

CONCLUDING THOUGHTS AND CAVEATS

The Real Challenge

Perhaps the most important thing to remember at this point is that strategic management is focused on improving firm-level performance. Put differently, the primary job of the strategic manager is to enhance the value of his or her organization, not to simply understand the forces affecting the organization's performance. Going all the way back to the preface of this text, we promised that this would be a book on strategic management, not merely a book about strategic management. The distinction is a subtle but important one, as many business theorists, consultants, and philosophers will talk at length about the importance of change, about cases where businesses failed because of their inability to adapt, or about examples of how disruption in society or the economy enabled great success or wealth by someone else. And all of that is important, certainly, but none of it excuses the strategic manager from the fundamental responsibility of improving the value of his or her specific firm, competition, change, and megatrends notwithstanding.

The key then is not to simply understand the nature and impact of these megatrends but to understand how to build organizational systems and processes that will facilitate ongoing competitive advantage, as these and other megatrends of the future continue to emerge. In this chapter and the proceeding one, we have mentioned the industry lifecycle, the concepts of adaptive fit and dynamic capabilities, real options-based thinking, as well as scenario-based planning as models and tools that facilitate such sustainable competitive advantage. As noted in Chapter 8, the concept presents something of a paradox to the strategist. Sustaining a competitive advantage requires more planning, while putting less confidence in those plans. It necessitates greater focus on value but with reduced concern for affluence. Ultimately, it requires greater discipline within the organization but less consistency in the operations from day to day. Managing those sets of contradictory imperatives is difficult in the best of times, but it is made especially difficult amidst the pressures of competition, innovation, organizational inertia, and uncertainty about the future.

Throughout the text we have sought to use Alphabet and its components (Google, Other Bets, and X) as examples of how this ongoing process might look in practice and how it might all be managed in a large organization. But the truth is that even Alphabet may one day be displaced by some disruptive megatrend, currently unforeseen by their management and beyond the current capability of their practices. For the strategist, then, the challenge is to stay vigilant, to understand and to anticipate the ebbs and flows of competitive dynamics, to create flexibility, to build dynamic capabilities throughout the organization and to create options for a future that is not fully knowable, while at the same time, doing what is required to create value, to satisfy customers, and to provide a good return on investment amidst the real and tangible competitive forces of the present.

Method and Myth

An interesting but somewhat obscure book from the early 1990s, entitled *Scientific Literacy and the Myth of the Scientific Method*, argued that scientific literacy was not always the key to certainty and good decision making that many expected it should be. The author, Henry Bauer, was a controversial and somewhat unorthodox figure in the mainstream philosophy of science literature. Nevertheless, his premise in this 1992 work was insightful, instructive, and broadly generalizable. Put simply, Bauer argued that good science is more about questions than answers. Scientific inquiry can and does resolve some issues, but in so doing, it often leads to others. Like a decision tree, each answer creates more questions, pulling the inquiry forward and often shifting it into unforeseen territory. The scientist then must be bound less by the desire for a particular answer than by the practice of the method, following the process where it leads, even if that means living in a state of perpetual uncertainty.

That rather esoteric lesson is often overlooked in the casual application of popular science as well as in the modern-day practice of business and business education. A great many managers and students alike are obsessed with the idea that some specific technique, formula, business model, or analytical method will unlock the mysteries of strategic management and yield a sustainable competitive advantage. Unfortunately, just as there is no perpetual motion machine, there is no single formula that will yield competitive advantage or that will guide the strategist in that pursuit. Indeed, think for just a moment about the very idea that such a formula even exists. If there was such a formula, if the solution to sustainable competitive advantage was as simple as just defining yourself in the right way, as easy as merely gathering the right data or applying the right analytical technique, or as straightforward as crafting the right slogan or mission statement and then promoting it in the market, if it was really that easy, then wouldn't everyone apply the same formula and method? And, if everyone applied the same formula and method, wouldn't they all get, more or less, the same result? This myth of the method has been the bane of many MBA classes and programs and is one of the reasons the MBA degree has lost some of its luster and value over the past decade. A thoughtful and well-educated strategic manager understands the complexity of the challenge as well as the difficulty of the solution. Strategies that work for one firm may not work for another, and effective initiatives in one setting may be completely ineffective in another.

In the context of our discussion of these large, disruptive megatrends, it is important to remember that no two disruptions are quite the same. The pattern of the effect, creating opportunity for some, while destroying the status quo for others, may be the same. But the specifics of each particular instance and for any particular firm will be very different. Hence, the key again is to create and combine sensitivity for change with the flexibility to adapt. And all of that has to be done within an organization where the culture and strategy are focused outward, on the customer and the market and on the challenge of continuously creating value. Any effort to shortcut this challenge through the creation of or reliance on a single tool or methodology will, ultimately, lead to disappointment and poor results.

Mega and Micro, Aggregation, and Causality

Megatrends are "mega" or extraordinarily large because they impact a large number of people or create effects that stretch across whole societies and economies. Think for a moment about globalization, the first example mentioned in this chapter. Globalizing is less a singular thing than it is the aggregated result of many individual things. The automobile business globalized, largely during the 1960s and 1970s, because international manufacturers began importing cars into the U.S., where buyers found them to offer greater value, in terms of overall price, quality, reliability, and so on than the domestically built alternatives. Hence, the globalization of this industry was a mega-result of a great many microcosmic actions on the part of individual buyers and sellers. The same would be true of the internet, of the growth in mobile devices, or in any of the potential, future trends discussed in this chapter. Ultimately, their mega-impact was the result of many, single, micro-impacts created and felt and the individual level.

Why is this important? Because, while the megatrends are easier to see and to describe at the aggregated, macro-levels, their implications for firm-level strategic management are better understood at the disaggregated, micro-level. For example, the emerging phenomenon of climate change presents a substantial challenge to humanity at large. But, how should a single firm respond, in light of this challenge? Shutting down would reduce the firm's carbon footprint but shutting down wouldn't be good for the firm's employees, investors, suppliers, or customers. So, the question is how to respond to climate change in a way that also fulfills the firm's mission. The answer would depend on the specifics of the firm, of course. For every firm, though, the solution would lie in the micro-level transactions among the firm, its customers, and its suppliers. Perhaps the firm could find newer, closer suppliers, whose products were valuable because of their proximity and because the shorter supply lines reduced costs, increased quality, or added some element of local value. That is surely been the case among the many "farm to table" restaurants and food markets that have emerged in the marketplace. These firms have addressed this "mega" trend by focusing on micro relationships and transactions.

Another example comes again from Alphabet and its subsidiary Waymo. Waymo is building the technology and infrastructure necessary to enable self-driving cars. The move towards autonomous vehicles could have tremendous implications for climate change, by enabling people to move around efficiently, without each individual having to own his or her own car, by reducing inefficiency in routing and traffic, and by enabling transportation as good or better than is possible today, with far fewer cars in total. The aggregated impacts on climate change could be huge. But the impact on climate change is not what is driving Waymo's value proposition. That value proposition comes from the micro-impact on each consumer who chooses not to own and drive his or her own car or who chooses to allow autonomous technology to control the routing. The value comes from the micro-impact on the fleet owners, who see Waymo's technology as more reliable, safer and, in the aggregate, less expensive than a fleet of individual human drivers. While Waymo's success may impact climate change positively and dramatically, its commercial success will be driven by the value it represents to many individual users.

For managers, then, the challenge is to develop the sensitivity to see and understand megatrends like those discussed in this chapter but also to be able to translate them into the sorts of micro-level actions and transactions through which the firm walks out its strategy. Large, mega changes like those discussed in this chapter, changes that affect societies and economies around the world, will represent some combination of opportunities and some threats to virtually every firm. The challenge for the manager is to find those linkages, between the mega and the micro, and to then act in the realm of the micro, so as to capitalize on and to contribute positively to the macro.

KEY TERMS

Artificial intelligence is the ability of computers to perform tasks that normally require human intelligence.

Creative destruction happens when waves or forces of destruction, such as megatrends, that result in the demise of products, companies, or industries also provides opportunities for new products, companies, or industries to emerge.

Demographic dividend is the potential for economic growth that can occur when the age-demographic patterns shift within a country, usually driven by a decline in the fertility and death rates, resulting in an increased proportion of the population in the working age bracket.

Forecasting is a prediction of what will happen in the future based on historical data and trends.

Internet of Things is the connection of computer devices embedded in everyday objects to the internet, enabling them to collect, receive, and transmit data.

Megatrends are significant forces that will have a profound impact on society over the coming years.

Scenario planning is an approach designed to create visions, or scenarios, of the future for the purpose of creating flexible long-term plans for the organization.

QUESTIONS FOR REVIEW

1. What are the three megatrends discussed in the chapter that have caused disruption over the past several decades? How have they caused disruption?
2. What are some of the opportunities that have arisen from these three megatrends, and what are some of the Fortune 500 companies that have been created as a result of these opportunities?
3. What are the 8 coming megatrends discussed in this chapter? What disruption might they cause? What industries might be particularly vulnerable to disruption? What opportunities might evolve from them?
4. What is the difference between scenario planning and forecasting? Under what circumstances might each approach be the most suitable for a manager to use?
5. What is a typical process for building scenarios? How are scenarios useful in developing strategy? How do scenarios serve in building resilience in a company?
6. Why is it important for a manager to conceptualize their company appropriately when building scenarios?

NOTES

1   Statista Print and Media in the United States dossier: www.statista.com/study/12527/print-media-in-the-united-states-statista-dossier/
2   eMarketer. "Time Spent on Mobile Devices Every Day in The United States from 2014 to 2021 (in Minutes)." *Statista*, Statista Inc., 30 May 2019, www.statista.com/statistics/1045353/mobile-device-daily-usage-time-in-the-us/
3   Statista Smartphones in the U.S. dossier: www.statista.com/study/26643/smartphones-in-the-us-statista-dossier/
4   Statista: Department Stores in the U.S.: www.statista.com/study/48324/department-stores-in-the-us/
5   Statista: Most popular proximity mobile payment apps in the United States from 2018 to 2019, by number of users: www.statista.com/statistics/863946/user-base-of-leading-proximity-payment-apps-usa/
6   pymnts.com: Starbucks mobile order tool accounts for 13 percent of U.S. sales: www.pymnts.com/earnings/2018/starbucks-rewards-mobile-app-stocks-loyalty/
7   The Next Four Decades: The Older Population in the United States: 2010 to 2050. U.S. Census Bureau, 2010. www.census.gov/prod/2010pubs/p25-1138.pdf
8   X website: https://x.company/
9   A peek inside the moonshot factory operating manual: https://blog.x.company/a-peek-inside-the-moonshot-factory-operating-manual-f5c33c9ab4d7

Chapter 10

Issues of Context, Setting, and Application

A BROAD VALUE PROPOSITION

The Executive Assessment Institute (EAI) is a small boutique consulting firm specializing in talent management and leadership development. Based in North Carolina and with just 5 full-time employees, EAI's client list includes Fortune 50 firms in the automotive, healthcare, and computer fields, as well as entrepreneurial ventures in photo optics, private equity, and sustainable energy. While many of its clients are based in the U.S., many others are headquartered in places like Finland, Denmark, Germany, and Japan. Some are publicly held, with stocks traded on the NYSE and NASDAQ, while others are privately held, funded either by their own operations or through venture capital.

How can such a small firm service such a broad and varied array of clients? To understand the answer, it is important to understand that even firms that are very different share some very basic things in common. Indeed, at a fundamental level firms are far more similar than they are different. For example, all firms survive by creating value for their customers over and above what those customers can find elsewhere. That value leads to transactions, which translate into revenues and profits. This is true even for firms that survive on the investment financing they receive in the expectation of future revenues and profits. All firms share the imperative to create value and to translate that value into revenues and profits, either in the present or at some point in the future.

Recall from Chapter 4 that firms are open systems and so can be viewed in terms of a simple model, input => transformation => output. All firms gather resources and convert those resources to produce outputs in the form of goods and services. It is from understanding this open systems model that we derive the principle of fit, discussed throughout the book. Firms that fit their environments perform better than those that do not. In fact, firms that do not fit their environments do not long survive. Finally, all firms have value chains, reflecting the ways in which they source inputs, conduct transformations, and manage the flow of outputs. Thus, while the specific names and details of the different processes and operations will vary from firm to firm, the basic functions are always present.

These are just some examples of the many ways in which firms are alike. The point though is that by understanding the workings of these basic dynamics and functions, a student could understand a great deal about any firm, even if that firm was unfamiliar. In the same way, a manager who appreciates the similarity in these basic characteristics could come into a new firm and understand a great deal about it in a very short amount of time. And a consultant could work with many different firms, providing real value to each, by focusing on just those processes and operations that are present in and important to them all. This is how a firm like EAI adds value.

EAI leverages its understanding of two things, strategy along with the complexity and value of human capital, in providing services to all sorts of firms in all sorts of places. Every firm has a strategy, and every strategy depends heavily on having the right people to manage it. Moreover, strategies must change and evolve with the environment. That change and evolution requires leadership to push for the creation of options, to make hard decisions about resource allocations, and to connect the analytical and intuitive aspects of strategy formulation to the practical nuts and bolts of implementation. Every firm, then, whether large or small, public or private, international or domestic, must somehow connect its strategy to the abilities of its people and empower those people to take charge of and drive its strategy.

Helping firms to make those connections between strategy and human capital is the value proposition of EAI. Its consultants help firms develop the right kinds of talent for their own competitive environments and strategic challenges. They help firms construct models that guide the selection and succession of key executives. They help top executives diagnose dysfunction in their management teams and structure those teams to make better decisions. EAI has helped venture capitalists assess the potential of new ventures and new venture teams and has helped large multinationals to develop the leadership skills needed to facilitate success across a range of diverse markets. And it has done this by offering a value proposition that is of key importance to every firm. By understanding just one essential linkage, EAI has been able to service a wide array of clients and produce value across a wide range of settings.

A HIGHLY GENERALIZABLE DISCIPLINE

The challenge of fully understanding strategic management is complicated by the breadth and variety of the settings in which the discipline is practiced. From large, publicly held firms to new entrepreneurial ventures, from manufacturing firms that build heavy machinery to knowledge firms that deal in data and code, from companies in single businesses in single locations to large and diversified multinationals, all firms and managers stand to benefit from strategic management and strategic thinking. Of course, across these various and different settings, the specific applications and workings of strategic management's principles, models, and tools will appear somewhat different. Thus, it is tempting to think that the practice of strategy somehow changes from firm to firm and from setting and setting. While certainly true to an extent, such thinking can also cause problems. Indeed, everyone thinks that their firm and setting is completely unique. Nevertheless, it is important to understand that strategic management is a highly **generalizable** discipline, with a fundamental logic and framework that can be applied in some way to every firm, every industry, and every setting.

Take for example the concept of competitive advantage. As defined in Chapter 1, competitive advantage exists when a firm produces value for customers sufficient to motivate an exchange above the firm's costs. This basic mechanism is essential to profitability, essential to the survival of the firm, and based on a few simple elements present in every transaction. For every type of product or service and customer there will be some level of use value, some exchange value, some customer surplus, and some profit or loss. Moreover, every transaction will be influenced by the finite resources of the buyer, the alternatives available in the marketplace, and the unique attributes of the producing firm. Because all of these elements are present in every transaction, competitive advantage will hold the same meaning for every firm; it will be the key to success and survival in every setting, public or private, large or small, domestic or international. Firms with a competitive advantage will perform better than firms with no advantage and firms with no advantage will not be successful. That is why Jack Welch, former CEO of General Electric, once said, "if you don't have a competitive advantage, don't compete." While settings differ, that basic truth remains the same.

This is true for all the processes, concepts, and tools introduced in this book. For instance, firms of all different shapes and sizes are affected in much the same way by bargaining power. All else being equal, firms with great bargaining power will perform better than those without it. In the market for smart TVs, Samsung, Vizio, LG, TCL, and Sony are the five largest, and together they accounted for roughly 80% of all sales in 2018. The number and size of these competitors, combined with the high levels of similarity in product quality and features, creates an intensely competitive market, where the buyers have substantial bargaining power. Consider though the wireless telecommunication market, where only two competitors, Verizon and AT&T, control a similar share of the market (34.5% and 33%, respectively), while the other three nationwide providers control less than 25% together. This gives Verizon and AT&T significant market power, which they use to promote sales and profitability. The same is true of other, and very different, types of businesses and industries as well. Good and reputable surgeons benefit from great bargaining power. Patients will often wait longer and pay more for specific practitioners if they believe the physician is the best. Automobile makers like Lexus and BMW have great bargaining power because of their brand and their reputations for quality and luxury. That bargaining power enables them to sell cars at higher prices and with fewer incentives than their competitors, enhancing the bottom line. Even universities derive benefits from bargaining power. With more applicants than they can accept, a university can be selective in admissions, charge more in tuition, and ask more in terms of preparation than if it had fewer applicants. Bargaining power, then, along with its tendency to benefit those who have it and penalize those who do not is a constant across settings. As a result, understanding how bargaining power works and understanding how it is gained and lost provides a powerful tool that can transcend context.

Indeed, concepts like value creation, competition, buyer elasticity, scarcity, asset specificity, customization, resource attractiveness, cost of capital, option value, and fit are at work in every business, every industry, and every type of market, and they affect the performance of every firm. These concepts hold value for every business, in every setting, so it behooves managers to understand them well. The problem comes in translating the concepts from the abstract to the practical and from the classroom to the specific setting of interest. This has long been a stumbling block for many and has limited the ability of students, managers, and professors alike to reap the full benefit of strategic management. Too many managers view strategic principles as merely academic concepts that may work for others but that could not work for them. Students and professors often make the mistake of thinking one way in the classroom but then a different way in the business world, as if one part of the brain is used to think academically, while another is used to think practically. Realizing the full benefit of strategic management means understanding its generalizability and learning how to think strategically in every setting and across every type of firm.

The problem with this is complexity; there are so many different settings where strategic management and its principles can be applied that many find it overwhelming. And there are so many conditions and nuances that no one can be expert in them all. So, the field of strategic management has fragmented into a variety of sub-disciplines and topics, reflecting a wide range of specific issues, contexts, and settings. In related fashion, the practice of strategic management has fragmented, too, with experts in all sorts of different industries, technologies, and types of firms. While all of this specialization offers some advantages, it also comes at a cost, specifically, the inability to see similarity even in related things. Certainly, there are managers who are expert in the creation and launch of new ventures for instance. But are new ventures really all that different from existing firms? At a fundamental level, they are much more similar than they are different. The same could be said of international firms. There are distinct and important issues associated with doing business internationally. But do domestic and international firms share nothing in common? Certain not; they too are more similar than they are different. The challenge then is to understand what is similar and what is different, to take the best from the logic of strategic management and then apply it to the unique and particular setting of interest.

That translation process, from the general to the specific, is the subject of this chapter. This material is meant to connect four specific issues of context, setting, and application to the larger framework of strategic management. Each of these issues is important and so has given rise to its own body of academic research, its own vocabulary, and its own set of specialists. However, each of these issues is also important to firm performance and so is inextricably intertwined with the normal business of strategy. So, it is best then to think of each of these as areas of specialization nested within a larger field. With a good grasp of strategic principles and thinking, these issues can be more easily understood and better leveraged to greater benefit. However, focusing on just the issues themselves, without a firm foundation in the logic and framework of strategic management, would be like missing a forest for its trees and would be a disservice to students and managers alike.

ENTREPRENEURSHIP

Defined strictly, entrepreneurship is the initiation, organization, and operation of a business venture for the purpose of earning a profit. This definition reflects the origins of the word *entreprendre*, a French word that means to undertake or initiate. The term entrepreneurship though has grown to take on much broader connotations and now includes a host of issues involving innovation, private equity, new venture management, and small business management. Researchers who study entrepreneurship examine a range of varying issues including characteristics of entrepreneurs and entrepreneurial teams, strategies of new ventures, franchising, environmental influences on venture success, resource protection, and firm capitalization. Most business schools offer courses in entrepreneurship, at both the undergraduate and the graduate levels, and many business schools have entire programs and faculty devoted to entrepreneurship exclusively.

In both theory and practice, entrepreneurship is interdisciplinary. With scholarly roots in both economics and management, the field draws from finance, marketing, design, engineering, and many other disciplines as well. The earliest interest in entrepreneurship arose in economics, through the work of Joseph Schumpeter (1942). Recall that Schumpeter's concept of creative destruction was discussed in Chapter 8, in the context of innovation and change. This creatively destructive force that Schumpeter identified in economic systems was entrepreneurship. It was the collective manifestation of many individual entrepreneurs acting to seize opportunities in the environment that had yet been unrecognized. Entrepreneurs were able to discern gaps of unsatisfied demand or untapped potential. They then marshaled the resources and initiated the businesses to provide innovative products and services to fill those gaps. Sometimes it worked; the gap materialized as expected and the new products and services were valued and purchased by the customers. Other times it did not and the venture failed. That risk, though, of initiating and organizing was borne by the entrepreneur.

When it worked and the venture was successful, the result was both creative and destructive. These new ventures provided better value to customers, which led to new revenues and profits. In so doing, though, they set new standards, established new norms, and created new industries and markets. These new ventures, along with their new products and services, destroyed the status quo along with the competitive advantages of many existing firms, just as the emergence of Amazon and e-commerce destroyed the traditional approaches to retailing, along with many of the leaders in that industry. This phenomenon was of great interest to economists, who saw entrepreneurship as an ongoing source of economic growth. With each successful occurrence, entrepreneurs created new value for themselves and the economy, inspiring others to look for similar opportunities and creating the conditions in which new gaps could arise.

The recognition of entrepreneurship and the realization that it often led to the creation of new firms attracted interest and scrutiny from organizational scholars. These scholars were less concerned with the economic impact of entrepreneurship than they were with the normative issues associated with the operation and management of the new ventures. Management scholars interested in entrepreneurship examined issues like how entrepreneurs could be made more successful and how new ventures should be managed to yield greater success (Sandberg, 1986; Vesper, 1980). As a result, entrepreneurship came to be associated with strategic management. Indeed, at one level, the two are largely indistinct. Strategic management is concerned with the whole enterprise and with firm-level performance; the same is true of entrepreneurship. Thus, entrepreneurship along with the range of issues related to new venture management can be considered a special case within the larger field of strategy.

Parallel Models

Through observation and study, researchers have identified a series of key steps in the entrepreneurial process. The consistency of these steps has been validated through anecdotes and evidence and distilled into models used in teaching entrepreneurship. While the specifics of different models will vary, the basics remain largely the same and are illustrated in Figure 10.1: (1) opportunity recognition, (2) feasibility and environmental analysis, (3) business plan development, (4) gathering key resources, (5) promoting the plan to secure investment, and (6) launching the venture. That structure maps neatly onto the strategic management framework introduced earlier in this book (see Figure 3.1).

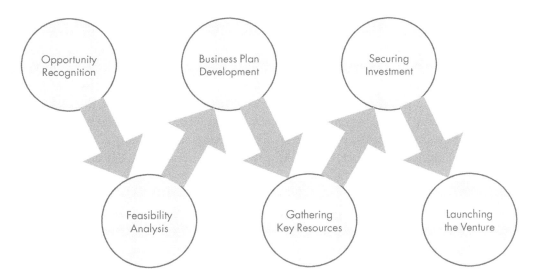

FIGURE 10.1 A General Model of the Entrepreneurial Process

To illustrate, consider that the entrepreneurial process begins with opportunity recognition. Academics have debated whether the entrepreneur actually creates the opportunity or simply identifies an opportunity that was there all along. In reality, there are likely cases of both. In the bigger picture, though, it is important to see the pursuit of this opportunity as the purpose of the entrepreneur. Recall that the process of strategic management also begins with a statement of the mission or purpose for the firm. In both cases, that purpose can be explicit and formalized in written statements or implied and understood through action and common direction. However, in both instances, the strategies of the firms, new and existing, will be directed by this basic purpose.

Next in the entrepreneurial process is the feasibility and environmental analysis. The challenge here is to evaluate the opportunity in light of the environmental forces. Will customers really value and buy the new product or service? Will the anticipated demand continue over time? Can a competitive advantage be achieved and sustained in light of anticipated competitor reactions? The whole approach is very similar to the sort of analysis depicted in the larger strategic model. Entrepreneurial ventures would certainly want to assess the state of the macro- and competitive environments, and they would do well to employ models like Porter's 5-Forces and the product/industry lifecycle. Moreover, it is important to understand that when doing this analysis, both entrepreneurs and existing firms are looking for the same sorts of things, evidence of opportunity and sustainability, insight into the elasticity and strength of the demand, and clues about the behavior of competitors, customers, and suppliers. Both are interested in identifying a space or a position within the environment that their firms can fill and, in so doing, generate revenues and earnings.

Having identified a position in the environment and having ascertained its potential for competitive advantage, both new and existing firms begin an assessment of their own resources and capabilities, in light of the conditions identified through the environmental analysis. In the strategic process, this happens as part of the resource-based assessment and involves the use of the value chain. In the entrepreneurial process, this happens during the development of the **business plan** and through the prioritization and securing of the key resources. In the world of entrepreneurship and new venture management, focus on the business plan is ubiquitous and intense. Business plans are an articulation of the strategy and are used to secure financing and support. Stated simply and practically, a business plan details how the new firm will make money by detailing how the venture will capitalize on opportunities in the environment. As a result, any good business plan will include an analysis of the resources and capabilities of the venture itself. Not surprisingly, that analysis will resemble the value chain analysis described in Chapter 5 and include some consideration of the resources needed to support the strategy, along with some assessment of the value, rarity, imitability, and substitutability of those resources going forward. A good business plan then will fulfill the same requirements as the basic competitive analyses described in Chapters 4 and 5. Both are designed to assess the opportunities and threats in the environment, both should capture the strengths and weaknesses of the firm or venture, and both are designed to articulate how the firm will make money through specific activities in a specific competitive environment.

With the business plan complete and with the conceptual part of the strategy in hand, the next step in the sequence is implementation. For entrepreneurs, that often means promoting and selling the plan to investors. In the world of entrepreneurship, these investors are called **venture capitalists** or **angels**. These investors are motivated by economic opportunity. Put simply, like the panelists on the popular TV show *Shark Tank*, they expect to make money off of their investments. Moreover, because these investors have many opportunities, they are typically deliberate and sophisticated in their assessment of each new firm. They study prospective entrepreneurs and their management teams closely, examining the technology and resources of the venture, considering the opportunities and threats in the environment, and estimating the value of the competitive advantage both now and into the future. Like any investor in the public market, what they want is a strong return. Thus, they search diligently, studying the business plans of prospective ventures and analyzing them for future growth and profitability. When they are convinced that the opportunity is right, they invest, providing capital, connections, and expertise in return for a portion of the equity and the future earnings.

While the process of obtaining new venture investment is complex, involving a great deal of specialized effort and knowledge, it still reflects the same basic elements as any other form of investment. There is the expectation of a positive return. Thus, the new venture must offer the prospect of future cash flows. There is an understanding that the investment must be competitive. Just as a private investor can choose among a variety of stocks, bonds, and real estate, so can a venture capitalist choose among a range of different entrepreneurs or other investments. Finally, there is a horizon over which the investment will be held and a terminal value if is sold. All of these elements factor into the value of any investment. As explained in Chapter 2 and elsewhere, that value can be estimated using net present value (NPV) analysis. So, while an entrepreneurial venture is a unique type of investment, it is still helpful to see it in terms of its net value, just as a good strategist views his or her firm in terms of its net value.

When viewed this way, the various steps in the entrepreneurial process make sense in more than just mechanical terms; they also make sense in strategic terms. Entrepreneurs ultimately face the same challenge as any other strategist; they must design a strategy that creates and delivers value, despite the friction of competitive forces and organizational processes. They must craft a plan that identifies the opportunity while addressing the threats. They must identify the sources of value and rareness and then acquire the resources necessary to bring their strategy about. They must take into account the potential for competitor response and the dangers of imitation and substitution. And they must do all of this in such a way that other potential stakeholders like investors, business partners, suppliers, and employees will see and understand the potential of the new venture. Finally, they must ultimately deliver on that potential, creating value in the form of transactions that lead to revenues and profits. Viewed in this way, entrepreneurs are strategists who operate in a special context and so grapple with a variety of special challenges unique to their setting.

New Complexities

Most of those special challenges fall under the heading of **liabilities of newness** (Stinchcombe, 1965). Newness, in any endeavor, carries with it some unique problems related to unfamiliarity and the lack of example or precedent. Entrepreneurs create new products and services or offer existing products and services in new places or in different ways. As a result, they often face greater uncertainty and ambiguity than others. Introducing new products or services means educating customers; it may also mean creating new processes, training new workers, or retraining existing workers in new methods. It may mean developing new supplier networks, introducing new business models, or educating investors on the risks and prospects of a new business model. The unique nature of the setting requires that entrepreneurs be good strategists while also dealing with heightened uncertainty on their own as well on the part of others.

Many of the special issues and topics that have been studied by scholars in the field of entrepreneurship are reflections of these challenges and liabilities. **Franchising**, for example, is an organizational form that enables growth by leveraging the financial resources of multiple independent owners, while also providing those independent owners access to a recognized name, to proven systems and to tested products and services. **Licensing** is a mechanism where new firms can commercialize an invention or a piece of intellectual property, without incurring the risk and uncertainty associated with market research and product development. Research into the various roles of venture capitalists reflects the fact that these individuals can often contribute more than just money to the success of their ventures. Having invested in other entrepreneurs and other new firms, these VCs will often have expertise and connections that can be leveraged to reduce uncertainty and to improve the chances of venture success.

For the purposes of this book though and for purpose of learning to apply the strategic framework and to think strategically, it is helpful to view entrepreneurship as a special case of strategic management. Returning to the example at the beginning of the chapter, EAI is an entrepreneurial venture, started to fill a niche and to seize upon an opportunity. Its success reflects a fit between the environment and a set of resources that are valuable and rare, and its continued success will depend upon the ongoing value of those resources in the face of potential imitation and substitution. Like any other firm, EAI must develop and nurture its competitive advantage through its day-to-day activities. It must sell services to clients who are seeking their own best interests, it must deliver value over and above its costs, and it must do all of this while creating new options for new competitive advantage in the future. In reality then, EAI's continued success will be a reflection of its strategy and the ability of its managers to learn, adapt, and implement the right strategy at the right time.

As mentioned earlier, specialization by academics and managers has become a necessary reality in the face of the complexities throughout the business world. However, specialization can be a double-edged sword when an intense focus on how things are different prevents seeing how they are still the same. Such is the case here; while different and specialized in many ways, entrepreneurship is still best understood as a special application of strategic management. It is still about creating value, still about competitive advantage, and still about providing a return on investment. While the terminology and issues may change and while the challenges may be somewhat unique, those basics remain the same.

INTERNATIONAL BUSINESS

There is an old saying that only two things are truly certain: death and taxes. Perhaps it is time to add a third item to this list of inevitabilities. Specifically, the world of business is becoming increasingly global. Table 10.1 provides a list of

Table 10.1
The World's Largest Companies: Now and Then

	2018	2009	2005
1	Walmart—USA	Royal Dutch Shell—Netherlands	Walmart—USA
2	State Grid—China	Exxon Mobil-USA	British Petroleum (BP)—Britain
3	Sinopec Group—China	Walmart—USA	Exxon Mobil—USA
4	China National Petroleum—China	British Petroleum (BP)—Britain	Royal Dutch Shell—Netherlands
5	Royal Dutch Shell—Netherlands	Chevron—USA	General Motors—USA

	2018	2009	2005
6	Toyota Motor—Japan	Total—France	DaimlerChrysler—Germany
7	Volkswagen—Germany	ConocoPhillips—USA	Toyota Motors—Japan
8	British Petroleum (BP)—Britain	ING Group—Netherlands	Ford—USA
9	Exxon Mobil—USA	Sinopec—China	General Electric—USA
10	Berkshire Hathaway—USA	Toyota Motors—Japan	Total—France
11	Apple—USA	Japan Post Holdings—Japan	Chevron—USA
12	Samsung Electronics—South Korea	General Electric—USA	ConocoPhillips —USA
13	McKesson—USA	China National Petroleum—China	AXA—France
14	Glencore—Switzerland	Volkswagen—Germany	Allianz—Germany
15	UnitedHealth Group—USA	State Grid—China	Volkswagen—Germany
16	Daimler—Germany	Dexia Group—Belgium	Citigroup—USA
17	CVS Health—USA	ENI—Italy	ING Group—Netherlands
18	Amazon.com—USA	General Motors—USA	Nippon Telegraph & Telephone—Japan
19	EXOR Group—Italy	Ford—USA	AIG—USA
20	AT&T—USA	Allianz—Germany	IBM—USA
21	General Motors—USA	HSBC Holdings—Britain	Siemens—Germany
22	Ford Motor—USA	Gazprom—Russia	Carrefour—France
23	China State Construction Engineering—China	Daimler—Germany	Hitachi—Japan
24	Hon Hai Precision Industry—Taiwan	BNP Paribas—France	Assicurazioni Generali—Italy
25	Amerisource Bergen—USA	Carrefour—France	Matsushita Electric—Japan

the world's 25 largest companies by revenue in 2005, 2009, and 2018. Of those on the list in 2005, 11 are from Europe, 10 are from the United States, and 4 are from Asia. Just 4 years later, in 2009 the list included 13 from Europe, 7 from the United States, and 5 from Asia. As of 2018, the list includes just 6 companies from Europe, 12 from the United States and 7 from Asia. Imagine how different this list would have looked 30 years ago and how different it may look 30 years from now. In addition, consider that there are many other large and well know companies with names like Axa, Honda, Gazprom, Pemex, LG, Petrobras, Tata, Rosneft, and Telefonica from countries like France, Japan, Mexico, Brazil, India, Russia, Spain, and South Korea among the Fortune Global 500 that are growing rapidly as leaders in their industries. And the birth of new industries may yet provide even more impetus for other new firms to expand and grow into global giants.

The amount of international business transacted by firms such as these, along with many others, is growing rapidly. Fifty years ago, international trade was barely more than 1% of world GDP. By 2015, it represented nearly 30%, and that number continues to grow. Direct investment in foreign assets by firms and individuals, called **foreign direct investment (FDI)**, has also risen drastically over the past 30 years, to over $1 trillion in 2018, or roughly 1.5% of gross world product. The past 20 years have seen an explosion of treaties, agreements, and new organizations intended to facilitate the ease of international business and trade. Perhaps the most significant of these was the establishment of the Euro as the standard currency among the majority of nations in the European Union. The Euro is now accepted and used in 19 **Eurozone** countries, making trade between individuals and businesses in those countries virtually seamless. But there have been other significant changes as well. The North American Free Trade Agreement (NAFTA), which was renegotiated and renamed the United States-Mexico-Canada Agreement, created and still maintains a free-trading block among the 3 participating countries. A similar arrangement has evolved in Southeast Asia, where 10 countries are members of the Association of Southeast Asian Nations (ASEAN), which is designed to leverage bargaining power and to facilitate trade and economic growth. Owing to the desire for a world body to promote, monitor, and facilitate international trade, the World Trade Organization was created in 1995, for the purpose of liberalizing world trade. The WTO now has 164 members, 85% of the 193 nations recognized by the United Nations.

Even amidst the recent and growing headwinds of increased nationalism, threatened tariff activity, the global COVID-19 pandemic, the rancor of Brexit and the failed Trans-Pacific Partnership, the trend towards globalization in the business world is persistent and pervasive. Consider that in 2002, worldwide containerized cargo traffic was roughly 225 million TEUs (20-foot equivalent container units). By 2017, that volume had roughly tripled to more than 776 million TEUs. And container traffic accounts only for the shipment of merchandise. Consider also the growth in services, energy, finance, and information. Indeed,

World Trade Organization data show that the value of all worldwide exports in 2017 was nearly $18 trillion. The total of all worldwide exports stood at only $1 trillion in 1976. Headwinds notwithstanding, then, the trend is towards greater international trade and greater growth in opportunities for business that do business internationally.

Two things then are abundantly clear. First, the **globalization** of business is pervasive and ongoing. Certainly, there has been international business and trade across national borders going back thousands of years. But the last century has seen that level of that trade grow exponentially, both in absolute terms and as a proportion of overall economic activity. While there will surely be periodic instances and momentary episodes in the future where the level of international business declines, the overall trend is strong and likely to continue. It is also clear that globalization is driving a trend towards **transnationalism**, where national identities are blurred and pose increasingly smaller constraints on the conduct of business. The second implication is that international business will be an increasingly common and important concern for strategic managers. Indeed, international business was once viewed as being so unusual and complex that it was the province of only the largest companies and only the most sophisticated and dedicated specialists. Today, however, international business is more and more a normal part of strategy, of increasing importance to the success of every firm and to the challenge of every strategic manager.

For the purposes of this discussion, international business is defined as transactions between individuals and businesses that cross national borders. A wide variety of issues and activities fall into that definition. Things like currency values and trading along with cultural differences and attitudes are significant parts of the international business landscape. Other issues too like patenting and intellectual property protection, ownership and taxation, labor practices, government regulation, and accounting rules on activities conducted in other countries, with other currencies, and according to different laws all fall within the boundaries this broad definition. Taken together, though, they all affect the performance of international firms, as well as the competitive environments of most non-international firms. Given this pervasive influence, international business must somehow fit into the larger framework and logic of strategic management.

As discussed earlier, though, strategic management is a highly generalizable discipline. So, while there is much about international business that is specialized, technical, and complex, there are also many issues that parallel the basic framework and logic of strategy. Understanding these common themes and leveraging the basic similarities can facilitate better management, with better performance as a result. This section then outlines some of those parallel issues along with some common implications meant to help students and managers translate across the contexts, from basic strategic management to international business and then back again.

International Strategies

One important similarity comes in the area of strategy and competitive advantage. Recall that competitive advantage derives from one of two basic sources, cost and differentiation. As discussed in Chapter 5, these generic strategies are really reflections of market conditions and demand elasticity. In cases where customers have strong preferences for a particular product, service, or supplier, their options are limited; they are less willing to substitute and more willing to pay a premium price. Thus, there is opportunity for competitive advantage based upon differentiation. Otherwise, in cases where customers have little or no preference among the suppliers of a particular product or service, their options are much broader; they are more willing to substitute and less willing to pay a premium price. Thus, in cases like this there is opportunity for competitive advantage based on low transaction costs. Across the range of all products, industries, and transactions, virtually every competitive advantage can be described and understood in terms of these two basic dimensions.

Not surprisingly, then, the same is true in the international context; elasticity of demand, along with issues like product substitutability and bargaining power still shape strategy and competitive advantage. In the international context, though, the scale and complexity of the market are much greater. Thus, the opportunity emerges for two different generic strategies, leveraging the same principles but doing so in a way that is unique to the international context. These two strategies are the **global** and the **multi-domestic** strategies. Both strategies reflect some basic realities about the international market and about how a firm plans to compete within it.

To illustrate, consider Vodafone, which is, together with its various subsidiaries and partners, one of the largest providers of mobile communications in the world. Based in the United Kingdom, Vodafone and its partners have over 300 million customers, in over 70 countries, such as South Africa, India, Chile, Turkey, New Zealand, Russia, Egypt, Italy, and Germany. In 25 of these countries, Vodafone owns much of the infrastructure needed to support its network. In the others, it operates through a series of partially owned subsidiaries and partners. In all of them, though, it uses the same or similar technologies to deliver the same basic services, with the same basic contracts and business models. In essence, Vodafone is a global company with the ability to treat the entire world as one huge marketplace, an approach which affords it tremendous economies of scale. That scale facilitates Vodafone's competitive advantage by providing seamless usage across regions, a wide range of plans and options, as well as a wide range of devices and functionality. More importantly, all of this capability and flexibility lowers the transaction costs for customers who often have many other options for the same basic services. These customers benefit from the range of their options and so are frequently elastic, able to shop from among a number of suppliers and choose the one that offers the features, equipment, functionality, and price that bests suits their needs. Vodafone's **global strategy** then leverages the same principles as the basic low-cost strategy. It is often the easiest choice, the choice offering the most options, the choice with the lowest price, and the choice with the greatest capability at a particular price point. Taking into account all of these things, it is the choice that meets the needs of the customer at the lowest overall transaction cost. By expanding its low-cost strategy globally and doing what it does on a worldwide scale, Vodafone is able to expand the size of its market, the scope of its capabilities, and the scale of its economies dramatically and exercise great competitive advantage over firms that lack similar size, scope, and scale.

The global strategy then follows an economic logic that is very similar to the low-cost strategy, leveraging things like efficiency, scale economy, and portability to offer products and services that appeal to elastic customers. But it does so by treating the world as a single, large, and seamless market where one product or product category can be adapted easily to suit all of the global demand. Standardization around one basic model provides enormous scale advantages, lowering costs per unit dramatically. Standardization and scale enable firms to source their materials at lower costs. Vodafone has enormous bargaining power over the suppliers of its equipment, the firms that deliver its advertising, and the institutions that finance its operations. It even has bargaining power over the governments and partners in the countries in which it operates. And it uses all of this bargaining power to lower its costs and to make its products and services more attractive to more and more customers, enabling greater competitiveness in a business marked by high elasticity of demand.

Other firms too have followed this same strategy. Numerous large financial institutions, like JPMorgan Chase, HSBC, BNP Paribas, and Deutsche Bank, have followed a similar path of trying to provide a seamless presence and consistent service across a wide range of national borders. The automobile industry has evolved towards global competition where a very few large manufacturers, like Ford, Toyota, Hyundai, GM, Volkswagen, and Honda, control the vast majority of the world's car and light truck market. These firms leverage common technologies, designs, and platforms; enjoy enormous bargaining power over their suppliers; and leverage tremendous economies of scale, as necessary to gain market share and profitability in an industry where substitutability and bargaining power of the buyer are high. Indeed, in every industry where the conditions are ripe for low-cost-based competitive advantage, there are also opportunities for a global strategy. In the aerospace industry and in petroleum production, in basic food commodities and in cement, even in industries as different as steel and computer assembly, there is the opportunity for advantage by employing a global strategy. Those opportunities reflect the realities of the markets, products, services, and customers. And, just as those same basic forces drive domestic competition towards low-cost strategies, so too do they drive international competition towards global strategies.

Consider though how different this is from a multi-domestic strategy. A good example of this approach can be seen in a firm like Johnson & Johnson. Like Vodafone, Johnson & Johnson is large, with tremendous international reach. Based in the U.S., Johnson & Johnson operates in nearly 60 countries around the world, like Argentina, Ukraine, Russia, France, China, Israel, and the United States, with millions of customers and billions of dollars in sales and infrastructure spread across the globe. However, as opposed to Vodafone, which produces just a few basic products, Johnson & Johnson produces hundreds of products in the areas of pharmaceuticals, consumer goods, and medical devices. Moreover, it operates through 250 semi-autonomous subsidiaries, organized into groups based upon product and geographic similarity. Both domestically and internationally, Johnson & Johnson seeks to be a premium provider. When its products have direct substitutes, it focuses on adding value through quality, reliability, service, and innovation. And it is reluctant to sacrifice price or margin simply to gain market share.

Operating with so many different products in so many different markets though, the challenge of this approach is enormous. Across a huge spectrum of tastes and preferences, across a maze of laws and regulations, amidst myriad different cultural norms and histories, Johnson & Johnson must position its brands and its many products as unique and different and so worthy of a premium price. To do this, it must do two things. First, it must recognize and understand those differences in all of the various different countries and regions in which it operates. Second, it must adjust its strategy to meet the specific needs of each of those various and different markets. In essence, it must see the world as a patchwork of different markets, each with its own characteristics and variations and each warranting its own strategic variations. This approach yields a host of different small strategies tailored to the contours of the local marketplace but together all part of the larger corporate whole.

As with the global strategy, the multi-domestic case is uniquely international. As the name implies, it involves operating in multiple different domestic environments. However, this strategy leverages some of the same principles as a domestic strategy based on differentiation, as it seeks to segment the demand and to match products and services to individual tastes and preferences. A multi-domestic strategy leans towards customization and away from standardization, again in an effort to appeal to the unique and varied preferences of different regions and groups. In doing all of this, a **multi-domestic strategy** seeks to capitalize on familiarity and loyalty, which can reduce elasticity of demand, increasing prices and margins. But doing all of that necessitates local information on the preferences and tastes of the different regions and customer groups as well as the systemic flexibility to provide products appealing to a wide array of tastes. For example, it requires the dexterity to design, make, and sell one type of product for the Chinese market and yet a very different sort of product for the South American market. And it requires the discipline to allow the business units in all of those different regions to evolve and adapt their own unique strategies, as necessary to appear differentiated in their own domestic contexts. This is the challenge that Johnson & Johnson faces, and this is the reason for its complex corporate-level strategy and structure.

Other firms though have adopted similar approaches. Yum! Brands, for instance, operates more than 48,000 restaurants, franchised and company owned, in 140 countries around the world. Its brands include Taco Bell, Pizza Hut, and WingStreet. While based in Louisville, Kentucky, only 38% of its locations are located inside the U.S., which means that Yum! has nearly 30,000 restaurants in countries outside of the U.S. Moreover, many of these international stores are frequently owned and run by local franchisees or joint-venture partners. These local owners and operators have limited autonomy over store concept and design as well as over menu variations and supply chains. As a result, each of the different brands can take on a uniquely local flavor, appropriate to its location and customers. A Pizza Hut in St. Petersburg, Russia, for instance, may feel very different from a Pizza Hut in Paris, France, and a KFC in Santiago, Chile, may look and feel very different from a KFC in Oxford, England. The result is a strategy adapted according to local knowledge and preference, a strategy designed to build familiarity and loyalty within particular markets, so as to support higher prices and margins. Indeed, anywhere there is opportunity for this sort of customization, there is the opportunity for a multi-domestic strategy.

The music industry, for example, is worldwide. Yet, the leading firms in the industry, firms like Sony, EMI, Warner Music, and Vivendi follow multi-domestic strategies, promoting artists and producing music that is tailored to specific national and regional tastes. The same is true in healthcare, where myriad laws, regulations, and payment practices necessitate wide variation in medical devices, pharmaceutical products, and service delivery practices, as necessary to suit the local markets. The prepared food and food products industries are often multi-domestic, given the wide variety of tastes and regulations in different countries and regions. For instance, Grupo Bimbo is a worldwide leader in baked goods. Based in Mexico City, Grupo Bimbo has annual sales of $15 billion, with operations in 32 countries, including Mexico, Brazil, Argentina, Peru, the U.S., Russia, Spain, France, and China. It markets over 150 different brands and delivers to 2.5 million locations daily. So, while it is a huge organization, Bimbo's operations are still largely local, as necessary to match local tastes and to assure freshness and high-quality service. Generally speaking, then, where there is opportunity for differentiation-based competitive advantage, there is often opportunity for a multi-domestic strategy. Both leverage individual differences and preferences; both capitalize on flexibility and customization so as to satisfy unique, local pockets of demand. And both seek to leverage inelasticity in an effort to increase profit and margin. So, just as the global strategy mapped onto economic principles similar to those underlying a low cost strategy, so does the multi-domestic strategy map onto economic principles similar to those underlying a differentiation strategy. As a result, understanding those basic principles can help a manager to better understand and function well in both domestic and international contexts.

Of course, this is not to say that all global strategies are entirely low-cost-based or that all multi-domestic strategies are based purely on differentiation. Indeed, as discussed in Chapter 5, all strategies and every competitive advantage combine elements of both. Even the most cost-conscious consumers have some concern for quality and some desire to have idiosyncratic preferences met. Thus, even pure low-cost strategies will make some effort at differentiating their products and services. For instance, Wal-Mart follows a strategy that is largely cost-based. Yet, it still invests in programs and features designed to build loyalty and to promote perceptions of quality and reliability. Likewise, even most discriminating and inelastic consumer, with the strongest preferences for specific products and services, will still have some desire to minimize costs. Thus, even a firm like Ritz Carlton, which pursues a strategy that is largely based on differentiation, will invest in cost-saving and convenience measures like computerized climate controls or points sharing packages. Indeed, this is an example of another similarity across the contexts; every strategy reflects a unique combination of attributes, specific to each firm's resources, position, and intent. And the success of each strategy will reflect the degree to which it fits the contours of its environment. Combining features and approaches that blend together elements of purely low-cost and differentiation strategies, each firm works to position itself in a way that will earn it the most and the most profitable transactions. What is different in the international context is the size and the complexity of market. And while that size and complexity offer new problems, they also offer new opportunities.

Implementation and Fit

Another similarity between the basic strategic framework and international business is the relationship between strategy and implementation. Recall from Chapter 8 that strategy drives the shape of the organization. Just as form follows function, so should the attributes of the organization reflect the imperatives of the strategy. This was the point of the 7-S model and the rationale underlying the idea of fit between strategy and things like structure, skills, style, staff, and shared values. Given the importance of this principle to organizational performance, it should come as no surprise that the relationship is just as important in the international context as it is domestically. Success still depends on having the right capabilities, the right people, and the right organization for the strategy.

To continue with the examples of Vodafone and Johnson & Johnson, it is clear how these two firms are different in terms of structure and approach and how those differences reflect differences in their strategies. Whereas Vodafone is largely centralized, Johnson & Johnson is highly decentralized. Where Johnson & Johnson employs specialists across a broad spectrum of technologies, functions, and disciplines, Vodafone is much more focused, specializing in a relatively narrow band of technologies, products, and services. Vodafone's marketing, contracting, billing, and accounting systems are also likely much more streamlined and simple than those of Johnson & Johnson, given its more limited product offerings and business models. Both firms though are tremendously successful and both would hold considerable advantages over most purely domestic competitors. Thus, by combining good understanding of basic strategic management principles, with the enormous opportunities of an increasingly worldwide marketplace, both firms have been successful.

To return to the example at the beginning of the chapter, it should come as no surprise that even a small firm like EAI could be successful internationally. It simply must match its capabilities to the nature of the opportunity, leveraging the logic and principles of strategy to create value for its customers around the world. As a small boutique firm, EAI emphasizes customized service. Thus, it interacts with each prospective client directly, designing solutions for each specific situation and problem. There is relatively little effort given to standardization or to leveraging economies of scale; each client and each problem are unique. This approach limits growth and overall volume. At the same time, it builds loyalty, limits substitutability, and promotes premium prices and margins. And, just like with larger organizations, its success depends upon how well its systems, people, skills, and capabilities fit its strategy. Just like Vodafone and Johnson & Johnson, EAI benefits from the expanded opportunities of an increasingly worldwide marketplace. However, it too must develop strategy appropriate to its position and market and it too must construct the sorts of structures and systems to that strategy. Whether in a global or a domestic market, these relationships are universal.

These parallels and similarities notwithstanding, no one should underestimate the complexity of the international marketplace. Cultural, legal, economic, even geographic distances can extract a tremendous toll on a firm's strategy and success. Ghemawat (2001) provides an insightful and instructive discussion of the various costs associated with these different dimensions of distance and concludes that, even in an increasingly small and integrated world, distance matters. Every manager and every student and academic would do well to heed this advice. But fear of the costs should never outweigh the opportunity. International competitors that follow the principles of strategic management will often enjoy substantial advantages over purely domestic firms. Thus, international business is a reality for virtually every manager, if not now, then in the not-so-distant future. The challenge is to understand what is similar and what is different, to adapt and apply what is similar, and to identify and account for the costs and risks of what is different. While a full examination is beyond the scope of this book, the matter is nevertheless central to performance and so fully within the purview and responsibility of the strategist.

LEADERSHIP

For years, leadership has been among the most popular topics in business schools. Students, managers, journalists, and academics have all contributed to the phenomenon of making leaders into celebrities and turning leadership into one of the featured classes in the business school. This fascination with leadership and with leaders themselves reflects the fact that many of these celebrities have real influence over their organizations. For example, the resignation of founders Bernie Marcus and Arthur Blank from Home Depot created an enormous shock, affecting the firm's growth, profitability, and stock price. Likewise, when Steve Jobs passed away in 2011, there was great concern about the direction of Apple and the ability of the company to continue its innovation and growth. And Jamie Dimon, CEO and Chairman of JPMorgan Chase, is commonly credited with leading the bank through the financial crisis of 2008 and into a position of market leadership in 2018. As these examples illustrate, leaders command attention because leadership matters to the success and performance of organizations.

But what is leadership and how does it relate to strategic management? As was the case with international business, a full and complete analysis of the topic would be beyond the scope of this book. Indeed, few topics have been studied so broadly, in such detail, and across so many settings. However, because leadership is so consequential in the minds of so many and because the topics of leadership and strategy are so frequently overlapped and confounded, it is important to sort out some basic parallels.

First of all, leadership is generally defined as influencing others towards the achievement of a common goal. By implication, leaders are the individuals who exercise that influence, setting goals and directing others towards their attainment. Under the umbrella of such a broad definition, research on leadership has proliferated, with perhaps thousands of articles having been published describing many different facets of leadership and often providing very different perspectives on its conduct and effects. Indeed, in an insightful review of that literature at the time, Pfeffer (1977) noted the ambiguities in the actual definition of leadership, along with ambiguities surrounding its effects and antecedents. More recently, Judge, Woolf, Hurst, and Livingston concluded that "not every scholar agrees on what is effective leadership or the behaviors that produce this effectiveness" (2008: 335). Other reviews of the research on leadership (Avolio, 2005; Yukl, 2006) conclude as well that it is a complex and multifaceted phenomenon, involving many layers of action, interaction, and response. As a consequence, studying leadership has proven to be a challenge, and understanding leadership in all of its various forms and appearances has proven especially difficult.

Basics of Leadership and Strategy

While different researchers, authors, and publications will emphasize different aspects of leadership, most will agree on the importance of some basic dimensions. These would include (1) casting a vision or purpose, (2) communicating with and motivating others, (3) catalyzing innovation and change, and (4) driving for results. Each of these activities has been associated with leadership and each is essential to long-term value and performance. As a result, each is inextricably linked to good strategic management.

Casting a Vision

Casting a vision or purpose is among the most familiar issues in leadership and it is one of the first challenges of strategic management. Recall that the mission was discussed in both Chapters 2 and 3 and depicted as a first step in the larger strategic management process in Figure 3.1. While scholars make fine-grained distinctions among visions, missions, and the core values of an organization, practically speaking, together, they serve a common purpose. That is to provide a common principle or rationale for the organization and its actions. Put differently, the purpose of the vision or mission is to answer the question, why does this organization exist and what principles govern its actions? For each organization, this purpose is a little different. For example, Coca-Cola follows a simple mission, "to refresh the world" through its portfolio of beverages. For ING, the Dutch financial services giant, the mission is to "deliver its financial products and services in the way customers want them delivered." Finally, for Procter & Gamble, the purpose is to "provide branded products and services of superior quality and value that improve the lives of the world's consumers." All of these statements provide a general sense of direction that serves to unify and guide decision making and action.

Of course, anyone can articulate a vision; simply writing down a statement about the purpose of the firm is no guarantee of success. For leadership to have its desired effect, this vision must activate and energize the efforts of the organization and its various stakeholders. It must tap into the basic needs of the customers and into unseen opportunities in the environment. Indeed, leadership looks very much like entrepreneurship in this regard. Good leaders articulate a message that resonates with the needs of their constituents, providing something new and different that heretofore had not been obvious and available elsewhere. This message has meaning not just for the customers or constituents but also for employees and internal stakeholders of the organization, serving to energize and rally their efforts. Employees of Wal-Mart used to love store visits by founder Sam Walton. He served as an inspiration, embodying the vision he cast for the company and visibly connecting the actions of rank-and-file employees to the corporate strategy and purpose. In casting a vision, leadership provides important value and momentum, both substantively and symbolically. It points the way forward, towards better opportunities; it provides guidance and direction for implementation; and it serves to motivate effort, connecting actions to outcomes and providing energy and enthusiasm.

The evidence is compelling that a well-crafted vision is important to organizational performance. However, simply understanding this is not enough. True visionaries are rare, and casting a meaningful vision is easier said than done. Thus, it helps for leaders or potential leaders to understand basic strategic management. At its core, strategy is about setting direction. The framework, models, and processes of strategic management are designed to facilitate that. Strategy then should serve the purposes of leadership, enabling the leader to better assess environmental conditions and to better identify needs and opportunities. It should help leaders understand organizational competencies and resources, so as to leverage them to full effect. And it should help to make clear the linkage between cause and effect, allowing every member of a firm to understand the relevance of their function to value creation and competitive advantage. Indeed, it is no exaggeration to say that good strategic management is the essence of leadership and that leadership is a key responsibility of strategic management. Nowhere is this more clear than in the role of casting a vision.

Communicating and Motivating

Of course, even the best vision is worth little until it is connected to the organization. As discussed earlier in this book, strategy cannot be separated from implementation because the two are judged together and by their end results. As a practical matter, it is simply not possible to have a great leader who does not deliver great outcomes. Thus, the vision, mission, and strategy are all inextricably linked to the communication and motivation that occur throughout the organization. Many great leaders have been noteworthy because of their communication skills and because of their ability to rally effort around their cause. Ronald Reagan and Barak Obama, presidents from different eras and different political parties have both been praised for their abilities to communicate and connect with voters in a way that inspires and activates. Google founders Larry Page and Sergey Brin created enormous value and wealth not just because of the vision they cast but also because of their ability to build and motivate an organization that could deliver on the promise to "organize the world's information and to make it universally accessible." Leadership is certainly about casting a vision, but it is also about building and managing an organization that can bring that vision into reality. Thus, it is also about communicating with and motivating others.

One prominent stream of academic research on leadership looks at the relationship between leaders and their followers. Called **leader-member exchange** (Diesnesch & Liden, 1986), this stream of research considers how leaders engage and motivate the support of their immediate followers. In this view, leadership occurs through a series of interpersonal relationships. Leaders may have some symbolic influence at the organizational level, through their visions and public statements. However, most of their effect is transmitted through their immediate followers. Thus the relationship between the leader and each member of this small circle is of key importance. Moreover, each of these lieutenants is also a leader of his or her own circle of followers, and so on throughout the organization. In this view, then, leadership can be seen as a series of interpersonal relationships, with leaders and followers taking on different roles and negotiating different responsibilities, as a function of their ability to influence, inspire, and deliver.

Because it focuses on individuals and dyads, this view is often seen as being outside scope of strategic management, but this is not the case. Indeed, the ability of a leader to connect with individuals and to influence them towards the right goals is a key driver of success. Research and practical experience have both shown that strategic management is a shared activity (Hambrick & Mason, 1984). CEOs in virtually every major corporation rely on a trusted inner circle of managers, called the **top management team**, who have substantial influence over the operation of the organization. This inner circle typically consists of vice-presidents, division managers, key board members, and various functional heads. Together they share the leadership of the firm, allocating responsibilities, promoting specific initiatives, and executing the vision through their various functional roles. Certainly the nature of the relationship between the CEO and these top management team members is strategically significant. Moreover, each member of the top management team likely has his or her team of followers, providing similar support and sharing similar responsibility.

As discussed in Chapter 8, the implementation of strategy can be viewed as a series of intraorganizational linkages and cascading responsibilities. One of the great deficiencies of many top managers is an inability to connect these dots; to understand the implications of a particular strategy to all those impacted; and to adequately divide, assign, and support the necessary roles and responsibilities. Too often, this detailed and tedious work can seem unglamorous and unworthy of a leader's time. However, the ability to make the necessary connections, to communicate the essential elements of the vision and strategy, and to relate those elements to the specific tasks of the various functions and roles within the organization is a key function of leadership. Leaders simply must be able to break down the strategy, to articulate it in terms of its operational implications, and to motivate every individual to make their needed contributions. This is true whether at Apple, JPMorgan Chase, Home Depot, or Wal-Mart; none of these firms would be what they are today were it not for the contributions of many individuals, all performing well in the roles outlined by the strategy. Thus, it is impossible to separate leadership from the need to communicate with and motivate followers in the behaviors necessary to make the vision a reality.

Catalyzing Innovation and Change

While individual behaviors are essential to strategic success, they are also a potential threat to innovation and change. Recall, from Chapter 8, the discussion of path dependence and the paradoxical nature of performance. Successful behaviors can be repeated and reinforced to the point that they become dysfunctional. Market leaders often defend the status quo against new technologies, fearing the loss of position and share. Key managers can grow defensive about new opportunities, as they fear erosion of their own influence or seek to leverage past investments. These tendencies, which were discussed in Chapter 8 and compared to the mythical story of Icarus, are a key challenge for leaders, who are to be catalysts for innovation and change.

Innovation and change are essential to strategic success. Without innovation, every firm will eventually stagnate and drift out of the mainstream. And without change, every capability will eventually grow calcified and obsolete, becoming irrelevant to customers and competitors alike and eventually losing all competitive advantage. Thus, innovation and change are keys to long-term success and key imperatives of any successful strategy. Unfortunately, innovation and change do not happen by themselves. Rather, firms naturally develop their own inertia, with all the weight of habit and history reinforcing practices from the past. Leaders then must find ways to break this momentum and shift the energies of the organization into new directions. Moreover, they must do this when the need for such change is less than fully obvious.

Among the many responsibilities of leadership, this one is perhaps the most important and yet least well understood (Heifetz & Laurie, 2001). Indeed, many who seek to be leaders fail to understand that the path to leadership is rarely popular and well-traveled. For example, although it is now taken for granted, there was a time when air conditioning was viewed with suspicion. At the turn of the century, the gases used in air conditioners were often toxic and flammable and malfunctions could easily result in serious injury or death. So, when firms like Frigidaire, Carrier, and GE began working to develop the technology and market for residential air conditioning, they met with little success and had difficulty sustaining their efforts in the face a tepid response from the market. More recently, the manufacture and sale of hybrid drive automobiles was a considerable risk. At least initially, consumers reacted negatively to the costs, to the size and limited power of the cars, and to their awkward appearance. Thus, many of the leading car makers were reluctant to invest or to invest heavily. However, Toyota did invest heavily, pushing the technology and design and promoting the vehicles despite their unpopularity. Of course, the Prius, Toyota's hybrid, became a resounding success, and 7 of the top 10 selling hybrid models in 2018 were made by Toyota. But that success was a result of Toyota's risk taking and leadership.

As mentioned, leadership is defined as influencing others toward a goal. But what is often missed in this definition is that these others needed to be influenced toward that goal because they were not going there by themselves. To put it differently, leadership involves directing and influencing others towards a goal that they did not know they wanted. Warren Buffet once said that "the chains of habit are too light to be felt until they are too heavy to be broken." The lesson is that the need for change is rarely obvious until it is too late. Leaders must recognize that need early and so be prepared to bear the frustrations of having to go it alone for a time. Here again, leadership looks very much like entrepreneurship in that both must anticipate and act based on anticipated realities and so both bear the risk of being wrong. Had the price of oil not increased, had the concerns of climate change not focused attention on carbon emissions, Toyota might not have looked so visionary. Alternatively, had Apple never introduced the iPod and had consumers never had the ability to take their music with them, Sirius/XM radio might have become a huge success. But the market did not evolve as they anticipated and satellite radio has struggled for profitability. The simple yet harsh reality is that leadership bears the responsibility for innovation and change and that implies a significant burden and risk.

Here again, a key dimension of leadership overlaps with strategic management. Recall that adaptation and change are a large part of the ongoing challenge of strategy implementation. Through interaction with the environment, a firm learns what works and what does not; through many trials and errors, firms introduce and perfect innovations, cultivating options and gathering information on which to base future strategies. This ongoing process of learning and adaptation is essential to success and so a fundamental component of strategy. However, it does not happen naturally. Rather, it must be catalyzed and directed and its value must be articulated. It must be institutionalized and promoted throughout the organization, encouraging managers at every level to innovate and take risks and reminding the organization's stakeholders of the hazards of inertia. Once again then, good strategic management is the imperative of leadership. Leaders must take action to make innovation and change happen, even when so doing is unpopular or seems unnatural. They must cast the vision, communicate the purpose, and motivate and direct others towards a goal that will likely not be obvious or well understood. They must understand when to change and when to stay the course so that the organization grows more valuable as a result. Like every facet of strategic management, change and innovation are tools for furthering competitive advantage.

Driving for Results

Focusing on success leads directly to the discussion of the final dimension of leadership. Leadership drives for success, both now and into the future. As discussed in several places throughout this book, conflicts between the short and the long term are commonplace. Should a firm invest and experiment with new innovations or should it focus its efforts and exploit an existing advantage? Should a firm go the extra mile and incur extra costs to please a customer or should it hold its ground and make only reasonable accommodations? Should a firm continue to leverage an asset until it is fully depreciated or should it invest now in a newer but uncertain technology? These sorts of questions are pervasive in day-to-day management and yet significant to overall performance, and they demand immediate answers. Thus, they are opportunities for leadership as well as the moments where real strategy is made.

As mentioned, leadership and strategy are judged on their end results. But end results are typically a function of many small actions and seemingly obscure decisions. As discussed in Chapter 5, competitive advantage and organizational performance are manifestations of many discrete, competitive episodes. Firms that perform well over time do so by doing well in these episodes. A strong competitive advantage and strong organizational performance are the aggregated outcomes of many individual instances of good decision making, where value is created for individual customers and where lessons about the purpose, commitment, and values of the firm are taught and learned.

Linking all of those discrete episodes together and connecting them to the overall mission and strategy of the firm is the job of leadership. In his seminal work, Phillip Selznick (1957) described this as the process of **institutionalization**. To an objective researcher or a detached theorist, a business is simply a collection of individuals and resources, performing routines and taking actions, based on the costs and benefits at hand. However, to real people, whether customers, employees, suppliers, or competitors, a business can seem much more. Firms can take on a personality and they can have clear and discernable styles. Their products can have a nostalgic value and they can make lasting contributions to society. Firms can have an identity and grow into positions of trust. In essence, through the consistency and value of their actions, firms can become more than mere collections of individuals, resources, and routines; instead, they can become institutions, whose place and value are recognized, understood, and even sought out by many. This process of institutionalization is a function of leadership but it is also the result of good strategic management.

As with other things, though, institutionalization does not occur on its own. Rather, it must be organized and directed. Like a starter turning an engine, leadership must provide the impetus and the energy to move a firm from a mere collection of individuals and actions to being an institution, where every job, every office, and every routine is infused with meaning and purpose. This is what it means to drive to results, to never be satisfied or complacent, to never be content with wasted effort or with lost opportunities, to always look for new options and to be one's own toughest competitor. This drive must come from somewhere because pushing against it will be the inertia of the firm along with the friction of habit. Firms can easily settle into a peaceful routine, especially when they are in a secure position. But that sort of peace can be misleading and that sort of settling can be dangerous.

Roger Enrico, former CEO of PepsiCo, Inc., once credited competition from Coca-Cola as providing the energy that Pepsi needed to stay "original and lively" (Enrico & Kornbluth, 1988). Without new challenges, without some recognized threat, without some purpose to unite the different specialists, departments, and locations of an organization, work quickly devolves into a routine, where no one provides extra effort and where creativity and initiative are quickly lost. Leadership provides that drive, identifying the threats, outlining the challenges, and connecting the solutions to day-to-day decisions and actions.

Recall from Chapter 2 that the mandate for every strategic manager is to increase the net present value of the firm, both now and into the future. Focusing on value creation removes the tension between the short and long term and provides a way to link discrete actions to long-term performance. Focusing on value provides a lens through which to assess the environment and identify opportunities and threats. By focusing on value, strategists are better able to assess and evaluate their resources and capabilities, to organize their own structures and systems, and to create and evaluate new options. Following the basic logic of strategic management, every action should enable value creation, and every decision should point towards competitive advantage. Thus, the most gifted leaders are also the most strategic, and the complete application of strategic management looks very much like leadership.

Adding Value

As a conclusion for this discussion, it is important to draw one final parallel. Leadership and strategy both are marked by the value they add and that value can be quantified and evaluated. Recall from Chapter 2 the discussion of Tobin's q, a key measure of firm performance. Tobin's q is calculated as the market value of the firm, divided by the replacement value of the firm's assets. A higher number reflects greater utilization of the assets and greater value associated with their use. So, if two firms, firm A and firm B, have similar assets and yet firm A has a higher Tobin's q, it would be fair to say that firm A is using its resources to better effect. For example, Toyota and GM are similar companies in terms of their investments, market, and facilities. Yet, Toyota has a much high market value and so a much higher Tobin's q. What does that mean? It means that Toyota is better positioned, with a strong brand, a strong balance sheet, and a stronger organization overall. It means that the past actions and decisions of Toyota's management created greater value than the past actions and decisions of GM's management. Put bluntly, it means that Toyota's leadership and strategy have been more effective. In essence, leadership and strategy serve a common purpose. Like the right hand complements the left, they are different but still part of the larger whole. They interact to guide the firm in a way that enhances its overall value and they are judged in the same way, by the results that they produce.

Leadership and strategic management then are inextricably linked together, such that each is incomplete without the other. Whether in large firms like Home Depot or PepsiCo or in smaller firms like EAI (see opening vignette), leadership is the driving force while strategy is the framework for action. Together they add intangible yet significant value to the assets and resources of the firm by providing a coherent vision of what the firm should be, by communicating that purpose and motivating and enabling others to work towards it, by initiating change and innovation as necessary to keep the firm current, and by pushing for continued improvement and value in every transaction. Make no mistake, leadership matters and it does so because of its effect on the strategic process.

CORPORATE GOVERNANCE

To fully appreciate the implications surrounding leadership and strategic management, it is also important to understand corporate governance. Governance refers collectively to the processes, structures, and systems by which firms are governed. Who has the authority to speak for the firm and to make key decisions? Who sets the agenda and the basic values that will drive the strategy? How are the goals and objectives set and whose interests does the firm serve? The answers to these questions describe how the firm is governed and identify the key sources of authority and responsibility in the strategic process. Given scandals over corporate ethics, concerns over stockholder rights, and recurring frustration over executive compensation, corporate governance has become an increasingly popular topic of academic research and political debate (see Box 10.1: Sarbanes-Oxley: A Seismic Event in Corporate Governance). But even before this heightened awareness, governance was important because of its effects on organizational action and performance. As such, it too is a key issue within the larger topic of strategic management.

Public and Private Ownership

To understand governance, it is important to understand some basics. The first and perhaps most fundamental of these is the distinction between **publicly held** and **privately held** firms. Privately held firms are those in which access to ownership rights is closed to the public. Ownership of these firms can be by a single individual, by members of a family, or even by a large number of individuals who are related in some other way. However, the stock of these firms is not listed on a public exchange nor is it available for public purchase. EAI, the small consulting firm mentioned at the beginning of this chapter is privately held, controlled entirely by and operated in the interests of its owner. While privately held firms are more commonly small, large firms can be privately held too. For example, Chick-fil-A is privately held. Yet,

Box 10.1
Sarbanes-Oxley

A SEISMIC EVENT IN CORPORATE GOVERNANCE

Enacted in 2002 and originally called the "Public Company Accounting Reform and Protection Act," Sarbanes-Oxley, or SOX as it has come to be known, was a response to a host of well-publicized corporate scandals in firms like Enron, WorldCom, Peregrine Systems, and Tyco International as well as the dramatic collapse of accounting firm Arthur Andersen. The size, scope, and nature of these scandals was such that confidence in the U.S. stock market and in many public corporations was badly shaken. As a result, SOX passed both the U.S. Senate and House of Representatives by a combined vote of 522–3, and it was signed into law quickly by the then President George W. Bush. SOX was described at the time and is still considered by many to be the most far-reaching legislation affecting corporate governance, oversight, and accounting standards since the Securities and Exchange Act of 1934.

The law sets new standards of behavior and accountability for public firms, top executives, the board of directors, and auditors. The law contains 11 different sections, covering things like additional responsibilities of the board, the amount and quality of information that must be made available to the public, standards for accounting firms that audit public companies, and criminal penalties. Some of these specific provisions include restrictions on auditors taking positions in firms that were formerly their clients; personal loans from a public company to its executives; and altering, falsifying, or destroying documents in an effort to influence a bankruptcy case or securities investigation. SOX also led to the creation of the Public Company Accounting Oversight Board, a private, non-profit organization charged with overseeing the auditors of public firms in order to protect the interests of investors.

Debate continues on the overall effects of SOX. Advocates argue that it has been beneficial, restoring confidence in the capital markets by strengthening corporate governance, oversight, and the system of accounting controls. Critics contend that, these benefits notwithstanding, SOX has had a detrimental effect on the competitiveness of U.S. firms by burdening them and the entire financial system with an overly complex, and expensive set of regulations. One unintended consequence of SOX was the chilling effect that it had on venture capital. Venture capitalists often recoup their investments when the firms in which they have invested go public. The added burden of SOX-related regulation has led some firms to delay or to scrap altogether any plans for public offerings. In addition, other larger and more established firms have chosen to exit the public capital markets, choosing to return to private ownership, so as to avoid the costly and complex requirements of SOX.

While certainly not all of its effects have been intended or beneficial, SOX still represents a major step toward open and honest corporate governance, which is essential for confidence in publicly held firms.

it has roughly 2,400 restaurants and sales of $10 billion. Some other privately held firms are even larger. Cargill, Inc. is a privately held commodities and food products firm, with nearly $115 billion in revenue, over 155,000 employees, and operations in 70 countries. Cox Enterprises is also a privately held, family-controlled media conglomerate, with interests in radio, newspapers, cable television, and automobile sales. Cox has roughly 60,000 employees and revenues exceeding $21 billion.

Privately held firms tend to have simpler structures than their publicly held counterparts. Because the ownership of privately held firms is less diffused, there is less opportunity for divisions among the interests of the owners. Also, because most or all of the shareholders will share some relationship, either as family members or employees, they are better known to one another and so less likely to act in ways injurious to the group at large. Moreover, because there is often a closer relationship between ownership and management in privately held firms, there is less concern with **agency problems**. As a result, privately held firms are typically subject to less restrictive regulation, at least in the U.S. Indeed, one consequence of increased oversight of publicly held firms that resulted from the scandals that occurred in the late 1990s and early 2000s is that many public corporations were taken private by their management teams or by private investors. So, while governance is still important in privately held firms, it is frequently less complicated because the number of owners is smaller, the interests of the owners are often more homogeneous, and the pressure from external regulators is lower.

On the other hand, publicly held firms are much more visible and complicated and so receive much more attention. Publicly held firms are those whose stocks are listed on public exchanges and so are accessible to the public. The largest of these firms may have billions of shares of stock outstanding, with millions of different owners. Coca-Cola, for example, has over 4.3 billion shares of stock in circulation. Microsoft has nearly 8 billion shares of stock outstanding, and Apple has roughly 5 billion shares of stock in the hands of its owners. With potentially millions of owners, controlling different amounts of stock and with different levels of attention and involvement, it is easy to see why governance in publicly held firms is so important and how it can become complicated.

Agency Problems

The issue of greatest concern in the governance of publicly held firms is the separation of ownership and control; this is the agency problem referenced earlier (Fama & Jensen, 1983). Typically, the principals do not directly manage the firm, despite the fact that they are its legal owners. Rather, managers are hired professionals, who act as agents of the owners. The managers control the firms but can bear few risks of ownership. As a result, their orientations can be quite different, which creates the potential for **moral hazard**. Managers may behave differently than owners, because of differences in their perceptions and motivations. Owners, for instance, might benefit from increased innovation, experimentation, and the cultivation of new options that could enhance the long-term value of the firm. Managers, on the other hand, might have a shorter-term perspective and so look to exploit existing positions, building market share and earnings in the present but doing so at the expense of longer-term initiatives. Alternatively, owners might entertain a takeover bid that offers a premium price for their shares. Managers though might see a takeover as a threat to their employment and so resist it, the premium price notwithstanding. The separation also creates asymmetries in knowledge. Managers will typically have much better information about the firm and its activities than the owners. And the owners must rely on the managers for the information they receive. Thus, a manager could be completely self-interested while effectively hiding that fact from the owners. This situation favors managers and creates a problem for owners. And so many of the issues in corporate governance deal with ways to overcome agency problems and make sure that agents act in the best interest of the principals they represent.

Two key mechanisms through which this occurs are the compensation system, which serves to incentivize managers to act in the interests of owners, and the oversight and regulatory system by which owners are kept informed of corporate action. To better understand these, it is important to identify and explain some of the key roles and actors. First is the **board of directors**. Every corporation has a board, charged with the **fiduciary responsibility** of representing the owners. The board recruits, hires, and oversees the chief executive officer, who then sets the strategy and is responsible for producing results that increase the value of the firm for its owners. The board monitors this performance, making sure that the firm operates within the law and in the best long-term interests of the stockholders.

While simple enough in concept, these mechanisms can be quite complex in practice. Fueling this complexity are number and variety of owners. Retirement funds and mutual funds, for instance, may invest heavily in a particular firm on behalf of their members. These **institutional investors**, as they are called, play an important role in governance by consolidating and giving weight to the voices of individual stockholders. They also exert pressure on firms, as their decisions to purchase or sell can substantially influence the perception and price of a stock in the marketplace. Other owners may represent themselves but control large blocks of voting shares. According to U.S. law, when the ownership of these large block-holders reaches 5%, they must be publicly disclosed, as large voting blocks can substantially influence board decisions and firm policy. Finally, firms can issue stock in different classes, some of which may include voting rights, some of which may not.

Of course, many owners are individual investors, with little expertise in the business, no direct knowledge of its operations, and little say in its strategy. Because these individual investors are seen as being so essential to the functioning of the capital markets and yet are so weak in terms of their influence, there is the Securities and Exchange Commission (SEC). Created by the Securities and Exchange Act of 1934, the mission of the SEC is "to protect investors, maintain fair orderly and efficient markets, and to facilitate capital formation." The SEC enforces rules on ownership, voting rights, proxies, stockholder protection, and what firms can and must disclose about their operations. Compliance with SEC regulations is the responsibility of the board, and various different committees within the board will typically be charged with different responsibilities.

For example, boards will typically have an audit committee. This committee will be responsible for hiring an independent auditor to review the firm's operations and performance. The audit committee will work with the independent auditor to make certain that all the information is current and correct and to disclose information as necessary to keep current and prospective owners informed about the firm's activities. The board may also have a governance committee, which will be responsible for nominating and overseeing the election of new board and committee members. This committee may also be responsible for setting compensation and retirement policy for board members as well as policies for resolving disputes. The governance committee is essentially responsible for assuring the independence of the board, as necessary for the board to fulfill its fiduciary obligations. Finally, boards will typically have a compensation committee, responsible for the compensation of the CEO and other key executives. This committee is charged with providing compensation sufficient to attract the best managers to the firm, while structuring that compensation so that it aligns the interests of the managers with the interests of the owners.

Compensation of the CEO and other top executives is an especially controversial issue. However, it is among the most important of the board's responsibilities as compensation is one of the primary tools for aligning the interests of managers and owners. To achieve its goals, compensation committees typically offer packages consisting of both present and deferred compensation, paid in the form of cash salary, incentive bonuses, stock, and options. The purpose of mixing various forms of compensation and paying them over an extended period is twofold. First, the board wants to hire the best and brightest managers to run their companies. But, because of agency problems, these hired managers may not think and act like owners. Thus, incentive-based compensation, often in the form of equity or options, can serve to align the interests of managers with the interest of owners.

Here again, the actual process can be very complex and often produce unintended consequences. Many executives have received extraordinary sums as the result of bonuses, stocks, and options. For example, Jamie Dimon, CEO of JPMorgan Chase received total compensation $31.5 million for 2019. Others have also been paid similarly extraordinary sums. Robert Iger, CEO of The Walt Disney Company, received $47.5 million in 2019, and Sundar Pichai, CEO of Google, received $281 million in salary and stock awards in 2019. Many have argued that these payments are justified based on gains in the companies' values, gains which benefitted stock-holders. Others though see these payments as evidence of agency problems gone amok (Dvorak, 2009). And there is evidence that the highest-paid CEOs also have the highest-paid followers (Graffin et al., 2008). All of this has contributed to an atmosphere of populist anger and a widely shared belief that effective oversight by many boards of directors is inadequate.

In response to such perceptions of boards and of publicly traded firms in general, the **ESG** (environmental, social, and governance) perspective has gained traction, especially in Europe but increasingly in the U.S. as well (Jan, 2019). Understanding that myriad issues like climate change, human rights, globalization, energy and material sustainability, and water scarcity can impact a firm's risk exposure, access to and cost of capital, operating practices, and regulatory pressures, an increasing number of firms are adopting a more holistic ESG approach to assessing the environmental and social outcomes from their decisions and actions. Various practical changes associated with this approach include things like increased transparency and responsiveness in response to risk events, broader and more deliberate measurement of societal impacts, in addition to financial outcomes, and greater focus on reputation as a long-term asset. The underlying principle is that a broad ESG perspective provides a firm with the legitimacy to operate. That legitimacy can then buffer the firm against negative events, but it can also serve as a differentiating, proactive, and positive attribute in the eyes of employees, customers, investors, and regulators. Indeed, recent studies (Kahn, 2019) suggest governance reflecting an ESG perspective is positively related to stock performance.

Governing the Board

Given the ability of the board to influence the firm, seats on the board are often coveted. So, maintaining the independence of the board can be a challenge. This is especially true when there is **duality**. Duality exists when the CEO and board chair are the same individual. While there are arguments for combining these roles and while a great many U.S. firms still operate with this duality, there are also strong arguments against it and most European firms have abandoned the practice. The primary argument against duality is the challenge to independence. As the CEO and the one most responsible for firm strategy and performance, the CEO cannot be expected to monitor his or her behavior effectively. Quite the contrary, it seems more likely that a CEO would want to influence opinion such that he or she looked good as a result. It would also seem that the CEO, as chairperson, could influence the governance committee, or whatever group was responsible for board and committee nominations. All of this could threaten the independence of the board and so the ability of the board to execute its responsibilities. Corporate governance experts often distinguish insiders from outsiders when discussing board membership. Insiders are board members who are also executives of the firm. Outsiders hold positions outside of the firm. The distinction speaks to the implied independence of two. Insiders are likely more beholden to the CEO and so more inclined to support his or her agenda and policies. In cases where there is duality, a high number of insiders could be especially problematic, allowing the CEO and other insiders to manage the firm for their benefit and in their own best interests, as opposed to the interest of the owners. Many shareholder watchdog groups, along with most institutional investors, use the number of outside directors as an indication of a board's independence, encouraging firms to increase the proportion of outside directors.

Certainly, there is a trend away from duality and towards the increasing use of outside directors. While well-intended, these moves may not necessarily increase the quality of the board. As mentioned, there are advantages to duality and the use of inside directors. The role of a board member entails understanding a great deal about the business and its industry. There may be high levels of specialized and technical knowledge required, as well as a considerable investment of time and energy. Outside directors may simply lack the knowledge or time to do a thorough and adequate job. There may also be conflicts of interest, where outside board members represent key suppliers, customers, or other constituents. Board members may be obliged to other board members because of appointments to other boards. These so-called **interlocks** may compromise independence, even among outside board members. Thus, while the question of board independence is an important one, no single or simple answer will satisfy the issue fully.

Governance, Value, and Strategic Management

As discussed previously, for the purposes of this chapter and text, governance should be seen simply as a means to an end, rather than as an end in itself. Instead, the end is the success of the firm, measured in relation to its mission and purpose. Viewed in this way, governance is just one more component of strategic management. Like international business, corporate governance is a highly specialized area, with its own vocabulary and requiring considerable and specialized understanding. Nevertheless, it is still just one of many issues of importance to strategic managers. And so it must be understood in the proper context. Good governance is necessary but is not sufficient for strong and sustained performance. Good governance can contribute to the development of a competitive advantage, but it is not a competitive advantage in and of itself. Good governance creates conditions in which competitive advantage can grow, but good governance alone cannot overcome a highly competitive environment, a poorly designed product, or a poorly marketed service, nor can it overcome a resource base that is outdated and easily imitated.

Rather, good governance is an intangible resource, something that interacts with and adds value to other things. Good governance undergirds a firm's reputation, providing assurance to suppliers, investors, employees, and customers. It facilitates trust and lasting relationships; it contributes to loyalty and commitment and it can promote involvement, investment, and effort. In this regard, good governance looks a lot like leadership. It adds new value, over and above the obvious value of a firm's assets. It enables others to succeed, encouraging them with resources and autonomy and then monitoring the results to assure accountability. Beyond these affirmative benefits, good governance can also help to prevent disasters. Many of the scandals that have shaken public confidence, in firms like Enron, Nortel, Volkswagen, Equifax, Lehman Brothers, and Tyco can be traced to a lack of vigilance. And the lack of vigilance is a failure of corporate governance. As a result of these types of scandals, many firms failed. While some others survived, they did so only after great turmoil. For every failure of governance, though, there is great embarrassment and substantial economic loss. Good governance then is like a healthy habit; it builds a stronger organization while also helping to prevent catastrophe. As a result, it is among the most important facets and key responsibilities of strategic management.

CONCLUSIONS

Throughout the book, every one of the chapters has ended with a series of caveats. These supplemental comments were meant to add additional breadth and depth, to offer some exceptions or special conditions, and to provide a measure of practical relevance to the concepts, tools, and frameworks presented. This chapter though will be different. The reason is that this chapter has itself been a series of exceptions and special conditions. In essence, this has been a whole chapter of caveats, offered to add additional depth and breadth to the material provided throughout the book. Each of the four topics, entrepreneurship, international business, leadership, and corporate governance, is both a discipline unto itself as well as an important part of the larger strategic management process. Each can be an important contributor to firm performance, but each is also sufficiently unique to justify its own vocabulary and its own scholarly identity and to be practiced by its own set of specialists. While this specialization offers advantages, it also comes at a cost. That cost comes in the form of redundancy, added complexity, and an inability to generalize across settings, the result of which is a more complicated landscape for students and less effective management overall. Thus, the purpose of this chapter has been to illustrate that, while these topics are specialized and important, they also share in common two essential things. They are all drivers of firm value and they are all among the responsibilities of strategic management.

Entrepreneurship, for instance, is all about creating value and providing a good return on investment. It seeks pockets of unsatisfied demand and looks for opportunities to apply innovative methods and technologies. Entrepreneurship requires planning and positioning, formulation and implementation, as well as learning and adaptation. Entrepreneurs create new ventures and those ventures have value chains through which products and services are created and distributed to the environment. Those ventures that succeed do so because they develop a competitive advantage, giving customers a reason to buy at a price above the venture's costs. And that competitive advantage enables revenues, profits, growth, and a positive return for the investors. It is important to see then that even though it is called by a different name, entrepreneurship is inseparable from the practice of strategy. Even inside of large and well-established firms, the energy, vitality, and creativity of entrepreneurship can be harnessed to promote growth, to provide incentives, and to sustain competitive advantage. So, it is important to see how entrepreneurship and strategy are fundamentally linked.

The same is true of international business. While involving a host of specialized concerns and technical issues, success in international business still rests on the basics of strategic management. Substitutability, bargaining power, and elasticity still characterize the competitiveness of the environment. Rare, valuable, and inimitable resources still drive uniqueness and competitive advantage across firms. And disconnects between the strategy and the various elements of a firm's systems, style, structures, and staff still represent the greatest threats to success. What happens as a firm moves from a domestic approach to an international one is that an additional layer of complexity is added. Processes that worked in one market may not work in another. The drivers of a product's value in one place may be very different than the drivers in another. Potentially everything about the way a firm goes to market and manages its structures and affairs may change as the landscape of laws, practices, and preferences change. But those changes do not alter the basic formula. In every context, whether domestic or international, in just one country, two countries, or dozens of countries simultaneously, success is still a function of value creation for customers and value capture through revenues over and above the firm's costs.

Success though does not come naturally; performing well requires hard and continuous effort as competitive pressure, customer aspirations, and organizational inertia combine to erode competitive advantage. Leadership then is necessary to envision the possibilities, to catalyze the resources, and to focus and motivate the effort. But leadership works with strategy, not independent of it. Leaders must understand their environments, they must understand the capabilities of their firms, and they must understand the opportunities and nature of competitive advantage. Leaders must understand that there are times to change radically, times to change subtly, and times to stay the course. To be effective in building long-term value, leaders must appreciate the need for investment and the trade-offs between exploiting strengths in the present and building options for the future. They must understand human behavior and motivation as well as organizational structures, systems, and processes. But more importantly, they must leverage all of this knowledge to get results and provide a return that is better than what investors can get elsewhere. That challenge to leadership is also fundamental to strategic management. Strategists are charged with getting results across the breadth of environmental exigencies and organizational conditions. In essence, strategists face the challenge of being leaders, just as leaders shoulder the burden of being strategists. So, while the tools and the terminology are different, the two functions are so close in practice as to make them indistinguishable.

Of course, enabling all the things that a leader or a strategist does is the governance of the firm. Governance, with all of its various structures and components, is the skeleton of the organization. Without effective governance, there would be no financing to enable the acquisition of resources. Without effective governance, there would be no authority to enable the formulation and implementation of strategy. More than anything else, governance provides an identity and direction for the firm. These two things form a foundation upon which a successful strategic process is built. Identity simply means the values and consciousness of the firm. What are the boundary conditions in which the strategy is made? What are the checks and balances that will govern decision making and the use of resources? Strategy gives a firm a personality that can be sensed and understood by the marketplace and the origins of that personality lie in the firm's governance. Strategy is about deciding where to go and how to get there, and governance should be seen as the starting point in that process. What is the mission of the firm, what are its goals, and how will it define and measure its own success? The answers to these questions will set the direction for the firm and govern the way it formulates and implements it strategy. Research has shown that patterns established early in a firm's development leave an **imprinting** effect on the people, processes, and structures of the firm for many years to come (Boeker, 1989). Governance controls the substance of that imprinted form and so understanding it is essential to understanding and managing strategy.

Ultimately, though, the point of all this is better management and better organizational performance. Recall from Chapter 1 that performance is the crux of business education. And knowing how to drive performance and deliver results is the goal of every business student, every manager, and every investor. Strategic management is nothing less than the single most valuable and generalizable framework for understanding, directing, and delivering that performance. Through all of its tools, models, and processes, strategic management provides an integrated picture of performance that incorporates all of the functions of the firm and applies across all sorts of contexts and settings.

KEY TERMS

Agency problems are the set of issues and complications arising from the separating of ownership and control. In particular are the asymmetries in decision-making power and information between owners and managers.

Angels are typically wealthy individuals who invest their own funds to finance entrepreneurial ventures in the earliest stages of development.

Board of directors refers to the group of individuals who oversee a company or organization. In publicly traded firms, the board has the fiduciary duty of representing the owners in hiring the CEO, setting policy, and monitoring the activities of the firm.

Duality exists when the CEO of a firm is also the chair of that firm's board of directors. This one individual then holds these dual offices simultaneously.

ESG stands for environmental, social, and governance and refers to a movement among firms, mostly in Europe but increasingly in the U.S., to take a broad, societal view in assessing the various risk and impacts of their operations.

Eurozone refers to the 19 European countries that are both members of the European Union (E.U.) and have also adopted the Euro as their official currency.

Fiduciary responsibility refers to a relationship of trust or obligation, where a party in power is charged with the obligation to act on behalf of and in the interests of another, more vulnerable party.

Foreign direct investment (FDI) is the ownership of business assets by a foreign party, either an individual or firm.

Franchising is a business model where a franchisor, who owns a concept, brand, and set of practices, sells the rights to use these assets to a franchisee, who pays in return an upfront fee and a royalty. This model facilitates rapid growth but involves shared ownership and profits and so the potential exists for conflicts of interests to arise between the franchisor and franchisee.

Generalizable is a term referring to the ability of a framework or principle to apply across a range of settings. Strategic management is a generalizable discipline because it provides a framework that can be useful across a range of firms, organizations, and settings.

Global Strategy is a type of international strategy that leverages standardization and economies of scale in building competitive advantage across multiple countries. With a focus on consistency and per-unit costs, a global strategy capitalizes on some of the same economic forces as a low-cost strategy.

Globalization is the name given to the homogenization of global markets, economies, and cultures. Notwithstanding some noteworthy ebbs and flows, the overall process and direction of globalization are undeniable over the course of time.

Institutional investors aggregate funds from individual investors and then invest collectively. Mutual funds and retirement funds are common institutional investors. Because they represent such large sums of money, these investors can be powerful actors in corporate governance.

Institutionalization is a term coined by Philip Selznick (1957) and refers to the process of infusing an organization with value, over and above the tangible value of their assets.

Interlocks exist when board members sit simultaneously on the boards of multiple different companies. By creating reciprocal interdependence among the board members, interlocks are thought to mitigate independence.

Leader-member exchange (LMX) refers to a body of academic research focusing on the dyadic relationships between leaders and their immediate followers. At the crux of this work is the understanding that leaders relate differently to different followers and that the nature of these relationships is key to leadership effectiveness.

Liabilities of newness refers to the various difficulties that arise from doing something new. Some examples would include the lack of precedent, the lack of familiarity in a role, or the lack of legitimacy in the eyes of a supplier or customer.

Licensing is a means of commercializing a product, technology, or piece of intellectual property. In a licensing arrangement, the license holder grants another party, for a fee the right to use, sell, or manufacture the licensed property.

Moral hazard occurs when decision makers are separated from the risks associated with their decisions. In the principal–agent relationship, for instance, the agent has the bulk of the decision making discretion and yet the principal bears the bulk of the risk of bad decisions.

Privately held firms are those whose ownership stock is not traded publicly or listed or traded on any public exchange.

Publicly held firms are those whose ownership stock is available to the public and is listed and traded on a public exchange.

Multi-domestic strategy is a type of international strategy that leverages customization and local responsiveness in building competitive advantage across multiple countries. With its focus on local preferences and branding, a multi-domestic strategy capitalizes on some of the same economic forces as a differentiation strategy.

Top management team refers to that small group of managers at the highest levels of the organization who make the majority of the strategic decisions and control the firm's operations. The CEO is typically the leader of the top management team.

Transnationalism is the name given to a social philosophy where national borders are largely inconsequential and so offer little resistance to the movement of people, goods, materials, and information. Large multinational firms may have no distinct national identity and so are said to be transnational.

Venture capitalists pool funds from individual investors to invest in entrepreneurial ventures. While specializing in different types of firms, at different stages of growth, venture capitalists are all accustomed to high risks, with the prospect of relatively short-term and large returns.

QUESTIONS FOR REVIEW

1. What is generalizability, and what does it mean to say that strategic management is a highly generalizable framework?
2. What are some of the basic similarities among all types of firms, whether they are selling products or services and are large or small?
3. How can an understanding of these similarities help one to be a better strategic manager?
4. How is a business plan for a new venture similar to the strategy of an existing business?
5. What are the two generic international strategies and how do they reflect economic principles similar to the generic strategies of low cost and differentiation?
6. Describe some differences you would likely find in comparing the structures and systems of two firms, one of which pursued a global strategy and the other a multi-domestic strategy.
7. What is globalization? What role have regional trading associations played in the role of globalization?

8. What is strategic leadership, and what is its connection to the larger framework of strategic management?

9. Why have scholars concluded that defining and measuring leadership is so complex and so ambiguous? How would you describe effective leadership?

10. What is institutionalization, and why is it important to strategic management and organizational performance?

11. What is corporate governance, and why is it important to distinguish between publicly and privately held firms in discussing governance structures?

12. How can executive compensation help to align the interests of managers and owners? Why is it necessary to incentivize managers to behave like owners?

13. What is meant by the independence of the board of directors? What are some common indicators of board independence?

References

Chapter 1

Amit, R. & Zott, C. 2001. Value creation in e-business. *Strategic Management Journal*, 22: 493–520.

Andrews, K. R. 1987. *The Concept of Corporate Strategy*. Homewood, IL: Irwin.

Chandler, A. D. 1962. *Strategy and Structure: Chapters in the History of the American Enterprise.* Cambridge, MA: The MIT Press.

Gilbert, D. R., Hartman, E., Mauriel, J. J. & Freeman, R. E. 1988. *A Logic for Strategy*. Cambridge, MA: Ballinger Publishing.

Hofer, C. W. & Schendel, D. 1978. *Strategy Formulation: Analytical Concepts*. New York: West Publishing.

Hoskisson, R. E., Hitt, M. A. & Ireland, R. D. 2008. *Competing for Advantage* (2nd ed.). Mason, OH: Thompson South-Western.

Mintzberg, H. 1987. The strategy concept I: Five Ps for strategy. *California Management Review*, 30: 11–24.

Ohmae, K. 1982. *The Mind of the Strategist: The Art of Japanese Business*. New York, NY: McGraw-Hill.

Porter, M. E. 1985. *Competitive Advantage: Creating and Sustaining Superior Performance*. New York, NY: Free Press.

Chapter 2

Abrahams, J. 1999. *The Mission Statement Book: 301 Corporate Mission Statements from America's Top Companies*. Berkeley, CA: Ten Speed Press.

Amason, A. C. & Mooney, A. C. 2008. Icarus' paradox revisited: How strong performance sows the seeds of dysfunction in future strategic decision making. *Strategic Organization*, 6: 407–434.

Audia, P. G., Locke, E. A. & Smith, K. G. 2000. The paradox of success: An archival and a laboratory study of strategic persistence following radical environmental change. *Academy of Management Journal*, 43: 837–854.

Chen, S., Matsumoto, D. & Rajgopal, S. 2011. Is silence golden? An empirical analysis of firms that stop giving quarterly earnings guidance. *Journal of Accounting and Economics*, 51: 134–150.

Collingwood, H. 2001. The earnings game: Everyone plays, nobody wins. *Harvard Business Review*, June.

Ford Motor Company. 2003. www.mycareer.ford.com/our company.

Jones, P. & Kahaner, L. 1995. *Say It and Live It: 50 Corporate Mission Statements That Hit the Mark*. New York, NY: Currency-Doubleday.

Land, J. K. 2010. CEO turnover around earnings restatements and fraud. *Pacific Accounting Review*, 22(3): 180–198.

Lindenburg, E. B. & Ross, S. A. 1981. Tobin's q ratio and industrial organization. *Journal of Business*, 54: 1–32.

Miller, D. 1990. *The Icarus Paradox: How Exceptional Companies Bring about Their Own Downfall*. New York, NY: Harper-Business.

Perfect, S. B. & Wiles, K. K. 1994. Alternative constructions of Tobin's q: An empirical comparison. *Journal of Empirical Finance*, 1: 313–341.

Weber, H. R. 2002. Coke drop earnings guidance: Soft-drink giant says move puts emphasis on long-term. Associated Press: 12/14/2002.

Chapter 3

Barney, J. B. 1991. Firm resources and sustained competitive advantage. *Journal of Management*, 17(1): 99–120.

Castrogiovanni, G. 1992. Environmental munificence: A theoretical assessment. *Academy of Management Review*, 16(3): 542–565.

Hedberg, B., Nystrom, P. & Starbuck, W. H. 1976. Camping on seesaws: Prescriptions for a self-designing organization. *Administrative Science Quarterly*, 21: 41–65.

Hunt, D. E. 1987. *Beginning with Ourselves: In Practice, Theory and Human Affairs*. Cambridge, MA: Brookline Books, pp. 4, 30.

Quinn, J. B. 1980. *Strategies for Change: Logical Incrementalism*. Homewood, IL: Irwin.

Chapter 4

Abell, 1980. *Defining the Business: The Starting Point of Strategic Planning*. Englewood Cliffs, NJ: Prentice-Hall.

Abernathy, W. J. & Clark, K. B. 1985. Innovation: Mapping the winds of creative destruction. *Research Policy*, 14: 3–22.

Boulding, K. E. 1956. General systems theory: The skeleton of science. *General Systems: Yearbook of the Society for the Advancement of General Systems Theory*, 1: 11–17.

Bourgeois, L. J. 1984. Strategic management and determinism. *Academy of Management Review*, 9: 586–596.

Button, K. 2002. Empty cores in airline markets. Paper presented at the 5th Hamburg Aviation Conference, Hamburg, Germany, February.

Cheah, H. B. 1990. Schumpeterian and Austrian entrepreneurship: Unity within duality. *Journal of Business Venturing*, 5: 341–347.

Chen, M., Smith, K. & Grimm, C. 1992. Action characteristics as predictors of competitive responses. *Management Science*, 33: 439–455.

Child, J. 1972. Organizational structure, environment, and performance: The role of strategic choice. *Sociology*, 6: 2–22.

D'Aveni, R. A. 1994. *Hyper-Competition: Managing the Dynamics of Strategic Maneuvering*. New York, NY: The Free Press.

Eldredge, N. & Gould, S. 1972. Punctuated equilibria: An alternative to phyletic gradualism. In T. J. Schoph (Ed.), *Models in Paleobiology*, pp. 82–115. San Francisco: Freeman, Cooper & Co.

Gersick, C. J. 1991. Revolutionary change theories: A multilevel exploration of the punctuated equilibrium paradigm. *Academy of Management Journal*, 16: 10–36.

Nelson, R. R. & Winter, S. G. 1973. Toward and evolutionary theory of economic capabilities. *American Economic Review*, 63: 440–449.

O'Neill, T. & Hymel, G. 1994. *All Politics Is Local and Other Rules of the Game*. Holbrook, MA: Bob Adams, Inc.

Porter, M. E. 1980. *Competitive Strategy*. New York, NY: The Free Press.

Schumpeter, J. 1942. *Capitalism, Socialism, and Democracy*. New York: Harper and Brothers.

Sjostrom, W. 1993. Antitrust immunity for shipping conferences: An empty core approach. *Antitrust Bulletin*, 38: 419–423.

Tushman, M. L. & Anderson, P. 1986. Technological discontinuities and organizational environments. *Administrative Science Quarterly*, 31: 439–465.

von Bertalanffy, L. 1950. The theory of open systems in physics and biology. *Science*, 111: 23–28.

Chapter 5

Andrews, 1971. *The Concept of Corporate Strategy*. Homewood, IL: Irwin.

Bach, G. L., Flanagan, R., Howell, J., Levy, F. & Lima, A. 1987. *Microeconomics* (11th ed.). Englewood Cliffs, NJ: Prentice-Hall.

Barney, J. B. 1991. Firm resources and sustained competitive advantage. *Journal of Management*, 17(1): 99–120.

Bowman, C. & Ambrosini, V. 2000. Value creation versus value capture: Towards a coherent definition of value in strategy. *British Journal of Management*, 11: 1–15.

Penrose, E. T. 1959. *The Theory of the Growth of the Firm*. New York: John Wiley.

Peteraf, M. A. 1993. The cornerstones of competitive advantage: A resource-based view. *Strategic Management Journal*, 14: 179–191.

Porter, M. E. 1985. *Competitive Advantage*. New York: Free Press.

Priem, R. L. 2007. A consumer perspective on value creation. *Academy of Management Review*, 32(1): 219–235.

Timmons, J. A. 1999. *New Venture Creation: Entrepreneurship for the 21st Century* (5th ed.). Boston: Irwin/McGraw-Hill.

Wernerfelt, B. 1984. A resource-based view of the firm. *Strategic Management Journal*, 5: 171–180.

Chapter 6

Barney, J. B. 1991. Firm resources and sustained competitive advantage. *Journal of Management*, 17(1): 99–120.

Hill, C. W. L. 1988. Differentiation versus low cost or differentiation and low cost: A contingency framework. *Academy of Management Review*, 13: 401–413.

Hofer, C. W. & Schendel, D. 1978. *Strategy Formulation: Analytical Concepts*. New York: West Publishing.

Porter, M. E. 1980. *Competitive Strategy*. New York, NY: The Free Press.

Priem, R. L. & Butler, J. E. 2001. Is the resource-based view a useful perspective for strategic management research? *Academy of Management Review*, 26: 1–22.

Teece, D. J., Pisano, G. & Shuen, A. 1997. Dynamic capabilities and strategic management. *Strategic Management Journal*, 18: 509–533.

Wernerfelt, B. 1984. A resource-based view of the firm. *Strategic Management Journal*, 5: 171–180.

Wright, P., Kroll, M., Tu, H. & Helms, M. 1991. Generic strategies and business performance: An empirical study of the screw machine products industry. *British Journal of Management*, 2: 57–65.

Chapter 7

Baum, J. & Korn, H. 1996. Competitive dynamics of interfirm rivalry. *Academy of Management Journal*, 39: 255–292.

Berger, P. & Ofek, E. 1995. Diversification's effect on firm value. *Journal of Financial Economics*, 37: 39–65.

Close, J. W. 2013. *A Giant Cow-Tipping by Savages: The Boom, Bust, and Boom Culture of M&A*. London: Palgrave Macmillan.

Gimeno, J. & Woo, C. 1996. Hypercompetition in a multimarket environment: The role of strategic similarity and multimarket contact in competitive de-escalation. *Organization Science*, 7: 322–341.

Hughes, A. & Singh, A. 1987. Takeovers and the stock market. *Contributions to Political Economy*, 6: 73–85.

Jensen, M. & Ruback, R. 1983. The market for corporate control: The scientific evidence. *Journal of Financial Economics*, 11: 5–50.

Karnani, A. & Wernerfelt, B. 1985. Multiple point competition. *Strategic Management Journal*, 6: 87–96.

Nielsen, J. F. & Melicher, R. W. 1973. A financial analysis of acquisition and merger premiums. *Journal of Financial and Quantitative Analysis*, 8: 139–148.

Porter, M. E. 1987. From competitive advantage to corporate strategy. *Harvard Business Review*, 65: 43–59.

Rosen, R. J. 2006. Merger momentum and investor sentiment: The stock market reaction to merger announcements. *Journal of Business*, 79: 987–1017.

Rumelt, R. 1974. *Strategy, Structure and Economic Performance*. Cambridge, MA: Harvard University Press.

Servaes, H. 1996. The value of diversification during the conglomerate merger wave. *Journal of Finance*, 51: 1201–1225.

Williamson, O. 1975. *Markets and Hierarchies, Analysis and Antitrust Implications: A Study in the Economics of Internal Organization*. New York: Free Press.

Chapter 8

Allison, G. T. 1971. *Essence of Decision*. New York, NY: Harper Collins Publishers.

Amason, A. C. & Mooney, A. C. 2008. The Icarus paradox revisited: How strong performance sows the seeds of dysfunction in future strategic decision making. *Strategic Organization*, 6: 407–434.

Burns, T. & Stalker, G. M. 1961. *The Management of Innovation*. London: Tavistock.

Chandler, A. D. 1962. *Strategy and Structure: Chapters in the History of the American Industrial Enterprise*. Cambridge, MA: MIT Press.

Chandy, R. K. & Tellis, G. J. 2000. The incumbent's curse? Incumbency, size and radical product innovation. *Journal of Marketing*, 64: 1–17.

Cyert, R. M. & March, J. G. 1963. *A Behavioral Theory of the Firm*. Upper Saddle River, NJ: Prentice Hall.

Demirag, I. 1995. Short term performance pressures: Is there a consensus view? *European Journal of Finance*, 1: 41–56.

Drucker, P. F. 1967. *The Effective Executive*. New York, NY: Harper & Row.

Duncan, R. B. 1974. Modifications in decision structure in adapting to the environment: Some implications for organizational learning. *Decision Sciences*, 705–725.

Dutton, J. E., Fahey, L. & Narayanan, V. K. 1983. Toward understanding strategic issue diagnosis. *Strategic Management Journal*, 4: 307–323.

Ferreira, N., Kar, J. & Trigeorgis, L. 2009. Option games. *Harvard Business Review*, 87: 101–107.

Fiol, C. M. & Lyles, M. A. 1985. Organizational learning. *Academy of Management Review*, 10: 803–813.

Foster, R. N. 2003. Corporate performance and technological change through investors' eyes. *Research Technology Management*, 46: 36–43.

Fredrickson, J. W. & Iaquinto, A. I. 1989. Inertia and creeping rationality in strategic decision processes. *Academy of Management Journal*, 32: 516–542.

Ghemewat, P. 1991. Marketing incumbency and technological inertia. *Marketing Science*, 10: 161–172.

Hedberg, B. L. T., Nystrom, P. C. & Starbuck, W. H. 1976. Camping on seesaws: Prescriptions for a self-designing organization. *Administrative Science Quarterly*, 21: 41–65.

Kahneman, D. & Tversky, A. 1979. Prospect theory: An analysis of decision under risk. *Econometrica*, 47: 263–291.

Lawrence, P. R. & Lorsch, J. W. 1967. *Organization and Environment: Managing Differentiation and Integration*. Boston, MA: HBS Press.

Luehrman, T. A. 1998. Strategy as a portfolio of real options. *Harvard Business Review*, September–October, 89–99.

McGrath, 1999. Falling forward: Real options reasoning and entrepreneurial failure. *Academy of Management Review*, 24: 13–30.

Miller, D. 1992. The Icarus paradox: How exceptional companies bring about their own downfall. *Business Horizons*, 35: 24–36.

Mintzberg, H. 1987. Crafting strategy. *Harvard Business Review*, 65: 65–75.

Nelson, R. R. & Winter, S. G. 1982. *An Evolutionary Theory of Economic Change*. Cambridge, MA: Belknap Press.

Pascale, R. & Athos, A. 1981. *The Art of Japanese Management*. London: Penguin Books.

Peters, T., Waterman, R. & Phillips, J. R. 1980. Structure is not organization. *Business Horizons*, 23: 14–26.

Rhoades, D. & Stelter, D. 2009. Seize advantage in a downturn. *Harvard Business Review*, 87: 1–8.

Scherpereel, C. M. 2008. The option-creating institution: A real options perspective on economic organization. *Strategic Management Journal*, 29: 455–470.

Schumpeter, J. A. 1942. *Capitalism, Socialism, and Democracy*. New York: Harper and Brothers.

Tayan, B. 2019. The Wells Fargo cross-selling scandal. Rock center for corporate governance at Stanford University: Topics, issues and controversies in corporate governance, no. CGRP-62. Research paper no. 17-1. https://ssrn.com/abstract=2879102.

Teece, D. J., Pisano, G. & Shuen, A. 1997. Dynamic capabilities and strategic management. *Strategic Management Journal*, 18: 509–533.

Chapter 9

Bauer, Henry. 1992. *Scientific Literacy and the Myth of the Scientific Method*. Champaign, IL: University of Illinois Press.

Gratton, L. & Scott, A. 2016. *The 100-Year Life: Living and Working in an Age of Longevity*. London: Bloomsbury.

Chapter 10

Avolio, B. J. 2005. *Leadership Development in the Balance*. Mahwah, NJ: Lawrence Erlbaum Associates Publishers.

Boeker, W. 1989. Strategic change: The effects of founding and history. *Academy of Management Journal*, 32: 489–515.

Diesnesch, R. M. & Liden, R. C. 1986. Leader-member exchange model of leadership: A critique and further development. *Academy of Management Review*, 11: 618–634.

Dvorak, P. 2009. Executive salaries remain under pressure in '09. *Wall Street Journal*, April 3.

Enrico, R. & Kornbluth, J. 1988. *The Other Guy Blinked: And Other Dispatches from the Cola Wars*. New York: Bantam Books.

Fama, E. F. & Jensen, M. C. 1983. Separation of ownership and control. *Journal of Law and Economics*, 26: 301–325.

Ghemawat, P. 2001. Distance still matters. *Harvard Business Review*, September 1–10.

Graffin, S. D., Wade, J. B., Porac, J. F. & McNamee, R. C. 2008. The impact of CEO status diffusion on the economic outcomes of other senior managers. *Organization Science*, 19: 457–474.

Hambrick, D. C. & Mason, P. A. 1984. Upper echelons: The organization as a reflection of its top managers. *Academy of Management Review*, 9: 193–206.

Heifetz, R. A. & Laurie, D. L. 2001. The work of leadership. *Harvard Business Review*, 79: 131–141.

Jan, O. 2019. The Board and ESG: Harvard Law School Forum on Corporate Governance and Financial Regulation, February, Cambridge, MA.

Judge, T. A., Woolf, E. F., Hurst, C. & Livingston, B. 2008. Leadership. In C. L. Cooper & J. Barling (Eds.), *Handbook of Organizational Behavior*, pp. 334–352. Thousand Oaks, CA: Sage Publications.

Kahn, M. 2019. Corporate governance, ESG, and stock returns around the world. *SSRN*, July. https://dx.doi.org/10.2139/ssrn.3279830.

Pfeffer, J. 1977. The ambiguity of leadership. *Academy of Management Review*, 2: 104–112.

Sandberg, W. R. 1986. *New Venture Performance: The Role of Strategy and Industry Structure*. Lexington, MA: Lexington Books.

Schumpeter, J. A. 1942. *Capitalism, Socialism, and Democracy*. New York: Harper and Brothers.

Selznick, P. 1957. *Leadership in Administration: A Sociological Interpretation*. Berkley, CA: University of California Press.

Stinchcombe, A. L. 1965. Social structure and organizations. In J. G. March (Ed.), *Handbook of Organizations*. Chicago: Rand McNally & Co.

Vesper, K. H. 1980. *New Venture Strategies*. Englewood Cliffs, NJ: Prentice Hall.

Yukl, G. 2006. *Leadership in Organizations* (6th ed.). Upper Saddle River, NJ: Prentice Hall.

Index

Note: Page numbers in *italic* indicate a figure and page numbers in **bold** indicate a table on the corresponding page.

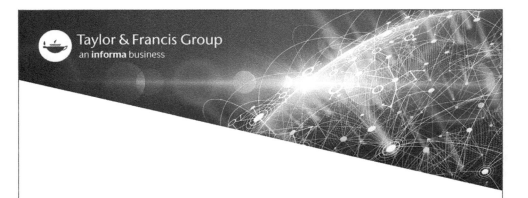